THAT GREECE
MIGHT STILL BE FREE

WILLIAM ST. CLAIR

THAT GREECE MIGHT STILL BE FREE

The Philhellenes in the War of Independence

The mountains look on Marathon—
And Marathon looks on the sea;
And musing there an hour alone,
I dream'd that Greece might still be free.
                                    Lord Byron

London
OXFORD UNIVERSITY PRESS
NEW YORK   TORONTO
1972

Oxford University Press, Ely House, London W.1.

GLASGOW   NEW YORK   TORONTO   MELBOURNE   WELLINGTON
CAPE TOWN   IBADAN   NAIROBI   DAR ES SALAAM   LUSAKA   ADDIS ABABA
DELHI   BOMBAY   CALCUTTA   MADRAS   KARACHI   LAHORE   DACCA
KUALA LUMPUR   SINGAPORE   HONG KONG   TOKYO

ISBN 0 19 215194 0

Printed in Great Britain by
The Camelot Press Ltd., London and Southampton

CONTENTS

ILLUSTRATIONS

ACKNOWLEDGEMENTS

I should like to record my gratitude to Dr. Francis Walton of the Gennadios Library, Athens, who has helped me in innumerable ways while I have been working on this book. Special thanks are also due to Mrs. Niemöller and the staff of the German Institute in London who scoured the libraries of Germany to find the rare books I was looking for.

I should like to acknowledge the help received, copies sent, and permissions given by the following libraries and institutions: the British Museum; the Public Record Office, London; the London Library; the National Library of Scotland; King's College, Aberdeen; the Bibliothèque Nationale, Paris; the Musée des Beaux Arts, Bordeaux; the British School at Athens; the Benaki Museum, Athens; the National Historical Museum, Athens; the Library of Congress, Washington; the New York Public Library; the Zentralbibliothek, Zurich; and the libraries at Heidelberg, Mainz, Tübingen, Bamberg, Marburg, Munich, Hanover, Bonn, Rostock, Darmstadt, and Nuremberg.

Miss Marjory Gordon, the great-granddaughter of the Philhellene, kindly gave me permission to consult and make use of her family papers. I should also like to record my thanks to Mr. Stephen de Winter, Mr. E. Finopoulos, Mrs. Marianne Fox, Mr. Peter Fraser, Mr. Peter Hopkirk, Mr. T. Lascarides, Professor Leslie Marchand, Mrs. Pearce and other staff of the British Council in Athens, Professor and Mrs. Robert Picken, and Mr. Stephen Robson for help on particular points.

I should like to thank Mr. A. C. Ward for preparing the Index, and Mr. Carl James for drawing the maps. The editorial and production staff of the Oxford University Press, London, have helped to improve the book in countless ways, and I am particularly grateful to Mr. Jon Stallworthy, with whom I first visited Greece years ago, for his encouragement and help from the time when the idea first took shape.

An especial thank you is due to my wife without whose participation the book could not have been attempted. Besides helping in innumerable other ways, she spent untold hours patiently translating to me all the German source books.

W. L. St. C.

October 1971

1. *The Outbreak*

The Turks of Greece left few traces. They disappeared suddenly and finally in the spring of 1821 unmourned and unnoticed by the rest of the world. Years later, when travellers asked about the heaps of stones, the old men would explain, 'There stood the tower of Ali Aga, and there we slew him, his harem, and his slaves.' It was hard to believe then that Greece had once contained a large population of Turkish descent, living in small communities all over the country, prosperous farmers, merchants, and officials, whose families had known no other home for hundreds of years. As the Greeks said, the moon devoured them.

Upwards of twenty thousand Turkish men, women, and children were murdered by their Greek neighbours in a few weeks of slaughter. They were killed deliberately, without qualm or scruple, and there were no regrets either then or later. Turkish families living in single farms or small isolated communities were summarily put to death and their homes burned down over their corpses. Others, when the disturbances began, abandoned home to seek the security of the nearest town, but the defenceless streams of refugees were overwhelmed by bands of armed Greeks.

In the smaller towns, the Turkish communities barricaded their houses and attempted to defend themselves as best they could, but few survived. In some places they were driven by hunger to surrender to their attackers on receiving promises of security, but these were seldom honoured. The men were killed at once and the women and children divided out as slaves, usually to be killed in their turn later. All over the Peloponnese roamed mobs of Greeks armed with clubs, scythes, and a few firearms, killing, plundering, and burning. They were often led by Christian priests, who exhorted them to greater efforts in their holy work.

In the larger towns and in a few fortresses there were garrisons of

Turkish and Albanian troops, and they were soon crammed with refugees who had escaped the massacres in the countryside. The troops made occasional sorties to try to break up the bands of Greeks and succeeded in bringing within the safety of the walls the inhabitants of a few Moslem communities, Turkish and Albanian, who had survived the first onslaught. They attempted to terrorize the population back into subjection by summary executions and demonstrations of force, but they could not turn the tide. Within a few weeks of the outbreak of the Revolution, the Turkish and Moslem Albanian population of the Peloponnese, previously about a ninth of the whole, had ceased to exist as a settled community. The towns on the coast which remained in Turkish hands had a precarious life-line to the outside world by sea but the others, including Tripolitsa, the biggest town of the Peloponnese, were under total siege.

During April the inhabitants of the important islands of Hydra, Spetsae, and Psara decided to join the revolutionaries. These islanders, who were mainly Christian Albanians by origin, had built up a strong merchant marine after the French were driven from the Eastern Mediterranean in the Napoleonic period. They armed their ships and began to attack traders flying the Turkish flag. They ranged all over the Aegean and beyond. Many Turkish merchant ships were captured, their crews killed, or thrown overboard, and the booty brought back to port. On several occasions ships crowded with Moslem pilgrims on their way to or from Mecca were seized and the crews and passengers put to death. The capture of a few treasure ships bound for Alexandria brought a rich haul of jewels and precious metals. The crew of a Turkish corvette, fifty-seven men in all, were brought back to Hydra in triumph and individually roasted to death over fires on the beach.

As the forays of the islanders became bolder, the appearance of their warships spread the conflict inexorably to every area where Greeks and Turks had lived together. In Crete it appears that the Turks struck the first blow in an attempt to save themselves, but soon the island was torn with massacres as the two communities tried desperately to overcome one another. In Northern Greece the garrisons were stronger, but in Thessaly, Macedonia, and Chalcidice many Greeks joined the Revolution and mercilessly attacked the Turks. In some areas their leaders deliberately instigated massacres of the Turks in order to try to involve the whole Greek population in the Revolution. Many communities were drawn into the terror against their better judgement. Others remained conspicuously loyal to the Turks or waited to see which way the wind would blow.

At about the same time as these massacres were occurring in Greece, a military revolt took place in the Turkish frontier provinces beyond the Danube, Wallachia and Moldavia, in the area of present-day Romania. Prince Alexander Hypsilantes, a high-ranking Russian officer of Greek descent, crossed the frontier from Russia with a small party of expatriate Greeks. Three local military commanders with whom he had made arrangements beforehand joined him with their troops, but the general rising in the Provinces on which he had staked his chance of success did not occur. The local population, Romanian and Slav, to whom Greeks and Russians were as alien as Turks, were actively hostile, and the only other local forces who joined him were a few bands of undisciplined mercenaries. Hypsilantes issued a proclamation which implied that he was leading an advance party of the Russian army, and that the main force was about to invade European Turkey to liberate the Christian population from the Turks. However, it soon became clear that the Russians had no intention of invading Turkey, and Hypsilantes was officially disowned as a traitor.

The revolt quickly lost momentum. Hypsilantes proved unable to control his motley army or even to persuade it to pursue a common strategy, and his troops were responsible for widespread pillage and murder including the gratuitous massacre of the Turkish merchant colony at Galatz. He decided to march to Bucharest but made no sensible plans to prepare to meet the Turkish army. After two months his revolt had made no progress. He had nowhere to retreat to and all he could do was await the Turkish counter-attack in the forlorn hope that something would turn up.

The Ottoman Government in Constantinople, faced with violent revolutions in different parts of the Empire, decided to answer terror with terror. A policy of exterminating all Greeks in the Ottoman Empire seems to have been seriously considered, as it had been at earlier periods of Turkish history, but when the Sultan remembered how great a proportion of the imperial revenues was derived from his Christian subjects, he decided upon a more selective policy.

The Patriarch of Constantinople occupied a special place in the administration of the Empire. He was regarded as their leader by all the Greek Orthodox community, but at the same time he was a high Ottoman official responsible to the Government for a wide range of administrative, legal, and educational subjects. He held his office on the appointment of the Government and was, according to Turkish practice, regarded as responsible for the good conduct of the Greeks. On Easter Sunday, the reigning Patriarch, Gregorios, was formally accused of being implicated in the Greek rebellion and was summarily hanged. His body remained for three days suspended from the gate of the Patriarchate, and was then dragged through the streets and thrown into the sea. On the same day three bishops and a dozen other Greeks who had held high office in the Ottoman Government service were publicly executed in various parts of the city. The Patriarch had played no active part in the preparations for the Revolution, although it could not be denied that he had known what was planned, and before his death he had pronounced a solemn excommunication on the rebels and called upon them to return to their allegiance. His successor repeated the excommunication. The Greek revolutionaries, therefore, although they regarded the Patriarch as a martyr, were in rebellion not only against the Turks but against their own ecclesiastical authorities.

During the few weeks after the hanging of Gregorios, the Ottoman Government sought out prominent Greeks from all over the capital, men in the Government service, men with high positions in the Church, men of noble family and men who were simply rich, and put them to death by hanging or beheading. Hardly a day passed without a public display. On 15 June five archbishops and three bishops were executed. In early July more than seventy Greeks shared their fate. In other cities the same policy was pursued. On 3 May at Adrianople an ex-patriarch, nine other priests, and twenty merchants were hanged outside the Metropolitan Church. Greeks of lesser importance were sent into exile to the remote provinces. Some were put to death on their arrival at their places of banishment, others were imprisoned. On one day four hundred and fifty Greek shop-keepers and tradesmen were rounded up in Constantinople and sent to work in the mines.

These were all deliberate official acts of the Ottoman Government decided upon by Sultan Mahmoud himself. The object was entirely political. The men concerned were put to death because they were Greeks and no serious attempt was made to show that they had been personally implicated in the revolts, although the opportunity was taken of purging the church of possible dissidents. Since the Greeks as a community had revolted, the Greeks as a community had to be punished, even if the individuals who had revolted and the individuals who were punished lived hundreds of miles apart and knew next to nothing of one another.

The official executions were only a prelude. When the first news of the revolt reached Constantinople, the Islamic religious authorities, with the acquiescence of the Government, called on all good Moslems to avenge the murders committed by the Christians. For three weeks anarchy was per-mitted in the city and in the villages nearby. Bands of Turks led by religious fanatics and insubordinate janissaries roamed the streets killing, plundering, and burning. The Greek quarter was abandoned to the mob. Hundreds of Greeks were slaughtered, churches and houses were broken into and looted, and fires raged uncontrolled. The streets were strewn with rotting corpses.

At Smyrna there was a still greater massacre. The city mob was joined by hordes of Turks from the interior who had banded together with the declared intention of marching to the scene of the revolt. Turkish troops stationed outside disobeyed their officers and entered the city. For a while the authorities attempted to keep control and, apart from sporadic murders and riots, some form of order was maintained. But when news arrived of the sinking of a Turkish ship, the situation got out of hand. The local

Turkish magistrates were called on by the mob to sign a document authorizing the extermination of the Christians. When they refused they were themselves murdered. Three thousand armed Turks entered the Greek quarter and sated their lust for revenge on the defenceless populace.

Similar scenes occurred throughout the Ottoman Empire wherever there were Greek minorities. At Cos some hundreds of Greeks were killed, at Rhodes some thousands. In Cyprus, which had enjoyed good community relations, there were at first only isolated murders, until the Pashas of Aleppo and Acre were ordered to send troops to secure the island. When their Syrian troops landed, law and order broke down. Nicosia and Famagusta were sacked and the island was given over to killing and pillage. The local Turks joined in. The archbishop, five bishops, and thirty-six other priests were put to death.

Kydonies, on the coast of Asia Minor, was a thriving Greek city of thirty thousand inhabitants, established forty years earlier by colonists from the islands. The local pasha stationed a corps of his troops in the neighbourhood with strict orders to prevent any Turkish mobs from entering, but the news of the hanging of the Patriarch convinced the fanatics that the Government was in favour of an extermination of the Christians. The Kydonians, fearing that the pasha's troops would not be able to give protection, appealed desperately for help to the Greek fleet and four or five thousand were taken off by Hydriote ships, but the appearance of the ships provoked the Turks beyond endurance. The town was burned to the ground and thousands of Greeks were massacred. The survivors, mostly women and children, were rounded up and sent to the slave markets at Smyrna and Constantinople.

Besides terrorizing the Christian minorities into obedience in this way, the Ottoman Government also set in hand military measures to deal with the Revolution itself. The various military governors gathered their forces to restore the Ottoman sovereignty in the revolted provinces.

Alexander Hypsilantes, isolated and exposed in the Danubian Provinces, never had much prospect of success. His army, which had been disunited and undisciplined from the start, became a rabble, splitting up into separate bands and ravaging the country. When the arrival of a Turkish army became imminent, many of his followers melted away with their plunder. Some crossed to Austria, where they were handed over to the Turks, others found a temporary refuge in Russia. Hypsilantes himself tried desperately to maintain his authority and even arranged the assassination of one of his local allies, but this merely caused others to take their troops back over to the Turkish side. Almost the only force which put up a sustained resistance to the advancing Turkish army was a small band of expatriate Greeks, mostly students from European universities without military experience. At Dragashan they were attacked by a superior force of Turkish cavalry, their squares were broken, and they suffered heavy losses. The survivors staggered back to the Pruth and on 29 June made a last stand behind trenches within sight of a Russian army on the other side of the river. Only a small remnant escaped across the river to Russia. Alexander Hypsilantes himself had left before the battle. He fled to Austria where the authorities, rather than extradite him to Russia to be shot as a deserter, put him in prison. In less than four months the ill-judged and badly executed revolt in the Danubian Provinces came to an end, and they played no further part in the Greek War of Independence.

In the northern parts of Greece, too, the Turks had little difficulty in reimposing their authority. In the north-west there was already a large army which had been engaged for several years in trying to put down a rebellion by Ali Pasha of Ioannina. By rapidly deploying troops in strategic places, the Turks were able to isolate most of Epirus from the rest of Greece and, by subsidies, managed to retain the loyalty of much of the Albanian population. The revolutionaries made several forays from the south, but in spite of some apparent success against detachments of the army, they made little progress in spreading the revolt. Gradually the Turks regained control over the whole region.

In the north-east the Turkish general, adopting the traditional strategy, led an army into the area of Mount Pelion, reoccupied without difficulty the towns that had joined the revolt, and burned them down. All the men that he could capture were put to death, and the women and children were carried off to the slave market at Salonika. Except for one isolated town which hung on until 1823, all of Thessaly reverted to Ottoman authority. In Macedonia the revolutionaries had murdered the Turks as they did elsewhere, but their numerical superiority was not so great and they were not so thorough. The Turkish troops succeeded in maintaining their authority in the streets of Salonika even when the revolutionaries appeared outside, and soon they had reconquered the whole area except for a few isolated pockets which were to be crushed before the winter, with the usual massacres of the men and removal of the women to the slave market. Only the revolutionaries of Mount Athos escaped by paying an indemnity at the time of their surrender.

When the Ottoman fleet returned to Constantinople after its first cruise against the rebels, a victory celebration was arranged for the delectation and terrorization of the populace. As each ship entered harbour, the prisoners herded on the decks with ropes round their necks were dropped from various parts of the rigging until all the bowsprits and yard-arms were crowded with men struggling in the agonies of death. It was said that most of these unfortunate Greeks were not rebels but seamen serving in the Ottoman fleet.

All these events occurred during the first months of the Revolution, most of them in the first few weeks. It is impossible to give a reliable estimate of the numbers who lost their lives. Even an order of magnitude is difficult to establish. Contemporary accounts are sparse and eye-witnesses notoriously untrustworthy in such confused situations. Many of those who apparently escaped the first massacres were soon involved in other outbreaks or died of starvation, exposure, or disease shortly afterwards. Others who survived as slaves were soon killed off as their usefulness diminished. It seems certain, however, that during the terrible summer of 1821 several tens of thousands of Turks were killed and several tens of thousands of Greeks. Only a tiny minority on either side were killed in battle in the usual sense of the term. In Southern Greece none of the settled Turkish or Moslem Albanian Communities survived, and in Constantinople and Asia Minor the Greek population was terrorized into such a state of submission that during the whole course of the war and for years later they were never again a threat to the Turkish power.

From many points of view the Greek population of the Ottoman Empire was better off in the years before the Revolution than it had ever been. As far as the Greeks of wealth and education were concerned, opportunities for advancement in the Ottoman service were steadily improving. A growing number of positions in the Government service were reserved for them, some on a hereditary basis, and in the two Danubian Provinces the Romanians and Slavs were ruled exclusively by Greeks. A large Greek mercantile class had grown up and most of the foreign trade and shipping was in the hands of Greeks. Thriving colonies of Greeks, often very rich, were establishing themselves in the cities and ports of Western Europe and Southern Russia. In the regions of the Empire where the Greeks were in the majority they had their own municipal institutions largely independent of Turkish interference. The Greek Church, with its headquarters at Constantinople, enjoyed wide-ranging privileges and was an integral part of the administration of the Empire. Even the Greek peasants could console themselves with the thought that they were exempt from some of the burdens, such as military service, which caused great suffering to the Moslem inhabitants of the Empire. They were considered by observers before the Revolution to be in a more fortunate position than the Catholic Irish.

In many areas of Greece, Greeks and Turks lived together on reasonably amicable terms. In some parts of the Peloponnese the population was almost entirely Greek, in others almost entirely Turkish. The Turkish garrisons were small and had been so little needed for internal security duties that they had long since neglected their training. The fortresses had been allowed to fall into disrepair and in some places the only armament was guns and powder left over from the Venetian occupation. Some of the Turks had been so long settled among the Greeks that they no longer could speak Turkish. When the history of the Greek Revolution came to be

B

written, the Greeks in their search for justification tended to recall many of the institutions of Turkish tyranny—such as forcible abduction of children to serve as janissaries—that had fallen into disuse long before the Revolution.

The Greeks had, of course, genuine and severe grievances. In the collection of taxes the Government was unjust, arbitrary, and oppressive, and the fact that the tax collectors were the local Greek leaders did not protect the Turkish Government from the blame. The taxes usually fell on the poorest classes, and Turkish governors regarded personal enrichment as a normal perquisite of their position. Much of the best land was owned by Turks and they were to a large extent shielded from this exploitation. In addition the Greeks were subjected to a range of humiliating regulations and restrictions deliberately designed to emphasize their inferior status: these could only be avoided by a change of religion.

The Government was unable to maintain effective law and order. Bands of robbers infested the mountains and often descended into the plains, causing great misery to the settled population both Greek and Turk. To try to control these robbers and to keep open the lines of communication, the Turkish authorities had for centuries permitted local leaders to maintain troops, but they were often as rapacious as the robbers themselves. The distinction between the *klephts*, the robbers, and the *armatoli*, the licensed armed Greeks, was hardly noticed by the Greeks of the plains, although later history was to build up an image of the *klephts* as patriots and freedom fighters.

In the eyes of the majority of Greeks in the Ottoman Empire, it was primarily their religion that distinguished them from the Turks, Arabs, Armenians, Jews, and others who made up the population of the Empire. All their feelings of being a community centred on the Orthodox Church with its Patriarch at Constantinople, and they felt themselves as alien to the Roman Catholic Greeks who inhabited some of the islands as to the Moslems. Their tradition led back to the great days when a Greek-speaking Roman Emperor sat on the throne of a Christian Empire at Constantinople and the Orthodox Church and the Patriarchate had an unbroken succession which had been little affected by the Turkish conquest. The Greek language which they spoke was known as 'Romaic' from the time when they had been citizens of the Eastern Roman Empire. They called their children after the saints of the Orthodox Church, Georgios, Demetrios, Spyridon.

Most Greeks in the Ottoman Empire had no comprehension of that complex of ideas relating to territorial boundaries and cultural and linguistic uniformity which makes up the European concept of a nation state. The concept was equally strange to the Turks who for long afterwards were to regard the name of Turk as a term of abuse. The animosity between the various communities arose predominantly from their religious differences.

Within the Ottoman system, advancement was open to an able man regardless of origin, provided only that he was a Moslem, and numerous Greeks had reached positions of great power by embracing Islam. Several generals on the Turkish side during the Greek Revolution were Moslem Greeks. The Albanians, some of whom were Christian and some Moslem, were torn by this dilemma, and when the need for decision became inescapable, they divided by religion and not by race. The Roman Catholic Greeks, who lived in the islands which had been under Venetian or Genoese rule, regarded themselves as a separate community. The Albanians of Hydra and Spetsae, many of whom could not even speak Greek, regarded themselves as Greek because their allegiance was to the Orthodox Church.

For centuries the leaders of the Greek and Moslem religions had preached hatred of one another. For an infidel of the opposed religion no contempt was too great, no feelings of humanity need intrude. If a man was hated by God, then mere human beings had a clear duty to do God's work for him. The simple Greek peasants who remorselessly killed their Turkish neighbours saw the Revolution as a war of religious extermination and, for the most part, the bishops and priests who led them shared this view. The first Greek revolutionary flags portrayed a cross over an upturned crescent or a cross over a severed Turkish head. Turkish boys who were not put to death were forcibly baptized, just as Greek boys captured by the Turks were forcibly circumcised. Under the banners of the Cross and the Crescent murder could be a religious duty.

The peasants of Greece were, however, merely the instrument of the Greek Revolution. The cause lay in a complex of ideas mostly imported from the West, which towards the end of the eighteenth century began to make their influence felt in Greece. During the late eighteenth century the colonies of Greeks in the cities of Italy, France, Austria, and Russia, grew and prospered. At first they were mainly communities of merchants interested principally in making money but, by the time of Napoleon, they had leisure for other activities. While remaining determinedly Greek, they became increasingly integrated into the countries where they had settled; their sons attended European universities, served in European armies, and absorbed the European political and intellectual ideas of the time. It was these overseas Greeks who first conceived a Greek Revolution as a nationalist movement on the European model. Their ideas were more complex than the simple wish to vent religious hatred which inspired the Greeks in Greece, and it was they who provided the initiative and organization which launched the Revolution.

Sometime around 1814 a few prominent Greeks living mainly in Russia formed a secret society, the 'Friendly Society', with the aim of promoting a revolution in the Ottoman Empire. Members were given the responsibility of finding new recruits who were admitted into the Society with awesome ceremonies of initiation and oaths of secrecy. The new members were told almost nothing of the nature of the controlling organization. Soon messengers were being sent over Europe to all communities where Greeks lived, and the leaders of the Greeks in the Ottoman Empire were initiated in increasing numbers—bishops, local landowners, municipal officials, shipowners, and robber chieftains. The conspiracy became widespread and indiscriminate, and few of its members had any clear idea of what was being planned. The ordinary Greeks, who did not understand the complex and alien political concepts of nationality put about by the educated Greeks, simply assumed that the overseas Greeks like themselves were interested in an extermination of their religious adversaries. If hardly anyone had much idea of the real nature of the Friendly Society, this merely served to make it appear more widespread and more powerful than it really was.

Meanwhile another force was moving in the opposite direction. Sultan Mahmoud, who in 1808 had taken over the government of the Empire, was a patient, determined, and ruthless ruler, who seemed to be reversing the long decline of the power of the Ottoman Empire. In 1820 Mahmoud decided that he was strong enough to bring back to obedience one of the last of the powerful independent pashas, Ali Pasha of Ioannina, who had ruled much of Albania and north-west Greece for nearly twenty years. In February 1820 Ali was ordered to Constantinople in person to give an account for certain crimes of which he had been accused. When he refused, he was declared a rebel and an army was mustered to restore the Ottoman authority. By midsummer, as a result of swift decisive action by the imperial authorities, Ali was surrounded by hostile forces and it was clear that a long struggle would be undertaken to subdue him.

It was Ali's rebellion in 1820 that precipitated the Greek Revolution. The conspirators overseas calculated that, if the Turks succeeded in putting down Ali Pasha, Turkish power throughout Greece would be immeasurably strengthened and a later Greek Revolution would have much less chance of success. If, however, they struck while Ali was still able to fight, then the Turkish forces would be divided and weakened. The Turks, for their part, feared that Ali might try to extend the area of rebellion. They noticed his overtures to the Greeks, promising political benefits if they would help him against the Turks, and found themselves obliged to make counter-offers in an attempt to maintain their loyalty. All over the Peninsula the Greeks, especially those who were permitted to have arms, found themselves being drawn into a position of having to declare either for Ali or for the Turkish Government.

The overseas conspirators decided suddenly to intensify their preparations. Messengers were sent all over Greece and thousands more Greeks were enrolled in the conspiracy. The building up of a treasury, the collection of arms, and the manufacture of gunpowder were speeded up. The *klephts* organized themselves to be ready for violence, and some of their leaders returned secretly from exile. The shipowners of the islands recalled their vessels to Greek harbours. A general air of expectancy built up all through 1820.

The sudden increase in tension was not lost on the Turks. They knew a good deal about the conspiracy, and rumours that a revolution was imminent were constantly being passed to them. They decided to take precautions. Orders were issued to repair some of the fortresses of the Peloponnese and, for the first time for many years, a start was actually made in putting these orders into effect.

In the Peloponnese, therefore, events moved inexorably towards the classic prelude to civil war. Both communities could see that the other was making preparations in case of trouble, and every act which each side took was a provocation to the other. It was increasingly obvious that whichever side dared to strike the first blow would give itself an overwhelming advantage. Both parties knew that the Turks did not have enough military resources in the area to hold down an armed population by normal means and that the usual Turkish policy in such circumstances was to try to head off trouble by making an example here and there. The Greeks were aware that, in the event of an unsuccessful revolt, the Turks were unlikely to distinguish between the innocent and the guilty when it came to restoring their authority. The overseas conspirators had no real appreciation of the situation in the Peloponnese. It was part of their plan that the revolution should break out simultaneously in all parts of the Ottoman Empire, but they unwisely decided to make their main effort in the Danubian Provinces.

The revolution in the Peloponnese broke out even before Alexander Hypsilantes raised his standard on the Danube. In February 1821 the chief Turkish officials met at Tripolitsa to consider how to contain the revolutionary fever which was everywhere in the air. They had basically two choices, either to do nothing provocative in the hope that the tension would die down or to take some strong action in the hope of forestalling trouble in advance. They chose the latter. Orders were issued for the Greek population to hand in their arms to the authorities, and the various local Greek leaders were asked to come in person to Tripolitsa.

The Turkish action, instead of quietening the situation, precipitated the tragedy it was intended to prevent. The Greek leaders were put in a dilemma. They were obliged to choose either revolution or submission; no middle course remained open. Even at this stage many would undoubtedly have preferred submission but almost at once the decision was taken out of their hands. The Greeks who were party to the conspiracy proclaimed a revolution and began to murder the Turkish population. Once the first blood was shed there was no going back. The revolutionaries believed that only by ruthlessness could they preserve their safety in the long run; once the murdering had begun, half measures would be fatal. Suddenly the pent-up hatreds, which had been deliberately intensified during the period of rising tension, were let loose. The bishops and priests exhorted their parishioners to exterminate the infidel Moslems. The *klephts* and *armatoli* came down from the mountains and ravaged the Turkish settlements. Control soon passed out of the hands of the leaders and the whole country was overrun by bands of armed men killing and plundering. The Turks of Greece paid the penalty for centuries of wrongs, real and imagined, and for their inherited religious beliefs. But the savage passion for revenge soon degenerated into a frenzied delight in killing and horror for their own sakes. The Turkish counter-terror which began with the hanging of the Patriarch at Constantinople on Easter day, started before the Ottoman Government realized the full extent of what was happening in the Peloponnese, but soon it was in full swing. Atrocity was answered by atrocity as Greeks and Turks struck mercilessly at their defenceless neighbours. The orgy of genocide exhausted itself in the Peloponnese only when there were no more Turks to kill.

2. The Return of the Ancient Hellenes

Shortly after the outbreak of the Revolution, one of the local Greek leaders in the Peloponnese, who was also a member of the conspiracy, issued a manifesto to the governments and peoples of Europe. A few extracts will give an indication of the style.

Reduced to a condition so pitiable, deprived of every right, we have, with unanimous voice, resolved to take up arms, and struggle against the tyrants. . . . In one word, we are unanimously resolved on Liberty or Death. Thus determined, we earnestly invite the united aid of all civilized nations to promote the attainment of our holy and legitimate purpose, the recovery of our rights, and the revival of our unhappy nation.

With every right does Hellas, our mother, whence ye also, O Nations, have become enlightened, anxiously request your friendly assistance with money, arms, and counsel, and we entertain the highest hope that our appeal will be listened to; promising to show ourselves deserving of your interest, and at the proper time to prove our gratitude by deeds.

> Given from the Spartan Head Quarters
> Calamata 23 March 1821 (O.S.)
> Signed Pietro Mauromichali, Commander-in-
> Chief of the Spartan and Messenian Forces[1]

To the average Peloponnesian Greek of 1821, even had he been able to read, the manifesto would have been incomprehensible. He would probably not have recognized the appellation of 'Hellene' as applying to himself and he would certainly have had no appreciation of the conception of 'Hellas' as a nation-state.

The direct tradition of knowledge of Ancient Greece had largely died out centuries before. The inhabitants of Olympia, Delphi, and Sparta knew little or nothing of the interesting history of the towns they occupied. Other famous ancient place names survived only in distorted Turkish or

Italian versions. A few manuscripts of ancient authors survived in the libraries of the monasteries hidden among heaps of theological adversaria but, with few exceptions, the libraries rotted undisturbed. The surviving ruins of ancient temples were ignored or used as building materials. The priests taught their parishioners to despise them as relics of the pagans.

In the eighteenth century a small change occurred. An increasing number of travellers from the West found their way to Greece. They were rich and educated and it was principally their interest in Ancient Greece that brought them. By the beginning of the nineteenth century the travelling gentle-man, with his pocket version of the classics, became a permanent feature of the Greek scene. These confident and successful men were amazed at the ignorance they found. They began to lecture the Greeks about their ancient history and established a regular circuit of famous sites to be visited. The Greeks picked up scraps of history and legend and repeated them back to subsequent visitors. In the towns frequented by tourists a superficial knowledge of Ancient Greece thus appeared, derived mainly from the West, but believed by many of the visitors, much to their delight, to be a genuine tradition from ancient times.

To the European reader, on the other hand, whether he agreed with the sentiments or not, the manifesto addressed by the Greeks to the peoples of Europe was an easily understandable political document. All the ideas were familiar to him, Liberty, Struggle against Tyrants, National Rights. The style is reminiscent of hundreds of proclamations that had poured from the presses all over Europe since the time of the French Revolution. The assumptions of the manifesto that Greece was inhabited by Hellenes and Spartans descended from the Ancient Hellenes would have caused no surprise.

The explanation for the apparent paradox was simple. Although the ideas in the manifesto appeared to come from Greece, they were, in reality, Western European ideas which had been taken back to Greece by Europeans and by Greeks educated in Europe. The classical tradition which lay at the heart of European civilization had been brought back to Greece after an absence of many centuries. The influence of the Ancient Greeks returned at last to the land of their birth.

At the time of the Greek Revolution, European interest in the Ancient Greeks had seldom been higher. Since the eighteenth century it had become increasingly recognized that the Roman writers and artists who had formerly been held up as models of excellence were themselves the intellectual descendants of the Greeks. The habit of regarding all of ancient civilization as equally 'classical' was refined. The distinction was increasingly drawn between the Greeks and the Romans, and very much in favour of the Greeks. Architects began to look to the monuments of the fifth century B.C. instead of the Roman Imperial Age. Artists—with less success—tried to extract the qualities that were intrinsically Greek from the surviving Greco-Roman copies. The Greek language and the Greek authors were studied more intensively. The new-found enthusiasm for the Greek became a political force. It was linked with the ideas of political liberty and national independence, which were spread so widely over Europe by the wars of the French Republic and Empire. The leaders of the movements that regarded themselves as representing all that was most humane and progressive claimed Ancient Greece as their model and their guide.

Unfortunately, in the refreshing rediscovery of Ancient Greek civilization and in the flood of propaganda, proper historical methods tended to be lost sight of. Much of the source material which gives life to our picture of Ancient Greece in the fifth and fourth centuries, particularly the biographical information about the great men, is of questionable value. In the eighteenth century all ancient authors tended to be regarded as of equal value as historical sources, even though some lived hundreds of years after the events they describe. The resulting picture was very different from what we now believe to have been the reality. Ancient history came to be regarded, like biblical history, as applying to an age inhabited by men larger than life, to whom ordinary human considerations meant less than at other times. The heroes were the bravest that had ever been, the philosophers the wisest, the political institutions the most enlightened, the artists the most sublime, the tyrants the most cruel, the enemies the most hateful, the traitors the most despicable; all the situations were clear cut, there was no difficulty in telling right from wrong; and every event had an edifying moral. [2]

A society in whose culture the Ancient Greeks played such an important part was bound to have a view about the Modern Greeks. The inhabitants of that famous land, whose language was still recognizably the same as that of Demosthenes, could not be regarded as just another remote tribe of natives or savages.* Western Europe could not escape being concerned with the nature of the relationship between the Ancient and the Modern Greeks. The question has teased, perplexed, and confused generations of Greeks and Europeans and it still stirs passions to an extent difficult for the rational to condone.

Whether the present inhabitants of Greece are descended from the Ancient Greeks is a profoundly unsatisfactory question. No method of subdividing the question makes much sense. On the one hand, one can attempt to trace the numerous incursions of immigrants to Greece and try to assess the extent to which the 'blood' of the Ancients has been diluted by outside races, Romans, barbarians, Franks, Turks, Venetians, Albanians, etc. On the other hand, one can point to the remarkable survival of ideas and customs and, in particular, to the astonishing strength of the linguistic tradition.

* The bloody revolt of the Serbs against the Turks in 1808 aroused no interest in Western Europe.

But neither approach seems to lead to the kind of answer which those who ask the question are seeking. What they seem to want to know is—Are the Modern Greeks the *same* as the Ancient Greeks? Are their racial and national characteristics the same? Do the Modern Greeks behave in the same kind of way as the Ancient Athenians, Spartans, and Corinthians behaved? If one looks among the Modern Greeks will one find the equivalents of Pericles and Sophocles and Plato? By their nature such questions are vague and contain within them a host of assumptions—about human nature, genetics and race, the influence of environment on behaviour, and the reliability of our knowledge of ancient history—all of which are questionable and some of which are simply unfounded.

And that is only part of the difficulty with the concept. Even if it were possible to devise some satisfactory way of disentangling the numerous intertwined thoughts, and if it were concluded that the Modern Greeks had a strong blood or cultural link with the Ancients, would this fact necessarily be of help in determining how to behave towards them in the nineteenth (or twentieth) century?

During the hundreds of years since the glorious age of Greece, various views have been held about the Modern Greeks. Europeans of the Middle Ages and Renaissance times may have assumed that the Modern Greeks were the descendants of the Ancients but they were far from regarding this as implying any continuity of character, let alone imposing any obligation. To be Greek was to be a drunkard, a lecher, and, especially, a cheat. It never seems to have occurred to the men who issued the calls to join in the defence of Byzantium, for example, to suggest that they were aiding the descendants of Pericles. Nor as Christians did the Western Europeans (of whatever sect) feel any instinctive sympathy for the schismatic Christians of the Orthodox Church.

By the seventeenth century, however, the literatures of Europe had already adopted a new convention. The image of the descendants of the once great Greeks living in humble cottages among the ruins of the magnificent buildings of antiquity offered innumerable opportunities for melancholy comment on the transience of human affairs. Equally, more hopeful writers could conjure up pictures of the Modern Greeks casting out the Turks and reviving a golden age. Most Europeans came to assume that the Ancient and Modern Greeks were the same without bothering unduly about the implications of the assumption. The philhellenic conventions gradually became accepted as self-evident truths. By 1770 they began to have the reassuring ring of the obvious and the few writers who questioned them were dismissed as crankish or malevolent.

The conventions of the poets and the essayists were repeated in the travel books, and the ideas which had started life as literary conceits seemed to be confirmed by direct observation. Travelling in Greece was expensive and dangerous and the authors tended to regard themselves as belonging to a club. They drew shamelessly on their predecessors to eke out their own information and often devoted part of their book to discussing the inadequacies of their rivals. Only a few were equipped to make more than superficial observations and many indulged in sweeping generalizations on the strength of a few weeks' visit.

The travellers were more interested in the Ancient than the Modern Greeks and a good deal of their effort was naturally devoted to describing the surviving ruins and charting the ancient topography. They delighted in drawing elaborate comparisons between the Ancients and Moderns. They picked out qualities which they thought were common to both—the quickness of wit, the love of arguing, even the habit of the siesta. They looked closely into the faces of the men and women and imagined that they saw features familiar from ancient sculpture and vases. In the wild and lawless district of Maina they were unanimous that the inhabitants were the direct descendants of the warlike Spartans. A few French writers carried their comparisons to a point of absurd sentimentality. On the whole, however, the travellers came to the conclusion that the Modern Greeks were a 'degenerate' version of the Ancient Greeks, and many while admitting the degeneration, were of the belief that a 'regeneration' was possible and even imminent. Most of the travellers devoted a section of their books to discussing the likelihood of the Greeks regaining their freedom and gave their opinion one way or the other.[3]

Lord Byron visited Greece in 1809 and 1810 and, on his return, published the first two cantos of *Childe Harold's Pilgrimage* based mainly on his experiences. Byron had read many of the travel books and the philhellenic sentiments which *Childe Harold* contains can be found in the works of dozens of earlier writers in prose and in verse, but never before had they been expressed in a best-seller. At least twelve editions of the poem were printed between 1812 and 1821 and it was translated into several European languages. Byron quickly became a European celebrity. From the first appearance of *Childe Harold* in 1812 until his death in 1824 his every act and every word was an object of interest—women threw themselves at him; the famous fought for his attention; friends, visitors, and snoopers dutifully recorded in their notebooks every overheard chance remark. The newspapers and reviews were full of anecdotes true and invented. His letters were assiduously preserved. It was obvious from the first that Byron was going to be one of the most famous men of the age and no detail about him seemed too trivial to be worth noting. His irreverence towards established authority and his tempestuous sexual life aroused intense indignation and envy, all of which contributed to the overwhelming public interest. Few, if any, Englishmen have had such a widespread influence or aroused such interest among their contemporaries at home and abroad.

After *Childe Harold's Pilgrimage* came a succession of 'Grecian' tales which sold in tens of thousands of copies. Many of them repeated philhellenic sentiments. The clichés of less talented travellers suddenly burst into life and the ruin and regeneration of classical Greece became a stirring romantic theme.

> Fair Greece! sad relic of departed worth!
> Immortal, though no more; though fallen, great!
> Who now shall lead thy scatter'd children forth,
> And long accustom'd bondage uncreate?
> Not such thy sons who whilome did await,
> The hopeless warriors of a willing doom,
> In bleak Thermopylae's sepulchral strait—
> Oh! who that gallant spirit shall resume,
> Leap from Eurotas' banks, and call thee from the tomb?
>
>   *   *   *
>
> When riseth Lacedemon's hardihood,
> When Thebes Epaminondas rears again,
> When Athens' children are with arts endued,
> When Grecian mothers shall give birth to men,
> Then mayst thou be restor'd; but not till then.
> A thousand years scarce serve to form a state;
> An hour may lay it in the dust: and when
> Can man its shatter'd splendour renovate,
> Recal its virtues back, and vanquish Time and Fate?

(*Childe Harold's Pilgrimage*, Canto 11, 1812)

> Despite of every yoke she bears,
> That land is glory's still and theirs!
> 'Tis still a watchword to the earth:
> When man would do a deed of worth
> He points to Greece, and turns to tread,
> So sanctioned, on the tyrant's head:
> He looks to her, and rushes on
> Where life is lost or freedom won.

(*The Siege of Corinth*, 1816)

After a few years Byron tired of the literary formula which had brought him such success, recognizing better than his friends that his talents were of a higher order. His audience was aghast and clamoured for more in the old style. We may be glad that Byron persevered with *Don Juan*, but even here, amid the humour and irreverence, he included the most famous of all philhellenic poems:

> The isles of Greece, the isles of Greece!
>   Where burning Sappho loved and sung,
> Where grew the arts of war and peace,—
>   Where Delos rose and Phoebus sprung!
> Eternal summer gilds them yet,
> But all, except their sun, is set.
>
>   *   *   *

The mountains look on Marathon—
  And Marathon looks on the sea;
And musing there an hour alone,
  I dream'd that Greece might still be free;
For standing on the Persian's grave,
I could not deem myself a slave.

  *   *   *

'Tis something, in the death of fame,
  Though link'd among a fetter'd race,
To feel at least a patriot's shame,
  Even as I sing, suffuse my face;
For what is left the poet here?
For Greeks a blush—for Greece a tear.

  *   *   *

Must *we* but weep o'er days more blest?
  Must *we* but blush?—Our fathers bled.
Earth! render back from out thy breast
  A remnant of our Spartan dead!
Of the three hundred grant but three,
To make a new Thermopylae.

        (*Don Juan*, Canto III, 1821)

With the advent of Byron, literary philhellenism became a widespread European movement. Hosts of imitators copied his rhetorical verses, and travellers who visited Greece after the appearance of *Childe Harold* in 1812 were even more enthusiastic than their predecessors.

By the time of the Greek Revolution in 1821 the educated public in Europe had been deeply immersed in three attractive ideas—that Ancient Greece had been a paradise inhabited by supermen; that the Modern Greeks were the true descendants of the Ancient Greeks; and that a war against the Turks could somehow 'regenerate' the Modern Greeks and restore the former glories. Not everyone believed in these ideas without qualification but there were few more sober ideas in circulation about the real state of Modern Greece.

As far as Western Europe was concerned, philhellenism remained until the outbreak of the Greek Revolution largely a literary phenomenon. It was sometimes employed as propaganda, for example by Napoleon in his attempts to instigate trouble against the Turks, but on the whole its appeal lay in the opportunities it presented of drawing moral lessons about the rise and fall of civilization and the romance of ruins. The responsibility for turning philhellenism into a political programme belongs to the Greeks themselves. The impetus came from the Greeks overseas.

By the late eighteenth century, the rich colonies of Greeks settled in Europe had become largely integrated into Western culture and had consciously absorbed many European customs and ideas. It was only natural that they should embrace the literary tradition of philhellenism and build on it. The new Greek literature which they began is full of themes and conventions which are essentially Western. The overseas Greeks adopted the belief that the best way of returning to antiquity was by imitation. They began to try to write in the language of the ancients, to revive the old grammar and to rid modern Greek of 'impurities'. They sometimes took to wearing antique clothes. In many European cities a Greek intelligentsia grew up, completely accepted into the local culture and yet losing no opportunity of advocating the cause of Greek freedom and regeneration.

Once the archaizing process was well established among the Greek colonies in Europe, they began to spread their ideas back to the Greeks in the Ottoman Empire. Money and books were sent to establish schools where ancient history and ancient Greek could be taught. European travellers were persuaded to give donations to charities in order to send Greek boys to Europe for education. The custom grew of adopting ancient names instead of the traditional saints' names. At Athens in 1813 the schoolmaster conducted a ceremony with laurel and olive leaves and formally exhorted his pupils to change their names from Ioannes and Pavlos to Pericles, Themistocles, and Xenophon. At the school in Kydonies (the city destroyed by the Turks in 1821) the pupils added the ancient names to the Greek names—Tzannos-Epaminondas, Charalantis-Pausanias.

Newspapers in Greek were published in Vienna and elsewhere and circulated in the Ottoman Empire. At Odessa a Greek theatre put on plays with such patriotic titles as *The Death of Demosthenes* and *Harmodius and Aristogeiton*. Voltaire, Alfieri, and other authors who preached Hellenism were translated into Modern Greek as were the ancient Greek authors.

The movement was mainly directed towards a return to Ancient Greece and yet the overseas Greeks, unlike the Europeans they copied, still retained a hankering for the Byzantine days as well. Constantine was a name adopted as often as Pericles and the revolution they dreamed of was not confined to establishing a nation in the area of present-day Greece—they instinctively felt that the centre of the Greek world was not Athens or Sparta or Corinth but Constantinople. And since Constantinople was now so clearly a Turkish city, with the Turks forming the majority of the population, the logic was inescapable that the Turks would have to go. Many of the overseas Greeks did not shrink from this conclusion. The famous war song said to be by Rhigas which Byron translated, so similar in style to many poems being written elsewhere, shows that he, at least, fully understood what philhellenism would really involve in practice.

> Sons of the Greeks! let us go
> In arms against the foe
> Till their hated blood shall flow
> In a river past our feet.

*   *   *

Hellenes of past ages,
  Oh, start again to life!
At the sound of my trumpet, breaking
  Your sleep, oh join with me!
And the seven-hill'd city* seeking
  Fight, conquer till we're free.

A great impetus was given to the spread of philhellenic ideas by the conquest of the Ionian Islands by the French and their subsequent virtual annexation by the British. The Ionian Islands had never been under Ottoman rule, having survived as outposts of Venice during the centuries of Turkish expansion, and their inhabitants were deeply affected by European customs and ideas. The Ionian Greeks, who now enjoyed a higher standard of education and a more just and settled government than the Greeks on the mainland, were well placed to advance the cause.

The occupying powers delighted in what they regarded as harmless archaizing. In 1809, within a year of the second French occupation, the local school of Corfu assumed the ancient name of the Academy of Korkyra and dated its prospectus the first year of the 647th Olympiad. The school was to devote itself to reviving the ancient Greek language and the prizes were to be an iron medal, 'the money of Lacedaemon', and crowns of wild olives. The practical British soldiers who succeeded the French as administrators were less enthusiastic about this antiquarianism but the process continued. The islands were renamed according to their ancient forms— Zante becoming Zacynthos, Santa Maura becoming Leukas—and a currency was established in obols in place of piastres. The islands became a testing-ground for English educational experiments and an advance base for protestant missionaries working throughout the Near East. A rich English eccentric, Lord Guilford, settled in Corfu, joined the Greek Church, and devoted his fortune to building up a Hellenic University. Lord Guilford, as chancellor of the university, invariably wore a purple robe in imitation of Socrates, with an ancient-style mantle tied round his shoulders with a gold clasp. Round his head he wore a velvet band embroidered with olives and the owl of Ancient Athens. The professors and students also wore ancient dress, including buskins, with different colours to denote the different faculties: citron and orange for medicine, green and violet for law, green and blue for philosophy, and so on. Lord Guilford's countrymen thought that he carried his colourful concern for the classics to the point of absurdity, but during the few years while the money lasted many Greeks attended his university and a steady stream of European books were made available in Modern Greek.

The Ionian Islands provided a useful bridge between the overseas Greeks and the Greeks of the Ottoman Empire, and in the years before the Revolution,

* Constantinople.

many agents passed to and from the mainland promoting the work of the 'Friendly Society'. But the apparent success of reviving Hellenism in the Ionian Islands and in a few towns elsewhere disguised from the conspirators how little they knew of the real conditions. The narrow strait between the Ionian Islands and the mainland of Greece was the dividing line between two worlds. The overseas Greeks and the higher classes of the Ionians were essentially Western European in outlook and the philhellenism which they adopted was a Western concept. In Greece itself the Greeks still thought of themselves as the Christian inhabitants of a Moslem Empire, not as the descendants of the Hellenes. The veneer of philhellenism in Greece was very thin indeed. The Greek leaders in Greece itself who joined the conspiracy were content to adopt the propaganda of the expatriates, but they knew that their power over their people depended on something else entirely. A policy of establishing a European nation-state based on ideas about Ancient Hellas formulated in Western Europe was far from their minds. Their aims were much simpler. They wanted to get rid of the Turks and take their place as rulers of the country. But they had no wish to set up European political institutions, to assume Western or ancient clothes, or to speak ancient Greek. They did not want to be 're-generated' at all. They were content with their primitive semi-barbarous Eastern way of life which they had always known. When the Revolution broke out in 1821, it was not apparent that there was a disparity of aims between the overseas Greeks who had instigated the Revolution and the local Greeks who had carried it out. The policy of both groups required the wholesale slaughter or expulsion of the Turks. Once that had been accomplished, events were soon to show that there were fundamental differences.

3. The Regiment

Indications that violence had broken out in Greece began to reach Western Europe when ships called at Marseilles, Trieste, and Ancona to buy arms and ammunition. Then letters arrived from Greeks at the scene of war and travellers hurried back with their impressions. The newspapers circulated such scraps of information as came their way with little means of checking them. Stories current in the ports were published in the local newspapers and then reprinted in other newspapers all over Europe.

Since the organization of the Revolution was in the hands of men educated in Europe, it was natural that their version of affairs should be the first to appear. They were conscious of the need to obtain international support and many of the proclamations and communiqués were drafted more with an eye to the European reader than to the Greeks to whom they were supposedly addressed.

While Alexander Hypsilantes should have been making military preparations to meet the Turks or trying to establish a secure base, he was devoting his efforts to issuing proclamations.

Let us recollect, brave and generous Greeks, the liberty of the classic land of Greece; the battles of Marathon and Thermopylae, let us combat upon the tombs of our ancestors who, to leave us free, fought and died. The blood of our tyrants is dear to the shades of the Theban Epaminondas, and of the Athenian Thasybulus who conquered and destroyed the thirty tyrants—to those of Harmodius and Aristogeiton who broke the yoke of Pisistratus—to that of Timoleon who restored liberty to Corinth and to Syracuse—above all, to those of Miltiades, Themistocles, Leonidas, and the three hundred who massacred so many times their number of the innumerable army of the barbarous Persians—the hour is come to destroy their successors, more barbarous and still more detestable. Let us do this or perish. To arms then, my friends, your country calls you.[1]

Only a tiny proportion of Greeks could have had any comprehension of these historical allusions.

A stream of false rumours poured from the Danubian Provinces—that Hypsilantes had won great victories, that tens of thousands of Bulgarians and Serbs had joined him, that important cities were being captured and that the Russians had invaded. Stories of Hypsilantes' successes were being printed in Europe long after his rash venture had been crushed.[2]

The news from Greece itself was even more misleading. The story was widely believed that on the outbreak of the Revolution the Greeks had offered the Turks rights of civic and religious freedom within a Greek state.[3] In May it was reported that the whole of the Peloponnese and Epirus was in Greek hands and that a Turkish army of 30,000 had been destroyed.[4] In July it was announced that the standard of the cross now flew on the Parthenon and that the Greeks had taken Athens without losing a man.[5] Two great naval battles were said to have been fought against the combined Turkish and Egyptian fleets, in one of which the Greeks sank eight ships.[6] Great victories were said to have been won, usually near sites famous in antiquity, in which thousands of Turks were killed and only a handful of Greeks. The newspapers delighted in drawing comparisons with the Ancient Greeks. The 'victories' of the Modern Greeks, according to the *Examiner*, enhanced even the glory of the Ancients:

It is hardly possible to name a spot in the scene of action, without starting some beautiful spirit of antiquity. Here are victories at Samos, the birthplace of Pythagoras; at Rhodes, famous for its roses and accomplishments; at Cos, the birthplace of Apelles, Hippocrates, and Simonides. But to behave as the Greeks have done at Malvasia is to dispute the glory even with those older names.[7]*

As the news became more detailed there was a search for heroes. The Mainotes were of course the Modern Spartans but Marco Botsaris, the Albanian Suliote leader, was usually taken as the Modern Leonidas. When stories appeared of a woman of Hydra, Boubolina, leading the Greeks in battle, she was dubbed the Modern Artemisia or the Greek Joan of Arc. It seemed impossible to represent any event in Modern Greece as an event in its own right without overwhelming it with misleading allusions.

The Turks were unaware of this aspect of international public opinion. They had no comprehension of the curious phenomenon of philhellenism which was returning full circle to the land where it was born. When the Revolution broke out, the Ottoman Government correctly diagnosed that the institution which gave a unity to the Greeks was the Church. There was a certain terrible logic in the Turkish policy of killing the patriarch and bishops and terrorizing the Christian inhabitants of Constantinople and Asia Minor. Most of the Greeks of the Ottoman Empire saw nothing strange

* For a description of what actually happened at Monemvasia see p. 41.

in the idea of taking revenge on a community as a whole for wrongs done by a few members. They shared this ethic themselves.

It did not occur to Europeans, as they read the news from Greece, that the Greeks of the Ottoman Empire shared the Eastern scale of values and the news arrived in such a way that the fact was not brought home to them. Constantinople and Smyrna were full of Europeans: diplomats, traders, and seamen. They were major communications centres from which ships regularly sailed to Europe. The Turkish atrocities against the Greek population were, as a result, witnessed with horror by many Europeans and soon reported all over Europe. The initial atrocities in Greece, on the other hand, were seen by very few Europeans. If any were reported they were put down to justifiable hatred arising from extreme provocation, and explained away in the same terms as the occasional atrocities committed by European armies. Few Europeans suspected the real forces that were at work.

Nobody was more deceived by the news from Greece than the overseas Greeks who had instigated the Revolution in the first place and who, by virtue of their superior education, regarded themselves as the obvious leaders. As soon as they heard of the Greek 'victories' in the Peloponnese, hundreds of Greeks studying in European universities or working in merchant houses made their way to the sea and embarked for the homeland which few of them had ever seen. Greeks who had survived the unsuccessful revolt in the Danubian provinces made the long journey through Russia and Austria to join them. The ports of Italy were soon crowded with Greeks looking for a passage to the Peloponnese. Many rich Greeks turned their assets into money and rushed to share the leadership of the newly independent country. Greeks from the Greek communities in Smyrna and Egypt left their families to join the cause, and many Ionians crossed to the Peloponnese before the British authorities put a stop to the exodus.

The overseas conspirators of the Friendly Society had appointed Demetrius Hypsilantes to lead the revolt in Greece. He arrived at Hydra with fifteen companions in June 1821 at about the same time as the revolt of his brother Alexander Hypsilantes was at its last gasp in the Danubian provinces. Like his brother, Demetrius Hypsilantes had been an officer in the Russian service, and at first sight he appeared to be the kind of leader the Greeks needed. Although only in his twenties he had a mature military look about him. His undoubted bravery and military experience won him respect. But, like his brother, he had launched himself into a situation which he could not control and did not really understand. On his arrival in Greece he declared himself regent on behalf of his brother whom he insisted would in due course take over the leadership of the new state. Like so many of the overseas Greeks he delighted in issuing grandiloquent proclamations aimed more at European opinion than the local Greeks. The tone of these pronouncements and the ceremoniousness with which he insisted on being treated made him appear ridiculous rather than impressive to the local populace. Since he had been appointed by the Society he never doubted his claims to complete sovereignty and seems to have been genuinely surprised that all classes of Greeks did not immediately rally to acclaim him as their leader. For many months he clung to the hope that Russia would invade Turkey and that all would turn out for the best. Partly as a result, rumours that the Russians had invaded European Turkey and that a Russian fleet was on its way to the Peloponnese were widely believed throughout the Peloponnese during the first year of the war. Shortly after his arrival, Hypsilantes announced that he would march on Constantinople during the next campaigning season.

Meanwhile, he devoted himself to attempting to graft the institutions of a modern European state on to the territories from which the Turks had been expelled. He distributed portfolios of imaginary departments of state to his followers and sent others as commissioners to proclaim his authority in the areas where the Revolution had broken out. The most pressing need, however, was to organize an army, to reduce the fortresses in Greece that were still in Turkish hands, and to prepare to defend the new state against the Turkish counter-attack which was bound to come.

Thousands of Greeks were in arms but they could not be called an army. They were simply the personal followers of the various leaders of the Revolution. It was clearly a first priority for any government to bring all the armed forces of the country under its direct control and to organize them so that their loyalty and discipline could be depended upon.

Hypsilantes had made his preparations before he left Italy. In Trieste he engaged a Frenchman called Baleste to raise and take command of a cadre which would provide the basis of a Greek national army. Baleste was eminently suited to the task. He had fought with distinction in Napoleon's armies and had no lack of military experience.[8] He had lived for many years in Crete where his father had been a merchant and therefore had first-hand knowledge of Greek conditions (before the Revolution) and he knew the language. Baleste engaged a party of former officers, French and Italian, and sailed for Calamata. There he began the task of recruiting and training the first regiment of the Greek army, known as the Regiment Baleste or simply as the Regiment.

The Regiment was to be organized as a European infantry battalion with muskets and bayonets and to be trained to fight in the standard European fashion by standing in line in close formation. Hypsilantes spent his fortune on equipping the force. Arms were bought in Europe and a uniform was distributed consisting of a black military dress with a black hat bearing a skull and the motto 'Liberty or Death'. Everything was provided, even drums and trumpets. Hypsilantes himself invariably wore the uniform of the Regiment which was the same as that adopted by his brother in the Danubian Provinces.

Some of the returning overseas Greeks who were familiar with European conditions joined the Regiment and began their training, and the Greeks from the Ionian Islands saw it as the natural focal point for their energies. There was a large contingent of Italians, but virtually none of the local armed Greeks could be persuaded to join. They much preferred the independent life of following a successful leader in search of plunder to the dull routine of discipline and drill. Most of the recruits were refugees, mainly Greeks who had escaped the destruction of Kydonies and had been landed destitute and friendless on the coast of the Morea. Altogether the Regiment Baleste was an unpromising basis on which to build a national army since the connections of most of its members with Greece were tenuous to say the least. However, since they were being fed and promised pay and since, for the most part, they had no other means of finding a livelihood, the recruits submitted willingly to the training of Baleste and his European officers. He was so successful that within a few weeks he had trained up a small force of about two hundred men to tolerable discipline able to execute European drill manoeuvres with reasonable confidence. Provided some means could be found of maintaining the flow of money to maintain the men and bring in new recruits, Baleste was confident that he had a nucleus on which to build an effective military organization.

Hypsilantes' arrival in Greece was soon followed by that of other prominent overseas Greeks each surrounded by a party of disciples and each expecting to be given a position of authority on his arrival. Many had served in European armies or government services and their ideas of the type of Greece they wanted were basically the same. The establishment of a national army on European lines featured in their plans and some of them engaged European officers to accompany them. One is said to have brought thirty German officers. Some of these overseas Greeks hastened back to Western Europe as soon as they saw the real conditions, but most attached themselves with more or less conviction to Hypsilantes.

The most important of the new arrivals was Alexander Mavrocordato, a member of a noble Constantinople family which had supplied the Turks with governors of the Danubian Provinces for the last century. Mavrocordato was a cultured man, thoroughly Europeanized, fluent in several languages, a friend of Byron and Shelley who had dedicated *Hellas* to him. Unlike Hypsilantes, who always wore the uniform of the Regiment and had an unmistakable military air about him, Mavrocordato usually dressed in a European frock coat. He was short, inclined to fatness, and wore spectacles. He looked like a civil servant or minor politician from one of the smaller European states. Many Europeans were drawn to him and looked upon him as an example of the kind of Greek who was most likely to bring about the regeneration of the country. Mavrocordato chartered a ship at the beginning of the Revolution and sailed from Marseilles with a large party of Greeks, several European officers, and a store of arms.

If the overseas Greeks had co-ordinated their activities and pooled their resources from the start they might have succeeded in asserting the leadership which they thought was their due. But the colonies of Greeks in European cities were quarrelling about their respective roles in the new state before they had even left Europe. When they reached Greece they gave one another the minimum of support and spread out to the various corners of the country to try to establish an area of influence for themselves. Mavrocordato, in particular, recognized very soon that Hypsilantes did not have the qualities necessary in a national leader and made no secret of his wish to supplant him. He had brought more money, more arms, and more European officers than Hypsilantes and he too wanted to begin the process of establishing an army on the European model.

The Regiment Baleste never exceeded three hundred men. But, as usual, by the time news of Hypsilantes' decision to form an army reached Europe, it was hopelessly distorted. Across the narrow strait in the Ionian Islands it was believed that 'several regiments were organizing at Kalamata, commanded by French and Italian generals'.[9] In August the Greeks of Leghorn were saying that there were 'four thousand organized European troops' in Greece.[10] By the time the news reached Sweden the newspapers were reporting that Hypsilantes was going to raise 10,000 infantry, cavalry and artillery on the European model.[11] The great 'victories' of the Greeks in the first days of the Revolution were attributed to the Greek 'Army'. The Moreotes were reported to be singing the *Marseillaise*.[12] The projected march on Constantinople was said to be imminent[13] and Ali Pasha to have changed his name to Constantine.[14]

It was not surprising that this good news, lavishly sown on ground already well fertilized with philhellenic sentiment, should produce a harvest of volunteers from Europe eager to join the cause. Europe was full of men for whom war offered the only hope of advancement. During the great upheavals of the French wars vast armies had been mobilized and after Waterloo they had been quickly demobilized. Tens of thousands of men had spent years in fighting, knew no other trade, and were now out of work. Many officers were in that familiar category of men who had served with credit but not distinction, men who had been long enough in the wars to realize that they were good at the military profession but for whom the peace had come before they had obtained any benefit. There were also many in the uncomfortable position of having just finished their training, with no experience of active service, when peace came; all they had to look forward to were years of dreary garrison duty and slow promotion among comrades who would bore them with tales of their exploits in the glorious days of war. Even for those who had served and who were still retained in the army when it was run down, the prospect was not always promising; the various governments were anxious to rid their armies of elements which were politically unwelcome.

The French army was steadily being purged of prominent Bonapartists. Many officers who had fought for Napoleon had hoped against hope that the Emperor might still return from St. Helena as he had from Elba and were thrown into despair by the news of his death, which arrived at the same time as the news of the Revolution in Greece. The governments of the German states, more conscious than before of their nationality, looked with disfavour on men who had worked with the French. Many officers lived in exile from their native countries subsisting as best they could, sometimes taking service as mercenaries in the less sophisticated armies and sometimes actively plotting to stage a return to the old system. The secret police in several countries kept a close watch on men who had been prominent during the wars.

Many of the Europeans who set out to take part in the Greek Revolution in the first year came from this great pool of unemployed or underemployed military talent. The war in Greece seemed to promise not only the chance to serve in a cause which was intrinsically good and honourable but an opportunity of reviving their own fortunes. As with the crusaders of other days, to whom they often compared themselves, the path of religious duty seemed to offer solid economic advantages. The overseas Greeks, in their rush to the Peloponnese from Trieste, Leghorn, Marseilles and other European ports, found themselves being jostled at the quayside by volunteers eager to go with them. Most were officers with some means of their own, ready to buy their own arms and pay their passage. Many had read reports of the Appeal which called on Europe to support the cause with 'money, arms and counsel' and which seemed to promise practical gratitude. They confidently expected that they would be enrolled as officers in the Greek Army and given the chance to distinguish themselves. The overseas Greeks, suffering from the same delusion themselves, encouraged them to come and almost every shipload of returning expatriate Greeks contained a number of Europeans. Other volunteers with means of their own set out from Europe independently. They drew out money from their banks, bought a personal set of arms, equipped themselves with uniforms (usually of their own design as they had read in the old travel books was the best method) and took passage on merchant vessels. If they knew any prominent Greeks settled in Europe they asked them for letters of introduction.

The governments of Europe were only slightly better informed about the circumstances of the outbreak of the Greek Revolution than the newspapers. The British Government with its officials in the Ionian Islands and warships ranging round the Levant coasts had access to first-hand reports, but the other governments depended to a large extent on despatches from their missions in Constantinople. The governments, in any case, were in no mood to respond to any romantic view of the Revolution. They judged the events in Eastern Europe in the context of their general European policy and in the light of their own national interest.

In 1821 the European system which had been set up after the final defeat of Napoleon looked distinctly shaky. Although the forces let loose by the French Revolution had been crushed, and Europe restored had a superficial resemblance to the Europe of 1789, the ideas which had led to the French Revolution could not be eradicated from men's minds. Post-war Europe did not seem to provide the kind of society that the peoples had fought for. In state after state the restoration had turned out to be not merely the return of the old monarchs but the old system of oppression by nobility and intolerance by the Church. Large sections of the public in France, Spain, Germany, and Italy had liked their first taste of liberal institutions which they had experienced during the war or seen applied elsewhere. The new generation had formed an exaggerated view of the benefits which could be expected by changes in the political system. 'Liberty' was an intoxicating and still novel concept embracing both national independence and freedom for the individual. The liberals all over Europe looked enviously at the English parliamentary system of government (although during this time many of the safeguards of English personal freedom were in suspense), but pinned their own hopes on constitutions and especially the Spanish constitution of 1812. The call for 'The Constitution' became a slogan and a rallying cry for liberal opinion in lands far from Spain.

The restored governments of Europe, conscious that they did not rule by general consent, were inclined to resort to repressive measures to keep their subjects in order. Liberty seemed to be a euphemism for revolution and they feared and detested revolution like an epidemic disease which would not respect national frontiers. Attempts were made to bind the five great powers—Britain, France, Austria, Prussia, and Russia—to an agreement to help one another to put down revolutions in their dominions and elsewhere in Europe. Britain refused and France was unenthusiastic, but the three others were determined to enforce their policy.

By 1821 it looked as if this policy was failing. In early 1820 a military revolution in favour of 'The Constitution' was proclaimed in Spain followed shortly afterwards by a similar movement in Portugal. Then in July revolution broke out in the kingdom of Naples and in March 1821 it spread to Piedmont. A separatist movement also broke out in Sicily. The news of the Greek Revolution coming shortly afterwards seemed to indicate that the whole political system was in danger. The governments of Europe felt bound to regard all these revolutions as examples of the same phenomenon. There were, it was true, superficial resemblances. All had been

instigated by secret societies, usually lumped together as carbonari and freemasons, and the Friendly Society had used roughly the same methods of
spreading their membership and laying their plans. All proclaimed their
aim as Liberty. All were enthusiastically acclaimed in Northern Europe by
the political opponents of the governments. In the eyes of the absolute
monarchs of Austria, Russia, and Prussia, all were revolts of ungrateful
subjects against their legitimate sovereigns.

While the overseas Greeks and unemployed officers were scrambling to
go to Greece, the revolutions in Italy suddenly collapsed. On the approach
of an Austrian Army the Italian revolutionaries lost their nerve and dispersed with hardly a fight. The revolts in favour of the constitution in
Naples and Piedmont, and the separatist revolt in Sicily, were quickly put
down. Throughout Italy Metternich's policy was to prevail. These movements had all been, in the main, revolts by the military rather than popular
or nationalist insurrections. When the Austrians arrived executions, im-
prisonments, and purges were ordered. Hundreds of men who had joined
the revolutions had to leave Italy at once to escape the repression. Suddenly
another large body of military men had to find a means of earning a living.
Some, including the leader of the Neapolitan revolutionaries, General
Pepe, went to Spain where the constitutional government was still in
power, but most went in the first place to France or England. A few
believed that they could somehow continue the struggle in Greece.

Although the Greek Revolution was in fact totally different in kind from
the others, ironically the policy of the powers helped to make the connection closer. As, one by one, the revolutions in Italy and the Iberian Peninsula were put down, and as the monarchs elsewhere progressively purged
their own societies of men whom they found undesirable citizens, an
increasing body of discontents was created. No government wanted potential revolutionaries within its own borders; political refugees were therefore
continually being moved on, like bands of gypsies for whom no one would
accept responsibility. The number of places of refuge for these men became
progressively fewer. Even Switzerland, a traditional sanctuary for political
refugees, became debarred to them as the ambassadors of the powers put
pressure on the Swiss authorities. The refugees were driven by circumstances
to move further afield—to England, to the United States, to South America,
to Egypt, and of course to Greece. With each turn of the screw their plight
became more desperate, their means of earning money more limited. As
their numbers grew, the sympathy and practical charity with which they
were greeted at first became more attenuated.

As the years passed, more and more of the volunteers who came to fight
for the Greek cause were men who had been driven by circumstances of this
kind. This is not to say that many of them were not influenced also by
philhellenic motives, by genuine belief that the Greek cause was right and

good, and by feelings of self sacrifice, but for most of the volunteers who came to Greece in 1821 philhellenic sentiment was only one of the factors which contributed to their decision. An increasing number had been on the circuit of revolutions moving from one trouble spot to another, picking up new companions on the way, and becoming cynical at the liberal beliefs which had started them on their wandering lives in the first place. Already by the summer of 1821, when the Regiment Baleste was being formed, the tendency could be seen. Persat,[15] for example, one of the earliest volunteers, had been a disgraced Bonapartist officer. He had taken part in a plot to try to rescue Napoleon from St. Helena; he had fought with Bolivar in South America; he had joined in another Bonapartist plot on his return to France and been obliged to flee; he had fought for the constitutionalists in Naples against the Austrians; and had escaped from prison by killing his guards. Humphreys,[16] a young English officer, had graduated from Sandhurst in 1817 but had been unable to obtain a commission in the British Army. He had gone to Naples with the intention of fighting for the constitutionalists but arrived when it was too late. On reading in the newspapers that the Greeks seemed determined in their turn to breathe the air of liberty* he hastened to Greece, believing himself about to taste the reality of the fantasies he had acquired from reading Byron.

There were a number of Poles who had given loyal service to the French cause and, as so often in the history of their country, they found that they were unwelcome in Poland when the wars came to an end. One,[17] the son of a rich landowning family, left behind by the war, had already tried his luck in South America and as a fur-trader in a ship up the Mississippi. After a gun fight with the captain of the ship he had been abandoned on the shore and lived for a while on wild berries with an Indian woman in a cave before being taken to the Poor Hospital at Boston. He had then drifted back to Europe and taken a ship to Greece. Another Pole,[18] who had served in Napoleon's armies and followed the Emperor to Elba, had fought under Bolivar and taken part in the Piedmontese Revolution. 'I have grown old in the search for freedom', he told his comrades. The freeing of Greece from the Turks was to be a preparation for the freeing of Poland from the Russians.

By far the largest group who came to Greece in the summer of 1821 were Italian refugees. Mavrocordato's party included half a dozen Piedmontese 'victims of the troubles'.[19] Nine prominent citizens of the Papal States joined a ship carrying Greeks from Leghorn in August. One of them wrote that he went to Greece 'in the hope of assisting in recovering her freedom, and perhaps, one day, that of my poor country which groans under the sacerdotal yoke'.[20] A tenth man who was to have accompanied them, a half-pay captain 'deeply compromised in political matters', committed

* Probably a report of the *Appeal* quoted on page 13 in which the phrase occurs.

suicide when he was refused a passport to go to Greece.[21] Crowds of Italians of all classes, misled by the news from Greece, made the short journey to Calamata 'in hopes of finding employment, in teaching languages, or getting situations as secretaries, commissaries, and clerks'.[22] Most of the Italians were military men, officers of the lower and middle ranks, captains, majors, and a few colonels. Tarella, a Piedmontese refugee under sentence of death, had served in the French Army in many of its successful campaigns, had been a battalion commander in 1815, and stuck with Napoleon to the end. Dania, a Genoese, also exiled, had been a successful cavalry officer in the French Army. Staraba, a Sicilian colonel, is said to have brought a party of volunteers to Calamata after the failure of the revolution in Naples.[23]

As these volunteers from all over Europe arrived on the coast of Greece by their various routes in the summer of 1821, their first act was to ask to be directed to the 'Greek Army'. They were met by uncomprehending stares at many places, but soon so many Greeks had heard about this Army that it was believed that it actually existed. Since only a tiny minority of the newcomers spoke any Greek, the scope for misunderstanding was great. All through 1821 and 1822 foreign volunteers were to be found wandering from village to village in the Peloponnese expecting that they would soon find the regiments which existed only in the imagination of the newspaper writers. Three travelling gentlemen, a German and two Englishmen, were in the Ionian Islands when they decided to join 'with heart and hand in the contest' and crossed to the mainland.[24] Soon after their arrival they encountered a band of about thirty armed Greeks. The Greeks could not understand their talk about being on the way to join the Army and shot at them, killing their servant. They then robbed them, tied them to trees, and left them to die. By good luck they managed to escape and even persevered on their way to Calamata.

When these men and the scores of other volunteers actually saw the Regiment Baleste, their disappointment can be imagined. Instead of the 'Army' they found Baleste and half a dozen European officers and three half-trained companies of recruits, mainly Greek refugees almost as unfamiliar with the conditions of the Peloponnese as they were themselves. There was no military treasury, no commissariat, none of the conveniences which they associated with an army. Far from being given the high commands they had been led to expect, there was clearly no room for the newcomers even as junior officers. Even if, as was still hoped, the Regiment was to be expanded, there was already a queue of other volunteeers with a prior claim.

Many of the volunteers took one look and decided at once to take the first available ship back. A high-ranking Bavarian cavalry officer[25] declared that he was leaving because he had heard that the Turks were offering 1,500 piastres for the heads of Franks. A Piedmontese major[26] was offended most of all by the lack of paybooks and the absence of arrangements for providing underwear and footwear. These excuses were reasonable enough considering what the volunteers had been led to expect. Inevitably, however their decision to go home was in these early days put down to cowardice or softness or unfulfilled ambition. And so there began a process that was to be seen at various times throughout the Greek Revolution. Volunteers, waiting in the European ports, were continually meeting disillusioned volunteers on their way back. Volunteers, arriving in Greek ports, were met at the quay by other volunteers eager to leave. It is a measure of the deep-rooted strength of the philhellenic impulse and of the other motives that drove men to Greece, that volunteers continued to arrive. The new-comers could not bring themselves to believe the accounts of the men who had been on the spot, the first-hand information was discounted as biased by personal disappointment. Every new volunteer felt that somehow he knew more about the real situation from his reading in the newspapers; that somehow he was more hardy or more enthusiastic or more likely to be welcomed than the weaklings who were turning back. For many, a return was out of the question. By taking part in the constitutionalist revolts and plots they had become stateless persons and in many cases deprived of their livelihood as well. The more prominent were sentenced to death in their absence to emphasize the point. Somehow they had to make the best of it. Forty Italians agreed to serve in the ranks of the Regiment Baleste in the hope that they might later have a chance of becoming officers when the Army was expanded. Others hung around nursing the belief that once they succeeded in meeting Hypsilantes personally, their special talents or qualifications would be recognized and they would be given positions of responsibility.

The number of volunteers who made the journey to Greece in the summer of 1821 is unknown. By September it was estimated that there were already two hundred.[27] The arrival of these men—many of them well-born, well-educated, well-armed, often splendidly uniformed, and by local standards apparently quite rich—made an impression on the local Greeks. Coming after the massive influx of Europeanized Greeks with whom they had so much in common, their arrival seemed to indicate that the world was deeply interested in the Greek Revolution and that it could not be regarded as a purely local Greek affair. The Greeks of the Peloponnese soon became used to the presence of foreigners among them and ceased to remark on the fact. Because the foreigners were there almost from the first, it soon ceased to occur to the Greeks that there was anything strange in volunteers coming from the other end of Europe to help them in their fight. They regarded it as entirely natural that the affairs of Greece should command such interest.

4. *Two Kinds of War*

The Greeks who had actually carried out the killings that made the Revolution possible had little sympathy with the Greeks from overseas and their Frankish colleagues who assumed so readily that they would take over the leadership. They disliked their Western manners and Western clothes and the fact that so many of them were more at home speaking French, German, or Italian than Greek. They preferred squatting on the floor to sitting on chairs, they loved extravagant flowing clothes of the Eastern variety, covered with embroidery. Their most prized personal possessions were daggers and firearms decorated, if they could afford it, with precious metal and jewels. To the local Greeks those from overseas were Franks almost as much as the Europeans by whom they were usually surrounded; and to be regarded with the same mixture of contempt and respect as travelling gentlemen.

To most of the Greeks who lived in Greece it was by no means obvious that a national government or a regular army on the European model was necessary. The country had always been split geographically. The Moreotes or Peloponnesians felt themselves different from the Roumeliotes across the Corinthian Gulf, the islanders felt different from the mainlanders. Within these divisions there were innumerable smaller local loyalties. The inhabitants of Western Greece had little contact with those of Eastern Greece. Every island had its own character. There were age-old petty feuds between neighbouring communities. The mountains and seas of the Greek Archipelago divided the people so completely that virtually every town and plain had a distinct character of its own. Although the Turks had been disposed of, the regional and municipal institutions through which they had ruled the country still existed. Some of the local Greek leaders who had enjoyed great authority under the Turks were content that the institutions should remain unchanged. Many Greeks regarded these 'primates' as little better than the Turks with whom they had recently been in full co-operation. But after the massacres of the Turks in the spring of 1821 the country had reverted to virtual anarchy. Although the primates kept a tight grip over some areas, much of the country was now in the hands of war lords whose strength stemmed from simple armed violence. The Mainotes, the most barbarous of the Greek tribes, left their mountain peninsula where the Turks had kept them shut in for hundreds of years and descended into the plains of the Peloponnese. They had few of the civic virtues of their putative ancestors, the ancient Spartans. They ruthlessly plundered the settled Greek villages and left a trail of destruction in the areas through which they passed. Houses were burnt and flocks seized. Cultivation of the land became intermittent. The *klephts* and *armatoli*, freed from the restraints which Turkish Government had imposed, were equally undisciplined. Power depended on money, and money could only be found by forced exactions from the peasantry or by plunder. Any Greek who could pay for a band of comrades became a 'captain'. He simply announced that he was willing to accept recruits and took as many men into his service as he could afford. Some captains had a handful of men, others a few hundred or even thousands. Many Greeks moved from master to master in accordance with their success. Within a few months of the outbreak of the Revotion the economy of the Peloponnese was ruined and food had to be imported. The ruin was caused almost entirely by the Greeks themselves.

At the time of Demetrius Hypsilantes' arrival, Southern Greece was a patchwork of virtually independent communities, across which bands of armed men moved at will. Some villages and districts tried to isolate and defend themselves as best they could, hoping that somehow the troubles would pass them by. In other areas the local captains established their own bases for banditry and everywhere there were small bodies of armed men roaming about looking for targets. The leaders of the islands tried to keep themselves free from events on the mainland. A handful of captains had such large bands of armed men at their disposal that they were virtually independent chieftains prepared to operate over a wide area. Petro Bey,* who had signed the appeal to the peoples of Europe, was the undisputed leader of the Mainotes, Marco Botsaris led the Suliotes, a tribe of Albanians who had joined the Greeks, and Odysseus exercised a precarious sovereignty over much of Eastern Greece.

The most formidable of the war lords was Colocotrones. For generations his family had been *klephts* in the Morea and several of his close relatives had been killed or tortured by the Turks. Colocotrones himself spent the

---

* Throughout the Revolution the Greeks remained proud of the titles conferred on them by the Turks. Even Mavrocordato and Hypsilantes liked being addressed as 'Prince'—a title granted to their families for services to the Ottoman Empire.

early part of his life in violence, killing and robbing Turks and Greeks alike. Before the Revolution he tried to present himself as a Robin Hood defending the poor against their oppressors, but, for the most part, he was a simple bandit chief. At one time the Turks had driven him out of the Morea and he had served for a while with the British Army in the Ionian Islands. Thus, unlike many of the other Greek warlords who came to prominence during the Revolution, he had some knowledge of the world outside. He was able to make use of this knowledge while remaining all his life a Greek *klepht*. Colocotrones was admitted into the conspiracy while in the Ionian Islands and had crossed secretly to the Peloponnese before the outbreak of the Revolution. In the first weeks he and his small band of followers had been as quick and as ruthless as any in their killing and plundering of Turks. He was therefore sufficiently rich to maintain the biggest band of armed Greeks in the area, and at the time of Hypsilantes' arrival in June 1821, had about 3,000 men at his call who would remain loyal to him if he could continue to provide them with pay and opportunities for plunder. He had some difficulty in restraining them from killing Hypsilantes, the primates, and the other captains, which they were constantly pestering to be allowed to do.

The local Greek population, whether *klephts* or peasantry, watched the Regiment Baleste with incomprehension. Apart from a few leaders such as Colocotrones, most had never seen a European army and they regarded the bayonets, uniforms, and parade drill manœuvres with a mixture of admiration and contempt.

Their own concept of fighting was quite different. In their battles against Turks, Albanians, and one another in the old days and during the first battles against armed Turks during the Revolution they had employed a curious, highly stylized form of warfare. The limiting factor was the inaccuracy of the firearms and the poor quality of the gunpowder which could be obtained locally. Firing their weapons was a lengthy process and often as dangerous to themselves as to the enemy. They invariably fired from the hip and turned their back to the enemy as they pulled the trigger. When the terrain allowed they preferred to try to ambush the enemy in mountain passes or on rocky ground. They hid behind rocks and fired; when the enemy fired back they swiftly retreated behind other rocks, covering one another as they darted back. In more open ground, where there were no adequate rocks to hide behind, they prepared for a battle by building waist-high barricades of stones, from behind which they could fire. Much of their effort during a skirmish was devoted to undermining the enemy's confidence by vigorous shouting of abuse and taunts from behind cover. We hear of Greeks being shot in the bottom while making obscene gestures at the Turks. Casualties were almost always light on both sides. Sometimes a battle went on for many hours with hundreds of men engaged but without anyone being killed. If someone *was* killed then it became a matter of pride to try to capture and strip the body. After a battle the heads of the dead were invariably cut off and taken in triumph to be piled into pyramids as a trophy. Prisoners could always expect to have their heads cut off unless they were thought to be rich and influential enough to be worth ransoming. Both Greeks and Turks paid their men a bonus for the number of heads they brought in after a battle and the Turkish commanders sometimes sent sackfuls of ears and noses to Constantinople as proof of their military success. These incentive schemes encouraged the men on both sides to prefer cutting up the dead to pursuing the live enemy: they also made prisoners more valuable if they were killed off.

Occasionally a detachment of Turks could be entirely surrounded without means of retreat. In those circumstances they had little hope of escaping alive. Similarly, if a detachment of Greeks could be caught on open ground by Turkish cavalry, there was no defence. They had simply to run away as best they could and hope that the cavalrymen would be distracted from cutting them down by eagerness to strip the dead.

These fighting techniques had a certain resemblance to the modes of fighting described by Homer—a point immediately noticed by the Europeans—but they were characteristic of all Eastern guerrillas operating in mountainous regions. Most Europeans failed to realize that the Greek method of fighting was remarkably effective and that it was militarily sound for a small badly-armed force to employ hit-and-run tactics. They simply regarded the Greek methods as obsolete and barbarous; different from the methods used in Europe and therefore inferior. All societies tend to be conservative where their military customs are concerned. They often cling to methods that have been successful in the past which have been rendered obsolete by developing tactics and technology. It was generally realized, for example, that one of the main reasons for the drastic decline in the military effectiveness of the Turks was their insistence on employing the charge of uncoordinated soldiers in huge numbers, even although experience had shown, on dozens of battlefields, that trained European infantry standing in lines and regulating their fire could withstand them.

But these differences in military techniques were relatively unimportant. With experience and good will the advocates of both methods could have grown to understand the advantages and disadvantages which both involved and planned their strategy accordingly. What the Europeans failed to understand was that the Greek method of fighting was part of a total scale of values quite alien to their own. In Europe the model of military virtue was the man who would stand his ground in the line of battle as his comrades were shot down around him and obey his orders to the end. For the Greeks, exposing oneself unnecessarily to the enemy's fire was considered foolhardy and anti-social, not brave; it was also foolish to risk

PRINCE DEMITRIOS YPSILANTIS

ALEXANDER MAVROCORDATO

THEODORE COLOCOTRONI.

ODYSSEUS TRITZO.

1a Hypsilantes   b Mavrocordato
c Colocotrones   d Odysseus

EIN KAPITÄN MIT SEINEN PALLIKAREN IM GEFECHTE.

2 The Greeks defending the Ancient Ruins of Corinth

being surrounded—running away at a certain point in the battle was not cowardice but common prudence. When it was explained to the Greeks that in Europe it was a point of honour to disregard the enemy's fire and that sometimes whole regiments stood shooting at one another in open ground until almost everyone on both sides was killed, their prejudices about the intrinsic stupidity of the Franks seemed to be confirmed. Perhaps most important of all, the Europeans did not understand that in the East fighting was regarded as a communal, almost a family affair in which everyone of the religious community shared. The concepts of treating one's enemy with respect, of extending rights to prisoners of war, of looking after the enemy wounded, and all the other conventions of European warfare were unknown. The Turks, it was often remarked, did not seem to regard the horrible cruelties of the Greek revolutionaries as *unjust* any more than they regarded it as unjust if the Sultan should decide to cut off their own heads without any apparent cause. Cruelty and violent death were everyday occurrences throughout the Ottoman Empire to which a fatalistic religion saw little objection, and death at the hands of Christian infidels, it was believed, led immediately to the arms of the black-eyed houris of Paradise.

The Greeks shared much of this scale of values. Their version of Christianity allowed them to regard all Moslems, men, women, and children, as abhorrent to God and deserving of total extirpation. As in so many wars, a martyr's crown and eternal bliss were promised to anyone who was killed in fighting the enemies of the faith. As the war progressed, the similarities between the Greeks and the Turks became more apparent. The first symbolic act of both sides when they took possession of a mosque or a church was to ride in on their horses and foul the places which their enemies regarded as most holy. Members of the opposed religion had no rights and need only be spared if they had some commercial value. Men of fighting age were almost invariably killed as being the safest way of disposing of them. Women and girls had some value as slaves and concubines provided the market was not overloaded. Boys also had a value and were usually baptized or circumcised to emphasize their change of faith before being exposed for sale.

The Greeks were proud of their fighting techniques and affected to despise the discipline required by European methods as being unworthy of free men. Yet they were not ignorant of the intrinsic superiority in certain circumstances of regular forces. Some of the leaders who had served with the French and British armies had seen how small bodies of well trained and disciplined troops could cut their way through Eastern hordes many times their number; they had also seen the effects of European artillery both in the field and in storming defended positions. From the beginning, many Greeks realized that the Regiment Baleste with the help of the experienced European officers could be developed into an army

D

which would be far more effective than their own unreliable bands of half-
armed individualists. Even among the ordinary Greek population the
Europeans who arrived in Greece in the first months of the Revolution
enjoyed immense prestige. It was instinctively felt that officers who had
taken part in the great campaigns in Europe must have military secrets
and techniques at their disposal which would easily defeat the Turks.
Young men, full of philhellenic enthusiasm, were shocked soon after their
arrival by receiving invitations from captains to join their bands instead
of going to Hypsilantes.[1] Offers came through from Ali Pasha whom
Europe had been led to believe was a monster.[2] There were even dark hints
that a more satisfactory military career could be guaranteed if they joined
the Turks. All these offers were turned down with indignation and amazement by the newcomers.

The potential of the Regiment Baleste was dramatically demonstrated in
August when a Turkish fleet appeared off Calamata and prepared to attack
the town. The Greek inhabitants fled, prepared to abandon the place, but
Baleste led his tiny force to the beach and, with a great show of flashing
bayonets and calm proficiency, terrified the Turks and drove them off.
Again, when Mavrocordato arrived at the siege of Patras in August, with a
few pieces of artillery and two French artillery officers brought from
Marseilles, the nature of the fighting changed appreciably. Although
several thousand Greeks had been besieging Patras for some months they
had not been able to prevent the Turks from making sorties almost any
time they wanted. In August, when the Turks made a foray in force, they
were fired upon with such effect by two fieldguns manned by the French
officers that they were driven back in confusion to the safety of the castle.
They lost about a hundred men and fifteen others were captured and beheaded. This was their greatest defeat so far. By the time the news reached
Western Europe the Turkish loss was put at 1,200.

The Greek leaders looked with admiration and dismay at these and other
examples of European methods. They were in a dilemma. On the one hand,
it was obvious to all that the success of the Revolution was by no means
assured, all the resources that could be mustered from whatever source
would be needed if independence was to be consolidated. On the other
hand, the local Greek leaders wanted to ensure that it was they who would
inherit the new country, not the incomers. An uneasy compromise was the
result. The Greek leaders paid lip-service to the idea of national unity, they
chose to ignore temporarily the conflicts of interest among themselves, and
grudgingly acknowledged Hypsilantes' claim to the leadership. But they
refused to give him any active help. They refused him supplies and discouraged their men from joining his Regiment. Hypsilantes and the Regiment were forced to rely for their existence on the money which he had
brought from Europe and this was rapidly running out.

The first essential from a military point of view, if the Revolution was to survive, was to capture the towns and castles in the Peloponnese that were still in Turkish hands. There were not many of them and all had been besieged in desultory fashion since the early days of the Revolution. Having virtually no artillery, the Greeks' main hope of compelling a surrender was to starve the Turks out, but usually they were unable to maintain a close blockade. Some of the fortresses continued to be supplied by sea, either by the Turkish fleet or by European merchant vessels. Others were blockaded by land and by sea but the blockade was not continuous. At siesta time Greeks and Turks slept and there was no question of activity on either side at night. But the Turkish castles were badly equipped to withstand a siege. They had not been stocked with provisions during the years of civil peace, their walls were in poor repair, and the cannon were often unserviceable.

By August 1821 the small town of Monemvasia was at its last extremity. The Turks were driven to eat cotton seed and seaweed and were stricken with a terrible disease. They even made desperate sorties to pick up dead bodies for food. They were determined not to surrender to the Mainotes encamped outside and for good reason. The Greeks had shortly before brought ashore sixty men and women who had been captured at sea and killed them one by one in sight of the Turks behind the walls. Then Hypsilantes sent one of his officers, who had come with him from Trieste, to conclude a capitulation. He agreed that the lives and property of the Turks would be spared and that they should be taken by sea to Asia Minor. When the gates were opened, however, he was unable to restrain the Greeks. The town was plundered and many Turks were killed. About five hundred Turks were taken in Greek ships and landed on an uninhabited island off the coast of Asia Minor. Those who survived this second period of starvation were rescued by a French merchant.

The surrender of Monemvasia was the only case during the first year of the Revolution in which the majority of the Turkish population succeeded in escaping extermination. When the news reached Western Europe it was proclaimed[3] as a triumph of Liberalism and Christianity. In fact, it was the solitary example where the ideas of the Europeanized Greeks prevailed over the ideas of the local Greeks. More typical was the surrender of Navarino which occurred a few days later. The Turks there, who were also at the last extremity of starvation, offered to surrender on the same terms as Monemvasia, trusting that Hypsilantes' men would be able to save them. Baleste himself was present, and, knowing what had happened at Monemvasia, refused to be a party to the surrender agreement or to commit Hypsilantes. The Greeks, however, offered a convention whereby they would be granted a secure passage to Africa. They had neither the intention nor even the means of doing this and one of the Greek negotiators boasted

Fortresses remaining in Turkish hands after the outbreak of the Revolution

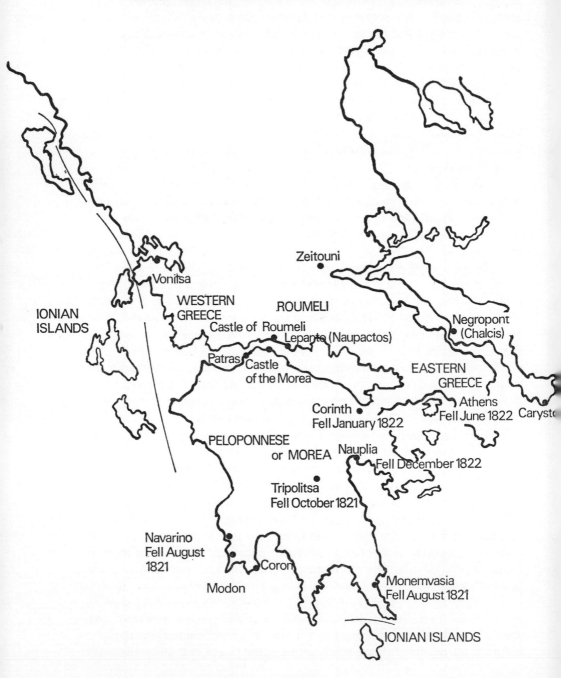

IONIAN ISLANDS

Zeitouni

Vonitsa

WESTERN GREECE

ROUMELI

Castle of Roumeli

Lepanto (Naupactos)

Negropont (Chalcis)

Patras Castle of the Morea

EASTERN GREECE

Athens Fell June 1822

Carysto

Corinth Fell January 1822

PELOPONNESE or MOREA

Nauplia Fell December 1822

Tripolitsa Fell October 1821

Navarino Fell August 1821

Coron

Modon

Monemvasia Fell August 1821

IONIAN ISLANDS

later that he destroyed the copy of the agreement so that no evidence should remain. When the gates were opened the Greeks rushed in and the whole population of between 2,000 and 3,000 were killed with the exception of about 160 who managed to escape. Some of the Turks were left to starve on an uninhabited island in the harbour. A Greek priest[4] who was an eye-witness described the scene as the Turkish women were stripped and searched to see if they were concealing any valuables. Naked women plunged into the sea and were shot in the water. Children of three and four were thrown in to drown, and babies were taken from their mothers and beaten against the rocks.

It seemed probable that the next town which would fall to the Greeks would be Tripolitsa. Situated in the middle of the Peloponnese, it was the biggest town in Southern Greece. It had a population of about 35,000 Turks and Albanians, many of whom had taken refuge there at the time of the outbreak of the Revolution. It had been the headquarters of the Turkish governor of the Morea and was therefore stocked with arms and money. Many rich Turks and Jews were also known to live there.

Hypsilantes and the Provisional Government of which he was head had gained nothing from the surrenders of Monemvasia and Navarino. Everything of value in these towns had been looted by the Greeks. Hypsilantes' own treasury was by now running very low and he was having difficulty even in maintaining the Regiment. The Greeks of Calamata who had been saved from the Turkish fleet by the Regiment refused to supply it with food.

Hypsilantes' hopes turned therefore to Tripolitsa. If Tripolitsa could be captured, its wealth, which was immense by Greek standards, could be used to replenish the national treasury and to pay and expand the Regiment. The city was surrounded by thousands of Greeks all waiting for their chance to share in the spoils. Colocotrones had the biggest contingent and there were numerous captains with smaller bands. But although the siege had been going on for several months its progress was slow. The Greeks were unable to maintain a continuous blockade and were often scattered by sorties of Turkish cavalry. They were even unable to prevent some of their number from selling provisions to the Turks. It seemed the kind of situation where European military methods and especially European artillery would be most useful. Hypsilantes therefore decided to summon the Regiment and the numerous European volunteers who were congregating at Calamata and elsewhere. Many Greeks now had their first sight of Europeans in action.

Two mortars and a few other pieces of artillery had been hauled with great difficulty from the coast and it was confidently expected that they would soon make an impression on the 12-foot-high wall which was the extent of Tripolitsa's fortifications. A plausible Italian called Tassi[5] volunteered to direct the fire. He claimed that he had been Napoleon's chief engineer and casually let it be known that he was a personal friend of Castlereagh and Metternich. The Greeks were taken in and entrusted him with the precious mortars. He assumed the title of 'Engineer-in-Chief'. But when he made his preparations to fire the first shot, it was obvious to the other Europeans that he knew nothing whatsoever about artillery. When the fuse was lit the mortar exploded. Tassi was nearly lynched on the spot. It emerged that he was not an officer but a saddler who had lived at Smyrna and had bankrupted himself by financial speculations.

The prestige of the Europeans suffered another blow when Hypsilantes' letter summoning the volunteers to Tripolitsa arrived at Calamata. There were about forty men of various nationalities in the town waiting to join the 'Greek Army'. Hypsilantes addressed his letter to Colonel Staraba, a Sicilian exile, who was the only one known to him by name, asking him to inform the other European officers of his wishes. This innocent action caused a great clamour. Several Frenchmen and Germans declared that they would never consent to serve under the command of an Italian (although this was not intended) and began to pick quarrels with the Italian volunteers. The Italians took offence at the insult and an affray broke out which lasted several hours. The Greeks looked on in amazement.

They were even more amazed when the letter was produced and it became clear that the whole episode was the result of a misunderstanding. The Italians demanded 'satisfaction'. A duel was arranged and a Frenchman was wounded and had to return to France. Such occurrences were common. The words 'Honour' and 'Satisfaction' were for ever on the lips of the volunteers, but it was a concept of honour which few Greeks could comprehend. 'Instead of fighting for the liberation of Greece,' said one of the Italian officers, 'we were constantly killing each other on the slightest provocation.'[6]

Tripolitsa fell to the Greeks on 5 October 1821. There were only about twenty Europeans present manning the artillery. Some fifty others on their way from Calamata did not arrive in time. Hypsilantes and the Regiment had been reduced to a desperate condition even before this. His money had run out, the fine uniforms of the Regiment were in shreds, many of the soldiers were now barefoot and near starvation for lack of supplies. Hypsilantes on a sudden impulse decided to march them to Patras on the strength of a rumour that it was about to fall. He seems to have realized that events were now beyond his control. While he was absent, Colocotrones and the other captains began to negotiate with the Turks for a capitulation. The Albanians made a separate agreement and were allowed to leave for Epirus with their arms, thus greatly reducing the strength of the defenders. Individual rich Turks began to offer to buy their way to safety and other groups within the walls made arrangements with Greek leaders that they had known before the Revolution. The armed Greeks who were waiting for their plunder began to notice cart-loads of goods coming out of the town at night, and the Greek leaders were constantly going to and fro for negotiations with the Turks. Whether or not any formal capitulation was signed is largely irrelevant. On 5 October the Greeks broke in and for two days the town was given over to the mob. Upwards of ten thousand Turks were put to death. European officers who were present described the scenes of horror. Prisoners who were suspected of having concealed their money were tortured. Their arms and legs were cut off and they were slowly roasted over fires. Pregnant women were cut open, their heads cut off, and dogs' heads stuck between their legs. From Friday to Sunday the air was filled with the sound of screams and laughter before Colocotrones called a halt. One Greek boasted that he had personally killed ninety people. The Jewish colony was systematically tortured. About two thousand prisoners, mainly women and children, were stripped and driven to a valley outside the town and then killed. The heap of bones could still be seen years later. For weeks afterwards starving Turkish children running helplessly about the ruins were being cut down and shot at by the exultant Greeks. The dead lay where they fell. An intolerable stench soon arose and flocks of scavenging birds settled on the town. Wild dogs roamed through the smouldering ruins feeding on the putrid corpses. The wells were poisoned by the bodies that had been thrown in. Soon plague broke out and spread so virulently that during the rest of the war the Peloponnese was never free of it.[7]

Thousands of Greeks enriched themselves with plunder and retired to their villages, leading a few Turkish women as slaves. Heaps of blood-stained clothing, arms, furniture, everything of value that could be found was put on sale. The price of slaves fell so low that they could not be sold, and all but the youngest women were killed off. The proceeds were divided amongst the various captains. But the greatest share of the booty went to Colocotrones. Fifty-two horses carried off the money, arms, and jewellery from the Turkish governor's palace which Colocotrones carefully preserved for himself. He became immensely rich, his money was sent to a bank in the Ionian Islands. He now had the resources to maintain himself and a band of men as an independent force for years to come.

Hypsilantes and the Greek national treasury gained nothing from the fall of Tripolitsa. What was worse in the long run, the prestige of his so-called government and of European military methods suffered a cruel blow. The captains now become openly hostile, refusing supplies to the Regiment and saying that the Franks should go home since no one had invited them to come to Greece. To keep alive, the Regiment began to make forays into the Greek countryside, seizing animals and food from the peasants, and thus increased the dislike in which they were held. Even so, men of the Regiment died of starvation and exposure with no help from the victorious Greeks. The plague claimed its victims. European volunteers sold their weapons in a desperate attempt to find money to buy their way back to Europe. Soon splendid uniforms were on sale in the bazaars, and wild Mainotes could be seen sporting golden epaulettes and European war medals over their rough sheepskin coats.

Probably a hundred Europeans saw either the fall of Tripolitsa or its immediate aftermath. For many, it was their first and last experience of the Greek War. Men who had taken part in numerous bloody campaigns in Europe found they had reached the limit of their tolerance. Those who had the money to pay for a passage and still had a homeland to return to made their way back to Europe. For some, their only military experience in Greece had been in fighting against the Greeks themselves to try to save a few Turks from the general massacre. Others, who had taken under their personal protection Turkish women and boys whom they had found starving in the ruins, sadly abandoned their protégés, well aware that they would not survive long. For those who had no home to go back to the prospects were terrible. They had only two choices, either to stay with Hypsilantes in hope that their comrades would support them until something turned up, or alternatively to enter the service of Colocotrones or one of the other captains. This second alternative amounted to a betrayal of their ideals and of their sense of military honour. It also meant embracing a life for which they were not fitted. They had somehow to learn a difficult language; to adapt themselves to live off the roughest of food consisting often merely of wild herbs; to live among men who never washed and who took pride in the amount of body lice they carried; and to accept the haphazard plundering and killing associated with the life of a brigand. Only a few had the stamina for this.

Baleste himself was disgusted and disillusioned by the events at Tripolitsa. Having seen the preambles at Monemvasia and Navarino, he felt that he understood the forces that were really at work. He proposed to Hypsilantes that the only course which could now save Greece would be to kill Colocotrones and the other captains and take their accumulated plunder into the national treasury. He suggested a plan to Hypsilantes for using the Regiment and the volunteers to do this, but Hypsilantes refused to contemplate it.[8]

Yet despite the exodus of many disgusted volunteers, more and more began to arrive. The older hands laughed at their polished boots, dress uniforms, and the ignorant stories they brought from Europe. The newcomers were shocked to find some of their friends whom they had last seen in officers' messes and ladies' salons in Europe now settling down to live like bandits surrounded by concubines and slaves. They could not shed their European habits so quickly. In particular they simply could not understand how the Regiment had proved so ineffective. They saw with contempt the puny fortifications and primitive arms with which the Turks had defended themselves at Triploitsa. These officers were certain from their own wide experience that with a few hundred disciplined European troops they could capture any fortress still held by the Turks; with a few hundred such troops they could clear the whole of Greece.

A month after the fall of Tripolitsa Hypsilantes and the Regiment Baleste were at Argos with about two hundred European officers who were waiting for the commissions and commands which the newspapers had led them to expect. Dania, a Piedmontese revolutionary in exile who had been a cavalry officer, drew up a scheme to try to restore the situation. His idea was that Hypsilantes and the Regiment would capture Nauplia by assault in the European style, occupy it themselves in such a way as to prevent looting, and so ensure that the wealth of the fortress should be used to replenish the national treasury. It was a bold scheme. Whereas Tripolitsa was a sprawling town on an inland plain surrounded with a single low wall, Nauplia was strategically situated on the coast, still on occasion being supplied by sea, and protected by a series of fortifications that are among the wonders of Venetian military architecture. Looking at the topography of the place one marvels at the daring of the plan and doubts whether it could ever have been carried out. But the European officers were experienced soldiers and from the subsequent history of Nauplia it seems likely that Dania's scheme was indeed feasible. It did, however, depend for its success on a degree of discipline and co-ordination which was unlikely to be achieved. The plan involved three main elements: ships were to attack the seaward side; the Regiment and the Europeans were to creep secretly up under the walls; and Colocotrones' Greeks were to make a mock diversionary attack elsewhere. While the Turks were distracted, the Regiment was to scale the walls with ladders and take the place by bayonet assault. Dania calculated that the Turks would be so terrified by the sudden unexpected appearance of a regiment of European troops in close order that they would be unable to resist. To make surprise doubly sure Dania arranged for the assault to be made at night several hours before daybreak since it was well known that neither Turks nor Greeks ever ventured out in the dark.

In the middle of December all the preparations were made. The many European volunteers waiting for commissions agreed to form themselves into a 'Sacred Company'. It was made up of Italians, Germans, French, Poles, and a sprinkling of other nationalities. Almost every member had been an officer in his own service with experience in the European wars. After some dispute the command was given to Colonel Tarella, a Piedmontese exile. The morale of the company was high. This was the kind of war they knew; this was what they had come for. They would be the first into the town and would take the glory for the capture of the famous city of Nauplia.

On the appointed night the Regiment and the Sacred Company silently crept up to the fortress, and two hours before daybreak they were all in position under the walls with their scaling ladders ready, without disturbing the sleeping Turks. It was a military accomplishment of which any professional army would have been proud. But the Greeks could not be brought to understand European military methods so quickly. Many of them simply refused to move at night, and had to be driven towards the town. When the signal was given for the attack to begin, all order broke down and the Greeks reverted to their traditional fighting methods. Everyone began firing at the same time, largely at random. The Regiment Baleste panicked and began to fire uselessly at the wall. The Turks were immediately alerted and quickly manned the defences. The Regiment and the Sacred Company were left crouching among the rocks under the walls caught in crossfire between Turks and Greeks. At this point virtually all the Greeks ran back in accordance with their normal tactics and daybreak revealed the isolated Europeans with a large expanse of open ground between them and safety, all of which was in the clear field of fire of the guns and muskets of the Turks. About thirty Europeans were killed or wounded and many more of the Regiment as one by one or in small parties they dashed across the open ground. The attack was a complete failure.

Hypsilantes' prestige and that of Europeans generally slumped again after this failure and another exodus of volunteers took place. The Sacred Company was disbanded. Virtually all the Germans left and many of the French, especially, as one of the others ruefully remarked,[9] 'those who had bread to eat in their own country'. As before, the volunteers who remained were mainly those who had nowhere else to go, the Italian revolutionaries, the Polish exiles, and the French Bonapartists.

Baleste now decided that he had had enough. It was clear that the vision of Greece which had made him sacrifice his career to follow Hypsilantes was not going to be realized. During the abortive assault on Nauplia he had been seen running about in full view of the Turks waving the standard which he had taken from the hands of the dying standard bearer of the Regiment, and hitting all the Greeks he could find among the rocks to try to make them move forward. Baleste and a few of the other officers left to join the revolt in Crete, the place where he had been brought up. He was later killed in a skirmish and his head sent to Constantinople. The command of the Regiment passed to the Piedmontese exile Tarella.

The Regiment by now was in a terrible state. Hypsilantes' money had long since run out, there was no pay and no help from the local population. Tarella, a harder and more desperate man than Baleste, somehow kept it together by making periodic raids on Greek villages and stealing food and animals. But the plague which had arisen from the unburied dead of Tripolitsa was now raging everywhere. Men of the Regiment died every day from malnutrition and disease. The wounded had little hope of recovery even from slight cuts, since these quickly became gangrenous. When the Regiment moved off, a few Greeks were given money to look after the sick and wounded who were left behind, but they stole their possessions and deserted them. A young doctor from Germany who arrived at this time with his head full of romantic philhellenic idealism committed suicide by taking poison.[10] On another occasion Tarella, recognizing the uniform and weapons of one of his Italian officers for sale in the bazaar, went to look for him and found him crawling round the streets of the town in a delirious condition with his tongue so swollen that he could not speak. The respect which the Greeks had for European methods and the enthusiasm of the Europeans for the Greek cause both ebbed rapidly away.

Even if Dania's bold plan to capture Nauplia had come off, it is doubtful whether it would have enabled Hypsilantes to occupy the town in an orderly manner and restore his treasury as he had hoped. It is more likely that the same pattern would have occurred as was seen at the surrender of Acrocorinth a few weeks later. Hypsilantes moved to Corinth on 24 December with the remnants of the Regiment, his suite of Europeanized Greeks, and the remaining volunteers. New volunteers from Europe, fresh and full of confidence, continued to arrive. Colocotrones and other captains followed with their bands. As with so many of the fortresses of the Peloponnese, the Acrocorinth would have been impregnable if it had been properly maintained and provisioned during the years of peace before the Revolution. But its garrison was small, consisting of a few hundred troops, mostly Albanians, and it was full of refugees who had gone there for protection during the early days of the outbreak. By December starvation was imminent.

As at Tripolitsa and elsewhere there were confused negotiations for a surrender. As at Tripolitsa the Albanians within the fortress made a separate capitulation whereby they were to be allowed to leave and return to Albania although on this occasion most of them were killed on the way. The remaining Turks, trusting in Hypsilantes and his European code of honour agreed to surrender on condition that they would be taken in neutral vessels to Asia Minor. Complex negotiations settled the amounts of clothing and money that each class of Turkish family was to be permitted to take. The Regiment Tarella was to occupy the fortress and no other Greeks were to be permitted to enter. At the end of January 1822 the Regiment marched in and the starving population began to limp down the road to the sea where they were to await the arrival of the neutral ships. But the two hundred or so men of the Regiment and the European volunteers were far too few to prevent Greek justice taking its course. The armed bands of Colocotrones and the other captains burst into the fortress and plundered all they could find, killing any Turk they met. Only the Bey and his harem were saved—as was usual with important prisoners, since there was a hope of ransom—but he was tortured mercilessly (although ineffectually) to make him reveal where the treasure was hidden. As for the other inhabitants, long before they reached the coast the stripping and killing had begun. A German officer[11] who was present describes how they staggered through a double rank of Greek women shouting and spitting at them. A Turkish couple, too starved and exhausted to carry their child any further, tried to hand it to a Greek. He immediately drew a long knife and cut off its head explaining, as the German officer tried to prevent him, that it was best to prevent Turks growing up. By the time the survivors reached the shore all control was lost, and when someone shouted a false alarm that Turkish soldiers from Nauplia were coming, almost all the prisoners, about 1,500 in all, were killed.

5. The Cause of Greece, the Cause of Europe

The news from Greece was reported throughout Western Europe, usually two months late. There was no means of following events in detail and reports had often to be revised later. The reaction of the public in the different countries of Europe is difficult to judge. The means by which opinion could be expressed were few. Newspapers had small circulations and were often subject to censorship. Parliaments where they existed were not representative. In all countries only a small proportion of the population were concerned with political questions.

It is clear, however, from the amount of writing on the Greek Revolution published in 1821 and 1822, that it roused intense interest in Britain, France, the Netherlands, the German states, Switzerland, the Scandinavian countries, and the United States. In Austria, Russia, and Italy the governments were even more authoritarian than elsewhere in Europe and the evidence for public interest in Greece harder to find. Yet it appears that in all countries where the classical tradition was strong, news of the Greek Revolution was eagerly sought.

Virtually none of the news emanating from Greece was free of distortion. The Turks had no great concern with international opinion, but their version of events was adequately put over with the help of the Austrians. News from Greece came almost exclusively from the Europeanized Greeks who had gone to join the Revolution and even at source it contained an element of propaganda. By the time it had passed through the Ionian Islands or through the Greek colonies in Europe several weeks later it had undergone a further transformation to make it more acceptable to Europeans.[1]

Even more distorting was the great burden of literary and historical allusions which everything Greek and Turkish carried with it. In the absence of real knowledge about the way of life, traditions, customs, and ideas of the Modern Greeks, the Europeans relied on their prejudices. Theories about the identity of the Ancient and Modern Greeks, about the nature of 'regeneration', about the similarity in outlook between Western Christians and Eastern Christians are implicit in much of the writing. All of these worked in favour of the Greeks. Similarly, inherited ideas about the Turks worked against them.

The notion that the Turks were a colourful backward people gradually being engulfed by a technologically superior Western civilization had not yet become general. Instead, older ideas that had lost their validity centuries before still held their power—that the Turks were a cruel, aggressive, barbarian race posing an active threat to Western civilization; and especially the idea that Christianity was bound to be in deadly conflict with Islam. Churchmen rediscovered and indulged an atavistic hatred against Turks and virulently demanded their expulsion or extirpation in the name of God. The features of Turkish life that were generally known had for centuries excited a fascinated horror: the Grand Seigneur in his Seraglio with his eunuchs, his harem, his slaves, and his janissaries; the custom of killing off one's brothers; of seizing infants for training for the armies; the bastinado and other highly sophisticated Oriental tortures. Much of the Western image of the Grand Turk was out of date or inaccurate, but the romantic poets had given it a new lease of life. Every word that came to mind in talking of Turks—pasha, scimitar, ataghan, spahi, dervish, turban—carried a weight of dreadful associations.

The official opinion of the powers on the Greek Revolution, pressed most strongly by Metternich and the Austrian Government, that the Sultan was the legitimate sovereign of the Greeks and that they were wrong to rebel against him, struck many people as hypocritical and cynical. Support for the Greek cause could be construed as disloyalty to the governments. It also meant, however, that political groups opposed to the governments for other reasons were tempted to embrace the Greek cause simply because the governments took a different view. The factors working in the Greek favour were overwhelming.

From Easter 1821 throughout the whole of Europe men in many walks of life were touched with a passionate sympathy for the Greeks and a desire to help them. The long years of repetition by poets and travellers had spread the ideas of philhellenism wide and deep, and suddenly it changed its character from being an intellectual, mainly literary concept, to a practical programme. When all allowance is made for the distortion of the news, the political situation in Europe, and other favourable factors, it remains an astonishing phenomenon. No country was unaffected. It was a European movement, springing up spontaneously in every society where European civilization was valued. The same sentiments occurred independently to men all over the Western world and drove them to action. It is not necessary to take the view that everyone who reiterated the themes of philhellenism believed implicitly in his own rhetoric. Yet the uniformity of all discussion of the Greek cause is one of its most significant features. Even those who opposed the efforts of the supporters of the cause seldom questioned the basis of the argument but only the political expediency of applying it.

There were important differences between the aims of philhellenism in different countries, but they were marginal additions to the solid nucleus of ideas which were common to all. The cause of Greece touched a nerve in people who had previously regarded themselves as outside politics. Many when they joined the philhellenic movement did not even realize that they were performing a political act. The cause seemed to be above politics. The idealism of youth was engaged and, for once, in a cause with which their elders could sympathize. It was said that the Swiss peasants, on their weekly journey into town asked eagerly for the latest news from Nauplia and never went home without dropping their contribution in the collecting box.[2] In the beer houses of Germany, it was said,[3] men who were never known to have been interested in events outside their village, talked eagerly about the war.

The exploits of the Greeks were extolled in verse. In France no less than nine books of philhellenic verse were published in 1821 and another eighteen in 1822.[4] In Germany one poet, Wilhelm Müller, had a great success. His first book of *Songs of the Greeks* sold a thousand copies in six weeks in the autumn of 1821 and three more books of new songs followed shortly afterwards before the censor intervened.[5] All over Western Europe and the United States newspapers and reviews published poems more or less in the style of Byron as well as selecting suitable passages from Byron's works for quotation.

The subject had an apparently irresistible attraction for mediocre poets. It allowed them to combine rich romance about slaves, viziers, pashas, camels, jewels, negroes, harems, and all the splendour and mystery of the East with the older conventions about the Ancient Greek heroes. The two main themes, the comparison between the Ancient and Modern Greeks and the struggle of the Christians against the Moslems, were present in almost all the poems, but the number of variations which can be made on these two ideas and still retain the reader's interest is limited. It is a measure of the receptiveness of the public that the demand for such poems continued unabated. Between 1821 and 1827 at least one hundred and twenty-eight separate books of philhellenic verses are known to have been published in France alone. The cause of the Greeks was a subject which stirred the feelings of many men who never attempted another poem in their lives. They felt that they must rise above everyday speech in dealing with this exciting, almost sacred subject.

Few of the poems of 1821 and 1822 are worth recalling except as evidence of the state of public opinion. Only one major poet joined the fashion. Shelley's *Hellas*, written in the autumn of 1821 and based on newspaper reports, contains in extreme form the ideas worked on by so many others. It epitomizes the deep sense of personal involvement in the Greek struggle which was so widely felt all over Europe. In the preface Shelley made the classic statement of philhellenism.

We are all Greeks. Our laws, our literature, our religion, our arts have their root in Greece. But for Greece . . . we might still have been savages and idolators. . . . The human form and the human mind attained to a perfection in Greece which has impressed its image on those faultless productions whose very fragments are the despair of modern art, and has propagated impulses which cannot cease, through a thousand channels of manifest or imperceptible operation, to ennoble and delight mankind until the extinction of the race. The Modern Greek is the descendant of those glorious beings whom the imagination almost refuses to figure to itself as belonging to our kind, and he inherits much of their sensibility, their rapidity of conception, their enthusiasm, and their courage.

In the drama itself all the other ingredients appear. The decay of Greece, the barbarism of the Turks, the hypocrisy of the governments. But the forces of evil are struck with terror when they see 'The panther, Freedom, fled to her old cover'. The final chorus is a paean for the longed-for regeneration:

> The world's great age begins anew,
>   The golden years return,
> The earth doth like a snake renew
>   Her winter weeds outworn:
> Heaven smiles, and faiths and empires gleam,
> Like wrecks of a dissolving dream.
>
> A brighter Hellas rears its mountains
>   From waves serener far.
> A new Peneus rolls his fountains
>   Against the morning star.
> Where fairer Tempes bloom, there sleep
> Young Cyclads on a sunnier deep.
>
> Another Athens shall arise
>   And to remoter time
> Bequeath, like sunset to the skies,
>   The splendour of its prime;
> And leave, if nought so bright may live,
> All earth can take or Heaven can give.

b Colonel Gordon

BALESTRA.

3a General Normann

c Baleste, First Commander of the Regiment

4 Scenes from the Massacres of Scio, by Delacroix

It was only to be expected that the false news from Greece feeding the strong philhellenic tradition that already flourished should lead to demands for action. The cause of the Greeks seemed to be so overwhelmingly good and the reprisals of the Turks so obviously barbarous and cruel that admiration from afar was not enough. Surely the governments of the great powers of civilized Europe could do something to help the Greeks? And if the governments would do nothing, surely individuals could help?

In France the interest was intense. The press, enjoying a precarious freedom, was split. On the one hand the voice of the liberals declared that the heroes of ancient Greece had arisen from the dead.

If our voice could be heard, the barbarians who are massacring the Greeks, slaughtering priests, and prostituting Christian virgins to the frenzied soldiery, would soon be punished, annihilated, and driven back to the deserts of Africa and Asia; if our voice could be heard the standard of the Cross would fly over the roofs of Constantinople or over the Parthenon, and the Church of St. Sophia would soon be restored to its former use.[6]

Other newspapers supporting the Government fulminated against the spirit of carbonarism having invaded the East.

The flood of books of verse in favour of the Greeks was matched by the publication of numerous pamphlets in the same style making ever more extreme claims on their behalf. Thirty pamphlets appeared in France during the first two years of the war. Some were thoughtful political tracts by journalists and ecclesiastics, some were by students, some were anonymous, some were fabrications of appeals said to come from Greece itself and some repeated the grandiloquent manifestoes which the Greeks were so fond of propounding. Many were intended simply to put pressure on the French Government to change its policy of support for Metternich's doctrine of legitimate sovereignty, and there was a good deal of discussion about French national interest—the chance of restoring French influence in the Levant, the danger of allowing the Russians to assume the leadership of the Greeks, and the possibility of new markets for French goods. Almost all the discussion however paid lip service at least to the clichés of philhellenism.

M. de Pradt, for example, a former bishop who published a steady stream of pamphlets on international affairs (with four on the Greek War alone), caught the popular mood:

Land of the arts and the sciences, mother of heroes, teacher of the Universe, at last after six centuries of slavery, you are raising the stone which barbarous hands had placed on your tomb to seal the entrance. O generous enterprise! What human soul could refuse to ally himself to your noble efforts, and would not offer you the tribute of his prayers in consolation for being unable to offer the help of his arm![7]

The professors were among the first to give a lead. Professors of Ancient Greek Literature in particular felt that they were well fitted to speak on Modern Greece, and professors of philosophy and theology were never far behind. Just as the cause of Greece inspired men to write poetry who never wrote another verse, so it inspired to political activity others who for the rest of their lives were content to have their opinions set by government and church.

The professor of Greek literature at Strasbourg held a public meeting in July 1821 in support of the Greek cause at which he delivered a lecture on the services which the Ancient Greeks had given to civilization. The themes of his closing remarks were all familiar:

> The Turks . . . have on several occasions threatened our own civilization with total destruction, and the Greeks have a proverb that wherever they put their feet the grass ceases to grow. This is the crushing yoke under which the mother-land of civilization is now groaning. These men are the children of the heroes, the poets, the philosophers, the artists, to whom we owe our civilization. Because they wished to restore a nation, they are the prey to the most terrible massacres, they are in danger of having to flee over the seas with only the memory of their ancient glory and of their efforts to restore to their lands and islands the fruits which modern progress has perfected.
>
> Could any sensitive and grateful man—especially the lover of letters and of the arts who owes to this country his most noble pleasures and sweetest inspiration—withhold his pity for the misfortunes that heap on them. Could any man suppress his desire to see reborn again in Greece the days of liberation of Marathon and Salamis, and if possible the blessed time when Plato listened to Socrates and when the songs of Homer and the choruses of Sophocles resounded through the court of Pericles and the temple of Phidias.[8]

A demand soon developed for practical help to be sent to the Greeks. And since it was clear that the Government was not prepared to do anything to help, it was left to private initiative to make a contribution. The most obvious way of helping was to raise money for the purchase of arms. Numerous public meetings were held and subscriptions and collections taken. Committees in support of the Greek cause sprang up in many towns quite independently of one another. Professors, priests, and student leaders made collections and handed the money over to the local Greek communities for forwarding to Greece. It was a spontaneous and wide-spread movement of sympathy and charity even though in many places the response was short-lived.

From the beginning the call was also made for volunteers to fight in the holy war. The proclamations of the Greeks themselves begged for help and they were soon being repeated in pamphlets. The *Appeal to the French People*, for example, which was published by 'an ex-student of law' in October 1821[9] has all the themes of philhellenism. 'Can you,' he asked the people of France, 'be the only people who will not help the descendants of Themistocles, Alcibiades, and Demosthenes? Can you allow your brothers in religion to be massacred? Are you no longer the descendants of the Crusading St. Louis?' The Voice of Greece is made to declare: 'Men of France, do not be deaf to my prayer, arm yourselves, go and join my son [Hypsilantes]. . . . My children will erect monuments to you, they will raise altars to you, their children will adore you and forever hold your names in the greatest veneration!' The student's answer to this appeal is clear: 'Let us form sacred battalions, let us arm ourselves with invincible weapons, let us march, and let us go and purge the earth of these barbarians just as long ago Hercules purged it of the monsters which were ravaging it.'

The French student's pamphlet contains all the elements that inspired volunteers all over Europe—the appeal to the Ancients, the appeal to Christianity, the appeal to be a latter-day crusader, the appeal to prospects of military advancement. The student reserves for his peroration a consideration which was distinctly French:

The Northern Powers no longer wait for us to advance. The perfidious Englishman trembles. But if, contrary to my expectation, he is bold enough to try and stop us, let us fall on him, and with the sword of God he will soon be crushed. Soon, as after the Pyramids, Marengo, and Austerlitz we will again come home in triumph.

Many Frenchmen felt that, somehow, by promoting the cause of Greece, they would atone for the disgrace of Waterloo; that somehow the war in Greece would give an opportunity of reasserting the old glories of France, uniting Royalists, Bonapartists, Orleanists, Liberals and all the other disparate sections of Restoration France with the nationalism that had been so strong and so comforting during the war years. The element of anti-British feeling was to persist throughout the war.

The French Government, from the beginning, took an ambivalent view of philhellenism. It could not help half believing that sending French volunteers to Greece must be in the French national interest, even if the Frenchmen concerned were those most bitterly opposed to the restored Bourbons. It calculated—correctly—that, despite their political views, Frenchmen would remain primarily Frenchmen. The French Government therefore was inclined to run several contradictory policies at the same time in the confident expectation that they could not all fail. It supported Metternich in theory and yet made little attempt to interfere with the help going to the Greeks; and it also gave help to the Turks, especially to the Sultan's subject and ally, the Pasha of Egypt. At Marseilles, volunteers on their way to Greece with the connivance of the French authorities could see frigates being built in the shipyards for the Egyptians. The ambivalence of French policy became even more pronounced later.

In Britain, which had at the time perhaps the most liberal political system and the most unrestrained press in Europe, the cause of the Greeks at first made less impression than elsewhere. An immense amount of writing sympathetic to the Greeks appeared in the newspapers and reviews, but suggestions that practical help should be sent met with little response. As elsewhere, the leadership of the movement was first taken up by scholars. Dr. Lemprière, the author of a dictionary of classical antiquities, began to campaign in the autumn of 1821 for a subscription to be raised to help the Greeks. A committee was formed and a few prominent men made a contribution, including Lords Lansdowne, Aberdeen, and Elgin, all famous for their collections of Greek sculpture. But only a few hundred pounds was collected and the committee was soon disbanded after a consignment of arms had been sent. [10]

But when in the middle of 1822 news arrived of the massacres of Chios, interest revived. About a dozen pamphlets on the Greek cause were published in addition to a vigorous campaign by several newspapers. All the familiar philhellenic arguments were reiterated:

> Greece . . . that land, the fostering nurse of civilization, where the spirit of antiquity still seems to linger amidst its olive groves, its myrtle bowers, and the precious relics of its splendid edifices; where both sacred and profane history unite in forming the most interesting associations; where Socrates taught the lessons of his incomparable ethics, and a still greater than Socrates disclosed the mysteries of the 'unknown God' to those that sat in darkness. [11]

Much effort was expended in disputing the doctrine of the legitimacy of the Ottoman Government, in explaining the commercial advantages of helping the Greeks to independence, and in raising fears of allowing Russian and French influence to predominate.

'You are solemnly and indispensably bound', wrote Lord Erskine in an open letter to the Foreign Secretary, 'by a duty paramount to that of a statesman, to make an *instant* effort to engage the nations in alliance with this country to overthrow the cruel dominion of unprincipled, incorrigible barbarians, over a Christian people struggling for freedom and independence.' [12]

In much of the writing on behalf of the Greeks there lies the unspoken belief that Britain, as the most powerful country in the world, the victor of Waterloo, had only to give the word and the dreadful war could be brought to an end. An unattractive assumption of superiority pervades the appeals. It was said that the countries which did nothing to stop the massacres of the Greeks were themselves equally guilty with the Turks. When the Foreign Secretary in trying to defend British neutrality in Parliament remarked that there had been atrocities on both sides, he was branded as pro-Turkish. It was seriously argued on a number of occasions that it was the Turks not the Greeks who should be blamed for the massacre at Tripolitsa since the Greeks 'may justly impute to the oppression of their conquerors not only the degradation of their persons but the debasement of their minds'.[13]

It is difficult to avoid the conclusion, in reading the English pamphlets, that the authors were more inspired by hatred of Turks and Moslems than by concern for the Greeks. They cheerfully demanded the wholesale expulsion of the millions of Turks settled in Europe. Thomas Hughes, a Church of England clergyman who had visited Greece before the Revolution and had written a book of travels, was perhaps the most violent, calling in two pamphlets for the extermination of 'the most weak, contemptible, vice-stained tyrants that ever polluted the earth on which they trod, vilifying and degrading the fairest part of the creation'. He quoted with approbation Lord Bacon's opinion that whereas no nations are wholly alien one to another, there are some races whom it is a human duty to 'suppress' since they 'have utterly degenerated from the laws of nature' and 'have in their very body and frame of estate a monstrosity . . . , they are common enemies of mankind . . . disgraces and reproaches to human nature'.[14]

But the English pamphleteers were their own enemies. Far from encouraging the widespread sympathy for the Greeks, they put people off by their extremism. The one balanced pamphleteer of the Greek Revolution, Sheridan, included in his list of causes of the relative indifference of the British towards the Greeks at this time 'the language of their partisans'.[15] Many men who would willingly have contributed money were ashamed to be allied with such unattractive purveyors of hatred. The sums raised in London were small and only a handful of volunteers set off to join the Greek army.

In the United States, too, the philhellenic movement made a strong start in 1821. At the same time as the *Appeal to the Nations of Europe* was allegedly issued from 'the Spartan Headquarters' at Calamata, another version was sent to the United States:

To the Citizens of the United States: Having formed the resolution to live or die for Freedom we are drawn toward you by a just sympathy since it is in your land that Liberty has fixed her abode, and by you that she is prized as by our fathers. . . . We esteem you nearer than the nations on our frontiers. . . . Free and prosperous yourselves you are desirous that all men should share the same blessings; that all should enjoy those rights to which all are by nature equally entitled. It is you who first proclaimed these rights; it is you who have been the first again to recognize them in rendering the rank of men to the Africans degraded to the level of brutes. . . . You will not assuredly imitate the culpable indifference or rather the long ingratitude of the Europeans. No. The fellow citizens of Penn, of Washington and of Franklin will not refuse their aid to descendants of Phocion and Thrasybulus or Aratus and Philopoemen.[16]*

* The modern reader is often surprised at the names chosen by the pamphleteers as examples of the great man of antiquity. Epaminondas was the clear favourite, but

This Appeal was widely circulated in the United States at the instigation of Edward Everett, a professor at Boston. It was specially drafted by Europeanized Greeks to flatter the image which Americans already had of themselves, although the reference to the American negroes must have failed to convince even in the United States. Yet among the sentiments which were common to philhellenic movements everywhere the Appeal identified and exploited a distinguishing national ingredient.

The Americans, confidently secure, even smug, in their own constitutional liberty could not conceal a feeling of superiority towards the unhappier political systems of the European nations. Throughout the war the American supporters of the Greek cause tended to feel that they alone were fitted to teach the Greeks about true liberty. In July 1821, at a dinner of Americans in Paris at which Washington Irving and Lafayette were present, the toast was given: 'The land of Minerva, the birthplace of Arts, Poetry, and Freedom—civilizing her conquerors in her decline, regenerating Europe in her fall. May her sons rebuild in her clime the home of Liberty.'[17] In 1824, at a benefit concert for the Greeks held in Cincinnati, an American general proclaimed, 'Humanity, policy, religion—all demand it. We must send our free-will offering. The Star-Spangled Banner must wave in the Aegean.'[18]

But it was in Germany during the early years of the war that philhellenism made its greatest impact. The response to the cause of the Greeks was more widespread in Germany than in any other country; the passions aroused were more deeply felt; and, as proof of this, greater efforts were made to provide practical assistance. German philhellenism, like philhellenism elsewhere, consisted of the two or three simple ideas common to all philhellenic movement plus national additions.

Nowhere in Europe was the classical tradition stronger. The enthusiasm for the Ancient Greeks in the late eighteenth and early nineteenth centuries had prepared the ground well. The political connotations of the classics were stronger than elsewhere because their impact was still recent. During the last years of the war against Napoleon a powerful idealistic and nationalist spirit had developed. The war had been fought for 'Freedom', a concept of intoxicating freshness and one closely connected with the new-found Ancient Greeks. The 'Freedom' had been mainly thought of as freedom from the foreign rule of the French, but many who took part in the last successful campaigns had dreamed of political freedom, of constitutional government, and they had been encouraged to do so by their leaders. The hopes of these liberals had been sadly disappointed in the years

they also had a strong preference for the obscure Philopoemen, since it was now possible to contradict the ancient tag that he was 'the last of the Greeks'. On the whole, the ancient names were used simply as incantations designed to evoke sympathetic responses with little attempt to find relevant comparisons.

after Waterloo. In one German country after another a chilling authoritarianism reasserted itself. The political liberties were withdrawn, the promised constitutions never implemented or stripped of their meaning. Only in the small South German states did recognizably free institutions survive, and they were being steadily eroded. The Governments of Prussia and Austria, fearful of any sign of revolution, resorted to ever sterner measures to suppress the remnants of liberalism and so created a growing body of discontents. Most of the forty or so governments which composed the German Confederation agreed with the views of the two large countries, or were too weak to resist pressure to conform.

The Germans knew less of the real conditions of Modern Greece than any of the other nationalities of Western Europe. Unlike the British and French, few of them had been taken to the Mediterranean by the wars. There were only a handful of travellers from Germany who made their way to Greece during the half century before the Revolution. Literary philhellenism, on the other hand, was there as elsewhere a well established genre. Kotzebue's 'Ruins of Athens' for example, to which Beethoven composed the music, is concerned with the theme of Minerva deserting the Parthenon to found a new temple of the Muses in Europe. Hölderlin's *Hyperion*, which first appeared in 1797, was curiously prophetic. It was the story of a German going to fight in a Greek War against the Turks. To Hölderlin it was not so much Greece that was being 'regenerated' as Germany in Greek dress. When the Greek Revolution broke out, this idea took on a new urgency. If the 'regeneration' of Greece meant violent revolution would not the regeneration of Germany mean the same? The Governments of Austria and Prussia, which saw a potential jacobin in every man who questioned monarchical absolutism, could not ignore the connection. Liberals tended to be philhellenes and philhellenes to be liberals.

In the German states, as elsewhere, the philhellenic movement of 1821 and 1822 was mainly inspired in the universities, and it was partly for this reason that it aroused such suspicion in the governments. The students of Germany, conscious of having played a leading part in the expulsion of the French, had made themselves into an important political force on the return of peace. They had demanded constitutional liberty and unification of Germany and had established an organization of students' unions covering the whole of Germany. In 1819, however, following the assassination by a student of Kotzebue, a Prussian minister whose name had become associated with reactionary policies (and incidentally the author of *The Ruins of Athens*), the Carlsbad decrees, applied all over the German Confederation, abolished the students' national union, reinstituted strict censorship, and imposed a range of other measures against the universities. It was only to be expected that the governments would treat with suspicion any new political movement originating in the universities which could provide an opportunity for evading the Carlsbad decrees.[19] Philhellenism, since it would provide an excuse for collecting money and for establishing connections all over the country, could perhaps be exploited for internal political purposes.

At Easter 1821 the professor of philology at Leipzig in the Kingdom of Saxony, Wilhelm Traugott Krug, issued a pamphlet under the title *Greece Regenerated,* which questioned the official doctrine that the Greeks were wrong to revolt against their legitimate sovereign. It was hardly a novel idea but the pamphlet seems to have aroused a great deal of interest simply because a professor had dared to question the government on such an important matter of policy.

Krug's pamphlet was only the first of many professorial pronouncements all over Germany. The theology professor at Leipzig published a pamphlet called *The Cause of Greece, the Cause of Europe.* Yet another quotation of the familiar sentiments will show how universally they were being repeated all over Europe:

> Would that the Greeks might rise from their political torpor, and with youthful vigour and glorious prospects re-enter the rank of European nations. This is the fervent wish of one who regards the event not only as a European but as a man and a Christian. . . . The Greeks have a powerful demand both on our gratitude and compassion. Though more than two thousand years have elapsed since Greece flowered, the Greeks of the present day are yet descendants of those whose immortal works still delight and form our minds; the descendants of those whose wisdom and science have become the common property of the world.[20]

Another Leipzig professor drew the parallel between the German and Greek Wars of Independence and hinted at the Germany he wanted to see. Remarks such as the following tended to reinforce the suspicion that the advocates of freedom for the Greeks had half their minds on the freedom of the Germans:

> We Germans see in the Greeks the image of ourselves. Our minds are taken back instinctively in an obscure way to the time when we were delivered from the French yoke. . . . The politician cannot see without a feeling of longing, the Amphictyons meeting again, and the estates assembling and deliberating in the interests of Greece. Already he thinks he can hear the harmonious speech of a new Demosthenes, of an Aeschines, or of an Isocrates. One wonders into whose hands Greece will fall if by herself or with the aid of another power, she recovers her liberty. Whatever the prince who raises claims to the throne of Greece it must be desired that the people have a liberal constitution with a system of representative estates, after the model of the American or the English or the present Polish constitution.[21]

Such sentiments were regarded as dangerously radical by the Austrian and Prussian Governments and all who took their lead from them.

From the beginning, calls went out for volunteers to fight. In June 1821 a prominent politician made a speech in the parliament of the Grand Duchy of Hesse at Darmstadt saying that Germany would be oppressed by blood guilt if help was not sent to the Greeks. By August, in several of the smaller German states the call had been made. In Aschaffenburg in Bavaria Baron Dalberg announced that he was forming a Corps of Volunteers. In the imperial city of Hamburg the following notice was taken round from door to door:

Proclamation to the Youth of Germany. The fight for Religion, Life and Freedom calls us to arms! Humanity and Duty challenge us to hurry to the aid of our brothers, the noble Greeks, to risk our blood, our lives for the Sacred Cause! The reign of the Moslems in Europe is nearing its end; Europe's most beautiful country must be freed, freed from the monsters! Let us throw our strength into the struggle! Seize your weapons, honourable youth of Germany, let us form a Greek-German Legion and soon bring support to our brothers! Officers with experience of service are ready to lead us!—God will be with us, for it is a sacred cause—the cause of Humanity—it is the fight for Religion, Life and Freedom, the fight against monsters! Our undertaking will be favoured by the Almighty. Then, victorious and crowned with glory, blessed by our Greek brothers and all Christendom and with the glorious knowledge that we have broken the chains of slavery of millions of our brothers, we shall see our German Fatherland again. Those interested should apply at once to Grosse Bäckerstrasse, No. 62, where they can find out more details. Deserters will not be accepted. A society will collect contributions for the support of this undertaking sacred to humanity.

Hamburg, August 1821[22]

As everywhere, it was the professors who set the pace. Professor Thiersch in Munich had actually been admitted to the Greek secret conspiracy, the Friendly Society, in 1814. In August 1821 he issued a call for German volunteers which was published throughout Bavaria suggesting that the volunteers could be paid from the lands they captured from the Turks. In Leipzig Krug issued a second pamphlet declaring that to fight for the Greeks would be to obey the first commandment. His scheme for private help appeared to be thoughtful and practical.

The private help would take the following form. Individuals with experience of fighting should go to Greece with the express or tacit permission of their governments and should there join the ranks of those fighting. This would in itself be a considerable help, for the Greeks are especially short of experienced soldiers and leaders. In particular they have few officers trained in artillery and military engineering. There are in Germany, as in most European states, many men with experience of fighting, who are inactive and unemployed but who long for activity and employment, and since they do not find this at home and are dissatisfied with their lot they are a nuisance or even a danger to their governments. These men would like to go to Greece, partly for love of the Greek cause, partly for the chance to do something, partly also perhaps from other considerations which may be less worthy but are not necessarily wholly disreputable. They would like to go to Greece and help to increase the Greek fighting forces provided they are given the means to do so. Without assistance most of them cannot go as the writer knows from countless examples. For this reason I suggest that the private help should also, wherever governments permit, take the form of societies of those who are deeply in sympathy with the great cause. These societies should find means of supporting the cause and ascertain who is ready to go and fight. The societies should not simply collect money to help the volunteers but should also establish contacts in Greece itself in order to prepare a favourable reception for them; and to procure suitable appointments, either with the forces already in existence or by forming new forces. . . . Obviously permission to go should not be given to men who are under age or who are lacking in military knowledge. There can therefore be no question of our students going.[23]

At Gotha in Thuringia Professor Jacobs and at Heidelberg in Baden Professor Voss put themselves at the head of the movement. Even in Prussia itself, at Berlin, Professor Zeune started a collection. In Switzerland and in Denmark it was again the professors of classics and theology who led the call for a practical expression of the sympathy for Greece which was so universally felt.

The Prussian Government had been prepared to tolerate philhellenism as long as it was mainly a literary theme or a subject for philosophical debate. The censor had allowed a good deal of sympathetic writing about the Greek Revolution within Prussia itself and even the Crown Prince had declared himself a supporter of the cause. But now there could be no disguising the political nature of the movement, dispersed and disorganized though it was. The Prussian Government took fright and decided to suppress this latest manifestation of liberal opposition. Permission was refused to circulate in Prussia any call for volunteers, and, as so often in German history, the professors caved in at the first touch of official pressure. Professor Krug was reprimanded by the Saxon Government, ordered to refrain from political activity, and his pamphlet was suppressed. Professor Zeune in Berlin was also reprimanded, and the money he had collected was confiscated and given to the poor fund. Throughout Prussia the censor tightened his grip. A query was submitted whether philhellenic poetry came within the terms of the ban as well as pamphlets. The answer came back that the Greek Revolution was inimical to the policy of Europe, the cause was being exploited for political purposes, and that poetry must be rigorously controlled.

In September and October 1821 the Prussian Government, with help from the Austrians, began to whip the other governments of Germany into line. A sharp protest was delivered to the Bavarian Government for permitting the publication of Professor Thiersch's manifesto. In other circumstances, their diplomatic note said, the best way of dealing with Thiersch's pamphlet would have been to ignore it, but the heads of many young German students had been seized with the madness, it was an evil influence on youth, it was stirring up revolutionary sentiment, and Thiersch should not go unpunished. He was accused of a long list of treasonable offences, but especially for plotting revolution and consorting with revolutionaries abroad under the excuse of being interested in freeing the Greeks. The Bavarian Government did not prosecute Thiersch or even revoke his call but the effect was much the same as if they had. Many supporters of the Greeks were frightened off, others continued their activities but more discreetly.

Most of the German governments agreed to follow the official Prussian and Austrian line and the professors obediently retracted what they had said about Greece. Zeune made a public statement in the newspapers that he could no longer be associated with receiving collections. Krug withdrew more graciously by issuing a third pamphlet which confined itself to asserting how united Europe was in the cause of the Greeks; the practical advice on how to help was deliberately omitted. Only in the smaller states of South West Germany did the supporters of the cause hold out. Baden, Württemberg, Hesse-Kassel, Hesse-Darmstadt, and the imperial city of Frankfurt were disinclined to take orders from the authoritarian Prussians. In this small area of Germany, the philhellenic movement was permitted to grow and the committees of Darmstadt, Stuttgart, and Frankfurt found themselves thrust into a position of leadership.

The Prussian ambassadors, reporting back to Berlin on their lack of success in these territories, drew an alarming picture of the philhellenic movement as a hotbed of revolution. Dalberg was described as a hypocrite with the name of humanity on his lips but revolution in his heart. From Frankfurt it was reported how the priests were inveigling women into the movement and preaching a crusade from the pulpit. The number of foreigners visiting the city was remarked on: the liberal banker Lafitte from Paris, a Frenchman travelling under a pseudonym who had been Robespierre's secretary during the Terror and was now claiming to be a papier-mâché salesman, another known revolutionary posing as a wine merchant, Italians thought to be carbonari and so on. Frankfurt was said to be keeping the ashes of revolution alight.

The results of the attempts to stop recruiting in Europe will be described later. The governments, however, had another important weapon besides suppression at home. It was decided to close the ports. Austria and its puppet governments in Italy put a stop to the exodus of expatriate Greeks from ports in their territories. The Pope co-operated by closing the ports in the Papal States. Only Marseilles, of all the ports of southern Europe, remained open owing to the ambivalent attitude of the French Government. From the autumn of 1821 young men from every corner of Europe, inspired by the rhetoric of professors and churchmen, packed their bags and set out for Marseilles, determined to play their part in the holy war for the regeneration of Greece.

6. The Road to Marseilles

Between November 1821 and August 1822 eight shiploads of volunteers left Marseilles for Greece. Over two hundred men took passage in these specially chartered vessels; others went independently, paying their own passage. They came from all parts of Europe: France, Italy, the Netherlands, Switzerland, Denmark, Sweden, Poland, and the Austrian Empire. There were a handful from Spain and Britain, and one American. The vast majority were Germans. As 1821 had been the year of the Italian volunteers, 1822 was to be the year of the Germans. In every region of the Confederation there were men who responded to the call and made their way to Greece despite all efforts on the part of their governments to stop them. Hundreds of others set off but changed their minds before it was too late to turn back.

More is known about the volunteers of 1822 than about any other group of the twelve hundred or so Philhellenes who took part in the Greek War of Independence. In many ways they are the most interesting. The majority were men of education and status in their own countries, men with a sense of service, men who felt that they were selflessly joining an honourable cause. No less than thirty of them have given accounts of their experiences. The third expedition in particular had nine authors among the forty or so volunteers.[1]

A young concert musician, who was also a doctor, read in a newspaper at Mannheim a call for German volunteers to assist in the regeneration of Greece and to take part in a sacred crusade against Islam. The call, he says, went through him like an electric shock; Fate wanted his arm for the cause of Freedom; he recognized a presentiment he had felt since boyhood; God was leading him; the finger was pointing to the East.[2] An army officer from Mecklenburg read the proclamation of Professor Krug and decided to give his 'Gut und Blut' to the sacred cause of Greece's struggle against tyranny. He had been looking for some means of again becoming an active soldier; had thought himself of going but until he read Krug's call it had seemed to be an impossible wish.[3] A Prussian theology student was swept away by the idea of fighting on the graves of Epaminondas and Themistocles.[4] The son of a schoolmaster at Dessau saw it as his duty to 'plant the tree of Freedom in the land where it first grew two thousand years ago' and 'like a knight of old' he left home without saying a word.[5] A young Württemberger from a well-to-do family pestered his parents for months to be allowed to go and finally obtained their assent when the newspapers began to publish accounts of the great victories of the Greeks.[6] An official in the Hamburg Government read the call of Thiersch, Krug, Dalberg, Iken, and others, sold up his furniture to raise money, and set off.[7] The students of Copenhagen raised money to send a few of their number and arranged to have further money sent to Marseilles. A young poet and painter from Schleswig was touched by the Greek enthusiasm in its most extreme form. He actually set out with the intention of being killed, seeing a vision of himself standing by an altar wearing vestments with the cross on his breast a target for the Moslems' bullets—'the blood would be the fruit of Freedom'.[8]

The movement attracted a few cranks and neer-do-wells. On the whole, however, the reasons for going were straightforward. A Danish student who later became a distinguished scientist describes his own feelings which were probably shared by most of his comrades:

I was completely dissatisfied with my position in Copenhagen. I was a nobody and seemed likely to remain so. . . . Added to this discontent at home was a strong desire to see the world. This inclination was partly instinctive like that of migrants but it had also been fed by reading travel books. Also a kind of warlike enthusiasm took hold of me and was daily fired by newspaper descriptions of the fighting between the Greeks and the Turks (unfortunately far too often incorrect). I had learned to admire the Greeks from my schooldays, and how could a man inclined to fight for freedom and justice find a better place than next to the oppressed Greeks? Against all this there seemed to be a decisive barrier in the impossibility of finding the necessary money for the journey. But here I was seduced by the continual newspaper reports on Greek Committees throughout Germany, Switzerland, and the South of France, which not only supported Philhellenes with travel money to Marseilles or Livorno, but also took them by sea to the Morea where they would at once be organized into regular corps according to the agreement between the Committees and the Greek Government, and looked after as regular soldiers.[9]

The professors and churchmen who had published the appeals and plans for volunteers to go to Greece were taken aback by the response. Men began to appear at Aschaffenburg and Boitzenburg and other places where it was reported that the volunteers were being collected. They found no one

Europe in 1821

to receive them. Some of the volunteers then made the journey to Leipzig to present themselves to the famous Professor Krug himself, but he did not know what to do with them. Having belatedly agreed to support the government, he advised the volunteers to go home, but when they insisted on their desire to go to Greece, he suggested they should go to Professor Thiersch at Munich. And so they set off for Munich. Thiersch was equally unable to help them; all he could do was recommend them to the Societies at Darmstadt, Stuttgart, and Frankfurt, the only ones in Germany which were still operating more or less openly.

For several months in late 1821 and early 1822 young men were to be found wandering over Germany looking for the organizations they had read about that were to send them to Greece. Students left their universities, officers gave up their commissions, clerks and apprentices obtained release from their contracts, the unemployed and the disillusioned from many walks of life found new hope, and set off to join the new crusade. Rumours and false stories appeared in the newspapers to keep alive their enthusiasm. It was said that a Crown Prince (unspecified) was going to take command of a German expedition.[10] A Nuremberg newspaper reported that 'a great court' (unspecified) had issued instructions to its diplomatic representatives abroad to issue passports to those wanting to go to Greece with no questions asked.[11] Two hundred students from Bonn were reported to have enrolled in a volunteer army to be paid for by a huge subscription raised in the town.[12] A treasury was said to have been established at Marseilles to pay them and the Greeks were eagerly awaiting their services.

Many governments issued directives to try to stop the volunteers crossing the frontiers, but they were easily evaded. The border officials were often sympathetic to the Greek cause and turned a blind eye. Passports could be obtained by inventing some convincing reason for wanting to go abroad. Soon a regular underground network came into existence. The word was passed around about which prominent citizens of a particular town were friendly to the cause and they secretly collected subscriptions. The volunteers moving from town to town called on these men—schoolmasters, clergymen, lawyers, merchants, officials, and others—and were given money and sent on their way with letters of recommendation to the next town. In Germany all roads led to Darmstadt, Stuttgart, and Frankfurt, but after that the going was easy. The volunteers made their way up the Rhine into Switzerland, where virtually every town had an active Greek Society, and then crossed into France to the Lyons Society, and then down the Rhône to Marseilles. The French officials seem to have been instructed to let them pass without question.

The South German and Swiss Societies, because they alone could act openly, and because they were conveniently situated on the philhellenic route, found themselves thrust into the leadership of the whole movement.

The Societies of Stuttgart and Zurich made arrangements to act as co-ordinators for all the Societies in Germany and Switzerland. They also arranged for a German banking house established in Marseilles to act as their agent for chartering ships and despatching the volunteers.

In the nature of things, the organization was very loose. The Societies had no control over the volunteers who presented themselves. Men would appear from remote towns in Germany or from even further afield with a letter of recommendation from some semi-clandestine Greek Society and very little else. Often they had set off with no more money than had been collected by passing round the hat after a students' meeting, or an advance of wages from a sympathetic employer. Subsidizing these men on their way drained the Societies' resources.

On the road to Marseilles there was a carnival atmosphere. The richer volunteers gave money to their poorer companions and paid for their passage in carriages and boats on the rivers, but most went on foot. Many joined simply for the fun of the journey. Volunteers were constantly meeting old friends that they had met earlier along the route. Little groups formed and broke up and joined up again. Some of the volunteers had extravagant uniforms made to their own design—one took seven uniforms decorated with badges inscribed 'Freedom or Death'.[13] The innocent were regularly fleeced and they sometimes showed their dislike of innkeepers by breaking up their furniture and leaving without paying. There was a good deal of drinking and singing of 'freedom' songs. Ordinary travellers found it difficult to find accommodation. 'In different parts of the country', wrote an English traveller, 'I met with numerous companies of young men on foot, with knapsacks at their backs, on their way to Marseilles, there to embark for Greece. These parties appeared to be composed chiefly of young German recruits and runaway students, and from the boisterous enthusiasm which they generally manifested, it was my endeavour always to avoid them as much as possible. On the roads this was easily managed, but not so easily at the inns, where it sometimes happened that I was unavoidably one of their party.'[14] This traveller was attacked in a brawl in an inn at Lausanne when he was foolish enough to become involved in a political argument with a few of these volunteers.

Many of the volunteers dropped out on the way but several hundred reached Marseilles. Many went no further. Although the South German and Swiss Societies were willing to pay the costs of the voyage to Greece and to provide arms and supplies, their resources were too limited to cope with the numbers. Rich volunteers could pay hotel bills as they waited for a passage, but the majority had virtually no money at all by the time they reached Marseilles. The Societies paid every man daily a small sum which was just about enough to live on but often weeks passed before enough money could be collected to charter a ship. A large empty house was hired as a kind of barracks for the less well-to-do. The volunteers hung around the harbour, some took work in the docks and in the quarries. Two cafés—one, the Café du Parc, was renamed the Café d'Hypsilanti—were taken over as the headquarters of different groups.* Some were content to sit there drinking and playing cards for weeks on end. The French secret police employed spies to keep an eye on them and two proscribed revolutionaries who tried to pass themselves off as volunteers for Greece were arrested and shot.[16] An offer from the ruler of Algiers to take a few mercenaries into his service was indignantly rejected. The Greek colony remained largely indifferent.

Every few weeks, as soon as enough money could be collected, a small ship was chartered to take the volunteers to Greece. The German bankers in Marseilles made the arrangement—the contract simply bound the captain of the vessel to land the men in some port in Greece in Greek hands. Food for the voyage was provided and sometimes arms were bought, but nothing else. There was no pay. There were no arrangements to receive them in Greece. The Societies' responsibility ended as soon as the ship reached Greece.

It was hardly an ideal preparation for a military expedition and many volunteers prudently swallowed their pride and went home. But the rest pressed on, trusting naïvely in their youth and strength and in the accounts they had read of the glittering commands awaiting them in Greece. Over half were retired officers, captains and lieutenants from the vast armies demobilized after the Napoleonic Wars, men who were out of work or bored with peacetime service. Some found they had taken part in the same battles on different sides. There were half a dozen counts and barons from France, Germany, and the Scandinavian countries and numerous officers from prestigious regiments of the French and Prussian armies. A few, whose military experience had been confined to garrison service in the smaller German militias, were inclined to add some elaboration to their record and others considered it helpful to add 'von' to their names. Non-commissioned officers became lieutenants and subalterns majors. Iron crosses and other medals were borrowed from fathers to add to the effect. These innocent aids to morale were always being exposed, however, as new volunteers appeared who had known the men at home.

The others who were not officers came from all walks of life: doctors, lawyers, clerks, students; a merchant from Luxemburg who hoped to set up a branch in Greece;[17] a Bavarian china manufacturer who wanted to found a factory;[18] two brothers from a cadet academy;[19] several boys still in their mid-teens;[20] a theology student from Tübingen;[21] an out-of-work

* The girl behind the cash desk at the Café du Parc was a great favourite among the volunteers. She was murdered one night by a tall blond Piedmontese who took the money and disappeared.[15]

F

French actor;[22] a forestry worker from Württemberg;[23] a Swiss professor of Ancient Greek who came from London;[24] a Swiss watchmaker;[25] a hairdresser from Frankfurt;[26] a dancing-master from Rostock;[27] a French fencing teacher who pretended to be a cavalry officer;[28] a gruff recruiting sergeant from Brunswick;[29] an old soldier from Baden deafened and stupefied by a life-time of fighting;[30] a Spanish girl dressed as a man.[31]

As always throughout the war, many of the volunteers were men whose lives had been ruined by the political upheavals: Poles who had fought in the French army, refugees from the revolutions in Italy, and French Bonapartists. Some of the German students flaunted revolutionary colours. A rich Hungarian officer,[32] who had served in the Neapolitan Army and was now living in retirement on the French Riviera, had been suspected of consorting with the Carbonari and decided to join the Greeks. Others had personal reasons for looking for military glory. A German baron,[33] who heard that his love intended to marry someone else, crossed Germany to dance with her at a ball and then set out for Marseilles. Another German of good family, travelling under a pseudonym, hinted at some dark but honourable affair that obliged him to leave home.[34] A Swiss medical student had recently been expelled from university.[35] A rich Englishman, the son of a general,[36] had been dismissed from the British Navy for challenging a superior officer to a duel.

Early in 1822 a young man appeared at the door of the Stuttgart Greek Society and claimed in deaf-and-dumb sign language to be Prince Alepso, a Greek prince from Argos, who wanted to go back to his country and his family.[37] He was a highly excitable, even hysterical, man much given to drunkenness, but this was put down to natural anxiety. He was subjected to various tests in Stuttgart by the Deaf and Dumb Institute and judged to be genuine. A few officers were asked to conduct him to Greece, and Alepso rode as they marched alongside. On the way to Marseilles he was greeted with reverence in the towns they passed through. A lady gave him a purse made of pearls, full of money, another lady gave him a gold ring. The volunteers found him extremely difficult to deal with, especially when in one of his tantrums he attempted to kill someone on board, threw the gifts into the sea, and appeared suicidal. But they stuck with him in accordance with their oaths in spite of his outbursts of hate against them. It was only after several months when the party reached Argos that his pretence broke down and he was overheard speaking in German after a bout of drinking. It turned out that he was a watchmaker's apprentice from Alsace who had run away from home after a family quarrel.

All these men passed through Marseilles on their way to Greece in the few months of hectic philhellenic activity in 1821–2, though they were not all there at the same time. For many there were weeks of waiting for a passage to be arranged, and occasionally there were more than a hundred volunteers in Marseilles all claiming to want to go to Greece. It was hardly surprising, with such a motley international collection of idealists, adventurers, and ragamuffins, that they should find it hard to co-operate among themselves. They were forever splitting up into hostile groups. At different times the French quarrelled with the Germans, the Danes with the Germans, the North Germans with the South Germans, the students with the soldiers, and so on. There were perpetual squabbles over money as the poor tried to sponge on the rich. The young idealists, busily revising their knowledge of Greece from their books, withdrew in disgust from their brash drunken comrades. The more thoughtful protested at the slender resources of the Societies being dissipated in gambling and on the women of the town.

There were no arrangements for appointing leaders. Every volunteer was an individualist and the cry was heard that, since they were to fight for Freedom, it was wrong to set one man above another. But even the most ethereal and the most independent had to recognize that someone would have to co-ordinate the basic arrangements of dealing with the bank, paying the ships' captains, and distributing the supplies. Elections were held from time to time to select commissioners but none of the leaders was able to keep everyone's loyalty for more than a short time. Some of the ships sailed with no one in charge at all.

Duels were frequent. Honour was a concept highly prized by almost everyone, but it meant different things to different people. The German students with their highly stylized code of conduct were forever taking offence at alleged insults, and there were a few trouble-makers who deliberately provoked quarrels to show off their swordsmanship. There were plenty of genuine points of honour to dispute over according to the conventions since so many of the volunteers were not quite what they claimed to be. Much of the quarrelling revolved round points of procedure on whether or not a particular man was of the right social status to give or receive challenges. But a great deal also seems to have been prompted by simple national hatreds and racial prejudices. The more sober volunteers tried to keep the peace and patch up the disputes, but deep grudges were formed and a few men swore that they would kill their adversary as soon as they landed in Greece.

All were sustained by the belief that their fortunes would be made as soon as they arrived. Even before they left Marseilles there was great rivalry to secure the best commissions, and the more forceful characters appointed themselves to high commands in the Greek forces on the strength of doubtful commendations from their local Societies. A French retired naval officer became a 'Greek admiral', a subaltern from a small German town guard was the 'Commander of the Greek Artillery'. They began to recruit their friends into a 'staff'.[38] The competition for mythical positions caused many quarrels. The worst was between Chevalier, a Swiss dandy who claimed to have been a major in the Hanseatic service (in fact he had been a corporal) and Lasky, an overbearing Prussian hussar officer who was also a poet.[39] Both claimed the right of dispensing appointments in the Greek army and new arrivals in Marseilles took them at their word and divided into two parties. The quarrel came to a duel with pistols—a method of fighting reserved for the most severe affairs of honour. Lasky was shot in the head and was lucky to survive. A Danish medical student[40] performed a trepanning operation and thereafter Lasky sported a silver plate in his skull. Although this added even more to his imposing appearance and to his prestige, it seems likely that his brain had been damaged and he was never the same man as before.

Early in 1822 the Societies decided to appoint a general to take command of the volunteers. They chose General Normann,[41] a Württemberg count who was related by marriage to Professor Orelli, a leading figure in the Zurich Society. Normann, in deciding to go to Greece, had much the same mixture of motives as many lesser men who followed him. On the one hand, he genuinely believed in the Greek cause and had a strong sense of duty and dedication; on the other, he was a casualty of the turbulent times in which he lived and had his own personal reasons for wanting to prove himself. His life had been a battleground of conflicting loyalties. Although born in Stuttgart, he had received his early military experience in the Austrian service. In 1803, however, when his native Württemberg became an ally of France, he was recalled and two years later was at war with his former Austrian comrades. To change sides was a painful ordeal for a young officer, but in 1813 there occurred a new crisis which was to ruin his life. Now he was a famous Major-General, already at the age of twenty-nine one of the most senior commanders of the Württemberg army, a veteran of innumerable campaigns, an officer of the Legion of Honour, and a personal friend of Napoleon whom he greatly admired. But the political situation was changing rapidly. After Napoleon's disastrous Russian campaign (in which Normann served), his German allies began to desert him and join the Allied cause. In May, Normann's forces fell in with a party of Prussians who were fighting on the Allied side. Normann was uncertain what to do, but during confused parleys shots were fired, a battle broke out, and several hundred Prussians were killed. Shortly afterwards Normann, under pressure from his officers, led his troops over to the Allied side, but by now it was both too soon and too late. The King of Württemberg, still loyal to the French, regarded his action as treasonable, and the Allies had little sympathy for a man who had so recently been their enemy. Normann was disgraced, cashiered, and forced to live in exile. His friends recognized that he had been the victim of a situation to which there was no honourable solution, but he could not live down the disgrace of having fired on Germans fighting for their independence. From that fateful day in 1813 he devoted himself to attempts to vindicate his reputation.

Normann's situation has many parallels. During a war it is common for generals to be unjustly treated, but afterwards it is difficult to interest public and official opinion in making amends. Wars cause so many unjust deaths and unjust injuries that an unjust loss of reputation seems unimportant.

Normann allowed himself to be persuaded that he could wipe out his past by leading an army of volunteers to liberate Greece. Some of his comrades of ten years before, now stiff and grey and bored, called on him at his castle and reminded him of the heroic days before 1813 when they had been successful dashing young officers. Other volunteers on the way to Marseilles were put up at the castle and helped to persuade him. The Societies promised men and money but their resources were being quickly dispersed in helping individuals on their road to Marseilles. As the displeasure of the Northern German governments made itself felt and the rate of money subscriptions tailed off, it was argued that Normann could revive the interest in the cause by publicizing his intention to lead the volunteers. Normann hesitated for a long time. He wanted to appear in Greece in the full splendour of a General with a staff and an army. He was conscious that he was no longer young and fit for harsh active campaigning and he still suffered from old war wounds. At last he decided that his duty was to go to Greece and he took leave of his sorrowing family and set off for Marseilles.

He took command of the fourth expedition to set sail. It was the best equipped which had left so far. There were two hundred and fifty people on board, mainly returning Greeks including women and children but also about forty-five European volunteers, the usual mixture of Germans, Frenchmen, Italians, and Poles from all kinds of backgrounds. One of the party, [42] who went as Normann's adjutant, described the scene as the ship set sail, with plentiful quotations from Schiller and Alfieri: 'The cannon thundered a farewell. Two hundred ships in Marseilles harbour saluted as Normann's ship sailed out. A thousand voices shouted "Long live Greece", "Long live the brave warriors of Germany".'

The news of Normann's departure had the expected effect. More volunteers set out from all over Europe to Marseilles hoping to join the main party in Greece. As ever the reports in the press were hopelessly exaggerated. Hundreds of officers were said to have gone; another five hundred paid by Dalberg were waiting at Leghorn; a citizen of The Hague had contributed a million and a half florins to the cause. [43]

But now the volunteers actually in Marseilles began to hear the first hints that they should not believe all that they heard and read. Men arriving in the town were accosted by strangers warning them not to go. The local Greek bishop stated publicly that volunteers would not be welcome. Already disillusioned volunteers were straggling back to Europe. In

April several French officers who had been present at the fall of Tripolitsa
arrived back at Marseilles and were so horrified at the idea of others following in their footsteps that they decided to publish an open letter in Marseilles
describing their experiences. A deputation of Germans interviewed them
as they stayed in quarantine and a curious record of the conversation was
published in a Marseilles newspaper. Only a few points survived the difficulties of communicating in a foreign language with men isolated in the
lazaret—that the Greeks were a despicable, cowardly, and ungrateful race;
that there was no cavalry, no artillery, no supplies, no pay; that Turkish
girls were taken as slaves; and that the Greeks had threatened to cut off
the Franks' heads at Patras. The Greeks of Marseilles spread a story that the
returning French officers had been expelled from Greece for misconduct
and were merely venting their spleen. The officers produced letters from
the Greek Government commending them for their brave services at
Tripolitsa and Nauplia but they could make little impression on public
opinion which remained unshakeably favourable to the Greeks. The Germans waiting to leave were unimpressed. They argued to themselves that
the French army had always insisted on extravagant commissariat arrangements unbecoming to true soldiers, and decided to press on. The French,
seething with frustration, decided to publish a pamphlet but were persuaded
to drop the idea by their old patron who promised them money if they would
do so. The French secret police in any case soon intervened and compelled
the returned officers—who were Bonapartists—to leave France. They
drifted off to join revolutions elsewhere. [44]

A Prussian officer who had sailed in the first expedition from Marseilles
and had been present at the massacre at Corinth also arrived back at Marseilles during 1822. He too tried to warn his comrades and published in
Marseilles itself an account of his experiences. The city, he wrote, is still
full of enthusiasts on their way to the abyss. 'You will only find misery,
death, and ingratitude. Do not believe what you are told in Germany and
Switzerland, but believe an old soldier.' [45]

Another Prussian officer on his return to Marseilles later in the year
also published a book there to tell of his experiences. [46] It was dedicated to
the Youth of Europe as a warning:

When I left my country I thought that with my twelve years' experience as an
artillery officer I would be able to help the Greeks and obtain a rapid advancement. Reading the sublime history of their fathers was the talisman that charmed
me to take an interest in these degenerate children . . . I said to myself, You are
going to fight under the standards of Achilles alongside the heroes of the siege
of Troy. But the Ancient Greeks no longer exist. Blind ignorance has succeeded
Solon, Socrates, and Demosthenes. Barbarism has replaced the wise laws of
Athens. . . . The Greeks do not honour the seductive promises they made to
foreigners in the newspapers.

This officer described the barbarities which he witnessed at Tripolitsa many months after the capture of the city: a young Turkish girl 'beautiful as Queen Helen of Troy' being summarily shot by Colocotrones' nephew; a Turkish boy led around by a rope, thrown into a ditch, stoned and stabbed, and then while still alive being tied to a plank and burned; three Turkish children being slowly burned to death over a bonfire while their mother and father were forced to watch; Hypsilantes standing helplessly by while atrocities were committed and weakly trying to explain away his shame to the Europeans by telling them that as old soldiers they should know the trade of war.

But an idea that had captivated Europe for centuries could not be so easily turned back by plain accounts of direct experience. The magic of the philhellenic dream continued to claim the youth of Europe. Somehow they managed to convince themselves that for them it would be different and the ships, laden with volunteers, continued to leave Marseilles on their way to Greece.

During the early months of 1822, although the news reaching Western Europe from Greece remained overwhelmingly slanted in the Greek favour, a few disturbing reports could also be heard, mingled with the propaganda. The massacres at Navarino, Tripolitsa, and elsewhere could not be denied. Explanations and excuses could be offered for the exuberance of a long-oppressed nation suddenly rending its chains, but massacres did not fit easily into the generally accepted notions of how the descendants of Pericles should behave. Nor could indiscriminate massacres easily be reconciled with the Christian ethic as understood in the West. But if there was ever a danger of the philhellenic enthusiasm being blunted, the Turks saw to it that their own reputation as the modern barbarian horde was maintained and enlarged.

Nowhere in the Ottoman Empire did the belief in the identity of the Ancient and Modern Greeks carry greater plausibility than in the island of Chios, or Scio as it then was universally called. A rich and fertile island, it was inhabited almost exclusively by Orthodox Greeks. There were over 100,000 of them and even during the most tyrannous periods of Turkish rule, the Sciotes seemed to stand out. From the early years of the seventeenth century travellers remarked on the gaiety and gentleness of the population. The European travellers, drawing on their predecessors' work for so many of their impressions, painted an ever more idyllic picture of life in Chios. The women in particular had a universal reputation for beauty and carelessness of morals. Their openness of manner and looseness of dress, in such stark contrast to the general situation in the East, stimulated the imagination and seemed to promise delights available elsewhere only in the South Sea Islands.

And in fact the Sciotes were in a highly enviable position. The island was prosperous and peaceful. Its government and tax gathering were exclusively in the hands of Greeks and the Turkish garrison was small and inconspicuous. The revival of Greek education had gone further in Chios than elsewhere in Greece and many Sciotes lived abroad in Western Europe maintaining close links with their homeland. The mainstay of the Sciote wealth and prosperity was the mastic crop which was grown to produce a kind of chewing gum. It was a luxury product exported to harems all over the Middle East, and innumerable bored Turkish ladies were as strongly addicted to it as their menfolk were to tobacco. As a result Chios was able to make a substantial contribution to the imperial treasury while at the same time maintaining only a light level of taxation. In the years before the Revolution, the island appeared to be a living example of the regeneration of Greece in action. The Ottoman Government enjoying secure revenues and untroubled by administrative costs regarded it as one of the most valuable provinces of the Empire.

When the Revolution broke out in Greece the leading Sciotes saw no reason to join the revolutionaries. They realized that no government of Europeanized Greeks and undisciplined Moreotes was likely to give them the undisturbed security, prosperity, and virtual independence which they enjoyed under the Turks. They also realized that they were situated far too close to the Turkish heartland in Asia Minor to be safe. At some points Chios is only two miles from the Asian mainland and the chief town is only seven miles from the Turkish port of Chesme. The Turkish main fleet, although harassed by the small ships of Hydra, Spetsae and Psara, was a formidable force. The Sciote leaders had little hesitation, therefore, in proclaiming their loyalty to the Ottoman Government and giving over prominent men as hostages for the good conduct of the islanders.

From the very beginning of the Revolution, however, it had been the aim of the revolutionaries to embroil as many Greek communities as possible in their struggle. Their technique was a simple one. It was to engineer some atrocity against the local Turkish population; after such an occurrence the Ottoman Government could no longer be expected to see a distinction between loyal and disloyal Greeks. The first revolutionaries, spurred on by the overseas conspirators, had ruthlessly exploited this method to draw into the conflict many Greek communities who would have preferred to stand aside. And many Greeks particularly in Northern Greece had paid the inevitable penalty in 1821. The prosperous and contented Sciotes were an obvious target for these tactics, especially as their happy condition was much envied by their poorer neighbours in Samos.

In March 1822 several hundred armed Samians landed in Chios, destroyed a few mosques, and proclaimed the Revolution. The Turks retired into the citadel. Reinforcements arrived from mainland Greece, including a few European officers, but they made little progress in besieging the citadel.

Many Sciotes decided to join the Revolution. When the news reached Constantinople, the Ottoman Government reacted in the normal way. Orders were given to put the hostages to death and Sciotes living in Constantinople were rounded up and imprisoned. The Ottoman fleet, which had just sailed from the Dardanelles, was given the task of recapturing the island from the insurgents. The Government, which had believed that it had by now successfully contained the Revolution within a small area, was especially indignant at the boldness of the revolutionaries. It was said that the ladies of Constantinople felt incensed at the prospect of losing their precious mastic supplies and encouraged the Sultan to take a severe line. More probably, the Government felt that an example had to be set to prevent Lesbos and other islands from going the same way and to maintain the precarious loyalty of the large Christian minorities in Constantinople and elsewhere in the Ottoman Empire.

The Turks of Asia Minor decided to take their revenge in their own way. When the Turkish forces landed in Chios from the fleet they were joined by thousands of armed undisciplined Turks who crossed in small boats from the mainland. And as on the previous occasions the Moslem religious authorities encouraged the people to look on the recapture of Chios as a holy war. An unofficial regiment of imams was even formed which crossed the narrow strait. At the first sign of the Turkish counter-attack the Samians abandoned their enterprise, pausing only to kill off all the Turks they had captured. The Sciotes, with no means of escape, were left to their fate.

In the first days after the Turkish troops landed, thousands were killed in the streets and thousands more were rounded up for transport to the slave markets. The main towns were given over to plunder. The Sciotes, who were largely unarmed, escaped as best they could or attempted a feeble resistance. Two parties, each of over two thousand, tried to protect themselves in monasteries in the hills but they all perished when the monasteries were set on fire.

It seems to have been the official Turkish policy to preserve as much of the island as possible and especially to leave untouched the mastic-growing villages on which the revenues of the island depended. But they were unable to restrain the appetites that had been let loose. The Turks on the mainland saw their comrades returning home laden with plunder and leading their slaves. No one wanted to be left out. Self interest and religious duty pointed in the same direction and thousands more Turks crossed to join in. They burst into the mastic villages and soon the whole of Chios was given over to massacre and destruction. One of the most peaceful and thriving communities in the Levant was utterly and irretrievably ruined. It has never properly recovered.

As always, it is impossible to assess accurately how many thousands were killed, left to die, or taken into slavery. The customs authorities gave official certificates for 41,000 slaves, mainly women and boys, and 5,000 of these were sent to the slave market at Constantinople to be sold at about 100 piastres each. The normal slave market was too small to cope with the numbers and many had to be exposed for sale in the fish market or on the street corners. The recalcitrant and the inconsolable were killed off as being of no commercial value and their bodies left to rot in the streets or by the water's edge in the usual Turkish way with their severed heads between their legs, to be devoured in time by the scavenging dogs which infested the city. Passers-by shuddered at the screams of boys being systematically circumcised in batches of forty or fifty to symbolize their forcible conversion to Mohamedanism. Large brothels of women and boys appeared all over the city.

The Christian population of Constantinople, Greeks and Armenians, had disappeared from the streets when the crisis broke out but, inevitably, many had nowhere to hide. As had happened a year before, bands of Turks, urged by the Moslem religious authorities to take up arms, roamed the streets killing any stragglers they could find. The Government, fearing that the Christians in Constantinople might be planning a revolution, took no steps to control the mobs of terrorists. The Patriarch of the Armenians had been ordered to prevent his people having any dealings with the Greeks: all Greeks were to be dismissed from employment with the sole exception of wet nurses, and even they were ordered to terminate the connection as soon as nature allowed.

In accordance with the Eastern custom of regarding every individual as sharing responsibility for the actions of his community, the Sciotes who lived in Constantinople were deliberately hunted down. For them simple death was not considered sufficient. They were taken to the torture house within the Seraglio and subjected to the highly refined punishments of the East, bastinadoed, hung upside down and beaten, suspended by hooks through the ears with weights attached to their feet, their finger nails pierced with needles, their limbs and joints broken by screws, or slowly burnt to death in huge ovens.

Trophies of the Sultan's great victory were exhibited to the people of Constantinople in the traditional manner. Sacks of human heads, noses, and ears from Chios were strewn around the streets. They lay where they fell sticking to the feet of pedestrians, and even in the food markets no Turk would deign to remove the putrefying masses of human flesh. The Sultan and his train of followers on their weekly procession to and from the mosque were too proud to step aside, and their horses unconcernedly trampled the ghastly remains of his Christian subjects into the mire.

8. *The Battalion of Philhellenes*

The eight shiploads of volunteers from Marseilles reached Greece at roughly monthly intervals beginning in November 1821. Other volunteers continued to arrive independently. They landed at different places, at Navarino, Calamata, Missolonghi, Monemvasia, and elsewhere. One party mistakenly put in to Modon which was still in Turkish hands, thinking they were at Navarino, and the volunteers who had begun to disembark, had to scuttle back on board when the Turks opened fire.[1]

The Greeks greeted their unexpected visitors with surprise and incomprehension although they were already accustomed to some extent to the bizarre notions of the Franks. Usually, after it had been explained through interpreters that the visitors had come to assist in the struggle for freedom, a cautious welcome was arranged. Muskets were fired in salute, wine was produced, and an empty house was set aside for quarters. The volunteers, in their multifarious uniforms, marched ashore with some appearance of European drill sometimes to the beat of a drum. The welcome, though friendly, did not match up to the enormous expectations of the Europeans. They were affronted, as officers, at having to unload their own baggage and they had expected more than a bare, ruinous, vermin-infested house to live in. One expedition was so sure that all their problems were over once they set foot in Greece that they made a present of all their provisions to the ship's captain and allowed the ship to leave, confident that they were free for ever from tedious ship's biscuit.

The first Greeks that the volunteers met did not resemble the race of men they had imagined from their schoolboy studies. To sit cross-legged on a bare floor swathed in shawls and smoking long pipes were manners more associated with Turks than with the descendants of Pericles. The attempts of the scholars to converse in Ancient Greek had no success.

More disturbing facts soon came to their attention. An unpleasant smell hung around the towns which they soon discovered arose from the headless corpses lying outside the walls. Emaciated and frightened young women and boys were to be seen running around, half naked, among the ruins. Wild dogs and scavenging birds were everywhere. The Greeks at Navarino, eager at first to impress, told boastfully of the great massacre of a few months before. One Greek claimed to have personally killed eighteen Turks, another said he had stabbed nine men, women, and children in their beds. The volunteers were proudly shown the bodies of Turkish women who had been thrown from the walls a few days previously after being raped and then having their arms and legs cut off.[2] Far from being impressed, as the Greeks intended they should be, the volunteers were shocked and distressed at these sights; they were equally horrified at the open prostitution of the surviving Turkish boys and the unashamed offers of the Greeks to share their pleasures—another aspect of life in which the customs of the East differed from those of the West.[3]

The Greeks found the behaviour of the volunteers equally incomprehensible. No sooner had they landed than quarrelling broke out. Duels were frequent,[4] fought after heavy drinking over abstruse points of honour as at Marseilles, and although no one was actually killed, a few men were wounded and unfit for further activity. Since none of the expeditions, with the exception of Normann's, had any acknowledged leader, the volunteers then split into the usual rival groups, French against Germans, Italians against French, Danes against Germans. Within days of their arrival some of the volunteers realized that they had made a mistake and decided to go home at the first opportunity. But as usual this was not easy to accomplish either because they had no money or because they were no longer welcome in their own countries. They clung to the belief that they had accidentally found themselves among untypical Greeks and that when they reached Hypsilantes or Mavrocordato their situations would improve. The expeditions quickly dispersed, some men preferring to wait on the coast, others choosing to go inland to try their fortune elsewhere.

The parties of volunteers who set off from the ports to seek the Greek Army soon found themselves in difficulties. In the early months, the Greek villages through which they passed welcomed them, gave them food and shelter, and guides for the next leg of their journey. By the spring of 1822, all over the Peloponnese small parties of Europeans and even one or two men travelling alone were to be found begging their way from village to village, either on their way to the Greek Army or on their way back. Food was already short, owing to the breakdown of the economy, and hospitality was given increasingly grudgingly. Besides, the country was covered by bands of armed Greeks, preying off the settled population. Although the newcomers did not realize it, many of the villages through which the

Europeans passed had already had to provide for the earlier generation of volunteers who had come and gone in 1821.

As 1822 went on, the volunteers found the Greek villagers more un-helpful—or, as they invariably termed it, ungrateful. At some places the strangers were refused entry. At others, attempts were made to steal from them. In the open countryside they were occasionally attacked by robber bands. The old soldiers became less scrupulous about their methods, demanding food and shelter at the point of their bayonets and helping themselves to any livestock that came their way.

The food was hard and the accommodation primitive, but most of the volunteers failed to appreciate that they were lucky to get any assistance at all. They could not forget that they were officers, and they had firm ideas about the treatment that officers were entitled to expect. They were per-petually reminding the Greeks that they had come to fight for them, and were perpetually being told that, as nobody had asked them to come they should not expect anything. One wise old Greek remarked that the Euro-peans had not come for the sake of Greek freedom but for their own, a comment which had a disconcerting ring of truth.[5]

Soon most volunteers in Greece were complaining bitterly about their situation, cursing their stupidity in setting out, and despising every aspect of Modern Greek life. One Greek characteristic in particular aroused disproportionately passionate indignation. In village after village the visitors would be promised food and horses if they would only have patience until tomorrow; when tomorrow came some further excuse would be found to delay matters; when eventually the volunteers reached the seat of government the same pattern was repeated. Everything would be arranged, they were assured, if they would only wait. The volunteers never understood that the habit of making unfulfillable promises was simply an Eastern way of being polite.

General Normann's expedition arrived at Navarino in February 1822. Many of the volunteers who had arrived in earlier ships made their way back to Navarino hoping to find a properly organized European force. They were sadly disappointed to find merely another disorganized band of individualists just as arrogant as they had been when they first arrived. When one of the old hands[6] passed an insulting remark about the Greeks, Normann said it was untrue and was at once challenged to a duel. A rich Hungarian nobleman[7] who had been several weeks in Greece was punched in the face and challenged to a duel to the death by a new arrival[8] when he claimed that he had heard him call his chief 'Normann' instead of 'General Graf von Normann'. Another fight broke out over the refusal of the officer to address another as Monsieur *de* A.[9] Such quarrels were frequent. Drum-head courts were held to try to deal with troublemakers but none of the accused would recognize their jurisdiction. Court proceedings soon developed into brawls between French and Germans. One or two unfortunates were beaten up and driven out of the town for alleged thefts or failure to pay debts. A pigsty was taken over as a place of punishment into which the drunken and the unruly could be thrown.[10] Normann looked on sadly and helplessly.

In spite of their curious behaviour, however, the volunteers still enjoyed great prestige simply because they were Europeans. The Greeks continued to believe that European military methods could somehow win victories and occasionally suggestions from the visitors were accepted. At Navarino Normann and about sixty volunteers were permitted to try to put their ideas into practice. An attempt was made to institute a regular watch on the walls of Navarino to guard against a surprise attack from Modon up the coast. The Greek leaders, however, were unable to prevail on the individual Greeks to obey. They insisted that there was no need to guard the walls at night or when it was raining since the Turks never ventured far at such times. To encourage the others, one Greek was bastinadoed for deserting his post, but the habits and beliefs of generations could not be altered by such simple methods. Soon the volunteers alone took over the whole defence of the town, sharing out the watch among themselves.

The usefulness of European military methods was soon put to the test. One day the watch reported that a Turkish fleet of sixty-three vessels had appeared off the town and a simultaneous attack by land was being mounted from Modon. The Greeks were terrified. The fortifications of the town had not been repaired and there were only provisions for two days. The town was filled with the noise of wailing as the inhabitants prepared to leave. But the volunteers, at last in a situation which they understood, greeted the opportunity of fighting with enthusiasm. The gates were shut to prevent the Greeks from leaving, the few cannon were manned by artillery officers, and with difficulty a few shots were fired. The Turks, astonished at this unexpected show of resistance, hastily retired.[11] Like Baleste's defence of Calamata in similar circumstances in August 1821 the action was pure bluff, but it was successful. It produced the same reaction among the Greeks—exaggerated respect for European military methods, coupled with a renewed suspicion that these methods might eventually be used to impose the sort of government on themselves which they would not welcome.

Normann had arrived in Greece expecting to be greeted as a saviour. He expected that the Government would make him Commander-in-Chief and give him general direction of the war. He sent a few officers to Hypsilantes to announce his arrival and the success of his first encounter. But he had no appreciation of the intense rivalry between the various Greek leaders. He did not understand that the Europeanized Greeks, Hypsilantes and Mavrocordato, who still nominally formed the government, had scarcely any resources and no authority; and that Colocotrones and the other captains had no wish to encourage the formation of a regular army. Normann waited impatiently at Navarino for the expected invitation.

While he waited it was decided to attempt an attack on Modon. His confident officers were sure that such a weakly defended fortress could easily be taken by a small disciplined and determined force. A plan was accordingly drawn up and a few hundred Greeks agreed to submit to the guidance of twenty-two Europeans. But as usual the two types of fighting could not be combined. The Greeks began to shout and fire off their weapons blindly from the hip before they were even within range of Modon. A Turk who had carelessly been walking outside the walls when they arrived was captured, stripped, and killed, but as soon as the alarm went up that the Turks were about to attack, the Greeks made a hasty retreat and the Europeans had to scramble home as best they could. That was the extent of the battle. The head of the Turk was taken back to Navarino on a pole and kicked around the streets.[12] A few days later the headless body of a young German lieutenant[13] who had been killed in the retreat was discovered by a shepherd, half eaten by dogs. The incident was hailed as a triumph by the Greeks. As for the Europeans it merely served to confirm their opinion that the Greeks were not only barbarians but cowards as well.

Meanwhile numerous small parties of volunteers had wandered all over Southern Greece. Generally they had gone to Argos (or later Corinth) where the Government and the remains of the Regiment Tarella were still maintaining a desultory siege on Nauplia. But when they discovered that there were no commissions to be had in the Regiment and that there was already a long waiting list for the Greek regular army (which showed no signs of being organized) they wandered off elsewhere. Some became little more than armed tourists. Inevitably, many drifted to Athens where the Acropolis—contrary to the reports in Europe—was still in Turkish hands. Everyone wanted to share the honour of being present at the capture of the most famous fortress in Greece. Attempts were made to mount artillery on the hills opposite the Acropolis but the few shots which they succeeded in firing over the wall caused no damage. Then in March 1822 about a dozen volunteers devised a bold scheme to take the fortress by storm. Like so many of their schemes it depended on a degree of co-ordination and discipline which it was unreasonable to expect. A mine was to be exploded under one part of the wall and the Greeks, led by the volunteers, were to make an immediate assault through the breach. The mine did explode according to plan and the volunteers rushed forward. An eighteen-year-old Prussian lieutenant was first up the ladder and succeeded in planting his lance in the breach.[14] But the Greeks could not overcome their aversion to venturing away from cover. As usual the handful of

Pl. II*a* Two Philhellenes with members of the Regiment Tarella. The one in the heavy greatcoat is probably General Normann.
  b Some of the Philhellenes of 1822

Deux Officiers Francs au milieu des soldats composant le célèbre Bataillon de Démétrius Ypsilanti.

Une Assemblée d'Officiers Européens, accourus au secours de la Grèce en 1822.

European volunteers were left to face the Turks alone and they had to retire at once. The Mecklenburg Count Stralendorf was killed in this encounter. He was given a splendid military funeral and the tomb of the scholar John Tweddell in the Theseum was broken open to provide a suitable grave. Several other Europeans were wounded.

Among the volunteers of 1822 there were a number of naval officers, who naturally hoped for commissions in the Greek fleet and made for Hydra. A French naval captain who had been retired in 1814, Count Jourdain, had set himself up as 'admiral' of the naval volunteers in Marseilles and claimed to be able to dispense commissions. But once they arrived in Greece his authority vanished and everyone tried to make his own claim. A dozen or so volunteers of all nationalities were taken on and joined the crews of the warships. But they were soon disgusted with the Greek methods of warfare. Hastings, a former British naval officer, saw a Turk being dragged round the deck by his beard then thrown overboard and struck at by boathooks. A Dutchman[15] was present when some Turks were rescued from the sea in an unconscious state. They were carefully revived and then tortured, killed, and mutilated.

As with the land forces, the Greek sailors were not inclined to put themselves under the guidance of their self-appointed advisers. The Europeans all had their own ideas about improving the navigation and the gunnery and the preparation of the ammunition but the Greeks, understandably in view of their consistent success, stuck to their own methods. Soon many of the naval volunteers had changed their minds and went off to try their fortune on land. Their general conclusion—apart from the usual complaints about Greek cowardice, barbarity, and ingratitude—was that the Greeks 'put the Franks in a position where it is impossible to be of any assistance to them and then complain of the uselessness of the Franks'.[16]

As in 1821, it was the universal belief of the volunteers landing at the various ports of Greece that they would soon find the Greek Army in which they would be given commissions. The aim of those who set off from the coast was to find this Army. In fact there were only the remains of the one battalion of regular troops that had been raised by Baleste and was now commanded by Colonel Tarella. After the failure of the attack on Nauplia in December 1821 and the fiasco when the Acrocorinth fell in January 1822, the Regiment had steadily lost prestige. Throughout the winter it had remained first at Argos and then at Corinth, the only force directly controlled by the Government of Hypsilantes and Mavrocordato. Throughout its short existence the Regiment had received no pay. It consisted only of about three hundred Greeks and Italians, half-clothed, half-starved, and half-armed, almost all refugees from the Turkish reprisals against the Greek communities in Asia Minor or from the unsuccessful Italian revolutions. They were men who stayed in the Regiment because they had no

G

choice. Many of the original Regiment had died of disease, malnutrition making them more vulnerable to the plagues which swept the country, others had joined the armed bands of the captains. But there were always enough wretches for whom the chance of an occasional meal was enough to sustain their loyalty. After the destruction of Chios hundreds more refugees had arrived in mainland Greece with no one to look after them and there was no shortage of recruits to replace the losses.

During the winter the Regiment had remained at Corinth making occasional foraging expeditions to find food from the surrounding villages. The officers, still for the most part the original Italian refugees, cursed the Greeks but continued to drill their men. Some of them had a few Turkish women and girls in their ménages whom they had saved by their own efforts from the various massacres or had bought in the sales of slaves for a few piastres.

This was the Greek Army about which they had read so much. But if it was not what they had been led to expect, at least it was a force recognizably on the European model being trained to fight according to European tactics. According to Hypsilantes and Mavrocordato, if the volunteers would only have patience, new regiments would be formed, and not only new regiments like the Regiment Tarella but artillery, cavalry, engineers, general staffs, and all the panoply of a national disciplined force. And so the European volunteers began to congregate at Corinth. Some tired of waiting and went off on sight-seeing excursions but they were soon drawn back to Corinth. By April 1822 there were about one hundred and fifty European volunteers in Corinth all expecting commissions in the prospective Greek Army.[17]

As the warm weather returned, life in this European colony was deceptively pleasant. Many were to look back on this period as the happiest they were to spend in Greece. Cafés were set up, wine was cheap, and the volunteers soon reverted to the carefree, confident, aimless type of life that they had enjoyed at Marseilles. Large sums changed hands at the gambling tables and there was perpetual quarrelling and duelling. Some of the more enterprising dug among the ancient ruins to find coins and there was always the hope that they might discover the fabled treasure which the Turks were thought to have buried before the fall of the fortress.

The Greek Government still asserted its intention of organizing an army of 30,000 regulars, but as the weeks passed and nothing happened the volunteers became increasingly impatient. The arrival of General Normann and Mavrocordato raised everyone's hopes that something was going to be done but still nothing happened. A formal letter of protest was drawn up and signed by sixty European officers but they were put off with promises. The Greeks produced pictures of the proposed uniforms for the various arms of the proposed army, but this ruse deceived nobody. Nor did an attempt to gain time by organizing a military choir meet with any success.

At Corinth the charlatans came into their own, gulling the simple volunteers and milking them of their money. Some now tried to translate into action the fantasies that had brought them to Greece. A tall thin bespectacled man with a huge cavalry sword became a favourite of Hypsilantes for a time. He called himself Baron Friedel von Friedelsburg and was forever talking about his castle at Friedelsburg in Denmark and his great connections in Europe.[18] It was not long before a genuine Danish count[19] arrived and exposed him. But although Friedel was not what he claimed and there was no such place as Friedelsburg, he was a man of talent. He had been a student, an actor, a musician, and an artist, and he now carried a lithographic press on his back. Like Paul Harro-Harring, another artist and poet who went to Greece, he seems genuinely to have had difficulty in keeping imagination separate from reality. He was to be found wandering over Greece through much of the war, good-humouredly attempting one unconvincing deception after another. Later he was to produce a magnificent series of portraits of the famous Greeks of the War of Independence.

More sinister was a Frenchman called Mari,[20] who had come with one of the expeditions from Marseilles. He claimed to have been an officer in Napoleon's guard but actually had been a drum major. At Corinth he lived with a Turkish woman with whom—to the suspicion of his comrades —he was heard to talk in Turkish. Like several of the volunteers active in Greece in 1821 and 1822 he had served in the army of Ali Pasha. Mari always seemed to have plenty of money and he occasionally took one or other of the volunteers aside and whispered confidentially that he knew Turkish officers in Salonika who would guarantee them a good job. Mari made three or four recruits and they all mysteriously disappeared. Later he was to fight against the Greeks as a battalion commander in the Egyptian army under the name of Bekir Aga.

By May the Greek Government—of whom Mavrocordato was now the nominal head—had largely given up its efforts to win the active co-operation of Colocotrones and the other captains. It was obvious that the armed bands of Greeks were not to be disciplined into a European army. A year after the outbreak of the Revolution the only forces who were prepared to take orders from the Government were the Regiment Tarella and the European volunteers. The day when all the volunteers could be given commands in the ranks which they expected was clearly a long way off. It was therefore suggested that the Europeans should form themselves into a regular unit of their own and await the day when the Greek army would be organized. Since there was no real alternative the great majority of the Europeans accepted the plan.

A commission of three Europeans, a Frenchman, a German, and an Italian, was appointed to look into the claims of the volunteers and grade them by rank. Since many of the volunteers had not told the whole truth about themselves, it was an invidious task. Many who had served in the famous regiments of Europe could not produce papers, others were exposed as impostors and their swords ceremonially broken. The charming but unconvincing Baron Friedel von Friedelsburg burst into tears when his pretensions were exploded and went off to try his skill at impersonation elsewhere in Greece. A party of German officers refused the indignity of serving as private soldiers and left for home. Inevitably there were accusations that the commission was being unfair—favouring the French—or the Germans—or undervaluing the experience of some battle-scarred officer. [21]

Eventually, about the middle of May, after a good deal of wrangling the volunteers were organized into a battalion of two companies of about fifty men each, the first company consisting mainly of French and Italians, the second of Germans. A few Greeks from Europeanized families were given commissions. The French system of ranks and commands was adopted. It was agreed that everyone would serve in lower ranks than they were entitled to. Officers of the higher ranks in their own armies were to be subalterns, middle-ranking officers were to be sergeants and corporals, lieutenants and others of no military experience were to be private soldiers. Similarly, within each group, rank was to be determined by the date on which a man arrived in Greece. All swore to serve for six months and were promised commands as officers as soon as the regular army was formed. There was to be a high rate of pay, but only a third was to be paid in cash, the rest in Government I.O.U.s to be honoured later. The first third of the pay was actually paid from the money which Mavrocordato and Normann had brought from Europe.

Mavrocordato himself, although he had no military experience, insisted on taking formal command with Normann as his chief of staff. The first company was commanded by the Piedmontese Dania, who had led the unsuccessful attack on Nauplia in December 1821; the second company was commanded by the Swiss Chevalier, who had taken part in the famous duel with Lasky at Marseilles. An artillery unit was organized to service two small field guns, and all the elements of a regular staff and supporting organization were set up, with paymasters, standard bearers, and medical teams. No permanent commander for the battalion was appointed but Dania was declared commander *ad interim*. He had such a strong impetuous nature and was so adept at attracting publicity to himself that he soon became the dominating figure.

There was a long debate about what the new battalion was to be called. Some wanted to call it the Sacred Battalion, the name adopted by the short-lived unit of foreign officers which had taken part in the attack on Nauplia. In the end it was decided to call it the Battalion of Philhellenes, a word which was already becoming general in all European languages to describe the volunteers who went to Greece.

On 24 May the Philhellenes were presented with their standard and reviewed by the ministers of the Greek Government. It was a proud moment. The disappointments, the broken promises, the atrocities, the national enmities and rivalries were all momentarily forgotten. The old idealism and enthusiasm surged again through their hearts. Here in the sunshine at Corinth, beside the stark pillars of the ruined Temple of Apollo, among the bishops, the captains, and the representatives of every part of Greece, it was again possible to believe in the cause of Hellas. As one Frenchman who was present remarked,[22] here was drawn up in the respective uniforms of their nations, men from the banks of the Seine and the Tagus, the Vistula and the Tiber, the Danube and the Po, even the Nile and the Dneiper, men from the Propontis and the Bosphorus side by side with men from the Baltic and the Zuyderzee, the conquerors and the conquered of Austerlitz, men who had come from all points of the compass to help an oppressed nation break its chains.

By the early summer of 1822 the Greek Revolution had cost the lives of upwards of 50,000 Turks, Greeks, Albanians, Jews, and others. Many more had been reduced to slavery or misery. Only a tiny minority had been killed in direct combat with the enemy. The Greek War of Independence hitherto was hardly a war at all in the conventional sense, but largely a series of opportunist massacres. The dead Turks were not for the most part the soldiers of the Sultan nor the dead Greeks the revolutionaries; the victims had simply paid the price of belonging in their respective circumstances to the weaker community and the wrong religion.

In the Peloponnese, apart from a few fortresses which were slowly being reduced by hunger, the Greeks had complete control. They also held a few of the islands. Elsewhere, however, the Revolution had been by no means successful. Despite the plans of the Friendly Society, it had not been joined by all the Christians of the Ottoman Empire. The Slavs, Bulgarians, Romanians, and Armenians had stood aloof and the Greeks of Northern Greece, of Constantinople, of Asia Minor, and of Egypt had all been terrorized or crushed into maintaining their loyalty to the Sultan and to the pro-Turkish patriarch at Constantinople. The Albanians, some tribes of whom were Christian and some Moslem, were torn by uncertainty as to where their best hope lay, but were untroubled by nationalist considerations. In the central part of present-day Greece, Epirus in the west, and Thessaly, Boeotia, and Attica in the east, the local leaders were ambiguous in their loyalties, well aware of the penalities of finding themselves on the losing side. At sea the huge Turkish fleet was still undefeated despite some striking but strategically unimportant successes of the Greek ships.

In early 1822 Ali Pasha of Ioannina, who had for so long defied the power of the Ottoman Government, was at last crushed. He had maintained his independence for so many years that many had thought he was invincible but his final defeat was total. The old man's head was sent to Constantinople, carefully washed and stuffed and exposed on a dish, as befitted his rank, outside the Seraglio. An inscription informed the passer-by that the head belonged to a 'traitor to religion' and included among the list of crimes that he had 'attempted the lives of a number of poor Rayas [Christians] who are a sacred deposit placed in our hands by Almighty Allah'. The heads of his four sons appeared there soon afterwards. [1] The formidable Turkish army which had been besieging Ioannina was now free in northwest Greece ready to march south against the revolutionaries.

On the other side of the country another large Turkish army of at least 20,000 including many cavalry was being prepared to march south. The ramshackle Ottoman Empire was mobilizing its immense resources for a massive attempt to reconquer the lands from which the Moslems had been so summarily extirpated. During the early months of 1822 it should have been obvious that the Greek revolutionaries were going to be put to a severe test. Instead of skirmishes outside besieged fortresses, tumble-down and isolated, crammed with refugees and defended by small poorly-armed garrisons, they were about to be invaded by two specially mobilized Turkish armies.

Greece was in no position to face such a challenge. Many of the Greeks who had massacred the Turks of the Peloponnese in 1821 seem to have assumed that the matter ended there; the Turks were gone, they now had taken over their lands: as far as they were concerned nothing more was called for. They made no attempt to provision and repair the fortresses that had been captured but were content to live their rough lives in their traditional way. The Greek leaders of the various districts devoted their efforts to imposing their authority as if they could now become independent potentates.

There still existed, however, the national Government which had been proclaimed by Demetrius Hypsilantes at the beginning of the Revolution. The less ignorant of the captains and local leaders had to recognize that some co-ordination of the activities of the revolutionaries was necessary although they had no wish to see an effective national Government which would cut their own powers. Colocotrones therefore and the other captains, while they would give no active support to the Government and in particular would not allow the formation of a regular European army, were ready to see the Government continue to be nominally in charge. There were also some incidental advantages to them in leaving the nominal direction of affairs in the hands of the Europeanized Greeks. For one thing they were literate, which was more than could be said for most of the captains, and they were adept at drafting the proclamations, laws and decrees which made such a favourable impression on international opinion.

The existence of a nominal national Government gave an air of respectability to the cruel and selfish policies of the captains.

Hypsilantes himself, after his repeated failures at Tripolitsa, Nauplia, and Corinth in 1821, had lost all authority although he still tried to maintain an attitude of superiority. And he had no money left. The Regiment could not be maintained and there was no prospect of his asserting enough authority to derive any revenues from the population. But just when Hypsilantes' authority reached its lowest point after his failure to prevent the pillage of Acrocorinth, Mavrocordato, who had been waiting in the wings, presented himself as his successor. Mavrocordato still had money and arms that he had brought from Europe and the remaining European volunteers had attached themselves to him.

In January 1822 the representatives of the various groups in Greece agreed to appoint Mavrocordato the first President and Chief Executive of independent Greece. Hypsilantes was given the honorific but even less authoritative post of Chief of the Legislature. The new arrangements were formalized in a written Constitution which was drafted by an Italian[2] to incorporate the philhellenic and liberal ideas of the time.

The Constitution of Epidaurus (the Greek village of Piada being renamed in its old form for the occasion) never existed in Greece except on paper. In the countries of Western Europe, however, where it was widely circulated, it played its part in maintaining the belief that the Greek Revolution was being conducted on progressive liberal principles.

When Mavrocordato was organizing the Philhellene Battalion in the spring of 1822 Greece was under this threat of invasion from two Turkish armies in the north-west and in the north-east. The Turkish fleet, reinforced with contingents from Egypt and the Barbary States, was being made ready to support them. It was a desperate situation. If Greece was to survive it was necessary for urgent measures to be taken to prevent the southward march of the two Turkish armies.

The Turkish army in the north-east posed the greater threat. Mavrocordato decided, however, to make his main effort in the north-west where the Turks were attempting, after their subjection of Ali Pasha, to conquer the Albanian Suliotes who had decided to join the Greeks. Mavrocordato probably felt that he had more chance of success in Epirus where he was already known from his activities in 1821 at Missolonghi. But the deep conflict of interest between the Government of Europeanized Greeks on the one hand and the various captains on the other was just as apparent as it had been when Hypsilantes was the nominal leader. Mavrocordato desperately needed a success. If he was to have a chance of building up Free Greece as a European-type nation state he must win a victory. Unless the regular troops, the Regiment Tarella, and the Battalion of Philhellenes, could be given a chance of showing their usefulness, Mavrocordato was doomed to seeing his authority and his army slip away from him as surely as it had done from Hypsilantes in 1821. Without victory there would be no chance of raising money and without money there could be no regular army. Without a regular army, Free Greece, if it survived at all, would inevitably be controlled by the wild self-seeking captains and local leaders. Two views of the Greek Revolution were in barely concealed conflict. Mavrocordato and the regulars represented the philhellenic ideal of a regenerated European state, the captains represented the simpler notion of a semi-barbaric Eastern theocracy in which the Moslems had simply been replaced by Christians, and where they would exercise the same kind of authority over their districts as Ali Pasha and innumerable other semi-independent potentates did all over the Middle East. The third (and original) view of the Revolution—that it was an attempt to restore a Christian Empire on the Byzantine model over the whole of the Ottoman Empire in Europe—had now lost all credibility, although the feeble Hypsilantes still paid it lip service. Few if any of the Philhellenes who set out proudly on Mavrocordato's expedition to Epirus understood the intricacies of the internal Greek political scene in which they were cast in such an important role.

At the end of May the Battalion set off from Corinth. The Philhellenes took affectionate farewells of the Turkish women in their ménages that they had rescued from the various massacres, knowing well that they would not survive long without their protection. They embarked on vessels at Corinth to take them to Vostitsa. As a result of bad weather the voyage took four days and, since they had only provisioned themselves for one day, they were famished when they arrived. Others went to Vostitsa by land. The Regiment Tarella accompanied them and on the way they were joined by several thousand irregular Greeks.

The old quarrels soon broke out. At Vostitsa the French company killed a sheep and refused to share it with the German company. It was agreed to settle the quarrel by a duel and two champions, a Frenchman and a German, were chosen. A ruined house without a roof was selected as the duelling ground and spectators lined the walls. After a short fight the Frenchman plunged his sword into the German's side and calmly asked if anyone else 'wanted satisfaction'. He was himself later killed in Spain.

Normann and the other more senior officers tried to patch up the quarrels but they had little success. The Germans complained that the French had been given more than their share of positions on the staff but Normann could only reply 'I am a German. When there is a battle we will show the French that we are better with the sword than with the tongue.' At Missolonghi there was another duel in which a German was shot dead by a Frenchman.[3]

The Greeks observed these duels with amazement and incomprehension.

They were also astonished when one of the Philhellenes decided to marry a Turkish women whom he had bought for two piastres. He had her baptized and married her in the church at Vostitsa. Then he dressed her in men's clothes intending to take her on the expedition. But the first time she went out to gather herbs to prepare his meal she was killed by the Greeks. [4]

At Missolonghi, however, it began to appear as if Mavrocordato's policy was going to work. Surrounded now with a disciplined and loyal force, he was able to persuade the Missolonghiotes to provide him with money and supplies. They had at first refused but agreed to co-operate when faced with the prospect of the troops helping themselves. At last the process of grafting a government on the country seemed to be showing some success. Whereas in 1821 Hypsilantes and his regulars had never exercised any authority over the population and had been obliged to subsist on their own resources, now there was a real chance that Mavrocordato might be able to harness the resources of the country little by little to his Government. If he could obtain resources from the country he would be able to strengthen the forces at the command of the Government, and as he strengthened the Government he had more chance of obtaining resources.

Before the process could be properly established, however, the army moved forward on its northward march into Epirus leaving only irregulars to guard the line of communication. The Missolonghiotes promised to continue to send supplies but once the regulars had gone, their co-operation drained away.

At Comboti there was another incident. A French fencing master, Mignac, who claimed to be an ex-cavalry captain, tried to punish (for some minor offence) a German lieutenant, who was serving as a corporal. When he appeared with a piece of rope intending to arrest the corporal, the Germans lost patience and, with the cry 'To arms', they surrounded Mignac with their bayonets. A full-scale fight between the two companies was only averted by promises of an inquiry and a decision that the two companies should proceed separately. However, when the inquiry came to the conclusion that a genuine mistake had been made they were not satisfied. A duel was inevitably the result. Mignac shot the Bavarian Baron Hobe at thirty paces and fatally wounded him. When Mignac went to shake hands with the dying man he refused. Mignac offered to fight another German, but Dania succeeded in having them both arrested before the duel could take place. Dania said they must put off their affairs of honour until after the battle for they were now entering enemy territory. [5]

On 22 June at Comboti the expedition had its first engagement with the Turks. They positioned themselves on some small hills near the plain and Normann himself with about twenty Philhellenes set out to reconnoitre the vicinity of the fortress of Arta. Soon after they set off they were sighted by a party of Turkish cavalry who galloped out to attack them. But now the Europeans were able to show that this was the kind of warfare which they really did understand. Tarella led his regiment swiftly along the base of the hills to cut off the Turkish retreat and Dania moved the Philhellenes to attack their flank. This was not the kind of strategy the Turks were used to—they expected only to meet the usual bands of irregular Greeks who were firing wildly from the hills. A momentary confusion seized them and the ever eager Dania gave the order to charge with the bayonet. The Philhellenes threw themselves eagerly at the enemy in good order and the Turks fled in confusion only to run into the fire of the Regiment Tarella, The Philhellenes pursued them for four miles killing many straggling horsemen without the loss of a single man. It was an astonishing vindication of European methods, and the Turks were convinced that they had come upon a foreign army 2,000 men strong.

The success of the affair at Comboti confirmed the belief of the Philhellenes in their intrinsic superiority and raised the confidence of the whole expedition. They moved forward and a few days later took up new positions in the village of Peta a few miles from the fortress of Arta.

But the long march from Corinth was already beginning to take its toll. A series of violent storms had soaked and chilled the men bivouacking on the open ground. Some had no more than rags on their backs and they found themselves scorched during the day and frozen at night. Fever broke out. A few Philhellenes were too ill to leave Missolonghi and at Comboti it was decided to evacuate seven more of the worst cases back to Missolonghi. Before this could be arranged, one of them, a captain from Hanover, died in convulsions.[6] A Dutch guards officer[7] was given the task of escorting the others back with the help of a few Greek muleteers. But no sooner had the rest of the expedition left Comboti than he took a horse and went off, leaving the sick men in charge of the muleteers. They abandoned them soon afterwards after taking their money. Two of the sick died that day of exposure and the other four, when found and brought to Peta, did not long survive.

An Italian, a former cavalry officer,[8] who had been showing signs of mental distress, also disappeared one night from the Battalion. It was thought that he had listened to the stories current in Corinth that the Turks were willing to take on European officers and had decided to desert to the enemy. Whether this was his intention or whether he, like the Dutchman, was merely trying to leave Greece is uncertain, but he was taken prisoner by a patrol and taken to the Turkish commander at Arta. There, in hopes of saving his life, he revealed all that he knew about Mavrocordato's forces and offered to join the Turks. He was summarily hanged.

In spite of these losses the numbers of the Philhellenes were kept up. At the end of June a party of volunteers, who had arrived in Greece too late to join the expedition at Corinth, reached Missolonghi. There they

found the sick who had been left behind by the expedition. In that unhealthy place there was little hope of recovery. A young Danish doctor,[9]
and the Spanish woman who had accompanied the Philhellenes all the way
from Marseilles[10] had already died but others felt well enough to rejoin
the army. Some of the new arrivals, already disgusted with the Greeks
for the usual reasons, were only too glad to abandon their enterprise and
cross from Missolonghi to the safety of the Ionian Islands. But eight men
set out to join the Philhellenes at Peta; only one was to survive the forthcoming battle.

Peta is on a low hill within sight of Arta with a few miles of plain and a
broad river between. The roads in and out of Arta can be clearly seen and
there are a number of other smaller hills covered with rough scrub between
the two towns. It is a strong defensive position provided all the hills are
held. The expedition spread out its forces on these hills round Peta with the
Battalion of Philhellenes claiming the post of honour on the low hills
nearest the plain. Normann and his headquarters lay further back. The
Greek irregular bands, as was their custom, built small entrenchments but
the Philhellenes, anxious for the opportunity of manœuvring in the
European style, despised such methods. All their hopes were on staging a
pitched battle in which their discipline and superior fire power could be
turned to advantage. It seemed to be only a matter of time before the
Turks would come out from Arta to try to dislodge them. Every morning
the Philhellenes at Peta could see the Turkish cavalry leaving the gate of
Arta and practising manœuvres on the nearby plain. They itched to be
allowed to attack. Some of them even suggested that they should abandon
their position on the hills but Normann insisted on their remaining on the
defensive. Dania, ever the dashing cavalry officer, was eager to the point of
insubordination and led a strong patrol into Turkish-held territory beyond
Arta before he was called back.

As the days passed, however, the situation of the troops at Peta became
increasingly uncomfortable. The food was bad—coarse corn mixed with
peppercorns and baked into hard bread. Water had to be fetched from two
hours' distance away. An enterprising Frenchman bought a quantity of
wine in the village but he would not give any to men who could not pay. It
was now obvious that the Greeks of Missolonghi were deliberately refusing
to send the supplies that they had promised. The Greek irregulars who
had accompanied the expedition began to melt away.

More worrying still was the curious behaviour of the local Greek leader
Gogos. He had for years maintained his strong band of armed Greeks in
the region, sometimes allying himself with Ali Pasha sometimes with the
Turks. It was thought, because of his vigorous fighting against the Turks
in 1821, that he had irretrievably committed himself to the Greek cause.
In fact, however, Gogos was typical of many of the Greek captains. He had

no interest in the aims of the Greek Revolution as propounded by the Europeanized Greeks, although from time to time he pretended the contrary; he was only concerned to maintain his personal position as a quasi-independent leader. If possible he would have preferred the Turks to be driven out or killed off, but if that was not possible, then his first priority was to make sure he was not caught on the losing side. In Epirus, unlike in the Peloponnese, the Greeks had not been able to massacre the Turks in 1821. It was possible still to make use of that fact to hedge bets, a policy which several Albanian tribes successfully carried through to the end of the war.

It was obvious to the army encamped at Peta that Gogos was in communication with the Turks. Stietz, a Hessian colonel on the staff, on a visit to the front, found him in the presence of emissaries from the Turks. At night beasts loaded with supplies were seen leaving Arta for Gogos' camp, and returning later without their loads. While the rest of the army depended on a feeble supply of food from Missolonghi, Gogos and his men always seemed to have an abundance. When questioned about the strange situation, he boasted that he was deceiving the Turks into supplying his men by promising them his loyalty. The Philhellene officers made repeated representations to Mavrocordato that Gogos was unreliable but Mavrocordato refused to take any action. He probably did not himself believe his statement that he had every trust in Gogos' loyalty, but was in too weak a position to enforce his will over any of the captains.

One advantage of the continuous communications which Gogos and others kept with the Turks in Arta was the steady flow of intelligence about the Turkish intentions received in the Greek headquarters. Information was received well in advance that the Turks were going to launch an attack on 16 July. Mavrocordato held a council of war of European officers to ensure that their dispositions were right. Tarella and Stietz were of the opinion that the Regiment and the Philhellenes should be held back in reserve so that they could repeat the tactics that had been so successful at Comboti a few weeks before. Dania, on the other hand, insisted that his men should remain in the place of honour in the front of the position. Mavrocordato and Normann were more swayed by the consideration of the effect on the morale of the remaining Greeks if the Regiment and the Philhellenes seemed to be drawing back. In the end political arguments overruled the military arguments, and the various forces took up positions in a rough circle round Peta. Normann, however, remained profoundly unhappy at the decision and felt obliged to write a letter to Mavrocordato to put his misgivings on record. The Regiment, he said, was now reduced to 350 men; the Philhellenes to 90; the Ionians, the only other force on whom he could rely were only 75; Gogos would probably desert his post and the other more reliable Greeks would be unable to help. Mavrocordato replied that he was sure the position could be defended and that Gogos would maintain his post with honour.

On 15 July the final preparations were made. The two field guns were moved into place. The French were persuaded to divide out the wine and brandy so that everyone would have something to hearten him next morning. A suggestion was made that the sick Philhellenes—who now amounted to twenty-one—should be moved back but they were obliged to remain at Peta.

On the morning of the 16th there was a thick mist. As the sun rose it cleared. The Philhellenes were gradually able to see that their expectations were correct—an army of several thousand Turks and Albanians had left Arta and was advancing towards them.[11]

The Turks came forward by their age-old methods crossing the open ground for a frontal attack up the hillside. Their standard bearers would rush forward and plant the standard and the troops would follow regardless of danger, stopping to fire and then waiting for the standards to be moved forward again. It was the first time that the Regiment had been in a conventional action and there was a momentary fear, after the first Turkish fusillade, that they would revert to their instinct to turn back, but the long training of Baleste and Tarella had had its effect. The Regiment stood their ground, held their fire until the first Turks were within range and then calmly shot them down. The Philhellenes for their part could hardly believe their luck—here was a type of war where their experience could be exploited to the full. A thrill of excitement passed through the ranks. Time and again as the Turks came within range they were met by a steady, deadly fusillade from the Regiment and the Philhellenes. A Turk would seize the standard and run forward with it only to be shot down, another Turk would pick it up only to suffer the same fate. For two hours the Turks tried to come up the hill with their traditional fatalistic disregard of casualties and of danger, acting out to the death the obsolete tactics which had once been the terror of the world. The hillside was soon covered with dead and dying Turks and Albanians. Victory seemed certain. The Philhellenes laughed with excitement at their good fortune and shouted to one another that they would dine in Arta that night.

Suddenly they heard shouts behind them and, to their horror, they saw that the Turks had turned their flank and were bearing down on them from the rear. Gogos had deserted his section of the front and his men could already be seen retiring to the security of the mountains behind. Whether Gogos deliberately deserted his station in accordance with some treacherous arrangement with the Turks cannot be proved, although the Philhellenes certainly believed he had. Perhaps he was merely obeying the old convention of hasty retreat as soon as the enemy appeared.

In any case it was fatal for his comrades who were fighting the battle in the European style. The Regiment Tarella, as soon as they saw the danger, managed to retreat, but for nearly a third of them—about a hundred men in all—it was too late. They were killed as the Turks overran their position. The Philhellenes also tried to retreat but Dania, confident to the last, gave the order too late. Most of the Philhellene Battalion found itself isolated on a small hill entirely surrounded and being attacked from all sides by the imperturbable enemy. In the *mêlée* firearms could not be used and the battle was fought to the death with bayonets, swords, and daggers. The Philhellenes realized only too well that their fate was certain but in their supreme crisis they were seized by a mad desperate excitement. A party rallied round the Standard of the Philhellenes which had been presented to them by Mavrocordato and only let it go when they were all killed. The last survivor was still holding it aloft as he died. The Frenchman Mignac, who had killed the Bavarian Baron in the duel a few days before, became a favourite target because from his bright red cavalry coat the Albanians thought he was the leader. He is said to have killed nine men before his sabre broke and he was overcome. Twelve Poles tried to force their way through with their bayonets but they were all cut down. By the afternoon it was over. If the Turks and Albanians had not stopped to strip the dead even fewer would have survived. As it was, out of the Battalion of about a hundred men, probably less than thirty survived. When the Turks entered the village of Peta they burned it down and cut off the heads of the sick Philhellenes that had been left there. Tarella, Dania, and eighteen others were captured alive as a result of a deliberate decision. They were made to carry the heads of their comrades back to Arta and were then impaled. A German doctor alone was spared after promising to join the Turks.

The names are known of sixty-seven Philhellenes who lost their lives in the battle or its immediate aftermath. Thirty-four Germans, twelve Italians, nine Poles, six Frenchmen, three Swiss, a Dutchman, a Hungarian, and an Egyptian Mameluke who was naturalized French.[12] They include all the higher ranking officers of the Battalion, Lasky and Chevalier who had fought the famous duel at Marseilles, the impostor Tassi who had exploded the mortar at Tripolitsa, old soldiers, runaway students, mercenaries, political exiles, and simple adventurers.

In the days after the battle the survivors began to straggle back to Missolonghi. Normann was alive, although slightly wounded in the breast, and also some members of his headquarters which had been back from the main battle area. Most of the other survivors were wounded and ill. On 27 July twenty-five Philhellenes paraded at Missolonghi for the last time at a funeral service for their dead comrades. The Battalion was formally disbanded and those who still had the strength and the means prepared to leave for home.

In the next few months disease and neglect completed the toll of misery.

There still remained at Missolonghi the sick and the wounded and a few, as usual, who had no home to go back to. And there were other Philhellenes who had arrived too late to join the expedition at Peta. There were also the remnants of the Regiment, the command of which was now given to Gubernatis, an Italian who had once served Ali Pasha and a survivor of the battle.

Panic reigned in Missolonghi. It was obvious that the Turks, after their victory, would soon be on the march south. The Turkish fleet also appeared offshore. Many of the Missolonghiotes decided to leave either for the mountains or for the Peloponnese, but for the majority there was no choice but to try to put themselves in a position to resist a siege. Mavrocordato too believed that if the Revolution was to survive in western Greece, Missolonghi must be held. Gubernatis in command of the two hundred survivors of the Regiment offered to help in the defence if the Missolonghiotes would pay and supply his men. When they refused, Gubernatis marched his men to Amphissa leaving the ungrateful town to survive if it could.

It was late in the autumn of 1822 before the Turks reached the gates of Missolonghi. The interim was taken up with long complex negotiations as the various captains in the region mended their fences with the enemy. The Suliotes, to save whom the expedition had been mounted, were evacuated as a tribe to the Ionian Islands.

There were now only about a dozen Philhellenes left in Missolonghi. Several had already died of disease since the battle of Peta.[13] As the winter rains set in, the others began to succumb. Two brothers who had together left the Cadet School in Württemberg to come to Greece both died in November.[14] Another Bavarian died in December.[15] A Swiss lieutenant[16] went mad and had to be chained up like an animal. A Turkish slave woman gave him food until he too died, howling deliriously to the end.

At the end of November General Normann died. His personal servant who had accompanied him from Württemberg died soon after.[17] It was said by some that the Greeks refused to give Normann enough money to pay his fare to the Ionian Islands. Others more charitably said that he deliberately decided to stay in Greece. Whatever the truth, Normann's death in Missolonghi had a certain dignity. If it is possible to die of a broken heart, that was the cause of his death. Apart from his personal tragedy Normann felt (with some justice) that he must share the blame for the destruction of the Philhellene Battalion. He had been responsible for them; in many cases it was his name that had made them volunteer. If he had only been a little more firm with Mavrocordato, the defeat might have been averted. Normann tortured himself with the thought that he had foreseen it all, the wrong dispositions, the treachery of Gogos, and yet had done nothing to stop it.

10. *The Triumph of the Captains*

While Mavrocordato, the Regiment, and the Philhellene Battalion were on their disastrous expedition to Epirus in the summer of 1822, the main Turkish invasion from the north-east was under way at the other side of Greece. Almost all outbreaks of revolution north of Thessaly had by now been ruthlessly stamped out, culminating in the killing of many thousands of Greek prisoners at Salonika in May. At the end of June an army of over 20,000 men assembled at Larissa ready to march south to reconquer the revolted provinces. It was ordered to co-operate with the army in Epirus for a two-pronged invasion of Greece down both sides of the mountains.

The Greek Government at Corinth saw the threat developing with alarm but was largely impotent to do anything about it. Having virtually no forces at its own disposal—apart from the Regiment Tarella and the Philhellenes which had gone to Epirus—the Government could only function by securing the co-operation of the great captains and the other local leaders. If the Turkish invasion was to be resisted before it reached the Peloponnese, it was essential that the Greeks of eastern Greece should co-operate. The most powerful man in that region was Odysseus, a man as self-seeking, unscrupulous, and effective as Colocotrones. Since the outbreak of the Revolution Odysseus had established himself as a virtually independent potentate in most of the region between Thermopylae and the Isthmus of Corinth. Like Gogos and the other captains in Epirus, Odysseus, when confronted with a superior Turkish power, tried to hedge his bets. If he could not survive as an independent potentate in a free Greece, then he preferred to do so under Turkish suzerainty. Odysseus therefore, like his colleagues in Western Greece, began to have conversations with the Turks.

The Greek Government at Corinth, foreseeing treachery, tried to bring

him under their control, but they were powerless. In desperation they tried
to remove him from his command, ignoring the unpleasant fact that the
loyalty of most of the Greeks was a personal one to the leader of the moment
who could pay them, and not to any larger concept of a Hellenic nation
state. In June two emissaries from the Government who visited Odysseus
at his headquarters were summarily put to death by his express orders. He
afterwards claimed that, if he had not killed them, they would have killed
him, and this was probably a correct appreciation of the situation.

When the Turkish army began to move south from Larissa in July 1822
it seemed that the divisions among the Greeks would make their task an
easy one. The Turks reached Thebes without opposition and as they
approached the Isthmus the local Greeks of that region abandoned the
strategic passes and allowed them through. The great fortress of the
Acrocorinth, which had surrendered to the Greeks with much bloodshed a
few months before, was hastily abandoned and the Turks found themselves
established in the Peloponnese, in the very heartland of the Revolution,
with their huge army still intact.

They had not been in time, however, to save Athens. At the end of
June the Turks who had been besieged in the Acropolis of Athens were at
the last stages of hunger and thirst. There were about 1,200 of them,
mainly refugees and including less than 200 men able to bear arms. On
21 June they agreed to surrender. Knowing what to expect from Greek
promises, they succeeded in involving the Austrian, Dutch, and French
consuls in the terms of capitulation, stipulating that the consuls were to
arrange for European ships to take the Turks to Asia Minor after they had
surrendered their wealth and their arms. The consuls, equally sceptical of
Greek promises, immediately made arrangements for European warships
to be sent to supervise the surrender and they made all the Greek priests
and captains of armed bands of the besieging force swear the most solemn
oaths to respect the terms. The surrender, however, took place before the
warships could arrive and, although at first the terms were respected
(except for the settlement of a few old personal scores), the hatred of the
Greeks could not be contained. When a rumour reached Athens that the
Turkish army had reached Thebes, the usual general massacre began.
Within a few hours about 400 of the defenceless Turks had been killed in
the streets, the Greek leaders making no attempt to interfere. The rest
crowded into the compounds of the European consuls who were making
frantic efforts to stop the massacres. Soon two French warships arrived at
the Piraeus and the surviving Turks were escorted from the consulates to
the sea through the murderous crowds by armed French marines. They
were eventually sent to Asia Minor. A few other Turks were taken to
Salamis by the Athenians when they abandoned the town, and were killed
off at leisure.

The Turkish army meanwhile, having arrived at Corinth with hardly an attempt at resistance, were understandably confident that the Peloponnese would soon be reconquered. Their plan was to relieve the fortress of Nauplia, which was still in Turkish hands, and then march to Tripolitsa. The Turkish fleet, which could have given direct assistance to Nauplia, sailed instead round the Morea to send relief supplies into Coron and Modon, the other fortresses in the peninsula which were still in Turkish hands.

The Turks in Nauplia who had been under siege for over a year were in the last stages of starvation. At the end of June, before the Turkish invasion force had left Thessaly, they had offered to surrender, saying that it was better to be quickly massacred than to die slowly of hunger. An agreement was made whereby they were to be conveyed in neutral vessels to Asia Minor on condition that they gave up their arms and two-thirds of their property. The Greeks might have obtained possession of Nauplia at once but, as usual, when the prospect of booty was imminent, the divisions among the different interests made themselves felt. A few Greeks were allowed into the fortress to draw up lists of the property and they began to make bargains with individual Turks to spare their lives in exchange for their money. Other Greeks began to sell provisions to the Turks. And so the Turks were enabled to hang on a little longer.

When the news arrived in Nauplia that a relieving army was on its way, the Turks inside naturally determined to prolong their resistance even longer although it was obvious that they were by now very near breaking-point. The commanders of the invading army felt bound to make the attempt to relieve the fortress, and therefore imprudently marched out of Corinth across the mountain passes into the plain of Argos.

It is difficult to decide whether the Turks suffered more from over-confidence or from mismanagement. Their army had, since it left Thessaly, marched through several mountainous passes which it had neglected to secure. The Greeks had reoccupied them as soon as the army had gone through. If the Turkish fleet had co-ordinated its activities with the army, this would not have mattered much, but instead it had sailed off to reinforce Coron and Modon. The army was isolated on the plain of Argos. Few of the Greeks understood the full implications of the situation. The Government which had been established at Argos decamped in panic to the coast, ready to leave by ship when the Turks appeared. Thousands of Greek refugees from all over the plain of Argos followed and the Mainotes, preparing to return to their barren mountains in the Southern Peloponnese, plundered their countrymen mercilessly before leaving. It was left to Demetrius Hypsilantes, who had apparently lost all his authority, to show what could be achieved. With a few hundred Greeks he occupied the old castle of

Argos and prepared to defend it vigorously. The Turks could not advance to Nauplia while Argos was still held.

As the weeks passed it became clear that this was more than a temporary setback. The Turkish army running short of supplies, decided to retire to Corinth, but it was too late. Colocotrones and his men had occupied the passes. When the Turks reached the narrow defiles they came under fire from the Greeks above. They had foolishly put themselves in the situation where local Greek military methods were at their most effective. The Greeks securely protected behind the high rocks, were able to kill off the Turks with hardly an attempt at resistance. It was a massacre more than a battle, and the Dervenaki became yet another spot where travellers years later could see the heaps of Turkish bones. If the Greeks had not been concerned to strip the dead, the whole Turkish army would have perished there and then. As it was, the Turks who fought their way through and reached Corinth were little better off. They still had no supplies and other equally dangerous passes lay to their rear. Colocotrones occupied all these passes and the beaten Turkish army was isolated at Corinth. Starvation and disease did the rest. The commander himself died in November and only a tiny remnant of the army was eventually taken off by the Turkish fleet.

The failure of the invasion decided the fate of Nauplia. At the beginning of December starved children were frequently found dead in the streets and emaciated women were seen wandering about searching for the most disgusting nourishment. Finally everyone was so weak from hunger that the remaining food could not be carried up to the soldiers on the walls at the top of the fortress. When they came down they were too weak to go up again. A vast crowd of armed Greeks assembled by the gates ready to plunder the fortress.

It was at Nauplia that the Regiment stood to arms for the last time as an organized unit. At Peta it had lost about a third of its strength, but its new commander Gubernatis had somehow held the remnant together. When the people of Missolonghi refused the offer of help in the defence of the town, the Regiment had marched to Amphissa and then to Athens. At the end of October it took its place along with the thousands of armed Greeks outside Nauplia. Since Peta it had steadily been losing men through disease and desertion, but as had occurred throughout its short history there were still displaced Greeks to whom membership of the Regiment offered the only hope of keeping alive. And there were still Philhellenes arriving in Greece who made their way to the Regiment in the belief that they were joining an army.

When the Regiment reached the plain outside Nauplia in October it consisted of only 135 men. Gubernatis and the other European officers were half naked and half starved, but somehow by ruthless foraging expeditions they found enough food and plunder in the villages to keep together. The old hands were long since inured to Greek methods but, as always, the newcomers' philhellenism quickly turned to disgust. Kotsch, a German officer who was present at the last stages of the siege describes how a Greek priest, suspected of corresponding with the Turks had his fingers broken and his nails burned out. Boiling water was then poured over him, he was walled up to his neck and honey smeared on his face to attract the flies. He did not die until the sixth day. A Jew who tried to leave the town was stripped naked, and had his genitals cut off, after which he was driven round the town and hanged. At last, on 12 December, the Turks sent heralds to ask for a capitulation.

The Regiment, amazingly, still enjoyed the vestiges of the prestige with which European military methods had been regarded in Greece since the outbreak of the Revolution. It was decided that the Regiment should be given the task of taking over the fortress. All enthusiasm for the Greek cause had long since gone. Some of the European officers had recently died of disease or starvation, others were near death. But the Greeks, still afraid themselves to approach the walls, promised that if the Regiment would take the lead in entering the fortress that they would share in the booty.

Gubernatis therefore led 105 men of the Regiment up the rocks to the walls of the highest part of the fortress, retracing the steps which he himself had taken just a year earlier during Dania's unsuccessful attempt to seize Nauplia by storm. They went at night and were admitted over the wall by the starving Turks.

But as everyone half expected, the result was the same as at Monemvasia, Navarino, the Acrocorinth, and Athens. Once the Greeks were admitted to the fortress the killing began, and a pyramid of heads was erected. As it happened, however, there were few Turks remaining in the upper fortress. The majority were packed in the lower part of the fortress whose defences were still intact. Fortunately for them a British frigate, H.M.S. *Cambrian* arrived in time to supervise its surrender. The captain threatened to bombard the town if the Greeks approached the gates of the lower fortress and he landed troops to escort the prisoners out. Five hundred diseased and starving Turks of all ages—men, women, and children—were crammed on board the ship and although sixty-seven died on the voyage and typhus broke out even among the crew, the rest were landed alive at Smyrna. The captain of the *Cambrian* also ensured that several hundred others were embarked on neutral vessels before the Greeks could get at them.

As on all the earlier occasions the plunder of the fortress of Nauplia fell entirely to the hands of armed Greeks. The European officers of the Regiment were given two or three Turkish girls each as their share of the booty. They took them to Athens where the consuls were authorized to buy them and send them to Asia Minor along with the survivors of the massacres at Athens.

Shortly afterwards the Regiment was disbanded. Its first two commanders, Baleste and Tarella, had both been killed. Gubernatis, the third and last commander, had been with it almost from the beginning. He had seen his men abandoned on the battlefield by the Greeks at Nauplia in 1821, and at Peta in 1822. He had seen the massacres at the Acrocorinth and at Nauplia and innumerable atrocities elsewhere. He himself had been wounded at Nauplia in 1821 and only escaped at Peta by hiding for two days in a thorn bush. He had been sent to Chios before the massacre to help to put the defences in order but his offer had been turned down by the Sciotes. Gubernatis was only technically a Philhellene. He was more a professional soldier of fortune. He had fought for Ali Pasha, he knew the Greeks, Turks, and the Albanians, and the manners and languages of the East. He had a professional's instinct for survival. Italy and much of the rest of Europe were closed to him. As with so many of his countrymen, soldiering was his only means of livelihood. He took passage to Egypt, was given a commission by Mehemet Ali, and devoted himself to training Moslem troops who were preparing to reconquer Greece for the Sultan.

Meanwhile, on the other side of Greece, the first siege of Missolonghi by the Turks was about to reach its climax. When in the winter of 1822-3 the Turks were at last ready to make their attack on the hastily constructed ditches, they found the constant rain a severe impediment. They still had hopes of making some arrangement with the inhabitants as they had with the captains, and interminable confused negotiations were carried on, with a good deal of bluff by the leaders on both sides of the walls.

The Turks were particularly concerned, after their experience at Peta, to discover how many Europeans there were in Missolonghi. Marco Botsaris, the Suliote leader, in one of the negotiating sessions tried to persuade the Turks that there were eight hundred Franks and twenty-four pieces of artillery in the town. The Turks, offering to set Botsaris up as a local commander under Turkish suzerainty, proposed to pay every Frank 15,000 piastres and to provide vessels to take them back to Europe. There were in fact only about six Philhellenes left, but Mavrocordato tried to give the impression that he still had a sizeable regular force. In the magazines there were found the boxes of bayonets that he had brought with him on his first arrival in Greece in 1821. All the other arms had long since gone but the Greeks had seen no use for bayonets. These were polished, fastened to poles, and set at intervals round the walls to give the impression that regular soldiers were on guard. False artillery bastions were built and two old drums were constantly beaten to give the impression that troops were exercising.

The Turks tried several assaults on Missolonghi during the winter but they were repulsed with little difficulty. Through sheer mismanagement an army of over 10,000 men, after winning a decisive battle at Peta in July, proved unable by the next new year to capture a town defended by an earth wall five feet high. Like the other Turkish army at Corinth, once they had been halted, their power vanished. Disease broke out, food became short, and the captains in the area north of Missolonghi who had agreed to rejoin the Turks after Peta started to change sides yet again as the fortunes of the Greeks improved. When the Turks decided to retreat, it was too late. The Greeks made sorties from Missolonghi and came down from the mountains to attack them. They killed numerous stragglers and captured much of the baggage train. As in Eastern Greece, the Turkish fleet, whether through fear of the Greek ships or mismanagement, gave no support to the army.

One Turkish ship which went aground off Missolonghi was found to contain about a hundred and fifty Albanian soldiers being repatriated to Albania at the end of their service, having amassed a considerable fortune. The Albanians surrendered on the strength of promises by Mavrocordato, but he was unable to prevent one of the Greek captains from killing them all and taking their money.

When the Turks tried to retreat, they found the river Acheloos too swollen with rain to be forded. They were eventually compelled to attempt a crossing and hundreds of Albanians were swept away, having tied to their backs large metal pots which they had used to carry their plunder from the Greek villages. Hundreds more were killed or drowned when the Greeks attacked, catching them in a classic situation in which their tactics of ambush from defended positions could cause greatest damage. Only a remnant of the Turkish army escaped across the mountains to Epirus. The Turkish commander anticipated by suicide an order from Constantinople for his execution.

The three great events of the campaign of 1822, the destruction of Chios, the expedition to Epirus, and the Turkish invasion of the Peloponnese, had all occurred largely independently of one another. By an incredible mixture of good luck on the part of the Greeks and incompetence on the part of the Turks, the Revolution had survived the first attempt of the Ottoman Government to reinforce its authority. By the winter of 1822-3 the Peloponnese remained firmly in the hands of the Greeks with the exception of the fortresses of Patras (and its subsidiaries the castles of Roumeli and of the Morea) and of Coron and Modon. In the west, Aetolia was also in the hands of the Greeks, and in the east most of the territory south of Thermopylae. At sea, in the waters near the Greek mainland, the Turkish fleet had proved unable to influence the situation. It was hardly the re-establishment of the Byzantine Empire which some had dreamed of, but nevertheless an astonishing result.

The captains had made it possible. It was Colocotrones who had destroyed a Turkish army by employing traditional methods of hit and run and ambush. Odysseus had survived as an independent potentate by skilful double-dealing. The captains of the west had destroyed the army attacking Missolonghi. The much vaunted European military methods, which had appeared so much superior had (however unluckily) led only to a disastrous defeat. Now there was not even the cadre of a regular disciplined force.

An immense booty had been seized from two Turkish armies and from Athens and Nauplia but it had gone entirely to the captains. The Europeanized Greeks of the Government had failed in almost everything they had set out to do. The military reputation of the Franks had been exploded. Colocotrones and Odysseus and innumerable lesser men had established themselves as they had wanted from the beginning: they had expelled the Turks and taken their lands; they were now ready to enjoy their status of rich successful warlords, ruling their regions as they pleased, answerable to no one but themselves. The ideal of establishing a regenerated nation state with a regular army, central administration, uniform laws and taxation, and all the other characteristics of a liberal Western European country seemed to have been destroyed for ever on the hills of Peta.

5 A European View of the First Siege of Missolonghi

6 Part of a Philhellenic Calendar for 1823, with Saints' Days and Anniversa

RECS POUR 1823.

Passage des Thermopyles par Marcos Botzaris.

PATRIE

Botzaris   Gordato   Sturnar

AVRIL	MAI	JUIN
D.Q. le 3. P.Q. le 18.	D.Q. le 3. P.Q. le 17.	D.Q. le 2. P.Q. le 15.
N.L. le 11. P.L. le 25.	N.L. le 10. P.L. le 24.	N.L. le 8. P.L. le 23.

Mytilene   Aivali   Samos

Louis Gouget, Graveur, Rue de la Calandre, N°44.

of the Battles of the Greek Revolution. The latter are mostly imaginary

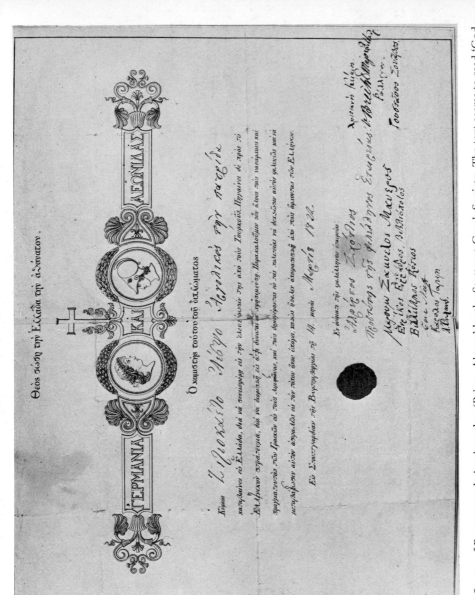

7a Commandant Dania, Commander of the Battalion of Philhellenes

b Letter of Recommendation issued to 'Prince Alepso' by the Stuttgart Greek Society. The text seems to read 'God save immortal Hellas. Germany and Leonidas. The bearer of this letter, Mr. Ziziokaeto Aebpso, a native of Argos, is on his way to Hellas to help in freeing her from the Turks. He is going to the Hellenic army in which he intends to serve. We call on all ships' captains and harbour masters of the Greeks and elders of the towns to give him a friendly welcome, and convey him safely to the place where he is going as if the Government of the Hellenes had authorized it. At Stuttgart in Württemberg the 4 March 1822'. There follows the names of the signatories, transliterated into

Of the eight expeditions of individual Philhellenes which sailed from Marseilles in 1821 and 1822 five arrived in Greece in time for the disastrous battle of Peta in July 1822. The sixth arrived in time for a few members to reach Missolonghi and meet the survivors. The last three expeditions, containing altogether between fifty and sixty Philhellenes, arrived in the midst of the terrible events related in the last chapter. There was also a small but continuous stream of other individual volunteers reaching Greece at their own expense by a variety of routes. Many of these men were to suffer miseries in Greece greater even than their predecessors.

After the battle of Peta and the dissolution of the Philhellene Battalion it was the wish of virtually all the Europeans in Greece to go home as quickly as possible. But this was by no means easy. The ports of Southern Europe, with the exception of Marseilles, were all controlled by governments hostile to the Greek cause. The Peloponnese was ravaged by plagues which sometimes died down but always sprang up again as new massacres renewed the supply of unburied bodies. The British Government in the Ionian Islands, besides trying to enforce a precarious neutrality towards the events on the mainland, maintained a tight quarantine to try to keep the islands free of the epidemics. It was said that they would not allow Philhellenes to land, but even so escape to the Ionian Islands seemed the most promising way home.

During the last months of 1822 several parties and a few individuals crossed the straits and threw themselves on the mercy of the British authorities. Contrary to their expectation they were well received, and given food and clothing. Subscriptions were raised for them among the British troops and they eventually made their way back to Italy, disguising from the port authorities that they had been in Greece. One party stole a boat

at Missolonghi; another party, after roaming round the coast like a miniature band of robbers, seized a boat after a battle with some Greeks in which
two of the Philhellenes were killed.[1] Eventually after long quarantines in
the islands and again in European ports they made their way home.

The island of Syra in the middle of the Aegean was almost entirely
inhabited by Roman Catholic Greeks. It had remained neutral in the war,
paying tribute, on occasion, both to the Turks and to the Revolutionary
Greeks. The French Government claimed an age-old right of protecting
the Roman Catholic inhabitants of the Ottoman Empire and the island
was virtually a French protectorate defended by French warships. It became
a thriving commercial centre at which European vessels called. Many
Philhellenes aimed to get to Syra and try to find a passage on a European
ship.

The Consuls at Athens, although almost all hostile to the Greek Revolution and to philhellenism, managed to arrange passages for some of
their countrymen to Syra. The French Consul General in Smyrna, also,
spent a great deal of money in helping to repatriate Philhellenes of all
nationalities. Some picked up ships going to Smyrna, to Constantinople,
to Odessa, to Egypt, to Marseilles, to Malta, and to Italy. Individuals who
turned up in Constantinople lived in terror of having their identity discovered by the Government. The Ambassadors of the European countries
helped them on their way, and if—like the Prussian Ambassador—they
were forbidden by their governments to do so, they helped them out of their
own pockets. The King of Denmark personally paid the debts of the Danish
Philhellenes.[2] Some merchant captains gave free passage or temporarily
enrolled Philhellenes in their crews.

Gradually through 1822 and 1823 numerous Philhellenes made their
way home by circuitous routes, often taking many months on their journey.
As on the way out, they were constantly meeting old comrades. But many
were not so lucky. Understandably, the captains of ships were unwilling
to take anyone who was diseased. Several men who reached the islands had
to be abandoned to die. On other occasions the ships would only take their
own nationals, leaving the rest to their fate. One captain said he could only
take three out of a party of about ten and lots had to be drawn to select the
lucky ones.[3] The citizens of Britain, France, Sweden, and Holland had the
best chances of escape since they had effective diplomatic representatives
on the spot and numerous ships passing through. The worst placed were
the citizens of the smaller German states who had little chance of meeting
countrymen able to help them.

The Philhellenes escaped from the scene of the war in a state of extreme
exhaustion and starvation. The European merchant colony at Smyrna
nursed a few back to health in their hospital in terror that the Turks would
discover what they were doing. One German officer,[4] who reached Smyrna

alone in a state of collapse, tried to earn a living as a gardener to an Armenian family and then as a porter in the docks but was too weak to continue. He was eventually given money by a British naval officer. Another German who had been a musician earned money until his health recovered by giving concerts and music lessons to the European colony.[5]

The first of the returning Philhellenes had the best treatment. Charity is strained if it is called upon too frequently, and the Philhellenes were an increasing embarrassment to their governments. The Turkish Government had protested to the powers about the activities of their nationals in Greece. Helping distressed Philhellenes could not easily be reconciled with a policy of aiding the Sultan to reassert his legitimate authority over his rebellious Greek subjects. In February 1823 the consuls throughout the Levant were informed that Europeans who fought for the Greeks would be treated as rebels.[6] Fortunately for the Philhellenes this did not prevent private charity from being given.

The Philhellenes who arrived in Greece in late 1822 suffered most. In many ways they are the most pathetic of the men who went to join the crusade during the early period. There were fewer unemployed professional officers than on earlier expeditions. There were clerks, students, merchants, apprentices, men who had been recruited late in the philhellenic campaign in Germany. They had been warned by returning volunteers even before they left Marseilles but they had not turned back. With the dissolution of the Philhellene Battalion there was no obvious point for them to make for when they arrived in Greece. So, like the first volunteers, they tended to wander over southern Greece in small groups looking for someone in authority to employ them. But the hospitable feelings of the Greek peasants had long since been exhausted by the ravages of the captains. Philhellenes were no longer strange figures from another world to be welcomed as guests. The respect which all Europeans had at first enjoyed in the villages had been squandered by their predecessors. After the exploding of the Europeans' pretensions to superiority (as the captains regarded it) at Peta, indifference turned to hostility. The Philhellenes found that the gates of towns were closed to them and they were driven away from some villages with stones. Soon their money ran out and they were obliged to sell their weapons and then their clothes. It was usually their feet which finally let them down. Their shoes would wear out in marching over the rough ground, they would try to walk by binding bandages on their feet, their feet would swell up, and they would be immobilized. They would then have to hang around the towns as beggars until they recovered or (more usually) died of disease.

Five suicides are recorded in 1822: two French officers and an Italian at Missolonghi, a German doctor from Mecklenburg at Argos, and a young German from Hamburg who disembarked soon after the battle of Peta.

Another German officer tried to shoot himself but the ball stuck in his nose bone.[7]

There were several instances of Philhellenes being robbed and murdered by the Greeks.[8] The worst case occurred after the fall of Nauplia when it was discovered that some Greeks had been inviting Philhellenes into a Turkish bath in the town and then murdering them. By persuading the visitors to strip, the bathkeeper was able to acquire their clothes without the inconvenience of having to wash their blood out later.[9]

Many who arrived in the latter part of 1822 died without ever seeing a Turk. Others, on being refused money to go home, took the course which had always been regarded as the last resort—they tried to join one of the captains. This, in many cases, merely postponed their fate. With their swollen feet they were unable to keep up with the bands and in skirmishes with the Turks they were the first to be cut down.

The rumour had been passed among the Philhellenes right from the beginning of the Revolution that the Turks were interested in engaging European officers to serve on the other side. The omens for this were not encouraging. The Italian who had tried to desert before Peta had been hanged.[10] The German doctor who had been taken prisoner by the Turks had been spared on condition that he joined them. When he later escaped and returned to the Peloponnese the Greeks said he was stupid to give up such a good position. He was reduced to beggary.[11] But as the misery of the surviving Philhellenes grew, the idea of changing sides became more attractive. An Italian who joined Odysseus' band tried to desert in early 1823 but his head was found shortly afterwards stuck on a pole.[12] A party of officers who reached Syra in safety wrote a letter to Constantinople offering their services but they never got a reply.[13]

There was, however, a way of changing sides which a few men discovered. The Pasha of Egypt was interested in recruiting officers to train his army in European methods. Philhellenes escaping from Greece in merchant ships to Egypt found that they were offered attractive terms at Alexandria. Gubernatis, who had commanded the Regiment, was the most famous of the renegades but a few others also joined the Egyptian service. Some of them were to return to Greece in 1825 as part of the Egyptian invading army.[14]

The survivors who began to reach home in 1822 and 1823 were scarred in body and mind. Having had exaggerated expectations in the first place, their disillusion was now unrestrained. Almost without exception they now hated the Greeks with a deep loathing, and cursed themselves for their stupidity in having been deceived. To their consternation they discovered on their return that their old friends were still as ignorant of what was occurring in Greece as when they had set out; that public opinion was overwhelmingly pro-Greek; and that volunteers were still leaving home to go to Greece with the same philhellenic slogans on their lips. Even more galling, when they told people of what they had seen and suffered, their stories were received with polite incredulity, discounted as the biased accounts of men with a personal grudge.

The Greek Societies seem at first to have deliberately tried to suppress any suggestion of unpleasantness. Returned Philhellenes were given a small sum of money with the broad hint that they were to go away and keep quiet. When letters appeared in the newspapers describing conditions in Greece, the Societies put about the story that the individuals concerned were untrustworthy and untypical. When the brother of the leader of the Stuttgart Greek Society returned from Greece and confirmed the reports, even he was silenced.[15]

Philhellenism was a sturdy plant with deep roots. It could not be easily eradicated. Although the leaders of the Societies were undoubtedly guilty of suppression of uncomfortable facts, they were honest men on the whole. As with so many believers in great causes, their minds could not readily assimilate the notion that the picture they imagined of Modern Greece was not the real one. Facts are poor weapons against such deep-seated beliefs. The returning Philhellenes for their part were in no mood to help the Societies to make the adjustment easily. They did not realize that they were victims of an idea. Their resentment needed a more concrete target. They turned on the Societies, on the professors, the priests, and the merchants, and accused them of every crime from maladministration to wilfully sending men to their deaths. Mainly, however, they were simply concerned to convince people that the common notion of Greece was wrong, to save others from falling into the same delusions as they had; and to clear their names of the implied stigma of having proved inadequate to the great ideal. They were seized with an overwhelming desire to shout 'It is not true' in the market place of every town with a Greek Society.

During the time when the Philhellenes were away, the Societies had continued their propaganda as best they could. In the countries where censorship was lax, absurd stories about the Greek Revolution had flowed from the presses. No story was too tall to be acceptable and one is tempted to believe the charge that some Societies deliberately manufactured their own news. As one writer put it, letters 'were fabricated at Augsburg, Paris, and London, the three great mints of Philhellenic mendacity. . . . Supplementary laboratories existed at Zante, Trieste, Frankfurt, and Stuttgart.'[16] A Swedish Philhellene, picking up a copy of an Augsburg newspaper of September 1822 on his way back, read with amused horror a letter allegedly by a Philhellene which put the size of Mavrocordato's army at 25,000 and described in detail the ribbons and medals issued to the troops.[17] The first reports of the Battle of Peta described it as a great victory. Its location was transferred to the more familiar Thermopylae, three pashas were said to have been captured, and General Normann's soldiers to have carried him in triumph from the battlefield on their shields![18] The engraving reproduced as Plate 5 shows a European view of what was happening in Greece. The Greeks and Philhellenes are standing in close order like a European army. The Turks are fighting with bows and arrows.

The Societies did, however, make an honest effort to publish genuine accounts by men who had gone to Greece. One of the first, published in Leipzig, consisted of a series of letters of a theology student, Feldhann, who accompanied General Normann. The author had, however, been killed at Peta before his confident descriptions of the voyage out and of the welcome in Greece appeared in Europe. The Societies also seized on an account by a young French naval officer, Voutier, which was published in Paris. It was translated twice into German with laudatory introductions by the Societies. Unfortunately this Frenchman was a shameless liar, describing himself as playing a leading role in many events at which he was not even present.*

Faced with a public intent on believing what it wanted, the disillusioned Philhellenes turned to the pen. Many had consoled themselves through their misery in Greece by keeping diaries. Although some who had promised themselves that they would tell their story when they went home later gave up their intention, an astonishing number of accounts were printed. In the two years after the expeditions had sailed from Marseilles virtually every district which had furnished Philhellenes had the opportunity of reading the story of a disappointed local hero. The map on page 118 shows the spread of such publications during this period over the area that had been the centre of the movement. They were printed on local presses and seldom circulated outside their area.[19]

These accounts make sad reading. Some are the disorganized productions of men unused to writing, others are ghost-written, others are anonymous to protect their authors from reprisals. The fact that so many did eventually appear in print attests the earnestness of the authors. The effort which it cost them to write these little books is described in the prefaces—how the authors abandoned and restarted the work but ultimately completed it out of indignation or pity for new victims, or how they had made solemn promises to their comrades in Greece to publish the truth. Almost without exception these books were written in ignorance that other such books were being published in neighbouring towns. They have an unmistakable ring of spontaneity. Again and again the same sentiments are repeated. 'I am writing this to warn others against the mistakes which I made'; 'Modern Greece is not the same as Ancient Greece'; 'The Greeks are a cruel, barbarian, ungrateful race'; 'I apologize for the unscholarly style of a simple

---

* See also p. 288.

soldier'. The writers are bitter, unrestrained, inaccurate, and unbalanced. Few showed that their experiences in Greece had really increased their understanding of the forces at work in the situation.

Gradually they had their effect. But they were not in time to prevent the last and greatest enterprise of the South German and Swiss Greek Societies.

Cities in which books by disillusioned Philhellenes were published 1822-1824

12. *The German Legion*

One of the disillusioned German Philhellenes on his way to a new career as an exile in the United States[1] records that on two occasions in the Peloponnese he was told a curious story. It was being said that two regiments of Swiss troops were on the way to help Greece, and that when they had finally expelled the Turks, the Swiss were to be given the best lands. The Philhellene noted the story merely as an example of the dozens of ridiculous rumours circulating when he was in Greece. In fact, however, there was more truth in this story than in most of the others. From various accounts it is possible to piece together what lay behind it.

While Mavrocordato had been enjoying his short period of ascendancy before his disastrous expedition to Epirus, he had personally given his approval to a scheme to bring an army of 6,000 German and Swiss volunteers to Greece. Almost alone of the principal Greeks, he understood the deeper implications of the political situation. He realized that without a regular army loyal to the central government his view of the aims of the Revolution would never prevail against the captains and their armed bands. If he could not raise a Greek army then he was ready to rely on foreign volunteers. He therefore authorized the scheme without telling the other members of the Government.

The scheme was put to him by a Greek called Kephalas and a Prussian called von Dittmar. These two men, although they were on bad terms, had decided to unite their fortunes in the belief that they would be more successful as a team than as two individuals. Their strategy was to exploit the mutual ignorance of Greeks and Germans.

In Greece Kephalas was a man of little importance, one of the many ambitious Greeks who had returned from Western Europe at the outbreak of the Revolution with exaggerated ideas about the reception that was his due. But he was accompanied by the famous Prussian cavalry officer, von Dittmar, who had won a high military reputation in the wars against the French and had subsequently proved his devotion to the freedom of oppressed peoples by taking part in the Piedmontese Revolution. Clearly he was an influential figure to recruit to the Greek cause and Kephalas basked in the reflected glory. The two adventurers explained to Mavrocordato that a rich Dutchman had made a huge donation to the Greek cause. With this money and the money at the disposal of the Greek Societies in South Germany and Switzerland, they claimed that a regular European force could be recruited in Württemberg and Switzerland and brought to Greece. This, they argued, would be far more effective than the expeditions of individual Philhellenes who were arriving in great numbers from Marseilles.

So at the very time when Mavrocordato's ambitions were being extinguished on the hills of Peta, Kephalas and Dittmar arrived back in Europe and put their scheme to the Darmstadt Greek Committee.

In Germany the picture looked very different. Von Dittmar (if he really was entitled to call himself von) was not to be taken seriously. He was simply another unemployed officer, one of the thousands who had not yet reconciled themselves to the changed conditions of Europe at peace and were hoping to resume their military careers by offering their services abroad. In Germany it was Kephalas who came into his own. He assumed the picturesque title of Baron Kephalas of Olympus, said he was a Senator of Greece, and the Victor of Tripolitsa (at which disgraceful episode he had not even been present). A runaway German apprentice had found little difficulty in convincing the Darmstadt Greek Society that he was Prince Alepso of Argos: how much easier was it for Kephalas to carry off his assumed role by flattering the Society and repeating the myths about Modern Greece which they so passionately wanted to believe. Kephalas seemed to the professors, churchmen, lawyers, merchants, and schoolmasters of the Societies to be exactly the kind of Greek for whose sake philhellenism existed. He spoke good German, had a German wife, and had served for a time in the Coburg militia; now he was one of the leaders of his regenerated country. For Dittmar, who had acquiesced in his own transfiguration in Greece, the pretensions of Kephalas were too much and he tried to warn the Societies against his partner. But the Societies had no ears for the complaints of a discontented officer, preferring to put their faith in a real Greek.

In September 1822 the Societies decided to make their biggest effort to date and to send a fully-equipped expedition of volunteers to Greece under Kephalas' command. Disillusioned Philhellenes had already returned from Greece protesting violently against the scheme, but Kephalas assured the Societies that they need not listen to them since they were merely disap-

pointed adventurers who had been expelled from Greece for incompetence
or worse. Under his command and with his influence with the Greek
Government, everything would be different. The Societies soon convinced
themselves that he was right. The trouble with the earlier expeditions, they
reasoned, had been that they had not been properly organized or equipped;
there had been no regular contract and command system, no acknowledged
leader, no official connection with the Greek Government. With a Greek
Senator in command, the whole situation would be different; was it not
universally agreed by even the most disgruntled of the returning volunteers
that a small European regular force would make short shrift of the Turks
given the minimum of support from the Greeks?

The Societies therefore turned their attention to ensuring that this
expedition would be properly organized, unlike the eight that had already
sailed. Considering that they were entirely dependent on public subscriptions for their funds and that the governments were unsympathetic to their
activities, they were remarkably successful. Recruiting was opened in the
states of south-west Germany and in Switzerland—the only areas where the
Governments still tolerated their activities. Maps of Greece were litho-
graphed and circulated to show the places where the volunteer army was
to be asked to operate. The credentials of all candidates were scrutinized.
A proclamation was drafted and issued in three languages under the auspices
of the Societies. It was even translated into Romansh for the benefit of the
citizens of the Engadine.[2]

It was decided that the new corps of Philhellenes should be called the
German Legion. It was to set sail for Greece in separate contingents at
monthly intervals as soon as the preparations could be made. Unlike the
earlier expeditions, the organization and equipping was to be the responsibility of the Societies and they would ensure that a proper contract was
made with the Greek Government to ensure that the force was properly
employed and maintained.

The response to the appeal was excellent. Within a few weeks about a
hundred and twenty volunteers had come forward and it was decided to
send them to Greece as the first contingent. By November 1822 all preparations were complete and the expedition made its way to Marseilles to embark
on the Brig *Scipio* chartered by the Societies. It was by far the best equipped
expedition that had left Europe to date, and was divided into four companies
representing infantry, artillery, sharpshooters, and chasseurs. 'Baron'
Kephalas was to be the commander, and officers and non-commissioned
officers were appointed for each of the four companies. Dittmar accompanied
the expedition but was not given any official position.

Every man was asked to swear to abide by the French military code, and
to promise obedience to Kephalas and to the Greek Government. He also
had to promise not to leave the Legion or join another unit or to dispose

of his weapons. Each man was issued with a uniform and another was promised. A large consignment of arms and ammunition was put on board, enough to equip not only the Legion but the regiments of Greeks who were expected to be entrusted to the Legion for training. The ship was also freighted with everything that the Societies thought necessary for the success of the expedition—food, money, medical supplies, and tools and materials to establish a workshop. There was even a consignment of ninety-two musical instruments for military bands.

The men who formed the expedition were almost all German and Swiss. They came from all sections of society and, in this respect, they were much more like a normal European military unit than the earlier expeditions, since the individuals who had gone to Greece in the first eight expeditions were mainly officers and men from the more educated classes. The Legion, on the other hand, although it had officers and students as well, was mainly composed of men of the lower orders of society. The earlier Philhellenes, ever conscious of the purity of their philhellenism and of their 'Honour', tended to disparage the men of the Legion as being more akin to mercenaries.

In December 1822 the leader of the Darmstadt Society went personally to Marseilles to take leave of his little army. In a tearful ceremony on board, in which he said that he wished he was going with them, he explained the terms of their service. As soon as they arrived in Greece a contract was to be signed with the Greek Government who would thereupon be responsible for their supplies and for their command. 'Baron' Kephalas had given assurances on behalf of the Greek Government that there would be no difficulty with the contract, but in case of difficulty, the expedition was supplied with enough money to come back if necessary. Other expeditions would follow at monthly intervals. In the middle of November the expedition set sail. A Philhellene, recently returned from Greece and now in quarantine in Marseilles, looked on helplessly, unable to persuade anyone to listen to his warnings.[3]

The Brig *Scipio* was far too small a vessel to accommodate a hundred and twenty men in any comfort. It was old, dirty, and unseaworthy. There was no room to stand up and the men had to sleep three to a mattress. Sea sickness added to the discomfort. Already there were murmurings against Kephalas, and the Legionaries for the first time had a chance to hear Dittmar's version of events, but order was maintained. A theology student, at Kephalas' suggestion, gave regular sermons on the Christian duty of the great crusade on which they were engaged.

At the beginning of December the *Scipio* reached Hydra. Much to the amusement of his men Kephalas donned a huge silver cloak with epaulettes and spurs and went ashore with a few officers to confer with the Hydriotes. None of the Germans could, of course, understand what was being said but it soon became obvious that something was amiss. Kephalas came back and announced that the Legion was not to be allowed ashore.

Days passed and still Kephalas seemed to be engaged in interminable discussions. The Legionaries, cooped up in their filthy ship in the middle of winter, became suspicious and then unruly. Permission was even refused to land a Swiss soldier[4] who had been taken ill on the voyage. Eventually the decision was reversed, but it came too late to save his life. To quieten the unrest it was agreed that they would be allowed ashore but only in small parties and on condition that they did not enter the town.

For the first time the Germans recognized the welcome that awaited them. One party that approached the town was driven away with stones. Another was taken to a hut outside the town, where one Legionary recognized two friends from his schooldays in Bremen. They had both been apprentices in a merchant house and had been released from their contracts to go to Greece on one of the earlier philhellenic expeditions. They lay in rags, filthy, covered with vermin and suffering severely from fever. One, who had been wounded near Nauplia had a huge swelling on his leg and had gone blind in one eye. They had no money and had long since sold their weapons and all their possessions. The Legionaries gave them money, but seem to have been so revolted by the filth and stench that they did little more to help. One of the two Philhellenes died within a few days.[5]

Meanwhile the Legionaries still stayed in their ship in the harbour. Kephalas was perpetually engaged in talks with the Hydriotes and was forever announcing that the contract with the Greek Government was about to be signed, but nothing happened, until at last the inevitable happened. A mutiny broke out. The commander of one of the companies threatened to blow up the ship by setting fire to the powder magazine unless they were allowed ashore. Calm was restored and then two weeks after their arrival at Hydra they were finally permitted to disembark.

By this time Kephalas had lost virtually all his authority. The Legion divided into two, a 'loyalist party' and the others. Dittmar became leader of the discontents, Kephalas issued arms to a few members of the loyalists and they acted as a kind of military police to keep the others in obedience. In one affray several men were badly wounded before peace was restored.

At last Kephalas announced that the contract had been signed and that the Legion was to leave Hydra and go to the mainland, leaving the consignment of arms at Hydra, but by this time the Legionaries were in no mood to believe anything that Kephalas said. They insisted on seeing the contract and refused to part with the store of arms. They addressed numerous angry protests to the Greeks but without result. The *Scipio* had left, they had spent their money, and realized that the store of arms was the only asset they had left to pay their passage home.

Gradually a compromise was worked out. The Legion agreed to leave the arms at Hydra under seal and go to the mainland hoping that there they would be able to make some arrangement with the Greeks. As one of them argued, in Germany they were an illegal force and, if they were not careful, they would be declared illegal in Greece as well. Their only hope was to stick together and try to insist on the terms of the contract being met. And so they left Hydra for the mainland. They offered to take with them the surviving sick Philhellene, who still lay in his hut outside the town, but he was too ill to be moved and was left behind.

It is clear that the arrival of the German Legion came as a complete surprise to the Greeks. The only man who might have been able to sort out the muddle was Mavrocordato but at this time he was at the other side of the country directing the defence of Missolonghi. In the Peloponnese the captains were entirely in control. They had defeated the Turkish invasion and taken over Nauplia: they had no need of a European regular force. Indeed, it was the last thing they wanted to see. They were not bothered by the arrival of the hundred and twenty men of the Legion: they were much more concerned at the talk of follow-up expeditions which were supposed to be on their way at monthly intervals, and the prospect of having these men settled, as the story ran, on the lands seized from the Turks. They were especially determined that the large store of arms should not fall into the hands of the Europeanized Greeks and so give them a new opportunity of interfering with their authority. The Hydriotes shared these interests and aspirations of the captains, content to pursue their profitable mixture of trade and piracy in conditions of local independence.

No one in the German Legion ever seems to have understood what lay behind the attitude of the Greeks. They protested that all they wanted was the opportunity to fight for Hellas, but their pathetic efforts to show off their military skill by staging parades merely reinforced the determination of the Greeks that they should never have an opportunity of exercising it. The Greek leaders could not, of course, reveal what they were really thinking. Instead they procrastinated, saying the Legion was welcome but there was no task for it just at the moment, saying how they wished they could be of help if they only had the resources, talking aimlessly of sending it to Crete or Euboea, but all the time spreading muddle, confusion, and distrust. The Legionaries, having consumed the supplies they had brought with them, asked to be given food but even this was refused. Food was undoubtedly short, but it was obvious that the protestations of the Greek leaders that they had none to spare was exaggerated to say the least. Perplexed and angry in a situation they did not understand the Legionaries could only conclude, as so many of the earlier Philhellenes had concluded, that the Greeks were a greedy, ungrateful, and untrustworthy race.

Hopefully, they awaited the arrival of the promised follow-up expeditions which were supposed to come every month, but events at the other end of Europe had supervened. The French authorities at Marseilles had been systematically taking statements from returning Philhellenes since they first began to appear back at Marseilles at the end of 1821. The wheels of bureaucracy turn slowly, but gradually the French Government built up a picture of what conditions were really like in Greece. After the departure of the German Legion in November 1822 the order came through that no more philhellenic expeditions were to be allowed to leave Marseilles. The French decision may be partly explained by the consideration that they no longer wanted to stand out against the policy of Metternich and the other powers. The evidence is, however, that the decision was taken mainly for humanitarian reasons. The returning Philhellenes were able to persuade the French Government (even if they never succeeded in persuading the Greek Societies) that to allow volunteers to go to Greece was to send young men uselessly to their death. At the end of 1822, with the closure of Marseilles, there was now no means whereby expeditions of Philhellenes could be sent to Greece from Mediterranean ports.

As 1823 went on, the men of the Legion, hanging uselessly around the streets of Nauplia, gradually gave way to despair. The old division between the loyalists and those who wanted to strike out on their own, opened and shut and opened again, but neither party had a credible line of action to suggest. They were gradually obliged to sell off their possessions and their weapons in defiance of the contract. Finally, abandoning all hope of continuing in Greece as a disciplined military force, the loyalists decided to pool their resources and send one of their members back to Darmstadt to ask the Societies for money to bring them home. Sergeant Kolbe was chosen and set off. Few expected to see him again.

By the summer the German Legion had ceased to exist. Man after man, as he felt he could bear no more, took his luck in his hands, and went off to try to hitchhike his way back to Europe. Some fifty or sixty joined the hundreds of disgruntled Philhellenes who were already to be found scattered all over the Levant and in the quarantines of Europe. The remainder gradually sank into misery. Plagues swept the town and at least twenty-five died of disease during 1823. Kephalas himself was one of the victims. A visitor who saw the remnant of the Legion in the autumn says that they were subsisting on tortoises.[6]

With the disintegration of the German Legion the first period of philhellenism comes to an end. Between the outbreak of the Greek Revolution in the spring of 1821 and the end of 1822 about six hundred men from the countries of Western Europe set out to join the cause. Of these, over one hundred and eighty are known by name to have died. If one excludes the German Legion, of whom a high proportion survived, the death-rate among the Philhellenes was about one in three, astonishingly high considering how many stayed only a few days or weeks in the country. With few exceptions the others acquired a hatred and disgust of the Greeks which they were to carry to their graves. At the end of this first period of philhellenism, only a few dozen volunteers were still active in Greece and they were mostly exiles with no other home.

It is difficult to claim that this huge sacrifice achieved anything. The Greek Revolution took its course during the first two years and was influenced only marginally by the activities of the volunteers. One must conclude gloomily that the results of their efforts were all negative— disillusionment of the Greeks with European military methods, disillusionment in Europe as reality obtruded into the philhellenic myths.

Yet in many ways the first period showed the philhellenic ideal at its most pure. The professors, lawyers, merchants, churchmen, and burghers of south-west Germany, Switzerland, and elsewhere who contributed to send the volunteers to Greece made their sacrifice in all innocence. They had no self interest to promote. They genuinely believed in the identity of the Ancient and Modern Greeks, in the ancient debt owed by Europe which Greece was at last calling in, in the concept of regeneration, in the benevolence of organized Christianity, in the hateful inferiority of Turks and Moslems, in the perfectibility of man by constitutions, in international liberalism, and no doubt in other attractive but questionable propositions. The volunteers themselves, for all their absurdities, generally went to Greece motivated in part at least by feelings of duty and sacrifice. They would have served Greece—as their successors were to do—despite everything, despite poor food and hard conditions, lack of pay, atrocities, anarchy, if only they had been given any encouragement to believe that their presence and sacrifice were welcome.

By the end of 1823 philhellenism in Germany and Switzerland, the regions where it had flourished most luxuriantly, had withered away. The reports of the returning Philhellenes and the constant pressure of the larger powers had taken their effect. By 1824 it had apparently been totally eradicated. Yet within two years another bloom was to appear.

13. *Knights and Crusaders*

The need for money in Greece was now desperate. In the early months of the Revolution much of the country's disposable wealth (such as it was) had been consumed. In the first flush of enthusiasm voluntary loans had been raised, then forced loans. The overseas Greeks had willingly contributed and loans had been successfully raised among the Greek merchant colonies in Italy and Germany. By the middle of 1822 many Greeks of all types were wiser and poorer men. The Greek government bonds which they had accepted in exchange for their money were worthless. Although great wealth had been seized from the Turks it had fallen into the hands of the captains. The whole economy was running down as armed bands helped themselves to the produce of the peasantry and as more and more of the peasantry decided to join them.

In theory there was one huge asset. The Turks of the Morea had occupied the best lands. Now that they were gone, these lands were supposed to belong to the Government to sell or rent as they decided. In fact the Government had no real control over these lands which nobody could afford to buy, and to the extent that they were used at all, they had been taken over by local Greeks or captains.

The possession of money now became the main source of power. The captains were able to pay their armed bands out of booty and enforced exactions in their chosen area. The Government, suffering constant humiliation but still in existence, could only hope to assert itself as an authority if it could provide a counter-attraction, in particular if it could match the pay offered by the captains. Thoughts turned to the prospect of raising money abroad, by tapping the vast reservoir of philhellenic sentiment which, in the eyes of most Greeks, had hitherto been misdirected.

Of all the means open to an individual citizen to influence events in a far country the handing over of money to its government is the least attractive. To see one's contribution thrown into the coffers of a national exchequer for general purposes fails to satisfy that feeling of personal participation and personal assistance which is such an important part of a donor's motivating force. Understandably, contributors prefer to see their money spent on some more limited and preferably more visible objective and to exercise some control over how it is spent after they have parted with it. The Greeks never had any real hope of being able to obtain by contribution the vast sums which were required, although donations would continue to be accepted with some show of grace. All their efforts were devoted to raising a loan. By contributing to a loan, it was judged, the friends of Greece could combine the sensation of making a sacrifice to a good cause with the hope that the sacrifice might turn out to be a lucrative investment.

The first attempts of the Greek Government to raise foreign money had been in Germany and Switzerland through the agency of 'Baron' Kephalas. But the revulsion against philhellenism caused by the return of the disillusioned volunteers had already eliminated this source. The agents reported ruefully that there was no chance of raising money on any terms. They were therefore sent further afield. They were met with sympathy but little else. The governments of Europe having reaffirmed at their Congress at Verona their determination not to recognize the Greek Government, anyone who risked money for the cause of Greece must regard it either as a gift or as a wild speculation.

The Greeks did receive a few offers. The French Count Alexandre Laborde offered to provide money by voluntary contributions, but in return the lenders were to be granted the free use of Navarino, to be allowed to occupy it with a force of 1,500 men, and ultimately to plant colonies in Greece. They also demanded the right to appoint political advisers to the Greek Government.[1] Another Frenchman, who claimed to be acting for the French liberal banker Lafitte, offered a loan of £4,000,000 on very onerous terms. The loan was to be discounted 50 per cent and to carry an annual interest of 6 per cent. As security, the Greek Government was to hand over to the lenders all the national lands—that is all the lands from which the Turks had been expelled, which were for many Greeks the prize for which the Revolution was being fought.

The schemes which came nearest to fruition at this time relied on one of the elements of philhellenism which had hitherto not been exploited to the full. The appeal to re-establish the Ancient Greeks and the appeal to defend Christians against Moslems had been reiterated so often that it was virtually impossible to reassert them without relapsing into cliché. The new schemes relied on a third element which had until now been very much subsidiary to the other two, the appeal to fight a new crusade.

The Order of the Knights Hospitaller of St. John of Jerusalem was established as a military religious order in the twelfth century. During the succeeding centuries the military aspects of its activities tended to take priority over the religious. In the name of Christianity (Roman Catholic version only) the Knights dutifully slaughtered, enslaved, and plundered the Moslems and schismatic Christians of the Eastern Mediterranean with remorseless efficiency. In 1522 the Knights were expelled from Rhodes, but were given the island of Malta as their sovereign domain and were henceforth known as the Knights of Malta. From Malta they continued their sporadic crusading until the eighteenth century. But as civilization spread in Europe it began to be questioned whether belief in Roman Catholicism need necessarily entail a duty to wage a perpetual war of hatred against those whose preference was for other beliefs and superstititions. The Knights themselves, increasingly conscious of the incongruity of their position, spent their ample accumulated wealth in improving and enjoying the amenities of their pleasant island. There was still a sufficient flow of rich recruits with the required sixteen quarterings of nobility ready to devote their lives to empty military ceremonial for the sake of the Faith. In 1798, however, the rump of the Knights was disdainfully expelled from Malta by Bonaparte and in 1815 their island was formally ceded to Britain at the Congress of Vienna. Now seven years later the Knights of Malta had lost even the fiction that they were performing a useful role, belief in which had sustained their boredom during the long years in the Maltese sunshine. The more anachronistic and ridiculous their situation, the more the Knights felt obliged to assert their dignity. They insisted on their status as a Sovereign Order, equal in status to the great kingdoms of Europe, and they dutifully maintained claims to a vast list of territories, rights, and privileges which they had temporarily enjoyed at some distant point in their ancient history, including incidentally sovereignty over the Morea. After their expulsion from Malta the members of the Order were now dispersed over Europe pursuing their unconvincing claims. The headquarters was in Russia but most prominent members lived in Paris.

The Sovereign Order was the first 'state' to accord recognition to the Greek Government. In July 1823 Count Jourdain, a French naval officer who had gone to Greece with one of the first philhellenic expeditions from Marseilles, concluded a 'treaty' with the Knights on behalf of the Greeks for a military alliance. The Knights undertook to raise a loan of 10,000,000 francs at 5 per cent, of which 4,000,000 francs was to go to the Greeks. With the remainder, the Knights were to raise a force of 4,000 men to campaign against the Turks. All conquests were to be shared between the Knights and the Greeks. There was a good deal of bargaining about providing the Knights with a base for their operations. The Greeks suggested Cyprus but in the end the Knights were promised perpetual sovereignty over Rhodes, from which they had been expelled in the sixteenth century. These islands were of course still firmly in the hands of the Turks and the negotiators were arguing over the division of conquests which they had yet to make. It was agreed, however, that until a permanent base could be found, the Knights were to be granted use of the island of Syra. This arrangement suited the Greeks since Syra was largely inhabited by Roman Catholic Greeks who preferred the rule of the Turks to that of schismatic Christian Greeks

When the treaty was concluded, a representative of the Knights, M. Chastelain, was despatched to Greece, a few Greeks were solemnly inducted into the Order, and Jourdain set about raising the money. The response in Paris was disappointing, but when the prospectus for a loan of £640,000 was circulated in London, it was subscribed within twenty-four hours. The Stock Exchange authorities, however, stepped in and the scheme could not proceed. The Grand Master was obliged to attempt to deny that the Order had signed the treaty and to disown the efforts of his representative. The Knights were obliged to postpone their plans but they did not give them up. M. Chastelain was still waiting in the wings in 1825, confident that events would eventually move in his favour. He occupied his time in conferring Knighthoods of Malta on rich Greeks for a fee of 600 francs each.

At about the same time a similar offer of a large loan was made to the Greeks. An Englishman called Peacock was despatched to Greece to explain the scheme to the Government, and other members of the syndicate, in particular a Montenegrin calling himself Count General de Wintz, pestered the Greek agents on their arrival in London. De Wintz had been an officer in the French service and was now employed by the East India Company. His plan involved the raising of money for the Greeks in return for help in the conquest of Cyprus. It never became clear who his backers were who were to supply the money, if in fact he had any. The Greek agents were of the opinion that his offer was simply that of the Knights of Malta in another guise. It was also said, however, that he was acting on behalf of the King of Sardinia who had inherited an old claim to the Kingdom of Cyprus and wanted to be in at the sharing out if the Ottoman Empire was to be dismembered. De Wintz's attempts to raise money on the London Stock Exchange were also deliberately frustrated by the authorities. He later floated another scheme involving the conquest of Crete in the name of the Knights of Malta: this too was prevented before any money was obtained, but representatives of the Knights were again in Greece in 1826 and 1827 pressing the Greeks to accept help which they were in no position to give.

On the face of it the idea of helping Greece by reviving the traditions and institutions of the Crusades was no more incongruous or anachronistic than some of the other manifestations of philhellenism that had appeared hitherto. The pamphlets and appeals for volunteers had described the cause as a crusade and many of the unfortunate young Germans who had died at Peta and elsewhere had fortified themselves in their torment by the belief that they were imitating the heroes of those supposedly splendid days.

There was also something to be said, from a political point of view, in having philhellenic activities controlled by the nearest equivalent to an international organization known at the time. The Knights had survived for so long as an independent force for that reason. However, to anyone who really understood the forces at work in international affairs at the beginning of the nineteenth century (a definition which excluded most Philhellenes), there were two overwhelming reasons against reviving the moribund Knights. The setting up of bases in the Eastern Mediterranean was certain to have an influence on the strategic situation and commercial opportunities in that part of the world. And the Knights, as they had been in their active days, were predominantly French.

Most of the attempts to involve the Knights of Malta in the affairs of Greece were aimed not at helping the Greeks but at establishing a French supremacy in the Levant. Once the Knights had established a military base somewhere in the area, the French Government could take over by affording the Knights 'protection'. Under one scheme the Knights were to develop Crete into a huge *entrepôt* from which all the trade of the East could be controlled. Just as the British had taken over India by establishing a few trading posts and forts, so the French, by the same methods, would establish a comparable empire in the Middle East. It was an old French dream and one that was to last well into the twentieth century.

For four years rumours about the Knights and their plans were passed about in Greece and elsewhere. The Knights were always there in the background, sailing in the Aegean in their yachts and waylaying prominent Philhellenes in London and Paris. In the end they achieved nothing.[2] The affair of the Knights is symptomatic of a change which was coming over philhellenism from 1823 onwards. Governments now began to play a more active part in the drama. Few people who occasionally heard stories about the schemes of the Knights or some other plot were aware of the secret international struggle that was being conducted beneath the surface of the polite diplomatic exchanges.

14. *Secrets of State*

Next to the General Post Office in Lombard Street in the City of London was a suite of offices with an inconspicuous door into Abchurch Lane. It consisted of three rooms, in one of which the fires and candles were never allowed to go out. The staff lived on the premises and, apart from them, only the Postmaster General himself had the right of entry. In these rooms a variety of highly specialized skills were exercised—letter-opening, seal-engraving, wax-mixing, deciphering—skills which had been developed and passed on from generation to generation.

This was the place where the diplomatic mail was intercepted. So skilfully was it done that His Majesty's Ministers often had the opportunity of reading deciphered diplomatic messages—the 'Long Packets'—even before the originals reached their destination. The recipients usually remained entirely ignorant that the seals had been broken and reset. The most difficult part of the operation was the deciphering but this had been developed to a fine art by the Willes family who had pursued lucrative careers simultaneously in the Church of England and in the decipherer's office for over a hundred years. Virtually no ciphers were safe from the men known in the Foreign Office as 'our Post Office friends' and the abolition of diplomatic interception in 1844 led to a marked deterioration in the success of British foreign policy.

Shortly after the outbreak of the Revolution in Greece a subsidiary intelligence centre was established in the Ionian Islands. Letters on their way from Greece to Western Europe were intercepted on their way through the quarantines in the Ionian Islands. The quarantine laws were carefully regulated to facilitate this service. At the same time the Ionian Government maintained a network of agents in Greece who regularly supplied documents and reports. Many of the letters were in code or in deliberately guarded terms, but the British authorities had little difficulty in reading and interpreting them. The danger of having communications intercepted is a constant concern of diplomacy and the main powers all had their individual systems supposedly designed to protect their security. Some also had successful intercept facilities, but the chancelleries of Europe would have been horrified if they had realized how many of their secrets were eventually finding their way to London. As far as Greek affairs were concerned, the British Government soon had the opportunity, by reason of its intelligence sources, of knowing more about Greek politics than anyone else. It knew more than the Greek Government since it was constantly discovering schemes and intrigues known only to small groups of leading Greeks. It knew more than any other European Government. It even had the material to make a judgement on the effectiveness of foreign intelligence systems, and realized, for example, from the reading of Russian and Austrian correspondence, how badly informed these two Governments were.

However good an intelligence system, it is bound to provide incomplete information, and there is always a temptation to regard information which has been obtained in secret and at great expense as of more value than straightforward open reporting. The British Government, being presented with a tantalizing series of glimpses of innumerable apparently sinister intrigues, was inclined to see the hand of a rival government behind every fatuous philhellenic scheme. Canning, the British Foreign Secretary, was convinced that the Knights of Malta were not only acting for French interests but were paid agents of the French Foreign Office. Others saw the hand of the Russians behind the schemes to revive the Knights—a natural presumption since their headquarters were in Russia—and there was some inclination to connect them with the Friendly Society itself, details of whose activities in Russia before the Revolution were gradually coming to light. When it was established beyond reasonable doubt that the Knights were acting on behalf of France, there still remained a suspicion that they might not be part of some vast Franco-Russian package deal to settle the affairs of the Levant to the exclusion of the British.

France was the only other country whose Government was well informed about the situation in Greece. Like the British, the French maintained agents to check on the open reports of their naval and diplomatic representatives. Although they had fewer opportunities of intercepting the mail, the French had other sources not used by the British. Throughout France and elsewhere a large secret police kept a close watch on prominent Frenchmen and foreigners. In particular they followed eagerly the activities of groups which might be hostile to the Bourbons. Disgruntled Bonapartist officers, a class from which many Philhellenes were inevitably drawn either by inclination or from force of circumstances, were so closely watched that some of them went to Greece simply to get away from the feeling of claustrophobia. The secret police charted the movements of potential opponents, allowed them to cross the frontiers if it suited the Government's policy, penetrated their aliases and compiled huge dossiers of miscellaneous information. It was inevitable in its investigation of all possible suspicions of conspiracy that the French Government should discover a good deal about philhellenic organizations in France and their correspondence with groups in Greece.

The French also made a systematic collection of information at the ports, and especially at Marseilles. By piecing together the different accounts of men passing through the quarantine a good deal of political information could be obtained. Like the British, the French had enough information on which to base a proper scepticism about the foreign policies of other powers and also enough to feed the wildest and most suspicious imaginations.

Governments rarely collect intelligence simply to enjoy the sensation of being well-informed. The urge to put secret information to practical use is usually irresistible. The intricacies of the Greek situation offered great attractions for an ambitious foreign policy. It was clear that the Greeks were desperately in need of help and that this could only be supplied from Europe. If the Greeks survived as an independent state, then the country which had won influence by giving aid in the war would be well placed to dominate later. Willy-nilly therefore the great powers were drawn in. However unwilling they might be to entangle themselves in the situation, they could not afford to let their rivals steal a march.

In 1823 practical philhellenism entered a new phase. The torch which had been carried during the first years by the German and Swiss Societies was taken up by the British and then by the French with other groups also playing important roles. But this new type of philhellenism, although in appearance simply a manifestation in new places of the familiar phenomenon, was in reality something much more complex. The secret activities and secret policies of the European governments henceforth added a new dimension.

The primary fear of both the British and the French Governments was that an independent Greece would be drawn into the orbit of Russia, that the Greek Revolution would fulfil for the Russians their ancient wish to establish themselves in the Mediterranean. The Russians were certainly well placed to take advantage of the situation not least because they were the only foreigners whom the Greeks regarded as fellow-Christians. All Europe knew too that there was one Greek who towered above all others in ability and reputation. Count Capodistria, born in the Ionian Islands, had entered the Russian service and risen to be Foreign Minister. He was now living in Switzerland. The British and French Governments were aware of correspondence designed to put Capodistria at the head of a Greek State and, with his background, they were bound to conclude that he would favour a close connection with Russia. If Russia was to be kept out of the Mediterranean, means would have to be found to prevent the growth of Russian influence in Greece. But also, taking a longer view, the Ottoman Empire must not be too much weakened since only the Turks seemed to stand in the way of a general Russian advance in the Middle East.

Both the British and French Governments were sufficiently well informed about events in Greece and elsewhere to realize that the Russians were not making the most of their advantages and opportunities. It became increasingly clear to both Governments that the main contenders for influence in Greece were Britain and France.

In 1823 both Britain and France were torn by conflicting interests in their foreign policies. On the one hand, they wanted to maintain the fragile agreement among the powers to treat the Greeks as rebels, or at least to remain strictly neutral in the conflict. This consideration was high in the minds of the French since they were about to send an army into Spain to put down the liberal constitutionalists there in the name of the Concert of Europe. On the other hand, both the British and the French could see that the nationals of the other country, whatever the public statements of the Governments, were working in Greece to establish a position of influence. On the French side there was a dilemma within a dilemma since they were also pursuing a policy of building up a special position in Egypt, still nominally part of the Ottoman Empire.

The two Governments resolved the dilemma by the classic method of pursuing all the policies at once, seizing any advantage to national interests that opportunity presented, and damning the contradictions. From 1823 onwards both Governments developed a habit of giving secret support to the philhellenic movements in their respective countries. Both based their policies on the fact that British and French people could be relied upon to lay aside their internal political differences in order to serve the national interest. But the support was not given consistently in pursuance of some well laid plan. The attitude of both Governments lurched gracelessly from one policy to another in accordance with the needs of the moment.

The exact extent therefore to which the Governments actively supported the philhellenic movements is difficult to measure. It is certain that various doubtful operations mounted by French Philhellenes in Greece enjoyed the backing of the French Government even although these Philhellenes were bitter opponents of the French régime.

In London too the Tory Government was in touch with the opposition who were organizing philhellenic activity. Many episodes can best be explained on the assumption that secret information was being passed to and fro. The help which the Government could provide, though severely

limited by their public commitment to neutrality, was well worth cultivating. In Britain, for example, the Foreign Enlistment Act made it a
crime for any British subject to join the armed forces of a foreign country.
If the Act had been applied strictly there would have been many fewer
Philhellenes. It was noticed, however, that the Act did not make it a crime
to *intend* to join a foreign army and all manner of facilities were provided to
allow volunteers to go to Greece when this was reckoned to be in the national
interest. Byron was to spend many weeks in the Ionian Islands as a virtual
guest of the British authorities before he went to Greece. Perhaps legally
they should have arrested him. Furthermore, although volunteers could be
allowed to go when it appeared to be in the national interest, the government
could occasionally prevent individuals who seemed unsuitable from going
or persuade or order others to come back if their actions in Greece were
not approved of.

A similar flexible use of government regulations could be used to control
or encourage the export of arms, another aspect of foreign policy which
governments neglect at their peril. Most important of all, the British
Government made no attempt to prevent the flow of money to Greece. They
defended this apparent breach of neutrality on the grounds that it was no
business of a government to interfere in how the individual spent his
money. Yet at the same time the Government co-operated actively with the
British Philhellenes to prevent interests thought to be pro-French from
raising money in London, passing the tip-offs they received to the Stock
Exchange authorities. It was direct British Government action which
frustrated the schemes of the Knights of Malta.

The French Government for its part used much the same range of
measures to advance the interests of French Philhellenes. It reopened
Marseilles to allow the passage of volunteers and arms to Greece. It permitted funds to be collected in support of the Greek cause and may have
secretly contributed to them. It tried to control the French Philhellenes
operating in Greece as if they were direct agents of the French Government. At the same time, however, even when Egyptian forces were fighting
in Greece on behalf of the Sultan, the French Government was giving aid
to the Egyptians, supplying them with warships and technical assistance,
allowing them to recruit trained soldiers in France, and probably doing
much else in secret. The French Ambassador in Constantinople was even
prepared to write letters of introduction to Mehemet Ali for disgruntled
French Philhellenes who wanted a change of service.

At the same time other governments and interest groups were similarly
enmeshing themselves in the intricacies of the Greek situation, each
believing that it was clever enough to extract an advantage but usually
doing little more than adding to the confusion and suspicion. The
American Government, in a smaller way than the French, found means of

backing both the Greeks and the Turks. The scattered exiles of the revolutions in Italy attempted to keep their own cause afloat by appearing to serve the Greeks. During this new phase of philhellenism, nothing was quite as straightforward as it seemed. This is not to say that all Philhellenes were consciously agents of a particular interest. They were not. The old rallying cries that had stirred Germany in 1821 and 1822 still had their magic, especially for those who did not appreciate the wider ramifications.

It is easy to exaggerate the effect of all this clandestine activity. Just as undue respect is often paid to secret intelligence, undue effectiveness can be attributed to secret policies. Organizations of naïve idealists are particularly vulnerable to being taken over by the politically aware, but although the governments attempted to control the activities of the Philhellenes they were not always successful in doing so.

The new factor was there all the time, and no understanding of the course of the war is possible without taking account of it. Whereas the Philhellenes of 1821 and 1822 were palpably acting for themselves whether for altruistic, selfish, or other motives, the later Philhellenes could never escape the suspicion that, consciously or unconsciously, they were part of the long arm of some sinister foreign policy.

One of the surprising features of the history of philhellenism during the Greek War of Independence is the slowness of the response in Britain. English literature had a long philhellenic tradition and the British people had a long tradition of espousing causes abroad, yet in 1821 and 1822 Britain was less affected by the calls to help the Greeks than any other part of Western Europe.

During the first two years there had been only a handful of British volunteers in Greece. The most important was Thomas Gordon of Cairness, a rich Scotsman who had been an officer in the British army and had travelled widely in the Near East.[1] Gordon was no empty-headed romantic but a sober, determined soldier. It seems likely that he knew something of the plans for the Greek Revolution before it broke out. He was in Paris when the news arrived and immediately chartered a ship at Marseilles, bought arms and ammunition, engaged a few French officers and sailed to Greece. Gordon was at Tripolitsa shortly after it fell in the autumn of 1821 and was an eye witness to the horrors. He left Greece shortly afterwards suffering severely from the plague which was sweeping the country. Constantly surrounded by a personal entourage of secretaries and servants—one, his old Sergeant Major, fell victim to the disease—he seemed to have all the attributes of the Milord: money, title, land and influence.

Frank Abney Hastings, a dismissed naval officer, was another of the earliest volunteers.[2] He too was rich and from a well-known family, and like Gordon, was looking for a field to try his talents. He sailed for Greece with Jarvis,[3] the son of the American consular agent in Hamburg in March 1822. Although he suffered the disappointments and frustrations of the 1822 generation of Philhellenes to which he belonged, Hastings was one of the few who stayed in Greece.

The other British Philhellenes who went to Greece during the early period are less well known, but all the familiar types were represented. Humphreys,[4] an English officer who could not find a commission in the British army after leaving Sandhurst, had set off to join the Revolution in Naples and had drifted on to Greece. He left in disgust after the fall of Tripolitsa but returned later. Haldenby,[5] a rich young man from Hull, came in one of the expeditions from Marseilles sponsored by the South German and Swiss Greek Societies, dressed in a splendid uniform and carrying pistols embossed in gold. Arriving after the destruction of the Philhellene Battalion, he was obliged to join the band of one of the Peloponnesian captains. On his first expedition his feet became so badly blistered that he straggled behind with a young French companion[6] and they were both cut down, killed, and stripped at the first encounter with the Turks. Another Englishman[7] who arrived from Malta with a huge cavalry sword and a case full of books, including Byron's *Don Juan*, prudently returned home when he discovered how useless his services were likely to be. The other British Philhellenes in Greece in 1821 and 1822 are shadowy figures, two travelling gentlemen[8] who made a brief visit to the Regiment Baleste in June 1821 with the (short lived) intention of enlisting, a sea captain[9] said to have survived the battle of Peta, and a rich young man[10] seeking consolation for an unsuccessful love affair, who was killed near Nauplia late in 1822. Altogether not more than a dozen British are recorded as having been in Greece in 1821 and 1822, compared with five or six hundred volunteers of other nationalities. And it is noteworthy that many of these men were living on the Continent when they took their decision to join the Greeks and should therefore to some extent, be regarded as the products of French or German philhellenism rather than of the British version.

The failure of the movement to establish itself in Britain during the early period is difficult to account for. There was no lack of news and propaganda in favour of the Greeks, and attempts were made, as on the Continent, to establish Greek societies, but with almost no success. One of the reasons suggested at the time[11] was that the advocates of the Greek cause in England were extremists and fanatics that repelled rather than attracted public support, and to judge from the pamphlets, there may be something in this explanation. More probably the main reason was the attitude of the Government. While Castlereagh was at the head of affairs, no open support for rebels could be tolerable to the Government and most moderates, even if sympathetic to the Greek cause, were not inclined to oppose the official policy. At the end of 1822, after Castlereagh had committed suicide in a fit of despair, a more subtle man re-entered the Foreign Office. George Canning was one of the most successful of British statesmen. Despite his subsequent elevation into the Pantheon of Modern Greece, it would be wrong to regard Canning as a Philhellene. It was largely through Canning's foresight, energy, and diplomatic skill, that an outcome to the Greek Revolution satisfactory to the powers was eventually arrived at. But there was never any question but that his chief concern was, quite properly, the advancement of British interests. It was because Canning considered that a more flexible foreign policy would be of benefit to Britain that British philhellenism was allowed to take root.

The London Greek Committee was founded in March 1823 and for the next two years was the most important philhellenic organization in the world. The London Committee was the centre for the movement all over the British Isles and for a time Europe and the United States also. Unlike the German, Swiss, and other societies of earlier years, its activities had an important effect on the course of the war. It is difficult to disentangle the various strands of events which led to its establishment. It is even more difficult to assess the complex motives in the minds of the men who involved themselves in its activities. The simple ideals about regenerating Ancient Greece and defending Christians against Infidels which had inspired the first philhellenic efforts on the Continent were now alloyed with apparently more sophisticated considerations.

At the same time as Count Jourdain was in Paris negotiating his treaty with the Knights of Malta, another Greek agent was in Spain. The Greeks calculated (wrongly) that the Spanish constitutionalists, as the last surviving liberal revolutionary government in Europe, might be inclined to help their fellow revolutionaries in Greece. The Spanish had no money to spare. On the contrary, their own position was now desperate. The Continental powers, having successfully quelled the revolutions in Italy, were turning their attention to the last surviving abscess of liberalism on the body of Europe and considering how best to lance it. A French army was prepared on the frontier ready to perform the surgery. The French Government only waited to be assured that the British would not interfere before sending their army across the border.

It was in Madrid, after his failure to secure help from the Spanish, that the Greek agent met a plausible young Irishman called Edward Blaquiere who was to play a decisive role in the philhellenic movement in Britain. Blaquiere persuaded him that, if he would go to London, money for the Greeks would be found, and that he himself had enough influential friends to be able to give him a virtual promise. The Greek agent left for London almost immediately.

Edward Blaquiere was a man of very pronounced convictions. During the war he had served in the British Navy in the Mediterranean and developed an interest in the peoples of the region, but he saw the complex political problems of Europe in the stark black and white moral terms beloved by the naïve and the fanatical. Blaquiere's strength lay in his energy and his obvious sincerity. He became a political propagandist, writing in quick succession a series of books about the political problems of various Mediterranean countries. On the whole his general sentiments would now be regarded as unexceptionable but his books are an unattractive mixture of instant history, conventional sentiment, and tired rhetoric. He was an example of the man who is so well meaning and so busy that he never has time to learn anything new, the propagandist whose mind genuinely cannot absorb information or make judgements that are at variance with his preconceptions. Energy became a substitute for thought. Throughout his short life Blaquiere continued to believe that all Mediterranean peoples were much the same and that the superficial knowledge picked up when he was a midshipman in Malta could be directly applied to Spain or Italy or Greece. In 1823 he had just finished a work of propaganda on the Spanish Revolution when the French troops were crossing the frontier. Abandoning the lost cause he now had energy to devote to the cause of the Greeks. Between 1823 when he first took it up and 1828 he published no less than three books and two pamphlets* on the Greek war at intervals between his frequent journeys across Europe and frenzied campaigning all over Britiain. He was also an indefatigable writer of letters and the clerks who intercepted the mail at British quarantine establishments must often have sighed with the weariness of copying out his effusions for transmission to London.

The other man who provided the driving force behind the London Greek Committee was a more complex character. John (later Sir John) Bowring, if his talents had not been so widely diffused, might have been one of the great Victorians. His philhellenism was an episode in the earlier part of his long career as financier, journalist, scholar, linguist, politician, economist, Eastern traveller, diplomat, and colonial administrator, and an episode of which in later life he was not proud. Yet even in 1823, when he was still only thirty-one, Bowring was a well-known figure in political circles in London and far beyond. He had an unusual proficiency in languages and as a boy had quickly learned French, Italian, Spanish, Portuguese, German, and Dutch and put the talent to good use by joining a London exporting company. As a young man he travelled extensively all over Europe, learning incidentally Danish, Swedish, Russian, Serbo-Croat, Polish, Czech, and Magyar. Later he was to learn Arabic and Chinese. But he was more than a successful merchant and scholar. Everywhere on his travels Bowring was introduced to the prominent men in literary and political circles and, once having made an acquaintance, he seems never to have let him go. In particular he got to know the liberals all over Europe. He must have been an affable young man and success bred success. Constantly on the move from one liberal drawing-room to another, he gave the

* Three if one counts the anonymous pamphlet by 'Crito', which is almost certainly edited by him.

appearance of being very well informed about the internal politics of several European countries. He was also deeply involved in complex financial transactions.

In 1821, Bowring was in Madrid trying to settle claims against the Spanish Government which dated back to the time when he was a contractor to Wellington's army in 1813. When the news of the Greek Revolution reached Madrid Bowring is said to have been the founder of a Spanish Philhellenic Committee,[12] a shadowy organization about whose activities, if any, nothing is known. It seems to have been an organization not so much of Spaniards as of dispersed unsuccessful revolutionaries from Italy and elsewhere and their well-wishers.

By his constant toing and froing among the liberals of Europe Bowring was one of the men who gave credibility to the belief that the revolutions in Spain, Italy, and Greece were the result of an international conspiracy. To others it seemed that Bowring must be a spy of the British Government.

In 1822 the French police in exasperation arrested him at Calais as he was about to return to England. Because of his known correspondence with opponents of the régime the French police had been secretly following him, searching his lodgings, and reading his papers. It was believed from other sources that he was implicated in a plot to spring from prison four soldiers who had been condemned to death for singing republican songs, the famous affair of the four Sergeants of La Rochelle. To add to the aura of intrigue and espionage which always surrounded Bowring, it was discovered when he was arrested that he was carrying despatches from the Portuguese Minister in Paris warning of the imminent French invasion of Spain. Bowring was fortunate to be released and expelled from France.

It was these two men, the simplistic journalist and the insidious omniscient merchant, who were responsible for establishing the Greek Committee in London. Blaquiere and Bowring were not spies. It was simply that their political activities took them into the twilight area of diplomacy. They picked up a great deal of useful intelligence and were prepared to pass it on to the British Government, but the co-operation or acquiescence of the Government, although helpful, was not essential to them. They needed no guidance in protecting British interests. On the contrary, one of the main considerations in their plans was to forestall attempts by other countries to exploit the Greek situation. It was they who warned the Government that the scheme to revive the Knights of Malta was a cover for French interference in Greece and so persuaded the Government to prevent the Knights concluding a loan on the London money market. It was they too who frustrated the various schemes of General de Wintz by persuading the Government to intervene. Canning, who already had experience of how useful Bowring could be, connived at the establishment of a philhellenic movement in Britain. The British Government, while remaining neutral in the Greek–Turkish conflict, thus had an instrument by which to assert influence. It was an indirect instrument, by no means under the control of the Government, but one nevertheless which could be guided and influenced and (with the help of the Ionian quarantine) closely watched. In exchange, the Government turned a blind eye to the activities of the London Committee, which were of doubtful legality, despite repeated representations from the Ottoman Government. It is too much to say that the London Greek Committee was in alliance with the Government, but on the other hand, it was not the independent charitable institution that it may have appeared.

The London Greek Committee issued its first circular signed by Bowring as secretary from the Crown and Anchor Tavern in the Strand on 3 March 1823. The original membership was twenty-six, almost all Members of Parliament. A public meeting was held on 15 May at which a series of resolutions were passed. The Chairman's opening address could have been culled from the dozens of philhellenic pamphlets which had circulated in Germany and France in 1821 and 1822:

The present state of Greece is highly interesting to the friends of humanity, civilization, and religion. . . . It is a matter of surprise and regret that hitherto they [the philhellenic feelings of the people of England] have produced so little active and beneficial result. At length, however, a numerous Committee has been formed of friends of Greece, and the time is arrived when they deem it right to make a public appeal. It is in the name of Greece. It is in behalf of a country associated with every sacred and sublime recollection:— it is for a people formerly free and enlightened, but long retained by foreign despots in the chains of ignorance and barbarism![13]

One of the motions, in the name of the young Lord John Russell, declared: 'That the liberation of that unhappy country affords the most cheering prospects of being able to enlarge the limit of Christianity and civilization.'[14]

For nearly two years afterwards the London Greek Committee showed enormous energy. Public meetings were held regularly in the Crown and Anchor at which impassioned philhellenic speeches were delivered after the audience had been suitably softened with alcohol. The Tavern was open every day to receive subscriptions. A campaign was mounted, with a good deal of success, to 'place' news and articles about Greece in the press. Some of the old philhellenic pamphlets which had come out at the beginning of the War, were republished with appropriate revisions. Others were written for the occasion.

Blaquiere himself made a long tour through England and Ireland to visit newspaper owners and to try to set up local committees. Gordon established a committee in Aberdeen. Gradually the programme became more ambitious. A 'sensational ascent' of a balloon was advertised and arranged, although on the day the balloon failed to rise. Blaquiere especially had an eye for the publicity gimmick. On one of his visits to Greece he brought back some cannon balls made from the marble of the Parthenon, thus combining the appeals of the modern war with the ancient glory. On other occasions a few frightened Greek and Turkish orphans were brought to England. The purpose was to provide them with education but the publicity opportunity was exploited to the full.

The Committee arranged for the publication of suitable books on Greece. A collection of Greek folk songs which had recently appeared in Paris was translated by way of the French into English. The resulting verses—such as this extract about the siege of Tripolitsa—made familiar reading for devotees of Sir Walter Scott:

> But when he came, the Grecian guns
>   Were shaking every tower,
> More close became the circling force
>   More thick the iron shower;
>
> Until Colocotroni cried,
>   From Graecia's nearest post:
> 'Yield freely, Kïamil, and trust
>   Colocotroni's host
>
> 'I pledge my word nor thou nor thine
>   Shall feel the sabre's edge.'
> 'Hellenes! Chiefs! I yield at once,
>   'And take the proffer'd pledge'
>
> A proud Boulouk-Bashèe exclaim'd,
>   From off a battery's height:
> 'No! Rayahs! unbelieving dogs!
>   We still defy your might!
>
> 'Our Sultan sits in Stambol yet,
>   'Unshaken on his throne;
> 'Unnumber'd forts and countless bands
>   'Of Turks are still our own.'[15]

The indefatigable Blaquiere, on top of all his other activities, produced a book called *The Greek Revolution, Its Origin and Progress*, a fitting companion to his earlier *Historical View of the Spanish Revolution*. Blaquiere's opportunities for discovering what actually occurred during the early months of the Greek Revolution were limited, and he certainly never understood the underlying causes. Yet, whatever allowances one may wish to make, he was guilty of every easy trick of suppression, distortion and smear that marks the unscrupulous partisan or the unshakeable fanatic. Every action of the Greeks was valorous, wise, and admirable; every action of the Turks— called throughout 'infidels'—was cruel, cowardly, and offensive. The atrocities committed by the Turks were related in loving detail; those committed by the Greeks were prudently omitted. Even the massacre of the Turks at Tripolitsa was blandly justified.

The publicity started by the London Greek Committee led to subsidiary committees being established in several provincial cities, although they seem to have been short-lived. Charities and missionary societies turned their attention to Greece in accordance with the new fashion. There even existed a 'Scottish Ladies Society for Promoting the Moral and Intellectual Improvement of Females in Greece'—a daunting programme even for Scottish ladies.[16]

Yet, in spite of all the energy of the London Greek Committee and the publicity for the Greek cause which they generated, the impact of the British Philhellenes on public opinion was slight. They never succeeded in stirring the conscience or capturing the imagination. At one of the meetings of the Committee the Chairman reported regretfully that hardly any replies had been received to the two thousand letters which had been sent out asking for subscriptions.[17] When Lord Byron's name was added to the membership of the Committee, interest picked up a little and by the end of 1823 its membership had risen to eighty-five. But the best measure of the public's commitment to political movements of this kind is the amount of money they are prepared to subscribe. By this measure, despite the Committee's apparent success in promoting publicity and securing Government co-operation, they failed in their prime purpose. The total sum of money collected by the Committee was only £11,241, far less than the monies collected by the Societies on the Continent and only slightly more than the sum sent for relief of Greek refugees by the British Quakers.

The reason why the British public were so unwilling to part with their money lay in the character of the Committee. On the face of it, the list of eighty-five men who formed membership of the London Greek Committee was representative of all that was great and good in British life. There were a few peers and numerous Members of Parliament, several lawyers including a former Lord Chancellor, two retired generals and other military men, a sprinkling of scholars, academics, and clergymen, the poets Byron, Moore, Rogers, and Campbell, and others whose names were familiar to the public for one reason or another.

But the Committee was primarily a political organization and it was judged for its politics. It was clear from the membership lists where its sympathies lay. There was only one Tory in the whole Committee and he was the unattractive pamphleteer who advocated extermination of the Turks in the name of religion, the Reverend Thomas Hughes. All the other members, insofar as their general political views could be identified, were Whigs and Radicals.

This fact by itself should not have put people off. Even without Tories the list could still be said to represent a fairly broad spectrum of opinion.

But from the beginning most of the members of the Committee took no active part in its affairs—they paid their subscription, allowed their name to be used, perhaps attended the first few meetings, but did nothing more. The driving force behind the Committee was a small group of about half a dozen, Joseph Hume, Sir Francis Burdett, Edward Ellice, and John Cam Hobhouse, all Members of Parliament and, of course, Bowring and Blaquiere. These men set the tone of the Committee and were mainly responsible for the impression it made on public opinion. Their reputation was not universally attractive. They were at the extreme left of the political spectrum within which British politics was then conducted. They regarded themselves as liberals, radicals, reformers or progressives, holders of advanced ideas, opponents of the established order.

Most of their policies have long since been implemented and have themselves entered the established traditions of British politics, but among the penalties of having ideas in advance of one's time is the risk of being dubbed a dangerous revolutionary or at best an irresponsible and impractical eccentric. Furthermore, the man with ideas in advance of his time is constantly finding more institutions in need of reform and is obliged to criticize, warn, and attack. As public opinion catches up, or alternatively as his unheeded warnings are seen to have been well founded, he is also constantly being presented with opportunities for saying 'I told you so'. It requires unusual political skill in these circumstances to avoid being considered destructive, priggish, or contrary. The leaders of the London Greek Committee did not have that skill. Admirable though their general political principles were, their self righteousness was insufferable. Year after year, as new liberal causes were thought of, the same names would appear before the public to advocate liberal solutions and often to ask for money. Committees would be set up to promote this or that good cause and the familiar names were sure to be found. Appeals from professional protesters and do-gooders are apt to raise a yawn. More easy-going men may be repelled from supporting a good cause by an unwillingness to ally themselves with such leaders. The cause of the Greeks in Britain appeared to most people to be simply the fashionable liberal cause of the hour, enjoying a brief month or two of public attention before its champions moved on to the cause of Spain, or Italy, or Ireland, or Catholic emancipation, or slavery, or capital punishment, or some other burning topic of the day.

The leaders of the London Greek Committee were particularly liable to provoke the wrong reactions. Not only did they believe that they were endowed with superior political wisdom (a venial fault in any politician who desires to be taken seriously) but they believed that they had discovered the key to all political questions. Liberalism to them was not merely an attitude of mind to be adopted in approaching political questions, but a complete and coherent political philosophy with its own rationale, its articles of faith, and its dogma. Among the original list of twenty-six members there was one name which seemed by its distinction to emphasize the insignificance of the others. Jeremy Bentham was now in his mid-seventies and had been pouring out his opinions on the troubles of the world for half a century. He was now a venerable old man but his mind and body were still far more active than many men half his age. He had attained the same kind of position as his direct spiritual descendant Bertrand Russell was to occupy in the nineteen-fifties, deeply and sincerely respected for his intelligence, his courage, and his energy even by men who had no understanding of his philosophy or despised his politics.

The true greatness of Bentham is usually underestimated. His concepts of liberty and utilitarianism, as refined by John Stuart Mill, remain probably the most civilized political principles that have been devised and are in need of revival. If the weaknesses in his philosophy, once they were recognized, seemed to be fatal, this was because he claimed too much. If Bentham had been content to expound a general guide to political conduct rather than establish a total coherent system of pure philosophy, his achievement would have been more widely recognized. The fault of Bentham was a tendency to retreat into dogma and his coterie exaggerated the fault. Bowring, who was to become Bentham's executor, was already in the habit of using the old man's name as a spiritual invocation to support his own ideas.* Other prominent Benthamites who joined the London Greek Committee were fawning and uncritical in the manner of disciples, regarding the master's chance remarks as mandatory pronouncements.

There were two aspects of Benthamite liberalism which especially attracted exaggerated respect. One was the belief that public opinion could ensure that the best policies would be identified and adopted, and the other was the belief that a good written constitution could guarantee the liberties of the governed. The Benthamites promoted both these articles of faith with particular intensity and some of the members of the London Greek Committee sometimes seemed to regard politics as being solely concerned with constitutions and communications methods. From the beginning the London Greek Committee gave off an odour of sanctimoniousness. Outsiders suspected, with a good deal of justice, that the Committee was less concerned with promoting the Greek war against the Turks than with using the unsettled situation in Greece as a practical testing ground for their political theories.

It is doubtful if the various representatives of the Greek Government who were sent to London from time to time to negotiate with the British

---

* Blaquiere introduced himself to Bentham by writing him a series of flattering letters. He introduced his friend Bowring to the great man after he had established himself as a disciple.

Philhellenes appreciated what kind of men they had fallen in with. At first they were simply bewildered. Blaquiere, who had brought the first Greek agent from Spain, adopted a proprietorial attitude and led his guest about London exhibiting him as the attraction of the hour. The Greek agents could only look on in wonderment as Blaquiere and Bowring protected them from the blandishments of this and that counter-offer, explaining how they alone had the true interests of Greece at heart.

But the Greek agents, for all their apparent willingness to be guided by their self-appointed friends and protectors, never lost sight of their main object. It was money that they needed most of all and they were ready to do all that was required to obtain it. The paltry sums raised by the Committee by subscription could never make any real difference to the course of the war. Their object was to use their contacts with the prominent men of the Committee to raise a loan on the London Stock Exchange. Talk about the proposed loan began as soon as the London Committee was formed— how it should be raised, whether in the name of the Committee or of the Greeks, how it should be spent. In the wildly speculative conditions of the London money market at the time the talk was almost enough, by itself, to ensure a successful flotation. By the end of the year Bowring was writing that he could raise a loan of £600,000 'by tomorrow morning' if it was decided to go ahead.[18] The prospect of a loan which would transform the chances of the Greeks winning the war was never far from people's minds.

Thus, partly through ignorance and partly by design, the Greek agents decided to humour the Committee. However bizarre the Committee's ideas seemed to be they decided to play along with them. Seldom have representatives of a supposedly independent country written such abjectly sycophantic thank-you letters as the Greek agents addressed to the members of the London Greek Committee. Anyone who might be in a position to render a service was presented with an effusive letter carefully drafted to appeal to his preconceptions. Much of the correspondence of the Greek Government and its agents overseas during this period is simply philhellenic waffle designed to ingratiate possible friends of the cause.

In particular the Greeks entered into a long correspondence with Jeremy Bentham about the exact terms of an ideal constitution for the country. They conveniently ignored the fact that the existing much-admired constitution was completely disregarded, and that the proposed delicate balances between the various constitutional instruments were hardly likely to function satisfactorily in a backward, largely illiterate, country where the chief source of political power was the ability to maintain bands of armed men at personal expense by plunder and extortion.

An official letter from the Greek Government thanked Bentham, 'the preceptor of the nineteenth century in the school of legislation' for suspending his labours 'which were embracing the general happiness of Europe' for the purpose of devoting himself to Greece. With the help of Bentham's advice, the Greek Government declared that Greece 'will make her advances with proportionately greater speed and better fortune, in the great work of that moral regeneration upon which her present and most permanent glory resides'.

The Greek agents took to addressing Bentham in their letters as 'Father and Protector of Greece', 'Friend and Father of our Country', 'Our faithful Friend and well-beloved Father'. Bentham was pleased to give his reply to 'My dear children' and to pass on his detailed suggestions on abstruse legal points to 'my son' Mavrocordato.[19] Bentham was made an honorary member of a (largely mythical) Learned Society in Nauplia which existed mainly for the purpose of having honorary members. The more extravagant the flattery, the more the Greek Committee came to believe it. Outsiders could only marvel and despair at the success of this new form of phil-hellenic humbug.

16. *Lord Byron joins the Cause*

The first success of the London Greek Committee was to recruit Lord Byron to its membership. He is the most famous and the most interesting Philhellene by such a large margin that it is now difficult to appreciate how much his expedition to Greece was a result of accident.

As usual Edward Blaquiere played an important role. The energy of this man never ceases to astonish. No sooner had he escorted the Greek agent safely from Madrid to London in the spring of 1823 and made the first moves towards the establishment of the London Greek Committee, than he rushed off to Greece itself. His purpose was allegedly to discover the facts of the situation in Greece (a task for which his prejudices made him quite unsuitable). In reality his main object was to forestall secret French moves to help the Greeks by making promises of money and other help on behalf of the English liberals. As he declared to the Government when he dutifully passed on to them the murky intelligence he had discovered about the Knights of Malta, he 'felt a natural solicitude that all the glory and advantages to be derived from Greek regeneration should belong to England'.[1]

Blaquiere asked to call on Byron at Genoa on his way to Greece and spent a few hours with him there in March 1823. He was armed with a letter of introduction from Byron's old friend John Cam Hobhouse, who was one of the original members of the London Greek Committee.* It is worth emphasizing, however, that at the time when Blaquiere called on Byron, the London Greek Committee hardly existed. All that had happened to date was that Blaquiere and Bowring had persuaded a few prominent liberal politicians including Hobhouse to give their permission to deal

* Trelawny also claims to have had a hand in introducing Blaquiere to Byron, but none of his statements can be accepted without confirmation.

with the agents of the Greek Government in their name and to hint that massive British help might be forthcoming.

In 1823 Byron was a more considerable man than he had been in the years before 1816 when his Grecian and Turkish tales had fanned a romantic literary philhellenism. He was more experienced, more tolerant, wiser. He was at work on his masterpiece, *Don Juan*, and, despite the continued adulation of a huge, mainly female, public for his earlier romantic poems, he now found them slightly juvenile and slightly shaming.

Byron was no longer a young man. He had largely given up the life of riot and sexual adventure which had shocked the English, and was living a settled, almost domestic, life with the Countess Guiccioli to whom he had a sincere and lasting attachment. The old panache was still there—he still loved extravagance—but he was now more conscious of the passing of time. He had a distressing tendency to run to fat and his hair was noticeably thinner. In a desperate effort to preserve the good looks of which he was so proud, he took to starving himself. Every morning he scrupulously measured his wrists and waist and, if there was any change, he took a large dose of Epsom salts. For breakfast he had only a dish of green tea, followed by several hours' hard exercise. Almost every day he took strong purgative pills and magnesia powders to try to cure the resulting indigestion. Some days he ate little or nothing but developed the habit of always having a glass of wine by him in the evening and of drinking immoderately late into the night. Byron felt life was slipping past him; that he had done nothing constructive since his disastrous scandal in 1816; that at the age of thirty-five he was fated to be simply a man of unfulfilled promise, a curiosity remarked by the tourists. Although he was writing brilliant poetry, it brought him little satisfaction and he seems to have no longer regarded poetry as a serious occupation.

The generosity of mind which, from the earliest days, had been one of his most attractive characteristics had not deserted him. The political idealism of his youth had not dried up as he grew older. His commitment to liberalism was totally sincere. Though he could see the absurdities of politicians and apparently sneer at them, this did not mean that he was not seriously concerned about political questions. He was a man who could see through the triviality, the pomposity, the injustice, the selfishness, and the tedium of the political process and yet was never tempted either to cynicism or to withdrawal. Unprotected by any comforting illusions, he never despaired and he never despised. These were rare and precious gifts.

In many ways, however, Byron was also very much a man of his time. Like hundreds of lesser men who had already been lured to Greece he was bored, he longed for action, and he still believed that war could be glorious. Greece appealed to him mainly as a fight for liberty, not as a fight for Greeks as such. He had seriously considered that South America and then Spain might be suitable theatres for his energies. And he had taken part in an abortive revolution in Italy. In all these respects Byron was a typical Philhellene, resembling hundreds of men from all over Europe whose names appear in the list of volunteers in the Greek cause.

Byron reacted to Blaquiere's enthusiastic proposals for helping the Greeks in the same way as the students and soldiers of Germany had reacted to the proclamations in the newspapers. He allowed himself to be persuaded that his half-suppressed imaginings could become a reality. Blaquiere encouraged him to believe that he could be practical and helpful and gave him a quite misleading account of conditions in Greece:

From all that I heard, it would be criminal in me to leave this without urging your Lordship to come up as soon as possible:— your presence will operate as a talisman and the field is too glorious, too closely associated with all that you hold dear to be any longer abandoned. . . . The cause is in a most flourishing state. I hope to be able to give your Lordship the result of the new elections in a few days. Meantime the effect produced by my mentioning the fact of *your* intention to join it, has been quite electric: need I say one word on the result to *yourself* of being *mainly instrumental* in resuscitating the Land already so happily illustrated by your sublime and energetic Muse. . . . Anxious to see your Lordship in this land of heroes, I remain most truly and devotedly yours, Edward Blaquiere.[2]

Blaquiere assured Byron that the British authorities in the Ionian Islands would all be delighted to see him, and that any money he spent on buying military or medical supplies would soon be reimbursed. He had even made arrangements for Byron to be received and entertained by 'a distinguished young poet' of the Ionian isles.

Flattery, combined with an ingenuous charm and apparently boundless energy, is a potent weapon. Shortly afterwards, Byron wrote to the Committee that he intended to go to Greece if the accounts in Blaquiere's letter could be confirmed.

Meanwhile in England, the London Committee, under Bowring's practised hand, skilfully exploited Byron's name to draw attention to themselves, leaking his confidential letters to the press without his approval. Nor did they see any objection to practising their publicist arts on Byron himself. It was seven years since Byron had left England; the posts were slow; news of home was scanty; and in any case Byron was not greatly interested in the day-to-day issues of English politics. With the exception of Hobhouse, the men who were organizing the London Greek Committee were largely unknown to him. He did not appreciate how small a section of British public opinion they represented and how difficult they were finding it to make any impact.

The Committee continued to overwhelm Byron with flattery. They encouraged him to write long letters about the Greek situation, implying that they valued his advice above all others. They even wrote to inform him

that he had been elected a member of the Committee in terms which implied
that this was a great honour open to few—a well-known recruiting trick of
unsuccessful organizations. For a time the bandwagon rolled as they had
hoped. Men allowed their names to be added to the Committee's membership out of respect or liking for Byron and the apparent widening of the
political base of the Committee induced others to join. But, despite appearances, the vast majority of the distinguished men whose names ornamented
the London Greek Committee took no part in its activities. Throughout
its life it was exclusively administered by a small group of doctrinaire
Benthamites. It was only when he reached Greece that Byron was to begin
to appreciate the true nature of the London Greek Committee with whom
he had tied his fortunes and his reputation. The process of disenchantment
was to be a painful one.

A few days after Blaquiere left Genoa, another episode turned Byron's
thoughts to Greece. Two German Philhellenes, a Württemberger and a
Bavarian, knowing his reputation for kindness, came to beg help to pay
for their journey back to Germany. They had both been members of General
Normann's party and the Württemberger had been present at Peta. Leaving
Greece together in September 1822 they had wandered from island to
island and eventually reached Smyrna. They had benefited from the kindness of the French Consul and had been given a free passage to Ancona,
but at Trieste they had been turned back by the Austrians. They now had
no money, clothes, or shoes.

Byron took a personal interest in the two men and invited them to his
house several times before sending them happily on their way. He was
able to converse about the places which he had visited in his youth and his
mind was drawn back to happier days. He examined them closely about
the state of affairs in Greece and learnt a good deal of more or less accurate
information about the attitude of the Greeks to foreigners and their aversion to European methods of warfare. The two young men were clearly
typical of the best of the 1822 generation of Philhellenes. As Byron wrote
in a letter to Bowring: 'Both are very simple, full of naïveté, and quite
unpretending: they say the foreigners quarrelled among themselves,
particularly the French with the Germans, which produced duels. . . . One
of them means to publish his Journal of the campaign.* The Bavarian
wonders a little that the Greeks are not quite the same with them of the
time of Themistocles.'[3]

After the visit of the Germans, Byron's enthusiasm for an expedition to
Greece grew rapidly. Everyone with whom he discussed the idea pressed
him to indulge his wishes. Count Gamba, the young brother of Byron's
mistress, who had shared in the débâcle of the revolution in Central Italy,
was bursting like so many of his countrymen to continue the struggle for

* This was perhaps Adolph von Lübtow whose book appeared in 1823 in Berne.

Italian independence in Greece. Blaquiere bombarded Byron with letters, urging him to go to Greece without delay and promising to meet him there.

At last on 13 July 1823 Byron left Genoa in a chartered vessel. He had on board a domestic retinue of nine servants—including a doctor specially recruited—five horses, two small cannon, a store of medicines, 10,000 Spanish dollars in cash and bills for a further 40,000. Passage was given to a few volunteers. [4] There is no doubt that Byron regarded the expedition as a serious one, almost as a sacrifice—any suggestions that he was simply out for adventure were firmly discounted. Yet it is no slur on his main motives to say that he also hoped that he would enjoy himself, that he would again be a figure in the land, and even that glory might come his way. Like many a lesser Philhellene, Byron gave himself away by his wardrobe. The fascination of the appurtenances of war just could not be resisted. He took half a dozen military uniforms in many colours and all lavishly decorated with gold and silver braid with sashes, epaulettes, waistcoats, and cocked hats to match. He took two gilded helmets decorated with the family motto 'Crede Byron' and at least ten swords. On the way he persuaded his friend Trelawny to give him his black American groom since he knew that it added to a man's dignity in the East to have a negro as a servant.

17. 'To bring Freedom and Knowledge to Greece'

The small caucus of ambitious men who directed the activities of the London Greek Committee took the grand view of their responsibilities. Whereas Greek Societies on the Continent had modestly and hopefully proclaimed their aim as to assist in the liberation of Greece from the Turks, the British Philhellenes felt no such limitation on their imagination. The fact that their political base was so narrow never caused them to hesitate or to doubt the correctness of their programme. Greece must be established as an independent nation state, they had no doubt of that. But the Greece they wanted to see was not so much some vague regeneration of Ancient Hellas as a practical example of the political principles of Jeremy Bentham. Philhellenism was to be an experiment in practical utilitarianism.

The first concern of the Committee was to send military help. Discussions and preparations began almost immediately after the Committee was set up in the middle of 1823. As always, Blaquiere was well to the fore with his own ideas. Although the avowed purpose of his visit to Greece was to discover what kind of aid would be most useful, it is clear that he had already made up his mind before he set out. 'A train of artillery', he suggested to Hobhouse, 'some old sergeants versed in the organization of light troops, and a few hospital supplies might give a new and immediate turn to the war if sent out at once.'[1] Byron too had not been slow in putting forward his own suggestions to the Committee, suggestions which were remarkably like Blaquiere's.

'The principal material wanted by the Greeks appears to be first, a park of field artillery—light and fit for mountain service; secondly gunpowder; thirdly, hospital or medical stores.' Byron also gave his views on the proposal that a cadre of a regular brigade should be established. 'A small body of good officers, especially artillery; an engineer with quantity (such as the

Committee might deem requisite) of stores, of the nature which Captain Blaquiere indicated as most wanted, would, I should conceive, be a highly useful accession.'[2] None of these ideas could be regarded as far-fetched or impracticable. On the contrary, the proposed spending of the Committee's few thousand pounds was the obvious way of trying to make an impact with scanty resources, so obvious indeed that it had been thought of and tried out before. Neither the Committee nor Byron ever realized fully that their own remedy for Greece was simply the mixture as before, the mixture administered unsuccessfully by the German and Swiss Societies, the mixture which, at the very time Blaquiere and Byron were prescribing it, was resulting in the deaths of the young men of the German Legion in the disease-infested streets of Nauplia.

Among the members of the London Greek Committee there was only one man who had any experience of the war in Greece. Thomas Gordon of Cairness,[3] who had sailed to Greece at the outbreak of the Revolution in 1821 with his own ship and his own store of weapons, had served as Chief of Staff to Hypsilantes at the time of the siege of Tripolitsa. He had left shortly afterwards, mainly as a result of illness, but had kept in touch with the situation ever since. Surprisingly, he had managed to keep on good personal terms with all the Greek leaders and at least one formal request had been made to him by the Greek Government to return. He maintained a correspondence with men all over Europe who were interested in the Greek cause or had recent information, and several distressed Philhellenes made the long journey to Aberdeenshire to beg from him. In later life he was to write a magnificent history of the Greek Revolution which still astonishes by its accuracy and judgement. Gordon was one of the few Philhellenes who really could have helped Greece. He was rich, independent, well-connected, and experienced. He knew the country and the people and he knew the Turks even better. He was a proven soldier and spoke both Greek and Turkish (as well as several European languages) with fluency. He never doubted the justice of the Greek cause, even after witnessing some of the worst massacres of the war, but he was no romantic. It was decided soon after the Committee was formed that Gordon should be in command of any expedition they should send to Greece.

Soon afterwards Gordon submitted a memorandum with his suggestions on the best way of helping the Greeks. A straight handing over of the money he said, although welcome to the Greeks, would be injudicious and would prove an apple of discord; sending out an armed European force, although the most efficacious method, could only be contemplated if the Committee had at least £30,000 at its disposal. As a practical scheme Gordon made two complementary proposals. A small body of artificers should be sent with all the necessary tools and equipment in order to provide Greece with an arsenal to manufacture and repair guns, muskets, and ammunition.

In addition, a brigade of light artillery should be equipped and sent to Greece. Gordon recommended that, apart from the cost of the arsenal and a few draught-animals for the guns, all the Committee's funds should be devoted to providing light artillery and artillerymen. His proposal had been thoroughly considered and costed in detail. He had already, at his own expense, engaged a former employee of Woolwich Arsenal, William Parry,[4] to draw up the necessary plans. Studies had been made of the guns best suited to Greek conditions, the supporting equipment and ammunition they would need, and the proper complement of artillerymen. Parry had even started to recruit provisionally about fifty veteran artillerymen and artificers, who would man the repair facility and the artillery brigade. In putting the scheme to the Committee Gordon proposed to pay one third of the total cost out of his own pocket if the Committee agreed to pay the remainder. It was a generous offer and a bold scheme. In the capable hands of Gordon it might possibly have succeeded, but in essentials the scheme resembled the disastrous project of the German Legion which had been equally well planned and well equipped.

The scheme was never put into effect. Gordon withdrew his offer to command the expedition and then his offer to pay a third of the cost, although he handed over free a few guns that he had already bought. In the long weeks of discussion between Gordon and the other leading members of the Committee the great difference of outlook between them became increasingly clear. The fulsome reports by Blaquiere of the conditions in Greece which were circulated by Bowring contrasted sharply with the information Gordon was receiving from his own sources. The confidence of the Committee that the Greeks would be delighted to accept their help and advice was contradicted by his own experience. But the main difference was over priorities. The Committee decided not to spend its money on the scheme suggested by Gordon but to send the arsenal without the artillery. Ten small mountain guns were bought in addition to a howitzer and larger guns donated by Gordon, but no crews of artillerymen were provided. They wanted the rest of the money to spend on other schemes aimed at the long-term regeneration of the country which will be described later. The conflict of opinion was between, on the one hand, the practical soldier who saw the first priority as helping to win the war against the Turks, and on the other, the doctrinaire Benthamites who prided themselves on taking the long view. Gordon's decision to withdraw was not caused by pique or by fear of being overshadowed by Lord Byron (whose intention to go to Greece had just been reported), but by a genuine belief that he could not be useful in the circumstances. He repeated his willingness 'to make every sacrifice' and he promised to go to Greece as soon as he saw the prospect of making a contribution to the success of the cause.

As a result, the expedition prepared by the British Philhellenes was unbalanced from the start. It was a civilian organization without a military force to serve and without a proper command. There were men to repair the guns but no men to use them. The whole conception rested on a misapprehension about the state of civil organization and military discipline in Greece. The Committee treated the expedition like a technical working party being sent as a reinforcement to a British military base overseas, assuming that all the necessary facilities already existed at the destination.

Apart from the fundamental lack of balance the expedition was well prepared. The items of direct military value consisted of twelve guns, 61 barrels of gunpowder, and various quantities of shot and shell. There was a store of medical supplies and equipment and a set of musical instruments for a military band—an item for which all philhellenic societies had an irresistible predilection. As for the arsenal, besides Parry who had supervised operations at Woolwich, eight other skilled men were engaged,[5] one of each trade needed in an arsenal, a clerk, a foreman of cartridge makers, a founder, a tinman, a smith, a turner, a wheelwright, and a carpenter. The list of tools, materials and instruments which accompanied them is astonishing for its variety and its comprehensiveness. Nothing was too great or too small to be dispensed with. Everything, it appeared, had been thought of. An entirely self-sufficient little factory was to be exported. The list of items runs for three pages in familiar military language ranging from furnace, blast, to iron bars, round; iron bars, flat; wheels, spare; tarpaulins, gun; and hammers, claw.

The expedition set sail from Gravesend in the *Ann* in November 1823. All the preparations had been made openly and the purpose for which the arms were being bought was well publicized. As if to emphasize the acquiescence of the British Government, the expedition was allowed to sail in a vessel which was also carrying stores to the British forces in Malta and the Ionian Islands. The authorities at London, Malta and Corfu were fully aware of the illegal purpose of the expedition but they had been instructed not to interfere unless they were officially informed on oath. There was a scare at Malta when one of the artificers, an Irishman, in a drunken quarrel aboard, threatened himself to inform the authorities, but he was dissuaded. The fiction was successfully maintained that the British authorities knew nothing of the destination of the arms and the soldiers. The *Ann* reached Greece in December 1823.

As it turned out, this was the only expedition which the London Greek Committee sent to Greece. But the establishment of a new centre of philhellenism led to a renewal of the flow of individual volunteers to Greece which had almost entirely ceased at the end of 1822. Blaquiere had been firmly advised on his own visit to Greece to discourage the sending of soldiers to Greece to add to the ranks of miserable wretches still subsisting there. But the Committee could not bear to refuse to give letters of introduction to the eager men who again began to step forward. Everyone who wanted to go to Greece now made his way in the first place to London. At first there was only a trickle. Doctors specially recruited by the Committee, unemployed military men from the Continent, former Philhellenes who wanted to give Greece a second chance. The Committee found itself being offered advice by self-appointed experts. Bellier de Launay, a dismissed Prussian subaltern who had made a brief visit to Greece in one of the early expeditions from Marseilles, now appeared in London as a Colonel, a Marquis, and a Knight of the Order of Minerva. When news arrived in Europe and America of Byron's intention to go to Greece, more volunteers stepped forward. A new episode of practical philhellenism began.

To be their principal agent in Greece the Committee chose a man of very different stamp from any who had ventured to Greece hitherto. The Honourable Leicester Stanhope, C.B., eldest son of the Earl of Harrington, was a lieutenant-colonel in the British Army. He was both an effective administrator and, at the same time, a doctrinaire Benthamite. Many of the Benthamites were speechifiers, literary men, thinkers, remote from reality, men who never really expected to see their theories realized in practice. Stanhope was as politically committed as any, ready always to defend his political theories in the face of the most recalcitrant of facts. And yet, perhaps because he always greatly underestimated the difficulties of carrying out his plans, he had remarkable practical success. His single-minded concentration on applying the principles of Jeremy Bentham to the regeneration of Greece was one of the strangest manifestations of philhellenism.

Stanhope's enthusiasm ranged over the whole spectrum of Benthamite doctrine and in Greece he was to try his energy in many fields. But there was one political principle which appealed to him above all the others— the freedom of the press. Stanhope believed in the absolute desirability of a free press with a passion bordering on monomania. Before he embraced the cause of Greece he had devoted much of his recent effort to trying to establish newspapers in India and had published a book on the subject. It was no doubt a laudable aim but Stanhope consistently damaged a good cause by grotesque overstatement. If a free press were to be established in India, he wrote, 'morals will be improved, superstitition and castes destroyed, women enfranchised and religion purified, the laws will be ameliorated, justice better administered, and cruelties prevented; slavery will be abolished, maladministration, seditions and wars checked, and invasions baffled; while the agriculture, trade and resources of the state will increase.'[6]

Stanhope's appointment emphasized the doctrinaire character of the London Greek Committee. Although, as a soldier himself, he recognized that there was a military problem to be solved—the winning of the war— he himself was much more interested in the longer-term objectives. The

regeneration of Greece, the old cry of the German professors, took on a
new meaning when adopted by the English. Consignments of bibles were
to be dispatched to Greece to convert the Greeks to the English version
of Christianity, or as it was generally put, to combat the superstitition of
the Greek Church. A system of public education was to be established in
Greece on the pattern introduced in England by Joseph Lancaster—books,
maps, mathematical instruments to equip the first classrooms were included
among the stores sent with Parry's expedition.

Most important of all, the Committee decided to send printing presses
to Greece with a view to establishing newspapers and so creating the
informed public opinion necessary for the health of political liberty.
Nothing could more clearly exemplify the supreme confidence of the Benthamites both in their political theories and in their practical abilities than
their plans to start newspapers in the barbarous and anarchic conditions of
Greece. Stanhope saw these printing presses as the most powerful weapon
which the Greeks could possess against the Turks.

In the autumn of 1823 he left England in company with Bellier de Launay
to establish himself in Greece as the appointed agent of the London Greek
Committee. The British Government, despite his commission in the British
Army, made no move to stop him in accordance with their policy of helping
British influence in Greece.

On the way Stanhope decided to call on the Swiss and South German
Greek Societies about whose existence the London Committee had heard,
with a view, as he himself put it, 'to establish an efficient system of co-
operation without shackling our efforts'. Stanhope met representatives of
the Greek Societies at Darmstadt, Zurich, Berne, and Geneva. He also met
Capodistria and other prominent overseas Greeks. Everywhere he was
courteously received as the representative of a powerful new philhellenic
organization through whose efforts the loan which would rejuvenate
Greece's fortunes was to be organized.

It would be fascinating to know what the solid burghers and pastors of
the German and Swiss Societies made of the aristocratic, republican,
slightly eccentric English officer who unexpectedly arrived among them
accompanied by the absurd Colonel Marquis Bellier de Launay (whose
pretensions impressed none of his own countrymen) in the autumn of 1823.
Although Stanhope was seeking their co-operation, it was clear that their
own period of pre-eminence was over; that the torch of philhellenism had
now passed from the Germans and Swiss to the British. Stanhope felt no
immodesty in taking the initiative.

One cannot help feeling sympathetic to the worthy men of the Societies.
For nearly two years, when the cause of the Greeks was neglected in
England, they had painstakingly collected subscriptions. In the face of the
consistent opposition of the great Continental governments, they had raised

huge sums of money, far more than was ever achieved by the London Greek Committee. Theirs had been no short-lived spurt of enthusiasm performed for a mixture of philanthropic and nationalistic motives, but a thorough and sustained effort based on a deeply-held belief in their debt to the Ancient Greeks and in their duty as Christians.

When Stanhope visited the Societies they were near the end of their resources. They were confused and perplexed and had suffered a series of shocks which had severely tested their courage and their charity. It will be remembered that, after the Societies had dispatched the German Legion to Greece in December 1822, the port of Marseilles had been closed and the Societies were unable to send further volunteers to Greece. But in the meantime another call on their philhellenism had appeared. As a result of the efforts of the English Quakers, the Austrian authorities decided to allow a large party of Greek refugees to cross the Austrian territories from Russia where they had taken refuge at the beginning of the Revolution. These refugees were penniless and, as 'rebels', politically untouchable. Many died of hunger, cold, and misery during their long trek across Eastern Europe, but one hundred and sixty reached the Austrian frontier in safety. They were thrown on the mercy of private charity and, as usual, it was the Swiss who were expected to be the conscience of Europe. The Greek Societies of Switzerland and South Germany somehow managed to raise the money to feed and clothe the refugees and arrange for them to be conveyed in parties to the Morea. It was an astonishing feat and it had strained the resources and the enthusiasm of the donors almost to breaking point.

The Societies were denied even the comfort of being thanked for their efforts. Throughout 1823 the flood of disillusioned volunteers had returned from Greece cursing the Societies and demanding money. Then in the middle of the year Sergeant Kolbe of the German Legion unexpectedly arrived back at Darmstadt. Kolbe, as has been related earlier, had been chosen by the survivors of the Legion to return to Germany to tell the Societies of the harsh unwelcoming reception they had suffered in Greece and to ask for money to pay for their passage home.

At the time when Stanhope was paying his visits, the Societies were still undecided about how to react to this painful news. Until Kolbe arrived they had been under the impression that the Legion was operating in Greece under 'Baron Kephalas of Olympus' according to the terms of the contract drawn up by the Societies. Even now they only knew a part of the story. Kolbe had left the Legion when it seemed to be breaking up. Since he had left Greece, the Legion had sunk from misery to misery and had by now ceased to exist as an organized force; many of its members were dead, others were reduced to beggary in the streets of Nauplia, and many more were scattered over the Eastern Mediterranean trying to beg their way home.

Stanhope discussed with the Societies what should be done about the German Legion. One of the leaders of the Darmstadt Society, Stanhope reported to Bowring, 'complained much of the conduct of the Greek Government towards the German corps: the Capitani, he said, were jealous of them; they had been left inactive and destitute of all succour. The German and Swiss Committees had, in consequence, come to a resolution to order the Legion home unless the Greek government would supply them with the means of subsistence.' To the self-assured English Colonel this was defeatist talk. The only reason for recalling the Legion, he declared, would be lack of funds and there was now no danger of that since the London Greek Committee had money and a loan was in the offing. Moreover, said the Colonel, the Societies had been wrong to send troops in the first place, and the Greeks were wise to be jealous of the interference of foreigners. 'So far from wishing to curb this spirit,' he advised, 'it should be fostered as calculated to root in the public mind a hatred of foreign dominion.' If the men of the Darmstadt Greek Society had been able to see at that moment what the 'wise jealousy' of the Greeks had done to the German Legion, they could perhaps have punctured his doctrinaire arrogance. But, in the false belief that the Legion was still operating in Greece, they decided to co-operate with Stanhope and to set up a Committee in Greece to control the Legion's activities consisting of one German and one Swiss member.

Stanhope, however, was never much interested in such short-term problems as the winning of the Greek War of Independence. 'The grand object of the Committee', he declared at Berne, 'is to give freedom and knowledge to Greece.' At Zurich he expanded on this theme:

To communicate knowledge to the Greeks was an object the Committee had near at heart. From this source spring order, morality, freedom and power. The venerable Bentham, with a spirit of philanthropy as fervent, and a mind as vast as ever, had employed his days and nights in contemplating and writing on the Constitution of Greece, and in framing for her a body of rational laws, the most useful of human offerings. The mighty power of the press of England had been exerted in favour of Greece.

On his Continental tour Stanhope collected ideas from everyone he met and bombarded the London Committee with his suggestions. The Swiss and United States systems of government, he decided, would be the most suitable for Greece, being at the same time democratic, republican, and unmilitaristic. For national defence, he suggested an army on the Swiss pattern was all that was needed: 60,000 reservists, consisting of military academies, staff, artillery, engineers, infantry, and sharp-shooters, who would be exercised for one month only per year. Stanhope obtained books on the subject for sending to Greece. The system of control of public expenditure adopted by the Canton of Geneva would, he suggested, be easily transferred to Greek conditions—again books were obtained. Books were also obtained on the legal system of Geneva, 'the nearest approximation to the system of Bentham that has yet been accomplished'. The cultivation of the silk worm should, he suggested, be introduced in Greece; museums and record offices should be established; Greece could be used as a colony for settling British 'superfluous population'.

'I found the Committees very much irritated against the Capitani and the people of Greece', he wrote to Bowring. 'It was my business to show them that a people long enslaved could not be all virtuous.' Stanhope, with his touchingly optimistic view of human nature, believed that the captains could be induced to co-operate with his Benthamite policies if only he had the opportunity of talking to them. He was also ready to believe the suggestion that the captains would be persuaded to obey the Government 'by the latter acting virtuously and deserving the confidence of the people'.

The Societies had learnt something from their two painful years of abortive philhellenic efforts. They had learnt the hard way that the facts of Modern Greece did not fit easily with their own predilections. Unfortunately, it was not a lesson that Stanhope was prepared to accept, and the portmanteau of preconceptions which he carried with him was heavier than that of any German philhellenic professor.

In reading the streams of advice which he poured out on his journey across Europe it is difficult to remember that this man who knew all the answers had never been in Greece or within a thousand miles of the country at any time in his life.

18. *Arrivals at Missolonghi*

The internal Greek political scene into which the British Philhellenes had so confidently thrust themselves was, as usual, complex and the temptation for the newcomer to see the situation in Western terms was as strong as ever. The Italian revolutionaries who joined the Regiment Baleste in 1821 had paid the penalty for this mistake. The Philhellenes sponsored by the Germans and the Swiss did the same in 1822. The British were now to follow their example.

Since the early months of 1822 there had existed a Provisional Government of Greece (called 'Hellas') and its activities were extensively reported in the newspapers in Western Europe. The Greek Government appeared to have all the appurtenances of sovereignty. There were Secretaries of State and Ministers for this and that. There were legislative and executive councils, representative apparently of the different regions and classes of Greece. There was provision for elections both locally and for the great offices of state. On paper, Greece had all the features which marked a mature, liberally-governed, European nation-state.

In reality, Greece was at best a compromise of various forces. There were the primates whose jurisdiction was mainly a local territorial one, often derived from the Turkish period. There were the various island communities and especially the leaders of the islands of Hydra, Psara, and Spetsae which provided the warships. There were the captains whose authority derived from their ability to maintain bands of irregular soldiers or bandits. There was the church. And there were the Greeks who had received their ideas overseas and had returned to share the prizes at the birth of a new nation. These forces were to a great extent independent of one another when not actually mutually antagonistic. The pronouncements of the Provisional Government carried no authority although they made impressive reading abroad.

The various groups all had their own interests but there were more fundamental differences. No unanimity existed even about what was the purpose of the Revolution. Various theories had had their adherents in the early days: that it was a simple war of religious extermination; that it was an attempt to re-establish a Greek Empire by displacing the Turks from Constantinople; that it was a restoration of Ancient Hellas. Now in 1823, two years after the outbreak, there were only two views of the Revolution that could be taken seriously, but they were irreconcilable. The first view, held mainly by the primates and captains, was that Greece should consist of a number of semi-independent principalities, little different from the Turkish district organization, except that the Turks had been ejected. The second view, held mainly by the Greeks with Western education, was that Greece should be established as a European nation-state with a strong central government. At the time the deep divergence between these views was obscured since the adherents of one policy often found it prudent to pay lip-service to the principles of the other and to compromise when it seemed expedient. Other extraneous factors were forever intruding to conceal the starkness of the difference.

In 1823 the captains were in the ascendant all over the mainland. It was they who had won the great victories over the Turkish invaders in the campaign of 1822 while the Government of Mavrocordato and its Western methods had been discredited at Peta. In 1823 the Turks attempted again to invade Greece but a disastrous fire in the arsenal at Constantinople had ensured that it was a feeble effort. And so, two years after the massacres of the Turkish population in the Morea, the Greeks had begun to take their independence for granted. The country was still dotted with fortresses in Turkish hands; Greek independence had been recognized by no foreign government (except the 'sovereign' Knights of Malta); a Turkish fleet still roamed the Aegean; and the Ottoman Government remained determined to crush the rebels at whatever cost, believing that its own future as a great power depended upon it. Nevertheless, the energies of most of the Greek leaders were now devoted to the internal power struggle. The clashes of interests and the wide divergences between attitudes of mind, which had been half-concealed in 1821 and 1822, now made themselves more apparent.

A meeting of the principal revolutionary leaders had taken place near Nauplia in April 1823 and gone through the motions of appointing men to the offices of state. The great captains of the Morea, with their bands of armed men in attendance to act as bullies, dominated the proceedings. Petro Bey, the leader of the Mainotes, was declared President and Colocotrones Vice-President. The Westernized Greeks were squeezed out as were the islanders. Mavrocordato, nominally President of the Assembly, was almost lynched at one point and was forced to flee to Hydra. The meeting eventually split into two rival factions. On the one hand were the captains of the Morea and their temporary allies, the primates. On the other was a rival government, established on the mainland near Spetsae, consisting of virtually all the others, the islanders and the remains of the Westernized party and a few captains from outside the Morea. Neither government had any money nor had they any authority outside their own areas. The captains and the primates ensured that all revenues that could be collected and all booty seized were devoted to maintaining their private armed bands. Greece was on the verge of civil war.

It was into this complex situation that the British Philhellenes now precipitated themselves. But whereas in earlier episodes the Philhellenes had been largely thrown about like flotsam and jetsam on political movements which they barely understood, the new Philhellenes were themselves a political force in Greece reacting on the others. The cause of the change was money.

One can only guess at the promises which Edward Blaquiere made on his first visit to Greece in the spring of 1823. Whatever he said, his visit had a profound effect. Blaquiere was regarded probably as an agent of the British Government and, in any case, as the agent of a rich and powerful group of British politicians. For the first time there was now a real chance of obtaining money—money, the source of power from which all else derived. The proposed English loan dominated the Greek internal scene long before it was concluded. If money became available, the differences between the various groups in Greece became more important, perhaps more worth fighting over. It was at once obvious to the Greeks that the party which took possession of the English money would be well placed to impose its will on the others. It would be that party's view of the Revolution which would prevail.

Sadly, few of the British Philhellenes grasped this simple fact. They realized in a vague way that the prospect of money in the background increased their bargaining power and perhaps assured them of a better hearing than they might otherwise have received. But it was a long time before they realized that the money in the background was the only thing their audiences were interested in. They fondly continued to believe that the various Greek parties were genuinely interested in the political experiments which they wanted to introduce. Some carried their comforting illusions to their graves; for others the process of disenchantment was long and painful.

Lord Byron was the first to realize what was happening. He had experience enough of being a celebrity not to take too seriously the grosser forms of sycophancy, and his secretary Lega Zambelli administered his financial affairs so closely as to deter all but the most brazen spongers. But Byron had first another illusion to discard. When he arrived in the Ionian Islands he had expected to meet Blaquiere who had played such an important part in persuading him to go to Greece. He was mortified therefore to discover that Blaquiere had already set off back to England with hardly an explanation of the change of plan. Blaquiere's flattering letters apparently stopped as soon as he had gained the object in hand. The true explanation did occur to Byron that Blaquiere was anxious to return to England to promote his own publicity campaign and especially to rush into print with his hasty observations on Greek affairs. This discourtesy on the part of the representative of the London Greek Committee was a symptom that Byron could not ignore. The realization soon dawned that the London Greek Committee were not really interested in him at all but only in the publicity value of his name. Instead of giving him a leading role, preferably a military role, the Committee saw Byron's presence as merely ornamental. He had been decoyed to Greece.[1]

In the light of this realization, Byron decided to proceed cautiously— in particular not to rush into Greek affairs without spending a little time learning about the situation from outside. At the time, this decision was dismissed as a typical relapse into lassitude. There may be some truth in the charge but the fact stands out that Byron, almost alone of the Philhellenes of the Greek War of Independence, did not rely on an unspoken assumption of superiority in knowledge and in ability. He tried to inform himself about Greek conditions.

The British Resident in Cephalonia with whom Byron stayed for a while in the autumn of 1823 was a self-declared expert on Greece. Charles James Napier was one of the heroes of the high noon of Victorian imperialism and at his death rated a statue in Trafalgar Square. He is still remembered for his panache in annexing tracts of India with a Latin pun on his lips. During his period of service in the Ionian Islands Napier was well placed to observe the situation in Greece. He seems to have been genuinely sympathetic to the Greek cause and he published anonymously two pamphlets on the subject.[2] It is difficult to escape the suspicion, however, that he looked on the Greek struggle principally as a stage on which he himself might perform, an opportunity for winning the military glory for which he craved.

Napier's attitude to the waging of war was, as military men say, robust. He believed in discipline above all and had the greatest contempt for Greek guerrilla methods. Like most other professional soldiers who observed the Greek scene he believed that, if only he had a few hundred trained and disciplined men, there was nothing he could not accomplish. The remedy which he prescribed for the ills of Greece was the gallows. He boasted that if he were put in command of a Greek force the gallows would be his most

M

effective weapon; he would use it so frequently that the price of hemp would be raised by fifty per cent in ten days. The exemplary execution of discontents was a feature of the British policy of imposing the rule of law on the Ionian Islands. The policy was successful but for many Philhellenes the line of gibbets at Zante, the first sight that met their eyes when they reached Grecian lands, confirmed their beliefs about the barbarity and hypocrisy of the English.

Napier, the enthusiastic, energetic, confident, ambitious professional, impressed Byron as soon as he became used to his arrogant manner. After several long talks with him Byron decided that Napier was the man to lead the Greeks and that disciplined regular forces were the answer. Napier treated Byron like an honoured guest on the little island which he was covering with macadamized roads as a substitute for more violent soldiering. It was doubtfully legal for a servant of the Crown to give assistance to a man whose avowed object was to enlist in a foreign cause, and Napier made sure that lesser Philhellenes were moved on. Byron decided to give Napier a formal commendation to the London Greek Committee and Napier took leave to return to London. To his disgust he discovered that the Committee really cared little for Byron and his views, and so far from accepting his proposals for vigorous military measures, were, as he said, freighting a ship with water colours to promote the art of painting in a regenerated Greece.

During his stay in the Ionian Islands Byron had many opportunities of discovering that the situation in Greece was more complex than could have been gathered from newspaper reports in the West or from Blaquiere's letters. The news that a great and rich English milord was on his way to Greece spread rapidly throughout the country. Few Greeks had perhaps heard of Byron the poet but the news made a great impression. He was the first rich Philhellene to arrive since Gordon's short visit in 1821 and his coming seemed to presage not only access to his own wealth but the much talked about loan. The various Greek leaders flooded him with attentions. Mavrocordato, whom Byron knew from his earlier days in Italy, wanted him to give his help to the alliance between himself and the islanders at Hydra. Colocotrones asked him to lend his weight to the Greek Government which he led. Others bluntly asked for money. If he had not been aware of it before, Byron now realized that it was simplistic to think of a Greek Government and people fighting against the Turks. He decided to take his time and to try not to commit himself to one party or another. For once indolence was the right policy.

Byron came to the conclusion early that the best solution was to raise a substantial loan and he began to press this proposal in a series of letters to Bowring. Meanwhile he was prepared to play along with the Committee's plans, although he never seems to have had much confidence in the likelihood of their success. He himself began to spend a good deal of his time in sight-seeing, talking, enjoying himself and trying, half seriously and half mockingly, to see whether he could adapt himself to the role of a military commander.

Byron was still at Cephalonia in November when the energetic Stanhope bustled through on his way from Italy. Stanhope only stayed long enough to hold a few of his conferences and to remark on Byron's lack of drive before he rushed on to Greece. Byron decided reluctantly that the time for deliberation was over and that he must make the move to Greece. He left Cephalonia, largely in response to the persistent pressure from the London Greek Committee, far from sure that he was doing the right thing.

At the end of December 1823 the principal actors in the British attempt to regenerate Greece began to arrive at Missolonghi. Stanhope was the first. His behaviour was like that of an insensitive colonial governor sent out with a mandate to restore discipline to an unruly province. No sooner had he completed the ceremonies of introduction than he launched into a long formal lecture to his hosts—which must have lasted several hours if he really delivered it in full as he says—on his plans to help Greece, the establishment of regular forces, a free press, posts, hospitals, schools, the strategy of reducing Turkish fortresses, and much else besides; the whole discourse embellished with much moralizing and discussion of instructive parallels from ancient and modern history.

Lord Byron reached Missolonghi a fortnight after Stanhope and his welcome was compared at the time to the advent of the Messiah. Certainly he did not under-rate the importance of appearances and he enjoyed the theatricality of the occasion. In the end he did not put on one of his golden helmets but relied on his impressive scarlet military cloak. A twenty-one gun salute was fired and crowds of Greeks and Philhellenes cheered him ashore. It must have been one of the best moments of his life. Parry's expedition on which the London Committee had placed such hopes and on which they had expended three quarters of their total resources was the last to arrive. Parry and the artificers with the cargo of arms, stores for an arsenal, printing presses and educational supplies reached Greece early in February 1824. At last the work of regeneration could begin. Stanhope characteristically demanded that priority should be given to landing the printing apparatus. Byron characteristically remarked, without sneering, on the incongruity of a blacksmith landing in Greece with 322 Greek Testaments. The local Greeks characteristically were totally indifferent and uncooperative. The Greek Government led by Mavrocordato, characteristically, for all his protestations of welcome did not even have the authority to arrange for the unloading of the ship.

Missolonghi in 1824, as now, was an unattractive featureless town. It is built on an alluvial plain on the edge of a huge lagoon, too shallow for all but the smallest vessels except through one dredged channel. The lagoon, which is little more than a muddy salt marsh choked with weeds, abounds with fish and it is the fish no doubt which account for Missolonghi's existence, for it remains one of the most unhealthy places in Greece, situated in the middle of a mosquito swamp. Although it was the most important town in Western Greece, it had attracted little notice before the Revolution. Travellers from Western Europe seldom stayed longer than they had to, for the town had no classical associations. Byron and Hobhouse spent three days there in November 1809. In 1821 the Greeks of Missolonghi killed all the Turks; in 1822 the town successfully defended itself during a winter siege; in 1824 for a few short months it became the centre of the world's interest in Greece, and thereafter was the most famous town associated with the Greek War of Independence.

It is difficult to judge how the two appointed agents of the London Greek Committee regarded one another. Stanhope later published extensive reminiscences of his dealings with Lord Byron which successively give the impression that Byron was a lightweight; that nevertheless Stanhope had condescended to deal with him on equal terms; and finally (after Byron's death) that Stanhope was a trusted personal friend of the great poet. But Stanhope shamelessly edited his material to suit his own purposes. Byron made many remarks about the 'typographical Colonel', which range from the playful to the exasperated, but like many others, he could not help respecting Stanhope despite all his absurdities. Stanhope was an eccentric, there was no doubt, but not a buffoon.

Their first meeting in the Ionian Islands had not augured well. Byron asked Stanhope whether he had brought any new publications with him and Stanhope immediately mentioned Jeremy Bentham's *Springs of Action*. 'What does the old fool know of springs of action', Byron is reported to have shouted. 'My —— has more spring in it.'[3] On another occasion, a quarrel between the two resulted in Stanhope calling Byron a Turk, and Byron saying that Stanhope deserved to be cashiered from the Army. The two men could tolerate one another and occasionally co-operate, but nothing more.

From almost every aspect their characters were opposites. Byron was wise and politically aware but at the same time hopelessly indecisive and impractical. Stanhope was insensitive and naïve but nevertheless immensely energetic and unexpectedly effective. Byron saw the humour even in subjects which he regarded most seriously. Stanhope was humourless as only fanatics can be.

The two were yoked together as colleagues and it is surprising that they managed to co-operate at all in the difficult conditions in which they were thrown. Fortunately on one fundamental point they were agreed—that they must use their influence to try to reconcile the Greek factions, who had already begun to fight one another.

Stanhope's method was to write letters and deliver speeches to everyone of importance he could find, exhorting them to be patriotic. Byron, insofar as he felt able to do anything about the political situation, preferred simply to be patient in the hope that matters would turn out for the best. But the two men differed on more than method. Byron, although he was scrupulously careful to avoid the appearance of committing himself to one Greek party rather than another, was naturally sympathetic to the claims of Mavrocordato who, since the beginning of the Revolution, had always attracted the Philhellenes arriving in Greece. His urbane manners, his facility in Western European languages, his European dress, had all worked in his favour. As the leader of the Greeks who saw the future of Greece as a European nation-state with European political institutions, he was also the nearest approximation to the type of hero they wanted, if hardly the 'Washington of the Greeks' which a few tried to dub him.

But with the arrival of the British Philhellenes at the end of 1823 a curious paradox occurred. Many of the Philhellenes who followed Byron to Greece were steeped in the Grecian tales. Mavrocordato, a fattish bespectacled man in a frock coat speaking French more fluently than Greek hardly measured up to their idea of a Greek hero. But when they met Colocotrones with his Homeric helmet or Odysseus with a clutch of jewelled pistols in his girdle or any of the other captains with their gaudy clothes and Eastern habits, they were enraptured. Here, they decided, were the 'true Greeks' to be distinguished from the 'intriguing Phanariotes' of Constantinople such as Mavrocordato. The phrase 'intriguing Phanariotes' became on their lips almost as conventional as the 'rosy-fingered dawn' of the Odyssey, although few of the Philhellenes can have known what a Phanariote was.

The captains, knowing of the prospect of the loan and realizing that their own future hung on the decision how to spend it, suddenly and for the first time became polite to foreigners. During the first two years of the Revolution, out of the hundreds of Philhellenes who went to Greece, there is hardly a record of a single one who preferred the captains to the Europeanized Greeks. Now that the captains exercised a little charm and hospitality, new Philhellenes were prepared to believe that these violent, greedy, and barbarous warlords were the men most worthy of their support.

Stanhope was no romantic—at least not in the sense of being fascinated by ataghans, turbans, long beards, and violence—but his brand of naïveté was just as vulnerable. He was charmed by the oriental hospitality of the captains, by their patience, and apparent readiness to listen to his theories. With Mavrocordato and 'the Phanariotes', who regarded him as a bore, he had little sympathy, recognizing in them the type of politicians he was used to in England. Virtually no foreigners understood the motives and complexities of Greek politics. Romantics and dreamers cannot therefore be blamed too much for falling into the illusion of seeing in the Greeks the features which they wanted to see. But among all the manifestations of philhellenism it is difficult to imagine a less promising means of regenerating Greece than to divide it up and hand it over to the warlords.

19. *The Byron Brigade*

By his first ceremonial appearance at Missolonghi in his scarlet uniform Byron had indicated that he saw his role in Greece as a military one. Before he had left the Ionian Islands he had even set about hiring a private army. The Albanian Suliotes had been spared by the Turks after Mavrocordato's disastrous expedition into Epirus in 1822 on condition that they went into exile. Byron now engaged to pay them to return to Greece to fight again. Soon he had a force of several hundred wild undisciplined Albanians on his pay roll at Missolonghi although, as was pointed out, only a proportion were genuine Suliotes, the others being unashamedly mercenaries pursuing the only trade for which their nation has ever been distinguished.

Byron would go riding in the plain outside Missolonghi at the head of this motley army, no doubt imagining himself as a future conquering hero. The rest of the day he spent in a kind of military headquarters which he had set up in a house near the shore, holding long inconclusive conferences about military plans. The room was festooned with all kinds of weapons to give the proper atmosphere.

It was here on 22 January 1824 that he composed the strange untypical poem 'On this day I complete my thirty-sixth year', some of whose verses express so well the conflicting motives that had brought him to Greece:

> 'Tis time this heart should be unmoved,
>   Since others it hath ceased to move;
> Yet, though I cannot be beloved,
>   Still let me love!
>
> My days are in the yellow leaf;
>   The flowers and fruits of love are gone;
> The worm, the canker, and the grief
>   Are mine alone!

> If thou regret'st thy youth, *why live?*
>   The land of honourable death
> Is here:— up to the field, and give
>   Away thy breath!
>
> Seek out—less often sought than found,
>   A soldier's grave—for thee the best;
> Then look around, and choose thy ground,
>   And take thy rest.

Byron's military plan seems to have been that Napier or Gordon or some other British professional soldier should take command of the Suliotes, of the Philhellenes in Greece, and of the artillery sent with Parry, and attack the fortresses still in Turkish hands—in particular Naupactus, Patras, and the Castles of Roumeli and the Morea. As philhellenic schemes went it was perhaps more promising than most, but that is to say little. As it was, the scheme never made any progress, for all the constitutent parts turned out to be failures.

Byron, like Stanhope, believed when he arrived in Missolonghi that the German Legion was still operating in the Morea. In his conversations with Napier in the Ionian Islands there had been talk of taking command of 'the corps of 200 Germans'. One of the first tasks therefore was to send Kolbe to Nauplia to tell the Legion that, although he had obtained money at Darmstadt to pay for their return, it was the wish of the Societies that they should go to Missolonghi and join the efforts of the British Philhellenes.

Kolbe returned to Missolonghi on 14 January with the news that out of the hundreds of Germans who had come to Greece in 1822, including the 115 or so men of the German Legion, only twenty-six remained. All the rest had set off for home or had died. The British Philhellenes watched with horror as the survivors straggled into Missolonghi, drawn and debilitated by a year of disappointment, starvation, disease, grief, and despair. Most of these men were only too glad to have the chance of going home but a few elected to stay. In addition a steady stream of new Philhellenes had begun to appear, attracted to Greece by the news of Lord Byron's expedition. Byron decided to provide pay for any officer who appeared with the object of building up a cadre on which a Greek regular force could be based. The news had an electrifying effect. Men began to appear from elsewhere in Greece, from the Ionian Islands, and from Western Europe anxious for commissions in Lord Byron's brigade. All roads led to Missolonghi. Almost all the Europeans who were still at large in Greece arrived to enjoy the hitherto unknown sensation of being paid.

Ten Germans who had been in Greece for two years became a personal bodyguard.[1] And, as Count Gamba records, every day there were offers of service from some foreigner or other. 'Thus we had them of all nations— English, Scotch, Irish, Americans, Germans, Swiss, Belgians, Russians,

Swedes, Danes, Hungarians and Italians. We were a sort of crusade in miniature.'[2] For a few weeks the atmosphere resembled that in Corinth in May 1822 when the original Battalion of Philhellenes was being formed. Life was pleasant and undemanding; food and wine were cheap and the comradeship good; there were next to no duties. But there were few links with 1822. A whole generation of Philhellenes had come and gone since then and only a few remained. The unabashed Baron Friedel von Friedelsburg was still wandering round with his lithographic press on his back, still impressing nobody (but charming everybody) with his fantastic claims to nobility and importance. There were a few men who had come in the early expeditions from Marseilles: Meyer a Swiss pharmacist who had married a Greek, Treiber a German doctor who had been at Peta, Komarones a Hungarian exile (now called Cameron), Bellier de Launay still posing as a Marquis, the younger Fels, a Saxon, who had come to avenge his brother killed at Peta, Jarvis, the rough American from Hamburg. There were also von Dittmar, who had led the sedition of the German Legion against Kephalas, and Humphreys, who had been with Gordon at the fall of Tripolitsa in October 1821 and was now again in Greece seeking an antidote to boredom.

Adolph von Sass,[3] a Swede, had had a remarkable history. He was one of that large class from whom many Philhellenes were drawn, men who had served in the Napoleonic wars long enough to realize that they were talented soldiers and then were suddenly dismissed at the coming of peace. Since soldiering was the only trade he knew, he had come to Greece as a volunteer in one of the expeditions from Marseilles in 1822 and had for a time joined the German Legion. But when the Legion broke up, Sass like so many others, tried to make his way home across the islands of the Aegean. A fellow Philhellene saw him in the Frank hospital at Smyrna. When he recovered he set out for Crete but the vessel in which he had taken passage was captured by the Turks. Sass was beaten and tortured and subjected to the usual unspecified because unmentionable Eastern insults. He was taken to Cairo and sold as a slave but was ransomed by an English traveller who also gave him money to go home. But no sooner did he reach Sweden than he hastened to London where he was given a letter of commendation and passage money to return to Greece.

Of the British who had arrived in Greece,[4] most of whom were now congregating at Missolonghi, a few names are known: Blackett, Hyler, Lypton, Hesketh, Tindall, Whitcombe, Winter, Hamilton Browne, Trelawny, Finlay, Millingen. Some are little more than names but it is clear that they included the usual soldiers of fortune and retired officers in search of employment, familiar from earlier periods. But enough can be pieced together to show that a new species of Philhellene had now made its appearance in Greece which was to become increasingly common in

1824 and 1825—the romantic Byronist. Men began to make their way to Greece as a direct result of hearing that Byron had gone there. They were romantics, but most Philhellenes had a touch of romanticism in them. The feature which distinguished this new species was that their main impetus came from reading Byron's poetry, the poetry which Byron himself no longer composed or admired. They were thus more Byronic than Byron, trying to find in Greece the exoticism which they loved, thinking they were copying Byron but actually behaving in a way which Byron himself never did.

Edward John Trelawny who had come with Byron from Genoa represented the extreme of this type of philhellenism. It is difficult to avoid the feeling in looking at some periods of his long and flamboyant career that he was simply a sycophantic liar of small talent who liked the company of the famous. In Greece he saw himself in the role of one of the heroes of Byron's tales to whom the prospect of violence and sensuality in oriental surroundings seemed justification enough for going to war.

A more complex character was George Finlay who set out for Greece as soon as he heard that Byron was going. Finlay was a romantic through and through and the papers about his early days are full of Byronic sentiments, some in Byronic verse, about 'the cause of freedom', 'heroes and deeds like Leonidas and Salamis', and 'eternal glory'. To his dying day Finlay was immensely proud that he had met Byron and conversed with him and that Byron had remarked on how he resembled the young Shelley. But as he became aware of the true situation in Greece, Finlay began to be ashamed of his romanticism. He fought against this strange force in his character with ever greater vigour until, by the end of his life, Finlay chose to appear crusty and cynical rather than tolerate even a suspicion that he sympathized with romantic philhellenism. Finlay's philhellenism developed in a way which Byron's might if he had lived. After a short initial romantic phase he somehow combined an apparent contempt for the Greeks with an over-powering interest in everything about them. Having quickly shed all his youthful illusions, he nevertheless devoted the remainder of his long life to Greece and to writing its history.

The romantic Byronists—as I have called them—were on the whole much more interested in playing a theatrical role than in fighting the Turks. And since the captains were now being exceedingly polite and attentive to foreigners, particularly English, it was possible to enjoy the sensation of being a Philhellene while being in reality a tourist.* We now find British volunteers appearing in Greece who reverted to the role of travelling gentlemen (entitled to protection from the Turks as soon as there was any prospect of danger). Others were more journalists than soldiers. The Phil-

---

* Finlay says (1824) that it was safer to ride from Athens to Missolonghi than from London to Edinburgh.

hellenes of 1821 and 1822, whose love of fighting was a chief motivation, would have despised their lack of enthusiasm. Nevertheless, to maintain one's beliefs and enjoy the sensation of being a romantic Byronist in the stark conditions of Greece—even without fighting—was a taxing business. Since a large measure of imagination was required even to go to Greece, some added a dash more and invented their philhellenic adventures after a quick trip into Greece from the safety of the Ionian Islands, or after a few trips ashore from the comfort of a British warship. The logical conclusion of romantic Byronism was of course not to bother to go to Greece at all but to supply the whole sensation from imagination. Edgar Allan Poe,[5] a fervent admirer of Byron, is the most famous of this last group. Despite his attempts to put about the story that he set out 'without a dollar on a quixotic expedition to join the Greeks then struggling for liberty', it is known that he got no nearer than Boston, Massachusetts.*

All the hopes of the Philhellenes of Lord Byron's Brigade, old and new, were centred on the expedition which had been dispatched by the London Greek Committee. William Parry with his artificers, his cannon, his gunpowder and his equipment for building an arsenal arrived amid great excitement in February 1824. Poor Parry suffered from overbilling. He had been a competent technician in Woolwich arsenal and Deptford dockyard and, as such, he had been selected by Gordon. But during the long interval between his announced departure from London and his arrival in Greece his reputation grew. He was credited with powers given to no man. He was the inventor of the Congreve rocket, he was a genius with artillery, he would provide the 'infernal fires' with which Byron, the Suliotes, and the Byron Brigade would batter down the Turkish fortresses. Much of this was simply Byron's habitual banter and exaggeration but many seem to have believed it.

The man who arrived in command of the London Committee's long-awaited expedition was hardly the type they expected. First of all he was a civilian but he was also unashamedly not a gentleman. He was blunt, uneducated, only partially literate, violent of temper, and overfond of strong spirits. Even so, he seems to have had more commonsense than all the sophisticated characters who were at Missolonghi in early 1824. Reading the numerous accounts of these exciting days one sometimes gets the impression that Parry was the only normal man among dozens of neurotics, men smothered in humbug and men desperately trying to find a compensation in philhellenism for some psychological inadequacy.

As so often in the past, the Philhellenes surrounding Byron who composed the Byron Brigade were not quite what they claimed. Of the four who boasted titles—Friedel, Bellier de Launay, Gilman, and Quass—perhaps

* Poe himself says that he failed to reach Greece but went to St. Petersburg. This is also imaginary.

not one was genuine. Trelawny's stories about his past life contained more fantasy than truth. Hamilton Brown claimed to have been dismissed from a post in the Ionian Islands for his philhellenic sympathies but had in fact committed the serious offence of passing official information to a member of the Opposition in Parliament.[6] 'Doctor' Meyer had been expelled from university before graduating. And, as so often in the past, dignity and honour were words always on their lips. Duels were arranged on abstruse points of protocol. Many of the Philhellenes, including von Dittmar and Finlay, refused to serve under Parry. When Kindermann, a Prussian officer, came to Byron to give up his commission Byron tried to dissuade him. 'He joked him not a little on the quarterings of his German escutcheon, and on the folly of introducing his prejudices into a country like Greece', but to no avail. Byron himself, of course, although an untypical Philhellene in some ways, was also distinguished by his punctilious sense of rank.

Among the strange international concourse of vain, prickly, and unbalanced men who formed the Byron Brigade, Lord Byron and William Parry struck up an unusual but sincere friendship. To the disgust of the well-bred officers and the romantic Byronists, Byron himself preferred the company and advice of the coarse artisan. The two men enjoyed one another's company, they found they could laugh together at the cant and hypocrisy with which they were surrounded. Parry's past is obscure and, as with his comrades in the Byron Brigade, his claims to have done this or that do not bear too close an examination. But there was no doubt that he had knocked about a bit and he could tell stories of a way of life from which Byron had been totally shut off. He also had a fund of droll anecdotes about his experiences with Jeremy Bentham and the members of the London Greek Committee when the expedition was being prepared. The *rapport* between Lord Byron and Captain (subsequently Major) Parry, the military Commander of the Byron Brigade, was perfect; but it did not advance the cause. Byron began to take Parry's advice on virtually everything, treating him as his chief military adviser. Parry as a result became even more conceited than he was before. He did not deliberately 'humbug' Byron—to use a favourite expression of the disgruntled Philhellenes—but he began to fancy himself in a role which the social conventions of the time could not tolerate. He referred to the officers of the Brigade as 'my officers' and began to refer to Lord Byron himself as 'my noble friend and protector'. Such pretensions to social equality on the part of a dockyard matie were an affront that could not be borne.

The energy expended in taking umbrage at Parry's vulgarity obscured a more important aspect of the situation. From a practical point of view he was a failure. The expedition, shorn of its main constituent by the decision to accept only part of Gordon's plan, never had much prospect of success in Greek conditions. What was to be expected, as often happens, did in fact occur. Parry himself seems to have made an effort to set up the arsenal and to drill the men, and the artificers worked hard enough for a while. But most of the Philhellenes thought it beneath their dignity to help in any such menial tasks and the Greeks absolutely refused to be disciplined. The Congreve rockets could not be used since the coal needed to fire them had not arrived.

The situation deteriorated and there was little that Byron could do to arrest the decline. The Suliotes became more and more unruly, mutinying for more pay. The disputes among the foreigners worsened. On several occasions shots were fired. Parry and Humphreys were both shot at. Lord Byron's life was threatened. One of the artificers was hit by a shot in the head and was accidentally saved by his hat. The arsenal had to be guarded to prevent it being pillaged by the Greeks and Suliotes. On 19 February an argument broke out between a Suliote and Sass, the Swedish officer, who was then on guard. Blows were exchanged and Sass was fatally wounded. He remained alive for an hour with a shot in the head and one arm almost severed from his body. The man who had endured disease, humiliation, slavery, and then had returned to Greece to try again, came to an ignominious end, killed in a brawl with one of the modern Spartiates, never having had an opportunity of serving the cause in any useful way.

After Sass's death all hope of building a credible military force at Missolonghi had finally to be abandoned. The artificers, who were (with every justification) afraid for their lives, demanded to be sent to the safety of the Ionian Islands and they were allowed to go. Parry himself and three others of the expedition remained to act as custodians of the stores. For a while there seemed to be a danger that Missolonghi would be entered and sacked by the Suliotes themselves and the guns which the London Committee had sent for use against the Turks, saw their first service in threatening the followers of the already legendary Marco Botsaris, the 'Leonidas' of Modern Greece so beloved by the pamphleteers. Shortly afterwards a mutiny broke out among the 'etiquette-soldiers', as Parry called the Germans who resented his elevation.

And so the expedition on which the London Greek Committee had placed such hopes disintegrated just as the German Legion had done a year earlier. Neither the prestige nor the money of Lord Byron could make up for the indifference of the Greeks and the quarrelsomeness of the Philhellenes, the two factors which had ruined all previous European attempts to help the Greeks. Like the German Legion, the Byron Brigade found that the only thing which the Greeks wanted from them was their stores. A stream of messengers arrived from various chieftains asking for a share of the cannon and gunpowder and other stores in the arsenal.

In retrospect, the death of Lord Byron in Missolonghi in April 1824 (like that of General Normann in the same town in 1822) seems to have a certain inevitability. In February Byron had suffered an epileptic fit and he seems never to have properly recovered. The combination of an unhealthy climate and an unhealthy diet brought on his last illness. The doctors finished him off, four or five of them vying with one another to apply more and more extreme bleeding. Among his delirious chattering as the end approached, his famous last words were thought to be 'Poor Greece'.

Six days after Byron's death an English merchant vessel, the *Florida*, arrived at Zante in the Ionian Islands. She had on board Edward Blaquiere with 30,000 English gold sovereigns and 50,000 Spanish silver dollars. The first instalment of the loan had arrived. At last Greece seemed to be about to receive the one thing which she wanted from European philhellenism—and enough of it to satisfy the most rapacious captain or ambitious Phanariote. The *Florida* turned round at Zante and conveyed the body of Lord Byron and the members of his party back to England. A few weeks later another vessel, the *Little Sally*, arrived with another 40,000 gold sovereigns, the second instalment of the loan.

The circumstances in which this money was obtained in England will be described in a later chapter. Here it is enough to mention that, under the contracts by which the first two instalments were sent to Greece, Lord Byron was (with Stanhope) named as one of the commissioners. It was stipulated that the money could not be handed over to the Greeks without his consent. Byron was dead and it was discovered that there was no provision for appointing a new commissioner without reference to London. The money had therefore to be put into a bank in Zante to await further instructions. The various Greek factions burned with frustration to see this vast wealth which was clearly intended for Greece locked up in Zante, only a few miles away but as inaccessible as if it had been in the vaults of the Bank of England.

It is usual at this point in the story of the Greek War of Independence to speculate on what might have happened if Byron had lived. Could he have used his personal influence and the influence of the vast English gold which he would have controlled to reconcile the Greek factions and to co-ordinate their efforts against the Turks? Could he even have become King or President of Greece as was rumoured at the time? At the very least, could he have prevented the civil war which began to spread over most of free Greece at about the time of his death? The questions are of course unanswerable, but the balance of probability is that Byron could have done none of these things. To imagine that any foreigner, however eminent and however respected, could have found a means of reconciling the political divisions of Greece is to fall into the philhellenic trap of underestimating these divisions, to see them in Western European terms as a kind of party politics conducted within a system where everyone's loyalty to the nation state can be assumed to override his loyalty to his particular interest group. Byron himself appreciated this fact more than most of his fellow Philhellenes, but it is difficult to imagine how he could have escaped further humiliating anticlimax whatever he chose to do. Even the greatest Philhellene could not have escaped the fact that the bases of philhellenism, numerous though they were, were almost all unsound.

With the death of the leader, the dissipation of their stores, and the ending of their pay, the Byron Brigade did not long survive, although the German Stitzelberger was appointed to take command in Byron's place. The resemblance to the fate of the German Legion became more and more evident to anyone who had the eyes to see it. Several Philhellenes decided to leave Greece altogether. Others drifted off to try their luck elsewhere. Two members of the Brigade, Jacobi and 'Baron' Gilman, were killed at the destruction of Psara in July 1824. Many, like Byron, simply succumbed to the strains of living in Greece. Parry went mad for a time after Byron's death and, although he later recovered, he finished his life in a lunatic asylum. Gill, one of the foremen who had come with Parry and had stayed in Greece to guard the stores, died of disease. One of the doctors, Forli, who attended Byron during his last illness died himself of disease at Missolonghi a few weeks later. The 'etiquette-soldier' Kinderman died of disease during the summer, as did the young Fels who had come back to Greece to avenge the twin brother he had lost at Peta. Dr. Bojons of Württemberg died in November. Two of the British volunteers who had refused to serve under Parry—Blackett and Winter—committed suicide during 1824. A Scottish volunteer, Fenton, who had come from Spain expressly to join Byron's Brigade was shot dead by a fellow Philhellene.*

Within a few months there were in Greece only a handful of survivors out of the proud Byron Brigade which at one time had contained about fifty Philhellenes. But the flow of new volunteers which had started again in mid-1823 with the news of Byron's intention to go to Greece was not stopped by the news of his death. From all over Europe, and increasingly from the United States, men set out on the long journey to Greece. Frellsen,[7] a Dane from Holstein, is said to have bought a gunboat as soon as he reached his majority and sailed to join Lord Byron. Two Hungarian musicians called Mangel,[8] father and son, arrived at Missolonghi thinking they might find a market for their talents. A Saxon diplomat, Meissel,[9] who had been purged from the foreign service for his liberal opinions, offered to teach international law but he died at Missolonghi shortly after his arrival. The year 1824 saw the deaths of more Philhellenes, in proportion to the number then in Greece, than any other of the war.

Lord Charles Murray,[10] a son of the Duke of Atholl, arrived at Missolonghi

* See pp. 239 f.

a few weeks after Byron's death. As he was rich and well connected there was some hope that he might in some way take Byron's place. He had been a travelling gentleman but had decided to become a Philhellene on reaching Greece. Few people knew that he had recently escaped from a private lunatic asylum in England. He translated a work on military fortification into Modern Greek and paid for a battery to be built at Missolonghi out of his own pocket, but by August 1824 he too was dead of disease brought on by sunstroke.

Three volunteers were sent by the London Committee in August 1824, Kahl and Müller, Germans, and Weller, an Englishman.[11] The two Germans died shortly after their arrival in Greece. Von Specht, an officer from Brunswick who had been with the Regiment Tarella at Peta and had then been disgraced for killing a fellow Philhellene in a duel,[12] finally succumbed to want and disease at Nauplia in October. Von Gruben,[13] a Prussian, committed suicide there in November. A romantic Englishman,[14] name unknown, who left his studies at Cambridge to join the Greeks, was also found in a dying state in October in the streets of Nauplia.

In August 1825 the British colony at Smyrna arranged for the funeral of another young Philhellene called Wright who had arrived on a warship in the last stages of emaciation.[15] The story of his adventures was told by his companion. Wright, the son of a rich gentleman in Dublin, had been a medical student. Next to the hospital where he attended lectures was the garden of a private mental hospital. One day Wright heard a girl singing in the garden and was so entranced that he climbed over the wall to talk to her. He repeated this exploit every day, and to his astonishment and delight the girl's sanity gradually returned. He fell deeply in love, but when the girl's sanity returned her memory faded and she remembered nothing of her affection for Wright. Soon she married someone else. Wright abandoned himself to melancholy, tried to break himself free by travel, but no novelty could soothe his aching heart.

> At length he joined the cause of the struggling Greeks and his name has been often and honourably mentioned amongst the companions of Lord Byron at Missolonghi. After his Lordship's death he still remained in Greece but his constitution was too weak to permit him to be of active service as a Palikari. He had, therefore, taken a post in the garrison which held possession of the castle and town of Navarino, in the Morea, and was wounded in the action at Sphacteria in the summer of 1825.

In fact Wright did not arrive in Greece until June 1825, nearly fourteen months after the death of Lord Byron, and during the few weeks he had actually spent in Greece he had been exposed both for exaggerating the time he had been in the country and for fraudulently assuming the rank of Colonel. We may therefore doubt the rest of the story. But, pathetic figure

Lord Byron attended by his Suliote guards.

8a Lord Byron and his suite riding outside Missolonghi, attended by his Suliotes

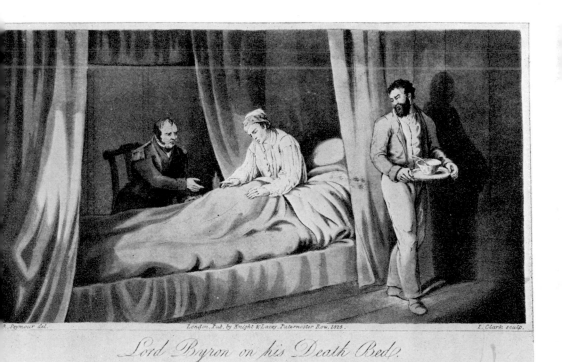

Lord Byron on his Death Bed.

b Lord Byron on his death bed. The figure at the bedside is William Parry

9 A Contemporary Cartoon on the Scandal of the Greek Loan. The figures represented are, left to right

though he is, Wright's fault was presumably merely to cross too blatantly the line between reality and fantasy around which so many of his comrades hovered. Philhellenism claimed its victims in unusual ways but destroyed them nonetheless.

But nobody was much interested in the fate of the Byron Brigade. Even in death Lord Byron himself monopolized attention. He at once entered the Pantheon of heroes of Modern Greece from which he has never been displaced. This was more than the well-known Greek characteristic of honouring a man more when he is dead than when he is alive. The British public, too, began to feel a nagging shame at the way in which Byron had been driven to leave England in a burst of cant and intolerance which foreshadowed the least attractive features of the Victorian era. After his death, the vile seducer and dangerous atheist became in the eyes of his detractors 'that celebrated, that talented, that erring nobleman, Lord Byron'.[16] Suddenly it was universally realized that he had been one of the most remarkable men of his time.

A flood of biographies appeared. Casual acquaintances rushed into print subtly trying to give the impression that they were among Byron's best friends. Hack writers were commissioned to produce biographical compilations from old press articles and from rival works. Literary men and aspirant arbiters of taste turned out elegant essays on the genius of the great departed. Byron's family and friends embarked on an attempt to control his posthumous reputation which was to tax their energies for fifty years.[17]

Within a few months of Byron's death several Philhellenes had attempted to cash in on the insatiable public demand. Gamba, Parry, Stanhope, and Blaquiere all produced books in 1825 based on their experiences in Greece which managed to drag the name of Lord Byron on to the title page. In the same year the dead Byron even enjoyed the ultimate flattery of having a three-volume life written (and invented) about him by an entirely fictitious 'English Gentleman in the Greek Military Service and Comrade of His Lordship'.[18] Every detail of the few weeks that Byron spent at Missolonghi was rehearsed and fought over in print. Stanhope brought a lawsuit against Parry in 1827. Even Doctor Millingen, who had helped to bleed Byron to death and who had subsequently joined the Turkish side, described himself in his book as 'Surgeon to the Byron Brigade at Mesolonghi'.

But, despite the plethora of biographical material, the myth of Lord Byron's death quickly obscured the reality. Byron became by his death the hero he would never have been if he had lived. The glory of his failure had a sweetness which could not have come from success. As the nineteenth century progressed, Byron became one of the cult figures of the romantic revolutionaries, the finest example of the union of thought and action, of art and politics. His example seemed to give respectability to national revolution in its most violent form and many a political scribbler advocating assassination and many a terrorist hurling his bombs felt he was partaking in a proud tradition. Byron, by his death, unwittingly played a part in promoting nationalism to the position (long held by religion) of being the most divisive and destructive element in Western civilization.

20. *Essays in Regeneration*

W hile Lord Byron was attempting to establish a military force at Missolonghi, the other agent of the London Greek Committee, Colonel Stanhope, continued to play his self-appointed role of the apostle of utilitarianism. The dogmatic self-assurance which had enabled him to impress and overawe the vastly more experienced Philhellenes of the Swiss and German Societies continued to be his principal strength. The reality of Greek conditions did not daunt him and it is to Stanhope that perhaps belongs the doubtful credit of being the only man who went to Greece during the war whose political ideas were not modified by the experience.

For Stanhope, his work in Greece was much the same as his work in India and his attitude was the mixture of tolerance and didacticism proper to a colonial trustee unashamedly representing a superior civilization. Yet even for Stanhope there remained the traces of philhellenic notions about the Ancient and Modern Greeks and the dreaded Moslems.

'It is my practice when natives visit me', he wrote to Bowring in a typical report, 'to draw their attention to those points which are most essential to their welfare, and to put the matter in a point of view that will interest them and set their minds in labour. For example, if I wish to recommend military discipline to them, I speak of the combined operations and close order observed by their ancestors in their arrays: speaking of education I lament that their Turkish masters should have deprived their children of the means of acquiring that knowledge which their great forefathers so eminently possessed.'

Stanhope's first concern on his arrival in Missolonghi was to establish a newspaper. Even before the *Ann* carrying Parry and the military stores had reached Greece, Stanhope was sending impatient letters demanding that first priority should be given to landing the printing presses. Within a few days he had set up the press, engaged the Swiss chemist Meyer to act as editor, and prepared to issue the prospectus. The newspaper was called the *Greek Chronicle* and its motto was the famous utilitarian slogan 'The greatest happiness of the greatest number'.

Not everyone was so certain that it was right to establish a newspaper, a thing unknown in Greece. Demetrius Hypsilantes had employed a press for a time at Calamata in 1821 to help promulgate his pronouncements and the Provisional Government had a press for printing its decrees and laws; but never before had there been an attempt to publish news and comment. The benefits which Stanhope foresaw seemed to prerequire a totally different set of conditions if they were to come to fruition. The creation of an informed public opinion and the encouragement of open and knowledgeable discussion of political matters were no doubt worthwhile aims, but could they be achieved by a single press controlled by foreigners and totally committed to a particular set of policies? As Byron was to point out when he arrived, in giving political judgements it is necessary to praise some men and censure others. In Greece men who felt they were insulted by word had the habit of replying by deed. So far from creating political unity the newspaper might encourage divisiveness and violence. And then only a small proportion of the Greek population could read. The newspaper was bound to find most of its readership abroad and in countries which were looking for excuses to condemn the Greek rebels.

When Mavrocordato's secretary, a Frenchman called Grasset, put some of these points to Stanhope he responded by invoking the dogma of the freedom of the press. 'Sophistry would not do', he reported to Bowring, 'from one who was slily acting as censor over the press, and attempting to suppress the thoughts of the finest genius of the most enlightened age— the thoughts of the immortal Bentham.' Stanhope gave Grasset several scoldings using a 'high and sturdy tone'; demanded whether he wanted to set up an inquisition in Greece; declared that he would set up another newspaper in the Morea and expose the whole affair; and reminded Grasset that no man's reputation would be safe without a free press.

Stanhope was the official representative of the British Philhellenes. He not only had money to dispose immediately on his own account and on that of the Committee, but also held out hopes of the fabled loan. For these reasons he was allowed to have his way. The first numbers of the *Greek Chronicle* of Missolonghi began to appear in January 1824. The first experiment in practical Benthamism had been successfully launched.

The early issues were largely taken up with extracts from the works of the great Jeremy and messages of good will from this or that well-wisher. But the tone and style of the paper, as it settled down to regular publication, were hardly in accordance with the best ideals of a free press. The so-called news which it printed was unscrupulously biased, and even invented, so that the smallest skirmishes with the Turks were represented as great and decisive battles. The comment was partisan and often libellous. When Byron arrived at Missolonghi he tried to use his influence to tone down the more offensive passages, and especially to prevent the newspaper from being used for gratuitous attacks on the policies of the great European powers. He insisted on the suppression of one issue which spoke with favour of the separatist movement in Hungary. Meyer, the editor, as his connection with Stanhope developed, became more radical in his views and seemed about to provide the evidence, which some of the powers had always wanted, that the Greek Revolution was inspired by the same liberals and even the same men as the revolutions in Italy and Spain.

Stanhope was never troubled by doubt. Newspapers were good in themselves whatever they printed. Soon afterwards a second newspaper, *The Greek Telegraph*, most of whose articles were in Italian, was established at Missolonghi. It too had a Benthamite motto, 'The world our country, and doing good our religion', but this generous sentiment proved to be obnoxious to the Methodist members of the London Greek Committee and a protest was lodged. With the establishment of *The Telegraph*, the unsalubrious unknown fishing town in Western Greece had more news-papers than the whole of the Ottoman Empire.

In April Stanhope established a third newspaper, *The Athens Free Press*, or *Ephemerides of Athens*, with the motto 'Publicity is the Soul of Justice'. At Hydra was established *The Friend of the Law*. For a few months Greece had four newspapers all proclaiming the virtues of free discussion, the need to keep public officials under scrutiny, the dangers of disunity, and the benefits of education. It was an astonishing achievement and, in the opinion of the best judges,[1] the experiment did more good than harm. But the newspapers throughout their life were regarded by the majority of the Greeks as playthings of the Philhellenes and they never put down roots or lost their connection with the foreigners. Once the subsidies ran out they all ceased publication.

Stanhope's absolute priority was the establishment of a newspaper but, as soon as the *Greek Chronicle* was appearing regularly, he turned his atten-tion and energy to other utilitarian projects. His method was to address long letters of advice to the multifarious authorities then operating in Greece and to back up his recommendations with judicious offers of money. As always his self-assurance was his strongest weapon. The Greeks had never met a man who had such a scant regard for difficulties, who apparently was not deterred from his plans by the fact that the country was still at war with the Turks and at the same time in the midst of a civil war; that there was no government with other than local power and that a large proportion of the people were quickly sinking towards misery. Stanhope for his part thought that with money he could accomplish anything. 'For £200 I can set the press to work', he wrote to the London Greek Committee, 'for £100 I can establish a post across the Morea; for £500 I could put a force in movement that would take Patras, Lepanto, and the Castles [of Roumeli and the Morea] which would free Greece.'

In pursuit of his conviction that 'in all countries the quick circulation of ideas must be conducive to the public good, but more especially so in a free and commercial state', Stanhope offered to set up and operate a postal service at his own expense. Clerks were to set up offices at the main towns, accounts were to be kept and submitted each month to headquarters. Every detail was laid down, including rates to be charged, the pay of the officials, the schedule of the service. It was even ordained that the runners were to run at five miles an hour and to perform twenty miles daily.

Education of the young was also to be started. Stanhope believed on his arrival in Greece that there were no schools at all and he was not far mistaken. A crash programme was therefore called for. It was natural that he should try to solve the problem by setting up 'Lancastrian' schools on the lines that had already been tried with some success in the Ionian Islands. 'Lancastrian' schools were schools run according to the theories of Joseph Lancaster, a prominent educational theorist of the day. The basic principle was that a small number of teachers would teach the elder pupils and they in their turn would teach the younger pupils. According to this principle, a poor community which was unable to afford the expense of a conventional school might acquire the rudiments of education. Stanhope was instrumental in setting up a number of Lancastrian schools in Greece, using the London Committee's money to help pay the wages of the schoolmaster and to buy schoolbooks. In the extreme conditions of Greece the principles on which the Lancastrian system worked had to be further diluted and sometimes boys sent to a central Lancastrian school were expected to return to their village and educate their comrades there.

A few selected Greek boys were sent to England to be educated at the expense of the London Greek Committee and of the Quakers mainly at the Lancastrian school in Lambeth. Jeremy Bentham contracted to pay the expenses of two boys out of his own pocket. It was intended that these boys should return to Greece as schoolmasters. 'We should,' declared one of the Greek newspapers in an anonymous article inspired and drafted by Stanhope, 'endeavour to obtain the offspring of parents who have been prominent in rescuing Greece from the Satanical rule of the Turks, and have been firm in promoting her liberties; . . . . We felicitate our countrymen [the Greeks] on having such a friend as Bentham. . . . He is the greatest civilian of this, or perhaps, of any age, and is renowned all over the world as a great public benefactor.' Altogether about twenty Greeks were sent to England for education in 1824 and 1825.

Stanhope also brought to England a Turkish boy of about nine or ten years old who was found prowling naked among the ruins of Argos, 'kicked or fondled as caprice dictated' until he was rescued by a Philhellene. His parents and family and the whole Turkish community had, as Stanhope put it, fallen 'victims to the fury of the enfranchised Greeks'. The boy, Mustapha Ali, was sent to the Lancastrian school in Lambeth where he was said to have earned his card of merit every day. He was dressed in Turkish dress complete with pistols and turban, although he hated to be called Turk and hated his name. He was said to have been 'very fond of dancing which he performs in a manner resembling that of the Ancient Greeks, deviating only by firing off his pistols while he twirls'.

A dispensary was set up at Missolonghi. The doctors sent out by the Committee were given a building and charge of the medicines brought in the *Ann*. A fee was paid if the patient could afford it but not otherwise. Stanhope reckoned that such dispensaries could be set up in other Greek towns at the trifling cost of £40 plus one foreign doctor.

Economic development, a subject in which the Benthamites were pioneers, was also to be encouraged. Stanhope sent home statistics of costs in Greece to try to encourage emigration from England. Land yielded ten per cent, he declared, a man could be hired for the equivalent of $7\frac{1}{2}$ pence per day, a woman for 5 pence, and a boy for $2\frac{1}{2}$ pence. Proposals were made for introducing more efficient agricultural methods. There was even a scheme for issuing a new coinage to replace the debased coins of many countries which circulated in the Eastern Mediterranean. According to the most advanced theories of the day in England, it was to be arranged on decimal principles.

In reading the reports to London, one gets the impression that Colonel Stanhope almost single-handed with only a few hundred pounds at his disposal accomplished more in a few months than the combined philhellenic activities of all nations hitherto. Even when one makes allowance for the fact that many of his schemes never came to anything or were soon abandoned, the record of his success is impressive, and in stark contrast to the abortive efforts of Lord Byron to form a military force at Missolonghi. Stanhope was eccentric, priggish, naïve, and presumably insufferable, but at the same time decisive and practical. Efficiency came naturally to him and he was attracted to men who shared his characteristics.

The area of Greece between Athens and Livadia seemed to be the most promising field for his activities. Unlike most of Greece, this part gave the appearance of being under an efficient government, well-policed, with reasonably fair local administration and access to justice. It was ruled as a personal domain by one of the most famous chieftains of Greece, Odysseus Androutses. Odysseus had picked up his proud classical name while a boy in the Ionian Islands. Like so many apparent classical survivals and revivals in Greece it was an importation from the West,* and yet, as if to emphasize the myth of philhellenism, he had an uncanny resemblance to one version of the Odysseus of antiquity. He was not the long-enduring, resourceful Odysseus of Homer, but the lying, cheating, double-dealer of later legend. Odysseus' commitment to the cause of Greek independence was never more than half-hearted. His hero was Ali Pasha and he seems to have tried consciously to model his own career on Ali's. Like Ali he was cruel, unscrupulous, and despotic in asserting his personal authority over his region. He did not much care whether he acknowledged Turkish suzerainty or not and he cared nothing at all for the euphuistic declarations about the regeneration of Greece. In 1821 and 1822 he actively co-operated with the Turks against the other Greeks when it suited him and he had on one occasion arranged the murder of two prominent Greeks on a mission to him from the Greek Government.

Like his mentor, Ali Pasha, Odysseus's policy for survival and aggrandizement was to suppress ruthlessly all opposition within and at the same time to accommodate quickly to the changing forces outside. Whether the outside forces were his fellow revolutionaries among the Greeks or his former colleagues among the Turks, Odysseus was ready to adapt. At the time when the British Philhellenes were active in Greece Odysseus was determined to ensure that he would be favoured when the money from the loan started to arrive. He decided to treat the British Philhellenes with courtesy.

Within a few days of meeting Odysseus for the first time Stanhope was completely won over. There are few more incongruous episodes in the history of philhellenism than this encounter between the unshakeable optimist and the cynical warlord. 'I have been constantly with Odysseus,' Stanhope wrote from Athens. 'He was a very strong mind, a good heart, and is brave as his sword; he is a doing man; he governs with a strong arm, and is the only man in Greece that can preserve order.' As a doing man himself, Stanhope was at once drawn to this rare phenomenon, an effective Greek. Soon he had convinced himself not only that Odysseus was a brave patriot but that he was a paragon of Benthamite liberalism. Stanhope, who had nothing but contempt for the romanticism of the militarists, of the archaizers, and of the Byronists, was caught by a romanticism of his own. On his first two days in Athens he had been taken to witness a scene that would have warmed the heart of any liberal idealist. As he wrote to Bowring:

---

* The Modern Greeks could understand a Greek assuming the name of Odysseus. But how many, one wonders, were so familiar with the history of the transmission of the classics that they could understand why some Europeans insisted on calling him Ulysses?

Yesterday a public meeting took place for the purpose of choosing three persons to serve as magistrates for Athens. The persons were named; their respective merits were canvassed and they were then ballotted for, and chosen by universal suffrage. This day another meeting took place for the purpose of choosing three judges. I attended the assembly held in the square opposite the port. Odysseus, with others, was seated on the hustings. Opposite stands an old tree, surrounded with a broad seat, from which the magistrates addressed the people, explained the objects for which they were assembled, and desired them to name their judges. A free debate then took place, it lasted long, became more and more animated, and at last, much difference of opinion existing, a ballot was demanded and the judges were chosen.

Stanhope was bowled over. The beauty of Athens, the simplicity of the ceremony, perhaps the old tree; it was a Benthamite idyll—political democracy returning to the land from which it had sprung. Stanhope began to report to the London Committee on the type of man he imagined (and wanted) Odysseus to be. 'He puts complete confidence in the people.' 'He is for strong government, for constitutional rights.' 'He professes himself of no faction.' 'He likes good foreigners . . . and courts instruction.' 'He . . . has taken the liberal course in politics.' 'He is a brave soldier, has great power, and promotes public liberty. Just such a man Greece requires.'

Odysseus was certainly the most unusual Benthamite ever to burn a village or slit a throat. Had it been possible to change an oriental brigand into an enlightened champion of constitutional liberty by addressing him flattering letters, then Stanhope would have succeeded. Jeremy Bentham himself might have demurred at the extravagance of some of Stanhope's remarks addressed to Odysseus, referring to his 'vast mind', his 'nobleness of soul to pursue the public good', and foretelling how he would 'soar above all his contemporaries' and 'entail on millions for ages to come the blessings of liberty'. There is something splendid in the matter-of-fact way in which Stanhope assumed that Odysseus shared his political outlook, as is shown in the following extract from a letter.

Dear General Odysseus
    I am desirous of obtaining your sanction to the formation of a utilitarian society in Athens. I propose to select its members from the most virtuous and able of her citizens. The end proposed is the formation of schools, museums, dispensaries, agricultural and horticultural societies—in short all the establishments connected with the advancement of useful knowledge.

In March 1824 the utilitarian society was established under the title of the Philomuse Society of Athens. There had been a Philomuse Society before. It had been founded probably in 1813 mainly by Western travellers visiting Athens and by Greeks of Western education. Rich travellers from England and France paid subscriptions to the Society, the proceeds of which went to buying school books and educating young Athenians. In return, the 'Friends of the Muses' were permitted to enjoy a little innocent flummery with mock antique ceremonies and clothes, gold and bronze rings with owls and Greek inscriptions, and grandiloquent speeches about the old days. The Philomuse Society was a manifestation of an earlier type of philhellenism, well known particularly in the Ionian Islands, which took pleasure in dreaming of a revival of Ancient Hellas without imagining that a revolution was a serious possibility.

As revised by Stanhope, the Philomuse Society declared in a letter to the newspaper (drafted of course by Stanhope) that its objects were to preserve the antiquities, to advance the knowledge and to improve the conditions of the Greeks. An appeal was issued to 'all useful societies in every part of the world' asking for information on 'education, the fine arts, legislation, political economy, agriculture, horticulture, commerce, mechanics, and public institutions'.

One writer in England, William Gell, who knew Greece as well as any man of his day, was so disgusted with the stream of philhellenic rubbish that purported to be news from Greece that he had in 1823 hastily published a book based on his own travels in the country to show what conditions were really like before the Revolution. The only circumstances which the philhellenic writers seem to have forgotten, he declared sarcastically, 'are the lighting of the Piraean road with gas lamps, the name of the Prima Donna of the opera at Thebes, and the notification of the reward offered by the Amphictyons for the discovery of the longitude'. Gell rounds off his list of absurdities with the remark that 'of all the hard pills to be swallowed . . . the Athenian Society of Philomusae . . . is the most difficult of digestion'.[2]

But Gell was wrong. Under Stanhope's impetus the Philomuse Society actually did convert some philhellenic dreams into reality. A church was equipped as a Lancastrian school, and another school was established to teach ancient Greek. Odysseus was even persuaded to lend some Turkish prisoners (slaves would be a more accurate description) to haul antiquities up to the Acropolis and so establish the first 'museum' in Greece.

Stanhope flattered Odysseus by lavishing on him the kind of praises which he would have liked to hear about himself. Odysseus flattered Stanhope in a more subtle way. He laid on occasional show-assemblies and show-elections, and listened particularly to the long-winded Colonel's theories. One morning when the two men were solemnly discussing the latest utilitarian scheme, a doctor entered and handed Odysseus a report on the state of the hospital and then answered various queries on it. No hospital existed, but Stanhope remained in ignorance.[3] Still less did it occur to him that this new-found champion of the people's rights was still in the habit of arbitrarily torturing and killing any men in his area of Greece who might appear to pose a threat to his power.

From Odysseus' point of view the policy was a complete success. His reputation for being the bravest and best of the Greeks spread far and wide through Europe. In Greece all the Philhellenes who shared Stanhope's beliefs naturally wanted to serve Odysseus. Other Philhellenes whose interest was simply to indulge their Byronic romanticism now found a justification for their apparently absurd preference. The attractive, but scarcely credible theory, that the barbarous mountain chieftains with their oriental dress and oriental habits were the 'true Greeks' received a curious reinforcement. Not only was Odysseus a 'true Greek' but a champion of constitutional liberty as well.

In the spring of 1824 Stanhope rushed about Greece trying to use his influence and to persuade Byron to use his influence to arrange a congress of the Greek leaders. The likelihood of success was never great. Mavrocordato and his friends at Missolonghi knew Odysseus better than Stanhope. With the death of Byron in April all hope of reconciliation passed.

But with the death of Byron Stanhope was now the sole agent of the London Greek Committee in Greece. This allowed him to make his last mistake. At Missolonghi there still lay the guns and gunpowder that had been sent out in the *Ann*, the armaments which had been donated by Gordon when his proposal to send an artillery brigade to Greece was overruled. These stores were now the only things of any value that remained from all the efforts of the London Greek Committee. To the consternation of Parry, who had shared many a laugh with Byron at the expense of the absurd Colonel, Stanhope now ordered that the gunpowder and guns should be handed over to Odysseus. With great difficulty the order was executed and the guns were hauled across Greece. Odysseus had no intention of using them against the Turks. He took them to a cave in Mount Parnassus where he had built a fortified redoubt from which he could conveniently control his little empire in Eastern Greece. The most lasting practical result of all the efforts of the British Benthamites was to reinforce the power of a cruel warlord.

But now one of the subterranean forces which have been described in earlier chapters gave a twist to events. The British Government had originally turned a blind eye to Colonel Stanhope, an officer in the British army (on half-pay) going to Greece. At the time they thought his activities would promote British interests. By early 1824, fortified by extensive intelligence from the intercepted mails in the Ionian Islands, they had changed their minds. To have such a vociferous republican liberal at large in Greece, Canning decided, far from advancing British interests, did damage to the monarchical principle. When Stanhope visited Zante in May 1824 he was handed a letter from the British army authorities in London ordering him to return home without delay. Since he depended on his army pension for his income he decided to obey.

Before he left Greece Stanhope decided to address one final appeal to the Greek people. His opening words, from a life-long passionate republican, must have added to the general belief among the Greeks that all Franks—and particularly the English—were either mad, or very, very devious. 'Greeks, The King, my sovereign, has commanded me immediately to return to England. I obey the royal mandate.' The rest of the letter was on familiar themes about their great ancestors, how money was less important than stout hearts and wise leaders, how faction and treachery were injurious to national unity. Stanhope listed a number of ways by which national evils could be averted, the last of which and the most important was for the people to respect their representatives 'who have hitherto been doomed to waste their talents and patriotism in obscurity, owing chiefly to their debates not having been published'.

And so Stanhope disappeared into obscurity, leaving Greece bewildered but essentially unchanged by his experiments.

21. *The New Apostles*

The subject of religion caused embarrassment among the followers of Jeremy Bentham. Those who thought most clearly about his philosophy and who recognized the social forces at work in the England of the day were bound to be opposed to the influence of the Churches (which was at the time unusually reactionary) and were by conviction atheists. On the other hand, the kind of men who liked the absolutist features of Benthamite philosophy and were attracted by the prospect of brainwashing their fellow men on the pretext of doing them good, were naturally prone to the similar attractions offered by organized religion.

It was a cruel dilemma for the leaders of the movement, made worse by the circumstances of the 1820s. Right-wing forces, both Church and State, tended at that time to condemn liberal ideas as seditious and blasphemous, as if the two offences were synonymous, and had some success in keeping the more ignorant classes in obedience as a result. Jeremy Bentham, rather than risk his important programmes for such a marginal subject as religion, adopted the device of being extremely circumspect in his open references to religion and thus succeeded in removing the impression that he was opposed to it.

Soon it became acceptable to be both an eager Christian and a Benthamite. Blaquiere and Stanhope belonged to this group and from the beginning the London Greek Committee had a distinctly Christian bias. Greece was not only to be regenerated in terms of English utilitarianism but converted to English Christianity as well. As Stanhope himself declared when the first consignment of Bibles arrived: 'They will save the priests the trouble of enlightening the darkness of their flocks. Flocks indeed! With the press and the Bibles, the whole mind of Greece may be put in labour.'[1] An alliance was formed between the London Greek Committee and various Christian groups, principally the missionary societies, to propagate in Greece the eternal truths of Christianity as understood in contemporary England.

The dispatch of missionaries to the technologically more backward areas of the world was one of the symptoms of the increasing power and arrogance of Western Europe in the nineteenth century. Earlier centuries had been unashamed of simple military conquest and economic exploitation. Now, it was felt, some higher justification was required. Cultural imperialism became the fashion, and the missionaries were its storm troopers. Soon these narrow intolerant men were to play a part in extinguishing primitive societies all over the world. In Greece, as ever, things were different.

Before the outbreak of the Greek Revolution the Levant was perhaps the most intractable area of the world with which the missionary societies had to deal. The few missionaries who ventured into the Ottoman Empire had scant success. Since under the Ottoman system a man's religion determined his place in the world, and it was their religion which gave the various national groups their distinctiveness, a change of religion was regarded by the authorities as a serious matter. Conversion to Mohamedanism was not discouraged for the able and ambitious, but attempts to convert Turks to Christianity could rightly be regarded as attempts to disrupt the social structure and were forbidden. For a Turk to renounce Mohamedanism was a capital offence. Jews were regarded by the Ottoman authorities as fair game and no impediment was put in the way of missions to them. But Jews, of course, proved to be almost impossible to convert. The Levant was sadly barren ground. The dozen or so authenticated examples of conversion all seem to have had unusual features and some were obtained by outright bribery. With the establishment of British rule in Malta and the Ionian Islands, secure bases were available for missionary forays and gradually missionaries ventured further afield. Two Americans visited Asia Minor, Egypt, and Palestine in the early 1820s. Some Germans penetrated to Georgia, and a Scottish expedition tried its luck in the Caucasus. The Rev. Joseph Wolff made numerous dangerous journeys all over the Levant in an attempt to convert the Jews. In spite of his repeated warnings that the Messiah was due to return in 1847—he and his wife intended to go to Jerusalem for the occasion—the various Jewish communities invariably greeted him with hostility and even from time to time tried to kill him. Wolff admitted that his immense efforts had resulted in almost total failure. From Malta the Rev. William Jowett made several visits to Greece and the Ionian Islands before the Revolution, but again with little success. In his book he examines the reasons for his failure and discusses ways in which missionary performance might be improved.[2] Extirpation of the Moslems, he concluded magnanimously, was not the answer to the problem.

When philhellenism was at its height in England in 1824, the men of the London Missionary Society decided to turn their attention to Greece.

When it was pointed out that the Greeks were already Christians, it was ruled that nevertheless they were eligible for conversion. The constitution of the Society, it was noticed, allowed it to help 'heathen and other unenlightened countries'.[3] Other British missionary groups soon joined in and a few American sects made a contribution, but none of any other nationality. Sending missionaries, like sending newspaper printing presses, was an elaboration of philhellenism unthought of elsewhere in Europe.

The British Christians surveyed the plight of their Greek brethren with sadness tinged with disgust. All observers were of the opinion that the Greek Church was ignorant, superstitious, and corrupt. Although the Church still contained honest and educated men among its leaders, these were few and far between. And the gap between the educated few and the generality of bishops and parish priests in Greece was immense. The Greek Church like the Greek people was degenerate and in need of regeneration.

Surprisingly, it was seldom noticed that the Greek Church contained some of the few indubitable examples of the survival of a tradition from ancient times. Demeter, Artemis, and Dionysus, to give only the most obvious examples, had lost few of their ancient characteristics in the course of their transmogrification into St. Demetrius (or Demetra), St. Artemidos, and St. Dionysus.

The connection between Modern Greece and Ancient Hellas, which was the inspiration of so much philhellenic activity, evoked no sympathetic response from the British Christians. Pre-Christian civilization was of no interest. They were so determined to avoid saying a good word about paganism that they practised a kind of anti-philhellenism. One missionary coming across the magnificent standing columns of the Temple of Apollo in Aegina dismissed it as 'an abominable fane'.[4] To him all the Ancient Greeks were 'sunk to the lowest grade of vice and woe'. Another claimed that the sight of Mount Parnassus left him cold until he recollected that the eye of St. Paul had rested on it and he could 'hold a species of distant communion with him by means of this classical mountain'.[5] The same missionary declared his faith that the honours of those who served God (meaning men like himself) would endure and increase in splendour when Classical Greece 'will have sunk in eternal oblivion or be consigned to merited insignificance'.[6] Another admitted sheepishly that, when he came upon a famous place, 'it must not be denied that we stopped to gaze a moment. . . . But rarely did we go out of our way to gratify our classical curiosity.'[7]

In matters of religious controversy, the more trivial the point of difference and the more unascertainable the answer to the question, the more uncontrolled the passions and the more puffed-up the indignation. The British Christians followed the usual pattern in their differences with the Greeks. One of the missionaries, after detailing lovingly the full horrors of

the errors of the Greek Church and clergy which he had discovered, summed
up his conclusions, conclusions with which most of his colleagues would
have agreed:

There is an infernal originality in apostate Christianity; it is the master effort
of the Prince of Darkness. The Church of Christ becomes the synagogue of
Satan. An attempt is made to combine light and darkness; to bring Heaven and
Hell into monstrous and impossible coalition; to mingle the Hallelujahs of
Paradise with the shrieks of the lost world; to place God and Satan conjointly
on the throne of the universe.[8]

The apparently more obvious topics of criticism were ignored. None of
the missionaries, as far as can be ascertained, remarked on the fact that the
Greek bishops and priests had exhorted their flocks to exterminate the
Turkish and Jewish minorities and had, in many cases, taken the lead and
personally assisted in piercing the bodies of their defenceless neighbours.
The missionaries sometimes acknowledged a thrill of inquisitive horror
when they addressed audiences known to have organized mass murders
but they prudently confined their sermons to safer topics.

The prime method chosen for bringing about the regeneration of the
Greek Church was to distribute the Bible. The Greeks who could read, it
was noticed, had little difficulty in obtaining translations of 'the ravings and
poisonous productions' of Rousseau and Voltaire.[9] Since the Church in
Greece was 'impious, ignorant, lifeless', one of the shocked missionaries
asked, 'Is it at all surprising that young Greeks educated in Italy, Germany,
France, or England, should return to the classic land disciples of Alfieri,
of Schiller, of Voltaire, of Lord Shaftesbury?'[10] The Bible was to be the
chief weapon against these hateful influences.

In addition to the cannon, tools, and printing presses sent by the London
Greek Committee in the *Ann* there was a consignment of 320 Greek Bibles
and tracts. These were to be the responsibility of one of the artificers, the
tinman Brownbill, called by Parry a 'hypocritical canting methodist'[11]
and by Byron, 'an elect blacksmith'.[12] When the artificers, including Brownbill, decamped to the Ionian Islands, the books were left on Lord Byron's
hands. He had them piled up outside his room at Missolonghi and offered
copies to his numerous visitors. But Byron was too intelligent and too
tolerant a man to make a good missionary.

The missionary societies donated bundles of Bibles to the captains of
British warships bound for Greek waters and urged them to distribute them.
The chaplain of H.M.S. *Cambrian*, who was in Greece in 1825, found that it
was almost impossible to find anyone who would accept a Bible as a gift.
A British merchant in Salonika explained that he had disposed of only
three out of a consignment of forty in four years. At Nauplia the chaplain
discovered that there were already many more Bibles than anyone wanted

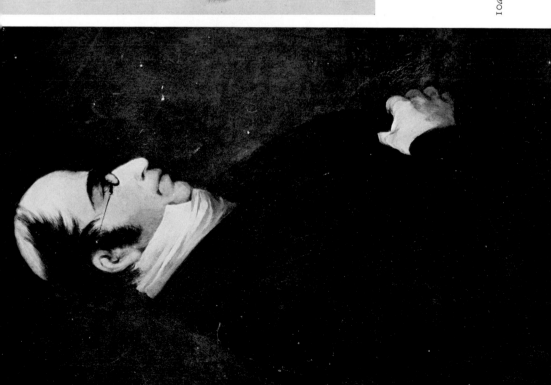

b Colonel Fabvier

10*a* Count Santa Rosa

11a A French Philhellenic Poster

b A Collection for the Greeks in 1826. On the wall is David's famous picture of Leonidas at Thermopylae

and new consignments were still arriving. The Greek priests refused his offers by showing him the heaps they already possessed.[13]

But the work of religious regeneration needed more direct methods. It was Colonel Stanhope who first suggested that missionaries should be sent. He named as his first choice the Reverend Sheridan Wilson who was already engaged on the futile task of trying to convert the Maltese from Roman Catholicism. Wilson is described by one of his English fellow priests as a Methodist and 'the most liberal of the sect I have met with'.[14] Liberalism of course is in the eye of the beholder.

Wilson was the first missionary to be employed full-time in Revolutionary Greece. When the directors of the London Missionary Society 'first turned a pitying eye on Greece'—as he explained—they began by establishing missionaries on the Ionian Islands. Already several missionaries had worked there and schools were established under their auspices in almost every town. The life was hard, two of the missionary wives died at their duty, but the missionary work had the full support of the British authorities in the islands.

It was quite another matter to venture alone into the anarchic conditions of Greece. Wilson himself was never lacking in courage. He was landed at Spetsae with his boxes of books just as night was falling on Christmas eve 1824. A Turkish fleet was in the offing and a stranger laden with unknown packages was bound to cause suspicion. 'I was in the utmost danger of assassination the moment I set foot ashore', Wilson explained later. 'Three hundred eyes and three hundred more flashed fire upon me. But when I pointed to my boxes and stated the benevolent object I had in view, their hands let go the grasped yatagan.'

Wilson spent the first night ashore terrified that he was about to be murdered since his host pointedly kept his long knife by his hand as he slept. But the Albanians and Greeks of the island, whatever else they may have thought about this strange beardless English priest, concluded that he was harmless. Soon Wilson was up and about round the island. In each of the island's forty warships he left two Bibles, one for the captain and one for the crew.

After a short stay he set off for the mainland and spent the next few months travelling all over Southern Greece. Often, as he reached a place that had been visited by St. Paul, he recalled that he too was an apostle to the gentiles. The church which St. Paul had planted still existed; it had 'retained its apostolic purity till carnal ascetics, light-headed monastics, lucre-loving hierophants, lordly prelates, and scripture-neglecting professors obscured the glory of the temple'.

Soon Wilson was giving his hosts practical advice on how the apostolic purity could be restored. The monasteries, he declared, should be swept away; they were 'hives of sanctimonious drones'. But most of his suggestions

o

had more limited aims. At Spetsae he finally induced an old Greek to take a glass of wine during Lent after giving him a sermon on the theory of fasting. The old man drank the wine out of a mixture of respect and fear of Wilson. Obviously the missionary was not getting his point across. 'This very man,' he commented indignantly later, 'who durst not drink a glass of wine on Saturday night, I saw *next* morning playing at cards!'

Wilson regularly insisted on the need to say grace at meals. The Greeks who were used to making the sign of the cross on these occasions were solemnly warned about the iniquity of this superstition. Profanation of the Sabbath, one need hardly add, was also a topic that caused great concern.

' "Captain Anthreas" said I, "you should not sing songs on Sunday"— "Why afendi?"—"It is wicked"—"But what must I do?"—"Sing psalms."'

The music of the Greek Church, he found, was 'intolerably nasal, full of most unmeaning and unedifying repetitions'. He discussed how it could be reformed with one of the bishops and the bishop promised that it would be done. But when the bishop demonstrated the new system, Wilson could only comment, 'Though I felt the condescension of this simple bishop, yet I honestly expressed to him my painful impression that his country had changed rather the character than the airs.' To explain what sacred music should really be like he sang him a little hymn:

> Gentle stranger, fare you well!
> Heavenly blessings with you dwell!
> Blessings such as you impart,
> To the orphan's bleeding heart.
> Gentle stranger, fare you well!
> Heavenly blessings with you dwell!

Sometimes Wilson's bland narrative unconsciously gives a glimpse of a more robust response to the missionary's self-assured advice. 'The Greeks . . . are ungallant enough to salute gentlemen before ladies. "We English," said I, "always take the ladies first." "Well," replied one of the party, "we *never* do." ' Such wilful unapologetic ignorance was difficult to condone.

It never occurred to Wilson to doubt that the ideas and customs current among his small English Christian sect in 1825 represented eternal truth and perfect morality. A man who brought such gifts to the Greeks need not underestimate himself. At one of his Sunday schools two Greek brothers presented themselves and gave their names as Leonidas and Lycurgus. 'Only imagine,' Wilson remarked, 'Leonidas and Lycurgus in a Sunday school! . . . Ah! I have said as I thought on those two dear boys, if your celebrated namesakes had enjoyed your privileges—had they sat at the feet of Jesus, what a happy land Lacedaemon might have been!' By sending him to Spetsae, he declared on another occasion, the British Churches had conferred 'grace' on the island. 'Yet by me you only paid your debts. From the learned ancestors of the modern Greeks, Britain received the writings of a Homer, a Plato, a Basil, and is repaying in these latter days her ancient obligations.' There can have been few besides himself who thought that the Rev. Sheridan Wilson was a fair exchange for Homer or Plato or even for Basil.

Wilson was the first missionary in Greece, but he was soon followed by other clergymen of other denominations sent by other missionary societies. Whatever the differences in dogma and doctrine that separated these men, they all seem to exhibit, in varying proportions, self-righteousness, insensitivity, intolerance, pomposity, and stolidity. Nothing they saw pleased them—perhaps occasionally the weather or the scenery but never the people and certainly not the classical remains. Even the colourful little jackets of the Greek women, one clergyman expostulated, were 'Staysless' and 'positively indecent and disgusting'.[15] Sometimes one gets the impression that the missionaries were competing with one another to see who could compile the longest list of Greek superstitions or who could find the grossest example. For all their talk of Christianity and for all their hard work in establishing mission schools, they showed hardly a spark of charity. Even their fellow countrymen felt that the 'utter unprofitableness of these gentlemen cannot be sufficiently pointed out'[16] and the Rev. Joseph Wolff, the missionary to the Jews, felt obliged to pass some criticisms on his fellow missionaries. It was said that they would arrive in the Levant knowing no language but English and that they seldom got beyond the stage of language training. One who was learning Greek at Tenos, gave up his missionary work to marry a local girl; another, who was intended for the interior of Asia Minor, decided instead to settle in the more congenial atmosphere of Smyrna; a third quietly pursued his own studies in order to equip himself for a post on his return to England.

The Rev. John Hartley, who was in Greece from 1826, was said to be an exception and there is no doubt of his vigour. But Hartley was a man who was more happy in being anti-Turk than pro-Christian. Like the Rev. Thomas Hughes, the philhellenic pamphleteer, Hartley was a survival of an earlier age when the Christian/Moslem confrontation seemed to be the most important international question of the day and when religious hatred was a respectable policy. Hartley was disposed to argue that the cruelties which the Turks had undergone at the hands of the Greeks and the bloody internal dissensions of the Ottoman Empire were the just retribution exacted by God for their failure to become Christians.[17]

By the late 1820s there were a dozen or so missionaries, English and American, operating in and around Greece. All the main denominations had their man to condemn and confuse the Greeks in accordance with their own especial doctrines. Virtually every town of Revolutionary Greece and every island in the Aegean was visited and numerous Lancastrian schools were established.

But the most important method of regenerating the Greek Church remained the distribution of books. 1 June 1825 was, according to the Rev. Sheridan Wilson, 'a memorable day, a happy one for poor Greece'. On that day, after his visit to Greece, Wilson set to work a Greek press at Malta and it ran almost continuously until 1834, printing nothing else but improving works in Greek. Apart from the Bible, the Mission Press published no less than thirty-six titles.

All ages and levels of education were catered for. Numerous simple religious story books were translated: *The Ladder of Learning*, *The Life of Robert Raikes*, *Tommy and Harry*, *The Cabin Boy*, *Well-spent Penny*, and *Jailor's Conversion*. Watts' *Divine Songs* were translated into Greek lyrics. The *Pilgrim's Progress* was said to be a great favourite. For the more highly educated Keith's *Evidences of Prophecy* was translated and another work, *The Clergyman's Guide*, was specially composed, containing a life of St. Paul, an address to missionaries published by the Scottish Missionary Society, commentaries on the Epistles from the most up-to-date scholars, a Sacred Chronology, notes on ancient and modern philosophers, and much else besides. A version of metrical psalms was published complete with music. There were also Anglo-Greek grammars, spelling books, Greek arithmetic books, and many others.

It was an impressive accomplishment. In addition, books in Greek, mainly Bibles and tracts, continued to arrive in ships direct from England and from the United States. The Americans also established their own press at Malta 'which never sleeps'. The Missionary Societies in England were delighted. As one of the reports stated explicitly,[18] the number of copies of the Bible distributed was the best measure of the success of their missionary efforts.

But something strange was occurring which the Societies had not noticed. In early 1825—that is *before* the mission press at Malta began printing—it had been difficult to find anyone willing to accept a Greek Bible as a gift. The market was already glutted. Now a remarkable change had occurred. There seemed suddenly to be no limit to the number of volumes that the Greeks would take. Not only would they accept them, they would even pay for them. One missionary sold four hundred copies of the New Testament in Aegina in four days and five hundred in Hydra in the same space of time. Others described how people came on immense journeys to buy from them and how they were surrounded by children begging for books. The number of Greek books distributed in Greece and the Aegean area was immense. It is impossible to compile complete statistics, but the order of magnitude can be illustrated by tabulating a few claims made at random by some of the missionaries.

Missionary	Volumes printed and distributed	Period
Wilson	240,200	1825–1834
Hartley	32,000	1826–1836
Brewer	32,000	1827–1828
Barker	2,500	Four months in 1830
Total	306,700	

This list is far from exhaustive. There are records of numerous other distributions for which no numbers are given. The total Greek population in the areas visited was probably not more than about a million and a half. There was thus probably at least one Greek book distributed for every two adult males and, of course, only a small fraction of Greeks were literate. It is clear that the missionaries, by their distribution of religious books, were practising cultural saturation bombing.

None of the missionaries found it surprising that there should be this sudden and apparently insatiable Greek demand for religious books. It was simply noted that, in 1826, 'Greece began to show an ardent thirst for missionary co-operation'. Perhaps, but it might have occurred to even the most optimistic that this was not a complete explanation. Travellers visiting Greece before the Revolution had traversed the length of the country without seeing more than a few dozen printed books in the whole course of their travels. It was *prima facie* unlikely, to say the least, that thousands of wild Greeks and Albanians should now find a sudden interest in the *Life of Robert Raikes*, let alone evince an eager desire to purchase a small library of similar works.

The explanation was simple. Anyone who had any real interest in the manners of the country could have discovered the answer if it had occurred to him to ask the question. Paper was a rare commodity in Greece and a valuable one. A twist of paper making a cartridge for the coarse gunpowder could improve the safety and perhaps the accuracy of the primitive muskets used by most of the Greeks. Among the stores sent with Parry in the *Ann* were forty reams of fine paper and thirty reams of coarse paper specifically intended for making cartridges for small arms and cannon. There can be no doubt that the vast majority of Greek books sent by the missionaries went straight into personal armouries. The fact was specifically noticed by at least one traveller.[19]

It was explained regretfully to the Reverend Sheridan Wilson when he inspected the paltry school library at Tripolitsa that many of the books had been torn up to provide cartridges, but it never seems to have occurred to him—or to any of his fellow missionaries—that their own productions were destined for a similar fate. A charitable observer might conjecture that the missionaries knowingly accepted a high wastage rate on the theory that the effort would be worthwhile if only a few shots of the barrage hit their target. But all the evidence suggests that the missionaries sincerely believed that the crowds of despised Greeks who showed such interest in their books genuinely wanted to read them (or to have them read aloud to them). If the missionaries did have their suspicions, they did not report them to the sponsoring societies in England who continued to measure their success by the numbers of books distributed.

Insensitivity to one's surroundings, however, is not necessarily a disadvantage to a missionary. Like Colonel Stanhope before them, the missionaries by their single-mindedness, their energy, and their absolute lack of doubt in the value of their activities, could not fail to accomplish something. There is no record of their having made converts. They had no success in substituting English customs and superstitions for the indigenous varieties which they found so appalling, but, with a few exceptions, they worked hard. Many Greeks did undoubtedly gain the rudiments of an education from schools established by the missionaries. As the numbers of the missionaries built up during the late 1820s and as more and more mission schools were established, it was natural that their influence should grow. For some years after the end of the war a few of the best men enjoyed a high reputation in Greece as teachers and genuine philanthropists, but the period was short-lived. As soon as the Greek clergy realized that the mission schools might prove a threat to their own authority, they were doomed. The famous school in Athens run by the Rev. John Hill, an American, survived for many years but only on the condition that religious subjects were not taught, and most missionaries felt that they could not help Greece on such terms. Later, the new state enacted that children of Greek orthodox parents could only be educated in schools controlled by the Greek priesthood. Soon the mission schools were closed or compelled to confine themselves to educating foreigners. And so the old-fashioned customs of the Greek Church—even including the survivals from pre-Christian times—were woven into the fabric of regenerated Greece. The influence of the new apostles, for all their high hopes and professions of faith, proved to be as ephemeral as the efforts of the other friends of the Greeks.

22. *The English Gold*

In 1822 the British Government decided to convert the rate of interest paid on government bonds from five per cent to four per cent. In 1824 the rate was further reduced to three and a half per cent. These actions had a profound—though of course unintended—effect upon the course of the Greek War of Independence. Indeed, it is difficult to see how Greek independence could have been achieved when it was but for the cupidity and short-sightedness of the British property-owning classes.

Philhellenism had taken many forms since the Greek Revolution broke out in 1821, but never before had it appeared that the best way to promote the Greek cause was also the best way to maximize the return on capital. For a short period in 1824 and 1825 a few rich Englishmen were to enjoy the delusion that by helping themselves to grow richer more quickly they were also helping the poor struggling Greeks to regain their freedom.

Because of the British lead in the industrial revolution, capital began to accumulate at a faster rate than domestic agriculture and industry could absorb it. In addition, many of the holders of government bonds began, as a result of the reduction in interest rates, to look for more lucrative forms of investment. During the early 1820s the most attractive investment seemed to be in foreign bonds. During these years, as the depression following the end of the long wars with France came to an end, several governments were in need of money to help pay for war debts to their nationals, and the only place where such money could be found was London.

The first major foreign loan was to France to allow her to defer some of the reparation payments due to the victorious allies. This was a huge success since not only was the rate of interest high but it appeared that the investment was guaranteed. When, on one occasion, Baring Brothers, the contractors for the loan, found that they could not pay, it was obvious to the governments concerned that it was more in their interest to give help to Baring Brothers than to allow them to default and so lose all chance of getting their money. Judicious bankers, especially Barings and Rothschilds, were thus in the comfortable position of having unlimited opportunities for making profits with no risk of loss.

After the French loan there was a rush of foreign loans on the London market. Nearly all took the same form. A firm of bankers was appointed contractors and they were responsible for selling the bonds. The interest rate was usually between five and eight per cent—a few percentage points above government stock—but the return was in fact much greater since the bonds were initially offered at a large discount. The contractors set their conditions for handling the loans, conditions which may have appeared to be details but which in practice were a charter for profiteering. It was usual for the contractors to take a large commission at every stage of the transaction and to insist on monopoly rights as buying agents for the foreign government. As one economic historian has commented, 'They received a commission for raising the money, a commission for spending it, and a commission for paying it back.'[1]

International economic relations was a subject little understood at the time but, even so, the contradictions were plain for all to see. For example the absolutist powers, Russia, Austria, Prussia, and France all had loans from the London market, and at least one of the loans was specifically and avowedly raised in order to equip forces to put down the revolutions in Naples and Spain. And yet simultaneously the Constitutionalist Government in Spain raised loans. Furthermore, a host of South and Central American countries which were in revolt against Spain—whether Constitutionalist or not they did not mind—also had no difficulty in raising money. The investing public seems to have believed that because governments were involved, as with the first French loans, their money was somehow guaranteed, and in the early years dividends were actually paid since the governments were constantly returning for second and third loans. Between 1822 and 1825 over £45 million was loaned to foreign governments, all of it ultimately from the few thousand men who formed the British wealthy class.[2]

In these circumstances, it is not surprising that the Greeks should have tried London in their attempt to find money, and that talk of a loan for Greece should have dominated the scene long before it was arranged. Bowring, who was well connected with the financial establishment in London, was not exaggerating when he told Hobhouse in December 1823 that he could 'engage to raise a loan of £600,000 by tomorrow morning if anybody invested with powers were here'.[3] The miserable state of South America had not prevented the countries there from obtaining a loan. How much more attractive was the Greek cause.

Yet the loan would probably not have been concluded if it had not been for the connivance and co-operation of the British Government. The Government on the whole was not much bothered if its citizens pursued commercial policies at variance with its own foreign policy, even if British money was being borrowed specifically to frustrate British policy on the Continent. But the Ottoman Empire was an ally of Great Britain. It was stretching even the most liberal interpretation of the rights of a subject to argue that he was entitled to exploit British institutions and British resources to organize and strengthen armed rebellion against a British ally. The loan would not have been permitted if the British Government had not been convinced from its intelligence sources that the rival schemes for loans being bandied about by the Knights of Malta, by the mysterious Robert Peacock and General de Wintz, and by Ruppental, were promoted by rival European powers.

It had been Edward Blaquiere who first brought the Greek agent Andreas Louriottis to London in early 1823 and he never lost the proprietorial tone which comes easily to those who regard themselves as leaders and founders of great movements. Louriottis and the other official agents of the Greek Government, known as the Greek Deputies, were at first treated as protégés of the London Greek Committee, to be protected from the temptations of the great city and guided and instructed like promising schoolboys. They were so overwhelmed at their good fortune, at the prospect of obtaining any money at all, that they willingly put up with this treatment. They were content to be led about as celebrities and to leave the policy-making to their self-appointed friends. When the Committee discussed plans to raise a loan they readily consented to leave the handling of it entirely to the men who seemed so well versed in these matters, the respectable Benthamites of the London Greek Committee.

When the decision to float a loan on behalf of Greece was taken, the Committee intensified its efforts to attract publicity. It was usual during these years when a loan was in the offing, to circulate prospectuses and to inspire puffs of one kind or another. There was of course no control over their accuracy. But of all the dubious claims for this or that country which were put about the City of London during the early 1820s to entice British money abroad, only one was more extravagant or more misleading than the Greek. The prize for effrontery must go to the Scottish impostor who raised a loan on behalf of the mythical Kingdom of Poyais in South America of which he had assumed the picturesque title of 'cazique'.

Edward Blaquiere's first pamphlet on Greece, which was rushed into print at the end of September 1823, claimed that nineteen-twentieths of the territory held by the Greeks was national land taken from the Turks and was being reserved as guarantee for a loan. Greece, Blaquiere declared, could 'calculate upon becoming one of the most opulent nations of Europe'.[4]

But Blaquiere reserved his main claims for his book *The Greek Revolution*, which was also rushed into print in the spring of 1824 when confidence in the loan was flagging.* Sometimes, in reading Blaquiere's description of the wealth of Greece, one is tempted to revise the judgement that he was simply a naïve and superficial busybody and conclude instead that he was a liar and a trickster. Surely no partisan of the Greeks, however unscrupulous, if like Blaquiere he had visited the country, would have thought of making such claims as are in this book.

The soil of Greece, he declared, was 'the most productive that could be named'.[5] The 'prospect of wealth and prosperity is almost boundless'.[6] Greece is 'a land flowing with milk and honey'.[7] Crete is 'the most prolific and beautiful spot on earth for its extent'.[8] Blaquiere carefully noted the advantages of Greece, its climate, its intelligent, educated, and industrious population, its harbours. 'I should have no hesitation whatever,' he decided, 'in estimating the physical strength of regenerated Greece to be fully equal to that of the whole South American continent.'[9] In choosing this particular comparison he no doubt had in mind that the London market had in the last year or so already extended credit to Chile, Peru, Buenos Aires, Mexico, Guatemala, Colombia, and Brazil, to say nothing of the Kingdom of Poyais.

If the public had any doubts about the loan, he said, this was because of their total ignorance of the state of Greece. The loan could have been raised and repaid by the smallest island in the Archipelago. The doubts must have been deliberately sown by the Jews, who were in league with the Levant Company merchants and had co-operated with the Turks in massacring the Greeks. In particular, Blaquiere claimed, 'a leading Jew capitalist',[10] meaning Rothschild, was behind the conspiracy. 'Surely that person must know that of all the countries or governments who have borrowed money in London within the last ten years, not excepting those for whom he has himself been the agent and the contractor, Greece possesses the surest and most ample means of repayment.'†[11] Blaquiere's anti-semitic smears were later to rebound on the London Greek Committee.

Blaquiere's third book on Greece, which came out in 1825 after he had been there again, was marginally less extravagant, but he repeated his claims that Greece was entitled to a high credit on the London Stock Exchange. The cause of Greece, he repeated, 'by far the most glorious that ever graced the page of history, should not be sacrificed at the unhallowed shrine of avarice, envy, or gratitude!'[12]

There can be no doubt that the effusions of Edward Blaquiere had their effect on promoting and sustaining the Greek loan although, as in the earlier

---

* See p. 212 below.

† If this rubbish means anything, it must mean that Blaquiere expected Rothschild to agree with him that Greece was a richer country even than France, than Prussia, than Austria, than Russia.

days when the London Greek Committee was campaigning for direct subscriptions on its own account, Blaquiere's enthusiasm must have actively repelled some potential supporters. But even such an expert and extravagant publicist would have had no success if he had not been telling many of his audience what they wanted to hear. Blaquiere was exploiting reliable emotions—a mild traditional philhellenism, a strong desire for profit; he persuaded the investing public that they could enjoy the rare sensation of serving God and Mammon simultaneously.

Ever since news had arrived in late 1823 of Lord Byron's new 'pilgrimage' to Greece, a climate of expectancy over the loan had been gradually building up. The final stimulus was given a few days before issue day when the Greek deputies were entertained at a banquet in the Guildhall in the City of London. The presence of the Lord Mayor and of Canning himself on this occasion confirmed the general view that the British Government tacitly approved of the whole transaction.

The first Greek loan was floated on the London Stock Exchange in February 1824, in the name of the London Greek Committee. It was heavily oversubscribed. The nominal value was £800,000, but it was issued at a forty-one per cent discount, so that the sale of £100 of stock only realized £59 in cash. The rate of interest was to be five per cent on the nominal capital. The contract also specified that one per cent should be set aside to establish a sinking fund and that a sum equivalent to the interest for the first two years should be withheld. Messrs. Loughnan, Son, and O'Brien, London bankers, the contractors, then proceeded to deduct at various times a sum of about £38,000 for commissions and expenses. And so by the time all the administrative deductions had been made in London, there only remained just over £300,000 to spend on behalf of Greece out of the £800,000 loan! As yet, even the £300,000 existed only on paper. Buyers of the Greek bonds had been required to put down only a first instalment of £10 per £100 bond with a promise to pay the remaining £49 in instalments over the next few months. This detail was to have important repercussions.

On the back of the bonds was the proud guarantee, 'To the payment of the annuities are appropriated all the revenues of Greece. The whole of the national property of Greece is hereby pledged to the holders of all obligations granted in virtue of this loan until the whole of the capital which such obligations represent shall be discharged.'[13]

The spending of the money was to be entrusted to three commissioners appointed by the Committee. At first they were to be Byron, Napier, and Stanhope. The Greek deputies were so anxious to get their hands on the money and send it to Greece that they seemed ready to agree to almost anything. But it soon occurred to them that if decisions about the spending of the money were to be entirely in the hands of Englishmen they would be accused of having sold Greece to the English. They felt they had been tricked; Bowring felt that they were trying to undo decisions that had already been taken. The first of many arguments between the Greek deputies and the Committee was on this occasion resolved by the intervention of Jeremy Bentham. It was decided as a compromise that one of the three commissioners should be a Greek.

With the launching of the Greek loan, the London Greek Committee abandoned almost completely its original objectives of raising money for the Greek cause by direct subscription. The Committee always had been dominated by a small caucus. Day-to-day control now passed entirely into the hands of a very small group, men with contacts in financial circles, Joseph Hume and Edward Ellice, both rich self-made Scotsmen and Members of Parliament, and Bowring, who hoped to emulate them. Hobhouse, Stanhope, and Blaquiere remained active but they seem to have been gradually excluded from some of the most important business. The occasional meeting was arranged to draw attention to the Greek cause—including on one occasion the presentation to the public of a Danish gentleman called Friedel, lately returned from Greece;[14] the impostor baron was apparently still doing business. But already the main focus of radical indignation and Benthamite energy had moved away from the cause of the Greeks. The familiar names were now issuing high moral appeals to the people of Britain in favour of the Spaniards who had been exiled from the country following the French invasion.

Within a few weeks of the flotation of the Greek loan the first consignment was ready to be sent to Greece. £30,000 in gold sovereigns and £10,000 in Spanish dollars was dispatched from London in the *Florida* at the end of March 1824. Edward Blaquiere, still feeling that the successful floating of the loans, if not the whole British philhellenic movement, was somehow his own property, decided to take passage to Greece and to try to assume the mantle of Stanhope. The *Florida* reached Zante after an especially quick voyage at the end of April.

Now there occurred a complex series of muddles to which allusion has already been made in an earlier chapter. The first news that greeted the *Florida* on its arrival was that Lord Byron was dead. Apart from all the other implications of that unexpected tragedy, what was to be done with the money? Byron was to have been one of the commissioners; Napier and Gordon who had also been named, had declined to come to Greece; Stanhope had received his letter of recall by the army authorities in London, and in any case was opposed to the money being paid over. There were thus not enough commissioners to receive the money officially. For the time being therefore it was consigned to Samuel Barff, a British banker established in Zante, to remain in his vault until instructions could be obtained from London. In spite of the pleadings of Blaquiere, Barff and the Ionian Government insisted that the money could not be released.

Since it usually took about six weeks to send a message from Zante to London (or in the other direction) the Committee and the Greek agents in London were taking their decisions on the basis of very out-of-date information. There was a further complication in that the Ionian Government was pursuing a different policy from the British Government, the Lord High Commissioner not being kept up to date with Canning's devious thinking. And so in June 1824 the second instalment of the loan, a further £40,000 in specie, arrived at Zante from London in the *Little Sally*. To the intense frustration and fury of all Greeks and Philhellenes, this money too was consigned to Samuel Barff's bank.

Meanwhile in London, the Committee was struggling with a quite different problem. Here again the slowness of communication between Greece and England was one of the most important factors. At the time when the loan was first floated in February 1824 the publicity situation was as favourable as it was ever likely to be. Not only had there been the build-up by Blaquiere's first pamphlet, and by the Guildhall banquet, but the British Government announcement of the reduction in interest rates on government bonds from four to three and a half per cent came the day after the announcement of the loan. In addition, it was at this time that Bowring, as secretary of the Committee, was receiving the voluminous letters from Colonel Stanhope describing his success in rapidly turning Greece into a model Benthamite state. These letters as they arrived were being fed to the press to such good effect that on the day that the loan was anounced one newspaper reported that Stanhope's corps, meaning the Byron Brigade, had 'succeeded to the utmost extent of his wishes'; that the Greeks had 'a force more than sufficient to reduce all the fortresses in the hands of the Turks'.[15]

As a result of the concurrence of all these favourable factors the value of the Greek bonds which had been issued at 59 rose to 63 and seemed set to rise further or, at worst, to stay above the issue price. The leading members of the Committee saw their chance to make some easy money. Hume and Ellice speculated heavily and it was partly because they were seen to be buying that the rate rose. Bowring was even more deeply involved. Not only did he accept an outright commission of £11,000 for his part in promoting the loan but he had contracted to buy at least £25,000 worth. He seemed set to make a killing. But they left it too late. During March as payments became due and investors began to sell off, the rate began to fall. By the end of the month it stood at 54—five per cent below the issue price. Instead of their expected gain, Bowring and the other members of the Committee who had speculated appeared likely to make a loss. The leaders of the Greek Committee now had a profound personal interest in the future of the Greek loan.

Bowring was later to protest vehemently that there had been no financial irregularities during his secretaryship of the London Greek Committee. The best that can be said in his favour is that different standards existed in 1824 from today. Bowring apparently saw nothing improper in making use of his official position and knowledge to promote his own interests. In April, Bowring, Hume, and the contractors put pressure on the Greek deputies to use some of the money already collected to buy up stock and so stimulate the market, and this was done. Blaquiere's book *The Greek Revolution*, which was published at this time, was apparently his contribution to trying to reflate the Greek cause on the Stock Exchange.

Then on 14 May came the news that Lord Byron was dead. The Greek scrip immediately fell and by 13 June it was down to 44¾. The situation was now becoming critical for the speculators. Relations between them and the Greek deputies worsened almost to breaking point. The deputies suspected, with good justification, that Bowring was now more interested in his own precarious financial position than in the troubles of Greece. Bowring and the others, on the other hand, were quite ready to call the kettle black. The Greek deputies had quickly shed the charming naïveté with which they had arrived in London. They had now set themselves up as gentlemen of leisure, enjoying the delights of London and drawing shamelessly and lavishly on the loan money. In addition the deputies and their friends were not only themselves deeply engaged in speculations in the Greek bonds, but were clearly enriching themselves by direct peculation of the money. A contest in mutual blackmail between Bowring and the deputies was the outcome.

Bowring was thoroughly impaled and the more he wriggled the deeper the hook entered. He considered resigning the secretaryship of the Committee but this would have meant the certainty of ruin. He began to campaign openly for the Greek agents to be recalled to Greece and replaced by more amenable men. His desperation can be clearly seen from his letters of the time. 'We are all of us very ill satisfied with the Greek deputies,' he wrote to Gordon. 'They are feeble, timid, suspicious, and impractical men wholly unfit for the post they occupy.'[16] To Hobhouse he wrote, 'I cannot obtain from Orlando and Luriottis even the civility of an answer to my letters—I will write no more. A man who has written three or four thousand letters to serve a cause (as I have done) and then by way of reward cannot get a civil word from the representatives of that cause must have passion for being so scorned if he bear it long.'[17]

Early in June a stormy meeting took place beetween Bowring and the Greek deputies. The date was approaching on which stockholders were due to pay the fourth instalment of money on their bonds. Despite the low rating of the bonds on the Stock Exchange the deputies were determined to press ahead in the belief that once the fourth payment had been made it would be too late for the stockholders to withdraw and that the bonds would be more secure as a result. Bowring, on the other hand, recommended that payment of the fourth instalment should be postponed until the situation in Greece itself was clarified. Bowring's advice was probably sound but by then he was personally far too deeply embroiled for his advice to have any claim to be objective.

His own financial position was now desperate. He was already in arrears on the payments for his bonds. He could not pay the fourth instalment and to sell the bonds at their current price would have been ruinous. He therefore swallowed his pride and begged the Greek deputies to lend him £5,000, offering his £25,000 of unpaid-for bonds as security. The deputies were affronted, but after pressure from other members of the Committee they reluctantly consented to a device to extricate Bowring from his embarrassment. In September they bought Bowring's £25,000 bonds at ten per cent discount, although the market stood at sixteen per cent below par, the difference being generously attributed to gratitude for Bowring's services to the Greek cause.

That was not the end of the matter. No sooner had the deal been concluded than a new factor appeared. Edward Blaquiere who had gone to Greece with the first instalment of the loan in the spring now reappeared on the scene. Blaquiere had spent his few months in Greece rushing around trying to continue the work of Colonel Stanhope. Although he had Stanhope's pomposity he lacked his ability. As Humphreys told Gordon in August 1824, 'Blaquiere . . . is a most extraordinary fellow. I should think he is a little cracked. He has a mania for writing letters of advice. He wrote one to the Lord High Commissioner which was a matchless production.'[18]

Blaquiere was, as ever, more interested in the appearance than the reality. His letters of advice may not have had any effect on the Greeks but that was not their sole purpose. They were carefully collected to be worked up into yet another book on his return to London. When he was due to leave Greece he had one of his most brilliant ideas—a true example of creative advertising. He persuaded the Greeks to send a Greek ship to England. The appearance of the first ship flying the colours of regenerated Greece in British waters would, he argued, be bound to cause a sensation and to resuscitate the flagging bonds. The *Amphitrite*, a Hydriote vessel with Blaquiere on board, duly reached the Medway in the middle of October. She had a cargo of currants and other Greek products to give the impression that Greece was a flourishing country easily able to repay the loan. She also carried nine frightened Greek boys (a tenth had died on the voyage) who were due to be sent to school as an example of practical regeneration in action.

One of Blaquiere's first actions on landing was to dress two of the Greek boys in expensive Greek costumes and parade them round London. They were naturally taken to the Stock Exchange where, it was said,[19] they were greeted with cheers. Blaquiere's theatricals had the intended effect. The discount on Greek bonds which was standing at sixteen per cent below par on 26 September before the arrival of the *Amphitrite*, had fallen to a mere four and a half per cent by the end of October. The speculators were not slow to seize their chance. Bowring, bold as brass, now wrote to the deputies asking to have his bonds back. The deputies were flabbergasted at his effrontery but again, after the usual pressure, they gave way. Bowring's bonds were given back to him at the old price and sold off on the market at the enhanced price.

Hume was also reimbursed by the deputies. He had bought £10,000 worth of scrip but had been obliged to sell in August at a loss of £1,300. From that day onward Hume never lost an opportunity of complaining that the deputies had treated him unjustly. At last, at the end of November, the deputies paid him a visit at his London house. After a good deal of sparring it emerged that the deputies were prepared to pay him £1,300, the amount of his loss, from their funds in return, presumably, for his silence. Hume accepted but only on condition that the deputies paid him a further £54, for interest for the period during which he had been without the money!

If the Greek deputies thought that by these expensive favours they could repurchase the co-operation of Bowring and the others, they were soon disabused. Early in December Bowring informed them officially that the London Greek Committee had decided to make direct representations to the Greek Government impeaching their public conduct. The news was passed to the Greek Government that there could be no question of another loan in the London market while Orlandos and Louriottis remained in London. But this time Bowring and his friends had over-estimated their strength. At the beginning of January 1825 the Greek deputies gleefully announced that arrangements had been made with Messrs J. & S. Ricardo, London bankers, to float a second loan on behalf of Greece, this time for £2,000,000. The whole affair had been concluded in secret without reference to the London Greek Committee. Orlandos and Louriottis were in a stronger position than ever.

Before the events of the Second Loan are described, the upshot of the other aspect of the muddle mentioned earlier should be explained. As the summer of 1824 progressed, the deputies and the Committee learnt that the two instalments of gold which had been sent to Greece had been sequestrated at Zante following the death of Lord Byron for lack of commissioners to receive it on behalf of the Greeks. The obvious solution was to send out new commissioners, but with Bowring and the Greek deputies engaged in a desperate struggle with one another over money and policy, it is hardly surprising that the obvious solution was not an easy one. Gordon, who had been named as commissioner to succeed Byron, saw what was happening and prudently refused to accept the commission. Hobhouse, who felt a deep sense of personal obligation to carry on the work begun by Lord Byron, was ready to go to Greece and even had his bags packed when he too realized that the interests of Greece, of the Greek Committee and of the Greek deputies could not be reconciled with one another, let alone reconciled with the interests of the bond holders. Furthermore, distressing news was arriving in London of a civil war raging in Greece. It was not at all clear that there was any longer a government in Greece to whom the money could properly be consigned.

In August 1824 the Committee at last found two commissioners willing to go to Greece to try to sort out the muddle. James Hamilton Browne, a dismissed official of the Ionian Government, had been in Greece before— he had accompanied Byron from Genoa—but he had no position or authority. The other, Henry Lytton Bulwer, the brother of the novelist, had been intending to go to Greece as a volunteer. Bulwer was later to achieve some distinction in the British foreign service. To judge from the book which he published about his visit to Greece, [20] in 1824 he was still a silly supercilious young man, proud of showing off his education, a romantic Byronist with a condescending manner. The London Greek Committee were sending a boy on a man's errand although, as events turned out, the situation was probably beyond correction in any case.

The exact nature of the mandate Browne and Bulwer were given cannot now be ascertained. They seem to have been instructed to hand over the money to the Greek Government if they found a Greek Government with roughly the same amount of authority in Greece as at the time when the loan was contracted for. But they also seem to have been instructed to persuade the Greek Government to accept conditions for the spending of the money and, in particular, to clarify the respective powers of the deputies and the Committee in London.

Browne and Bulwer crossed Europe by land to save time and reached Greece at about the same time as the *Florida* arrived at Nauplia with £50,000 worth of gold on board, the third instalment of the loan. To their surprise they found that the first two instalments, which were thought to be safely locked up at Zante, had already been paid over to the Greeks. Samuel Barff, taking the initiative into his own hands in a manner not to be encouraged in bankers, had disregarded the details of the contract and the law of the Ionian Islands, and exported the money with the simple excuse that the money was intended for Greece and to Greece it should go.

The task of Browne and Bulwer, which had seemed difficult enough before, was now rendered impossible. Once the Greeks had got their hands on the first £80,000 it was unlikely that they could consent to any conditions restricting their freedom of action. Browne and Bulwer's strongest bargaining counter—the fear that more loans would not be forthcoming without the co-operation of the British Philhellenes—was fast losing its

P

force. Not only were the deputies reporting fully from London on their negotiations with other bankers there, but the omnipresent Knights of Malta were renewing their offers to raise money for Greece in Paris. Browne and Bulwer hung around Nauplia week after week waiting for an answer to their overtures but were fobbed off with the old diplomatic trick of 'Tomorrow'. Then they both fell severely ill and their negotiating position declined from weakness to impotence. It seemed certain that they would die—as did the captain of the *Florida*—if they did not leave Nauplia at once for the fresher air of the islands. Abandoning the negotiations they sailed away and by great good fortune both survived. They did obtain a piece of paper from the Greek Government before being taken to safety by a British warship, but it was little more than a receipt for the money.

The abortive mission of Browne and Bulwer can be regarded as the last gasp of the London Greek Committee—their final feeble attempt to exercise some control over the Greek deputies in London and over the spending of the money. By the end of 1824 the deputies were in complete command. The launching of the second loan merely confirmed their supremacy. The Committee existed only in name—even minutes were no longer kept. The *Florida*, *Little Sally*, and *Nimble* plied a shuttle service through 1824 and 1825 conveying to Greece their cargoes of English gold.

The second Greek loan was floated in February 1825. Its terms were even more attractive to investors than the first. It was discounted to $55\frac{1}{2}$ instead of 59. As with the first loan, a sum equivalent to two years' interest at five per cent of the nominal capital was withheld along with a sum equivalent to one per cent to establish a sinking fund. The administration of the loan was in the hands of Messrs. J. and S. Ricardo, London bankers. Orlandos and Louriottis, the Greek deputies, had almost absolute control and the London Greek Committee was not officially concerned at all. However, the deputies continued to deal on an individual basis with several members of the Committee whom they believed to be their friends.

The sum realized was £980,000 but that takes no account of the 'commissions' and 'expenses'. If some of the dealings connected with the first loan were less than proper, the handling of the second loan was scandalous. Despite the voluminous information that was gradually drawn out by successive inquiries, the complete story still defies reconstruction. Hundreds of thousands of pounds were wasted on the schemes to build a fleet for Greece—a complex story told in a later chapter. But waste is one thing, corruption another. A sum of £113,000 was said to have been spent on 'rejuvenating' the stock of the first loan—in other words playing the market to try to keep the price up, an activity affording innumerable opportunities for the exchanging of favours and the lining of pockets. Bonds were bought when the market was low and accounted as if they had been bought when it was high. Other huge sums were put down as expenses or commissions for this or that which were little more than bribes. Bowring is said to have accepted a further payment as simple hush money. Many thousands of pounds remained entirely unaccounted for. The deputies were not subtle embezzlers. Not content to appropriate large sums by the safe method of making false purchases and sales, they could not resist taking a rake-off even when small sums passed through their hands and when the chances of detection were high. For example, a sum of £2,695 was charged as lost owing to the failure of a Greek merchant in London: the merchant's books showed only £500. The sum of £1,200 was credited as received from Calcutta from a subscription there, but the Calcutta accounts showed that £2,200 was sent. It is not even possible to discover how much money was remitted to Greece.

During most of 1824 and 1825 the British public and the holders of Greek bonds remained in ignorance of the sordid dramas being enacted behind the scenes with their money. They occasionally read in the newspapers that the *Florida* or one of the other vessels had left England with another consignment of gold and assumed that everything was going well. Then towards the end of 1825 a distressing series of events occurred. First, the South American mining speculations collapsed whereupon the Bank of England, becoming alarmed at the galloping speculation, stopped discounting commercial paper. Suddenly the country was in the grip of an economic crisis. There were a few dramatic bank failures and the gold poured from the Bank's reserves. In December the country was said to be 'within twenty four hours of barter' and only emergency government measures, allowing the Bank to exceed the legal limit on its note issue, saved the situation; but it did not prevent numerous business enterprises from bankruptcy. Foreign stocks followed soon afterwards. In January 1826 the agents for the Colombian Government loan stopped payment and the myth that stocks were safe just because they were 'government' exploded. Suddenly the horrible truth burst in on thousands of investors— the only interest they had received came out of the principal of successive loans and the only way they were likely to get any more payments from abroad was by making more loans. Within a few months a long list of foreign governments were in default—Spain, Portugal, every South American country except Brazil, and of course Greece.

It was natural, since the speculation boom had now clearly burst, that attention should again be directed towards the progress of the Greek loan. At the beginning of 1826 rumours that the loans were being mismanaged began to circulate, culminating in the publication of a book, *Greece Vindicated*, by an Italian Philhellene, Count Palma, which threw out a number of accusations and demanded an investigation into the conduct of the deputies. The bonds slipped down to eighteen per cent below par. At the same time frightening news began to arrive of the progress of the war in Greece.

In particular, accounts were gradually coming through of the fall of Missolonghi, the circumstances of which will be described in a later chapter.

The situation on the Stock Exchange was too bad even for 'rejuvenation' dealings to have much effect. Attempts were made to hush up or deny the reports from Greece. False reports* were deliberately published in order to

---

* It is perhaps worth quoting one of these false reports in full for the light it sheds on public opinion at the time. The reports are presumably an attempt to set down the kind of news the stockholders wanted to hear, but clearly if they had outraged public credulity too far they would not have been accepted for publication. The following composition from *The Examiner* emphasizes how profoundly ignorant the public still were about conditions in Greece. None of the brave Philhellenes mentioned in the letters (except Berton) are otherwise known to history, nor are the 1,500 French and Italian volunteers from Leghorn. General Lafayette took part in the American War of Independence, but exercised his philhellenism from Paris; at the age of 69 he is unlikely to have been successful with the bayonet. The battles described—ferocious enough for anyone's money—are equally imaginary:

Missolonghi, Jan. 2, 1826.—[From a Correspondent.]—On the morning of the 30th December, the Turks were seen advancing in three heavy columns in the direction of the George Franklin and Betzaris batteries, led on by German Officers, under a tremendous fire of artillery and mortars; at the same time their fleet commenced a most furious attack on the port. They were received by a destructive shower of grape and musquetry from the troops and batteries; at the same time a discharge of shells and rockets added to their dismay; but in spite of a heavy loss they advanced and carried two of the outports. The conflict now raged with the greatest fury, shot and shells spread death in every direction. Our gallant artillery and riflemen excited terror around them. It is impossible to describe the horrors of the scene; all around was obscured with clouds of smoke. At this moment two Turkish vessels blew up with a tremendous explosion; still they persisted, and, after two hours fighting, they succeeded in obtaining possession of the Franklin battery. After a heavy loss, an officer planted the Turkish colours on the rampart, when our gallant leader, St Aubyn, rushed forward and hurled him from the walls. The ground was now disputed inch by inch, the slaughter was tremendous on both sides, the Turks were three times driven back with immense loss, or they must have succeeded, when Admiral Miaulis entered the harbour, and commenced a furious attack on their fleet, which ended in their total defeat, with the loss of sixteen sail burnt or taken. The infidels were now totally routed, and flying in all directions, pursued by our victorious troops, leaving the ditches filled, and the wall covered with their dead. Two 24-pounders on the Franklin were literally covered with blood.

I regret to state, our brave Major St Aubyn lost his arm while cheering his men at the third attack. Our loss was severe; the Turks lost four thousand killed, eight hundred wounded, five hundred prisoners, fifteen German and other Officers, with fifteen cannon and mortars taken.

Had not Admiral Miaulis arrived to relieve us, it was the intention of the Governor and Officers to have blown up all together.

Camp of St. Anne's, near Lepanto, Jan. 17, 1826.
I take the first opportunity of writing you the account of the late victory. On the 12th there was a sharp skirmish, in which the Turks lost a number of their best men and officers, and fell back to the village. About seven o'clock next morning the contest began with the outposts, which fell back into line. A large body of Mamelukes were charged by our cavalry, headed by Colonel Berton, and totally routed. Our riflemen in front picked out the officers as they advanced to their post. Our artillery was

puff up the cause, as had been done in 1821 and 1822 from the famous 'mints of philhellenic mendacity'[22] in Germany and Italy. Blaquiere, always to be relied upon, rushed into print for the fourth time on the Greek cause, dropping encouraging hints that diplomatic action by the powers would soon restore the situation,[23] but gradually the pressure for an investigation became irresistible.

Most of the accusations were directed at the deputies, and the suspicious

served by French and English volunteers, who had orders not to fire till the Turks were within 200 yards. The enemy now endeavoured to turn our left wing, but were received at the point of the bayonet by General La Fayette, our second in command. The battle now raged along the whole line with the most deadly fury. The village of St John was three times taken and retaken, with great slaughter; their second in command fell in the last attack, when they gave up the contest, leaving 800 dead on the spot, besides prisoners and wounded. General Gouras, at the head of the Corinthian brigade, carried the village of St Anne's, and ordered a general attack with the whole force, when the Turks were completely routed, and fled in every direction, leaving 3000 dead, 900 prisoners, 400 wounded, 2 generals killed, 14 officers wounded, 25 taken, with 9 cannon, the Pacha's tent, 14 baggage and ammunition waggons, &c. Our loss was 800 killed and 700 wounded. A young man of the name of Herbert took two standards, for which he was made Captain on the field; three other standards were also taken. The Turkish force was 10,000 men; ours was 7,000. Make all the haste you can to join us. I hope the next will inform you that the Cross floats on the walls of Lepanto.

LETTER FROM COLONEL BERTON.

Camp at Lepanto, Jan. 25, 1826.

Dear —, After the affair of the 12th, we had a fatiguing march in pursuit of the runaway Ibrahim Pacha, who was collecting his troops at Lepanto and Patras, and talking very largely of putting us all to the sword, but we saved his Highness the trouble, by a signal defeat. We arrived under the walls of the above place, on the 20th, driving his picquets before us, and next morning blockaded the town. Generals La Fayette and Delcroux having surveyed the ground, we began our trenches, in spite of a heavy fire from the town and castle. On the 22nd we were joined by fifteen hundred French and Italian volunteers from Leghorn, consisting of lancers, hussars, &c. and a small battering train of eight thirty-six pounders and four mortars. On the same night, two German officers deserted to us, and informed us of the Pacha's intent of attacking us in the morning with 15,000 horse and foot. Our force was only 9,000. At daybreak, the Turks advanced, covered by a heavy fire from the fortification, with loud shouts of Alla and Mahomet. Our artillery and musquetry opened on them with tremendous effect, and in fifteen minutes the whole line was furiously engaged; our cavalry charged the enemy in grand style, cutting numbers of them to pieces. The battle had now raged seven hours with the greatest obstinacy, when the fine convent of St Mary's was blown up, and 700 Turks with it; their line was now broken and routed, they flying in every direction to the town, pursued by our cavalry to the gates; a part entered pell-mell with them, but not being supported, cut their way out, only losing six men in that daring exploit. A party of our cavalry had nearly taken the Pacha prisoner, who was carried off the field wounded by a carbine ball in his breast. The enemy lost 4,000 killed, 800 wounded, 2,000 prisoners, 8 standards, 10 cannon, 6 ammunition waggons. Our loss was 2,000 killed, 400 wounded. General Gouras was slightly wounded in the head by a musket ball. The Turks had orders to give no quarter. They lost 125 officers. I forgot to inform you, in my last, that the Pacha (Ibrahim's) tent and seraglio of ladies were taken.

B. BERTON.[21]

stockholders assumed that the London Greek Committee was the proper body to protect their interests. Bowring, sensing this, tried to forestall any criticism that might be levelled at himself for his part in the first loan, by joining the pack in attacks against the second loan. It was a mean device, and ultimately it failed, but Bowring rode the tiger for a surprisingly long time. The Greek deputies—hardened embezzlers and double-dealers though they were—must have felt that British hypocrisy was especially blessed when Bowring was appointed secretary of an investigating commission by the Greek Government. The commission made no discoveries since the deputies simply refused to accept their right to investigate their affairs.

Then in July 1826 Bowring published an anonymous article in the *Westminster Review* in defence of the London Greek Committee. It was a skilful piece of unscrupulous politics. As far as the first loan was concerned, he gave a categorical undertaking that the funds had been well applied with 'no waste, no jobbing in any state whatever'. In turning to attack the second loan for which the Committee had no responsibility he casually mentioned that the bondholders could expect 'total and final loss'. It was a brilliant stroke. The bondholders, worried though they were, had never feared this even in their deepest moments of depression. Indignantly they began to organize themselves to demand action, assisted by Bowring who gave them a paper on the results of the earlier abortive investigation. Then in September, led by the unsuspecting Colonel Stanhope, they decided to appoint a further investigating committee and again Bowring was made a member. As before no progress was possible since, naturally, the deputies and Messrs. Ricardo refused to co-operate. Bowring brazenly continued his bluff. 'We are going most courageously and determinedly', he wrote in statesmanlike terms to a friend, 'into the enquiries connected with the Greek loans. Whether any ultimate good will result I know not but the public shall know the facts.'[24] In October a further angry meeting of bondholders discussed a recent admission by Louriottis that £8,000 worth of bonds had been purchased at 54 when the market stood at less than half that figure. Bowring who was present joined in the chorus of condemnation and declared that the truth must be ruthlessly pursued 'no matter to whom it attached reproach'.[25] No gambler under strain was ever more cool or courageous. He staked his reputation on being able to stir up enough dust and cause enough bluster to obscure his own guilt.

By now Orlandos had left England but Louriottis, the other deputy, refused to be browbeaten. With the help of *The Times* he skilfully redirected the indignation of the bondholders. In disclosing that £8,000 had been bought at far higher than the market rate, Louriottis had declared cryptically that this had been done on behalf of a 'friend of Greece . . . whose name he could not possibly state'. *The Times* led the demand that the 'friend of Greece' should be named, thundering that 'the man who has done this is what we call in English a swindler'. Soon a lively correspondence developed in the newspapers with every day bringing new charges and counter-charges. It was *The Times* which in the end, from its own inquiries, published the apparently anticlimatic story that the 'friend of Greece' was a little-known man called Burton, a London broker. Once the circle of silence was broken the whole story became clearer. Burton, it seems, had made an agreement with the deputies that the transaction in which he was involved could only be made public in the context of a general revelation of all similar transactions, including the one in which Bowring was involved. The deputies had a strong motive for not making public the Burton transaction since Burton was only an agent for bonds owned by Louriottis' secretary, George Lee; Burton was in fact merely an instrument of the deputies' own embezzlement! Bowring may have been banking on this net of intrigue holding enough to preserve his own activities secret, but even when the full story of his transactions in 1824 was published he denied it with high disdain. It was not until *The Times* had published one of Bowring's letters of 1824 which left no room for doubt, that he was compelled to admit what had happened, and then he claimed lamely in his defence that he had been suffering from a family sorrow at the time and could not be held responsible.

Gradually one scandalous fact after another was dragged before the public gaze. The deputies' guilt was never in any doubt. They at first refused to give any account and then, when they did, their accounts had such huge 'miscellaneous' items and such dissimilar services lumped together that it was obvious that money had disappeared. But the British public was more interested in the revelations about the British.

Bowring, naturally, came in for more criticism than the others. Attempts were made to warn Bentham against his favourite disciple and chosen executor, but Bentham forgave him. Hume came out of the scandal with some scraps of dignity. He admitted openly what he had done and tried to give the impression that it was only what any red-blooded man of affairs would have done in similar circumstances. Ellice feebly feigned indignation at the accusations against him until overwhelming evidence was produced. Stanhope and Hobhouse, although they may not have been proved to have been directly involved in any malpractices, had been made to look thoroughly incompetent and simple. All the leaders of the London Greek Committee were either knaves or fools.

Numerous bankers and brokers were also exposed as enriching themselves by doubtfully proper activities. The embarrassment of Hume and Ellice, both rich self-made men from Scotland, and of the bankers provided a feast of opportunities for ritual attacks on those ogres ever present where finance is concerned, the Scots and the Jews.

The satirists poured out their doggerel on the theme:

Roused by the sound of liberty and scrip
To arms, to arms belligerent brokers skip:
Loud rings the cry of freedom far and wide;
Stocks and subscriptions pour on every side;
Contractors, weeping over Grecian wounds,
Pocket their four-and-sixty thousand pounds.

*   *   *

Here 'Brimful now is misery's fatal cup
The Turks have blown another fortress up'
There 'Forts blown up! I've heavier news to tell;
The scrip—the scrip will be blown up as well'
One cries 'The cause is lost', another 'Zounds!
Who cares: I've lost my four and fifty pounds'
Snuffles a saint 'I sorrow for the Cross!
But 19 discount is a serious loss'[26]

The chief victim of the Greek bubble was Benthamism. Joseph Hume had been the scourge of the Government in the House of Commons. He had employed clerks at his own expense to go through the public accounts to look for the smallest items of unnecessary expenditure. He had exploited his experience in making fortunes in India to attack the administration of the East India Company. Ellice had been a leader in criticizing the Government's methods of administration and seeing waste in every activity undertaken. Hobhouse and Stanhope had for years bored and exasperated the British public with their sermonizing.

At last the public had its own back. The radicals, the denigrators, the men who adopted a high moral tone, the men who were forever pushing fashionable liberal causes down the throats of the people, the men who saw nothing right with the community in which they lived but had a ready answer to every political problem, these men had been proved to be either corrupt or incompetent and in some cases both. The men who had assumed a superiority in wisdom, who never doubted that they were the best leaders for the British Empire, had shown themselves unable to handle even such a puny enterprise as the Greek loan without bungling it. The downfall of the Benthamites was enjoyed throughout Britain with a savage self-satisfied relish.

But in politics memories are short. The Benthamites had the kind of resilience which accompanies arrogance. Within months Hume, Ellice, and the others were attacking the Government as successfully as ever, undismayed by the affair of the Greek bubble. Within a few years Bowring's misdemeanours had been forgotten to the extent that he was being employed by the Government for commercial investigations on the Continent. If in the end the careers of these remarkable men did not match their ambitions, the reasons lay elsewhere.

What then did the loans achieve? The story of the £1,000,000 or so that was actually spent on behalf of Greece will be told in later chapters. Here it is enough to round off the story of the loans. No interest was ever paid on the bonds. The price fell steadily. Many investors lost heavily. The bonds were bought up from the original investors for a shilling or two by professional speculators, and for the next fifty years they were passed around the stock exchanges of Europe. They still had a value. As long as Greece was in default on her loans the holders of the bonds managed to keep the stock exchanges of Europe closed to her. Greece, along with the other countries who had defaulted in the speculative bubble of 1823–5, was virtually cut off from European credit and capital and her economic development was retarded as a result. The speculators calculated that a time would come when Greece would settle with the bond holders in order to have access to European capital.

It was not until 1878 that the time came. The sum owed by Greece for the two loans then amounted to no less than £10,030,000. Since the total revenue of the Greek Government for all purposes at that time was about £750,000 and the irreducible expenditure about £850,000, it was clear that the chances of the loans ever being repaid in full were slender. After long negotiations the bondholders accepted a complicated arrangement, the basis of which was that the accumulated debt would be cancelled on the issue of £1,200,000 worth of new bonds at five per cent. It was a generous settlement.

23. *The Coming of the Arabs*

At the end of 1823 it seemed to many observers that the Greek war was over; that Greek independence was secure; and that all that remained was for the facts to be internationally recognized and the appropriate treaties drawn up to regularize the new situation. Sultan Mahmoud had twice attempted to put down the Greek rebellion without success. In 1822 two huge armies had been sent down either side of Greece only to be destroyed when they reached the end of their journey. In 1823, owing partly to the fire in the arsenal at Constantinople, the attempt at reconquest from the north had been ill-prepared and half-hearted. It was true that the Turks still held a few important fortresses in Greece; that there was still a good deal of fighting and disputed sovereignty in the area north of the Corinthian Gulf; and that the Turks still had a large and undefeated fleet. Yet, on balance, it seemed reasonable to assume that the Turks would never again attempt a full-scale invasion. Several histories of the war were published in Western Europe at this time to coincide with the end of the war.

In reality, Sultan Mahmoud had not abandoned his hope of reconquest. The Ottoman Empire, despite the fashionable view that it was on the point of breaking up, still had immense resources. Mahmoud, one of the most effective rulers that the Empire had endured for generations, realized this. The weakness arose not from lack of resources but from lack of organization, from disorder, and from incompetence. This was a weakness which a determined ruler could put right and Mahmoud devoted himself—with no small success—to the attempt. But by its nature reorganization took time. It took time to wind up the war with Persia which always seemed to break out when there was trouble in the west of the Empire. It took time to restore relations with Russia, whose armies had menaced the northern borders since the outbreak of the Greek Revolution. It took time to reform the administration and the finances of the Empire. In particular, it took time to build up an army on the modern European model. Mahmoud realized that he would have to wait for an opportunity when he would be strong enough to impose modernization on the janissaries.

The situation in Greece could not wait. If the Ottoman Empire was obliged to recognize the independence of Free Greece, however unimportant and small the geographical area might be, then the way would be open for all the other nationalities of European Turkey to attempt revolt, to say nothing of the multifarious races of Asiatic Turkey. An example had to be made of the Greeks. The dangerous Western European idea of nationalism could not be permitted to implant itself in the East. Mahmoud needed an army and at once.

There was no question of finding allies. No Christian power, whatever the secret wishes of its government, would have dared to help the Sultan to crush his rebellious Christian subjects. There was only one man in a position to help.

Mehemet Ali, the Pasha of Egypt, was among the most remarkable men of the early nineteenth century. By birth an Albanian, born the son of a peasant in Thrace, his career was a supreme example of one of the great strengths of the Ottoman Empire. The Empire was a meritocracy right up to the highest positions, the merits being chiefly survivability and ruthlessness. Mehemet Ali had first made his mark in the Turkish army in the campaigns against Bonaparte in Egypt. He stayed in Egypt after the war and in 1805 became Pasha. Thereafter, his career went from success to success. In 1807 he inflicted a severe and humiliating defeat upon an invading British force. In 1811 he organized a systematic massacre of the Mamelukes who had ruled Egypt for some hundreds of years, and thereafter until 1849 he was the sole ruler of the country. With the help of his son, Ibrahim, who was equally effective, Mehemet imposed his will on long-suffering Egypt with tenacious ferocity. The country was beaten and cowed into order and discipline. Tens of thousands of men died in carrying out his grandiose works and the rate of tax on the fellaheen was raised by between 600 and 1,000 per cent. In Europe, Mehemet won a reputation as a benevolent reformer by the simple device, much employed by dictators, of being polite to foreign visitors and by making the public services appear to work efficiently. Modern European methods were systematically imposed on all walks of life and, for a few brief and intensely uncomfortable years, Egypt ceased to be a backward country. If the great powers of Europe had not become alarmed in the 1830s, then the whole Ottoman Empire might have been resuscitated under an Albanian dynasty; the technological and military gap between Europe and the East which had been widening since the seventeenth century might have been closed; and the Turks and their allies might again have become a terror to Europe.

Mehemet's first priority was the efficiency of his armed forces. The army was raised from 20,000 to 100,000 but it was unlike any other army in the East. From his experience in fighting Bonaparte, Mehemet had conceived a profound admiration for French military methods. His troops were therefore trained in the most modern European system, as regular troops in uniform with close discipline, ready as necessary to stand in line or charge with the bayonet. They were supplied with the best types of arms imported from France. French and other European officers were attracted by high pay to serve as instructors and as officers in the field. The navy too was rebuilt to modern standards with the help of French constructors. Orders were placed for naval vessels to be built in France and many a Philhellene had remarked on Mehemet's frigates building in the shipyard at Marseilles. Another of his best ships was built at Deptford near London. Mehemet's armies did not lack experience. Between 1811 and 1818 Ibrahim subdued the provinces of Arabia in a series of ferocious campaigns; and between 1821 and 1823 another of Mehemet's sons, Ismael, conquered and annexed the Sudan. It was clear that a formidable power was growing up in the East.

At the beginning of 1824, at about the same time as the Greek deputies Orlandos and Louriottis arrived in London, the Sultan put a proposal to Mehemet. Mehemet was still nominally the subject of the Sultan, and Egypt was still nominally a part of the Ottoman Empire, but neither party was much interested in appearances. The fact was that the Pasha was as powerful a man as the Sultan, and Mahmoud only turned to Mehemet out of desperation. It was agreed that the two should co-operate to crush the Greek rebellion. In return for the help of the Egyptians, the Sultan promised that Crete would be put under Mehemet's control and that Ibrahim would be made Pasha of the Morea. Mahmoud could have had little confidence that Greece would ever return to his control. If it was reconquered, Mehemet would be even more powerful, even more of a threat to the Sultan's own position. Not only would he have a large and underpopulated province on which to impose his accustomed methods of development but, more importantly, he would have a direct link with Albania and therefore an inexhaustible supply of cheap undiscriminating soldiers. Mahmoud's best hope was that he would buy time, that if the Greek Revolution could be extinguished, then something might have turned up or his own reforms might have borne fruit before he had himself to face a confrontation with the Pasha.

For the time being, thoughts of the future were put aside as the two rulers mobilized their strength against the Greeks. From the beginning of 1824 the dockyards at Constantinople were busy fitting out new warships and the Sultan himself made several visits to encourage the workers. Instructions were sent to all the provinces ordering levies of troops and armed gangs roamed the streets of the capital impressing men for the fleet. The Ottoman Government took out contracts for the hire of foreign merchant ships to act as transport vessels. In Egypt too the preparations were intense. Alexandria, hitherto a commercial port, was transformed into a vast naval dockyard. Thousands of trained soldiers, mainly Egyptians and Albanians, were collected and billeted in cantonments nearby in readiness to form the invading forces. And Mehemet too, by offering lucrative rates and squeezing normal trade, hired a fleet of foreign merchant ships—flying the flags of most European countries—to help transport his armies.

The signs were clear for all to see. Soon they became unmistakable. Crete was the first to feel the change. By the spring of 1824 Hussein, Mehemet's son-in-law, had extinguished all but a few mountain enclaves of resistance. An expedition was then mounted against the island of Casos whose inhabitants had since the outbreak of the Revolution and earlier earned their living by the murder, pillage, and piracy of Greeks, Turks, and Franks. One night of killing and burning put an end to the Casiote menace. Shortly afterwards, a similar scene was enacted at Psara, one of the three islands that provided the warships on which Free Greece depended. At the beginning of July the Ottoman fleet effected a landing and destroyed everything they found. During these dreadful months in 1824 the war again burst into life. It was the kind of war—if war it can be called—that had not been seen since the destruction of Chios in 1822. It is impossible to estimate how many tens of thousands of men, women and children were systematically and haphazardly butchered and left to die of exposure, wounds, starvation, and disease. Again the slave markets of the Empire were glutted with human cattle and a ghastly cargo of trophies, including 500 heads and 1,200 ears was sent to Constantinople for exhibition at the Seraglio Gate.

Meanwhile, the Greeks were behaving as if the war was already over. After the defeat of the invasion from the north in 1823 the country had split into numerous fragments as the original contradictions in the aims of the revolutionaries could no longer be concealed. For a few months from the end of 1823 till the spring of 1824 the country was in the grip of the first civil war. This name, however, gives a false picture of what was actually occurring. Sporadic acts of violence were committed between various groups in several areas of Greece but the casualties were small. The chief opponents were, on the one hand, a coalition of the islanders, some of the chieftains of Roumeli, the area north of the gulf of Corinth, and the remnants of the Westernized party which still hoped to build a unitary European state, and, on the other hand, Colocotrones and some of the other captains of the Morea. Some chieftains—notably Odysseus— remained neutral or indifferent.

The island party had some claim to be regarded as the legitimate Government—in so far as such terms have validity in a revolutionary situation—as the direct successor of the Government proclaimed at Epidaurus in 1822. The rich Hydriote ship-owner, Conduriottis, held the title of President of Greece. He was an Albanian, unable to speak Greek. And so the leaders of both armies in the war came—as did many of the fighting men—from that violent illiterate race who had not yet learned to prefer nationalism to other loyalties.

The chief aim of Conduriottis' Government was to assert its authority over Colocotrones and in particular to compel him to hand over Nauplia which his men had held since its fall. The Government brought armed men from Roumeli and by the spring of 1824 Colocotrones' son Panos was under siege at Nauplia. At the same time fighting between rival chieftains had broken out in Western Greece.

This was the situation at the end of June 1824 when, in quick succession, two pieces of news arrived which immediately transformed the politics of Greece. First of all it was learned that £40,000 worth of English gold intended for Greece had arrived at Zante. Then, soon afterwards, came the terrifying stories of the destruction of Casos and Psara. When the news of Psara reached Zante, Samuel Barff decided to send the money immediately to the Greek Government despite the prohibition of its export by the Ionian Government.

In war, so it has often been said, three things are required above all else, money, money, and more money. This had been the view of all intelligent observers of the Greek scene. Demetrius Hypsilantes had apparently failed because of lack of money to command national loyalty; the Regiment Baleste had failed for lack of money to pay and recruit its men; the German Legion had failed through lack of money to buy food; the Byron Brigade had failed when the poet paymaster died. Most important of all, successive attempts at imposing national unity on Greece had failed because the so-called governments had never had enough money to break local and personal loyalties buttressed by money. Now for the first time in the history of the war, money was available.

To any outsider used to Western European methods of thought there could be no doubt about the right policy in these circumstances. Greece lay under the imminent threat of invasion by a large, disciplined, well-tried army. The first priority must surely be to put aside the internal political divisions and unite against the common enemy. The British gold, judiciously dispensed, would act as the cement to keep the various groups together.

This policy was in fact attempted and eventually it can be said to have succeeded but only at enormous cost after two civil wars. The economic consequences of introducing a large amount of precious metal into Greece were not foreseen. It was simply assumed that the effects would be beneficial, that because in earlier phases of the war things might have been different if there had been a little more money available, then these situations could be repeated and the benefits multiplied by injecting larger sums. The arrival of the gold had a drastic effect not only on the economy of Greece but also on its political structure. Power in revolutionary Greece depended (more than it normally does in more settled countries) on the possession of money. Anyone with money could hire armed men and there was a large pool of underemployed armed men who felt no compunction about moving about offering their services from market to market.

The arrival at Nauplia in quick succession of three shiploads of gold caused a sensation throughout Greece. The Reverend Sheridan Wilson, who was present when the first ship arrived, records that 'the sight of beautiful English gold almost threw the poor penniless natives into extacies'. He describes how he met a party of Greeks on his travels shortly afterwards. '"Sir," they enquired, "is the loan arrived?" "Yes," said I, "the brig lies at Nauplia." Not a word more did the poor fellows utter; but, seizing each others' hands, they formed a circle, danced for a few moments on the green sward, and then, bidding me farewell . . . they set off for the golden fleece.'[1] At Nauplia itself each successive shipload was greeted with shouts of 'Long Live England!'[2] After the first three instalments were paid over in the autumn of 1824, further consignments continued to arrive at roughly two-monthly intervals far into 1825.

The exact amount of gold that was shipped to Greece from the proceeds of the two loans is unknown. It was probably in the range £400,000 to £500,000, and all in the form of fine gold or silver. In the context of the Greek economy at the time it was an enormous sum of money. Figures about the value of the products and about the revenues of Greece are of course sketchy and in any case comparisons based on exchange rates are notoriously difficult. Nevertheless, since there was a complete absence of exchange controls and English sovereigns and Spanish dollars, being made of fine metal, were eagerly accepted all over the Eastern Mediterranean in preference to the Ottoman coinage, it is possible to give a few indications of the value of the loan. In 1825 a gold sovereign (£1) was reckoned to be worth 50 piastres. A piastre and a half could hire a man's labour for a day. The total value of all marketed goods of the Morea in the peaceful prosperous conditions before the war was estimated at between 30,000,000 and 40,000,000 piastres taxed roughly at ten per cent. Since the war, that had probably been reduced by at least a half. In addition, the Government was unable to raise taxes in any systematic way over the whole area of Free Greece. Large regions were preserved for their own purposes by independent chiefs, and often the only method of raising revenue was to send armed bands into the country to seize a reasonable proportion of any assets they could find. In the most successful year for the Government, 1825, the revenue collected was about five and a half million piastres (about £90,000). It was hardly surprising therefore that the loan appeared to virtually all Greeks to be wealth beyond the dreams of avarice.

There seemed to be more than enough for everyone. The first civil war was quickly brought to an end by the simple expedient of paying 50,000 piastres to Colocotrones in exchange for his giving up the possession of Nauplia. All the public debts, real or imaginary, that had been built up since the outbreak of the Revolution were paid off, and all members of the Government helped themselves to large sums in payment for their own services. Corruption is the wrong word to describe the process. It was more a kind of financial anarchy.

Soon afterwards, all the leaders of revolutionary Greece began to arrive at Nauplia determined to have their share of the gold. Colocotrones was there, and Odysseus, and the great primates of the Morea, and dozens of lesser chieftains with a few men at their command, all eager to proclaim that they must have money to continue the war against the Turks which had, in fact, in mainland Greece largely ceased many months before.

Conduriottis and his Government hesitated, but political debts must be paid. The Government had been kept in power by the islanders, the ship-owners of Hydra and Spetsae of whom Conduriottis was one of the richest. They must have first claim. And it so happened that the policy of partisan selfishness could also be represented as the best policy for Greece as a whole. The dreadful news from Crete, Casos, and Psara made the threat all too clear; it was a maritime threat. What more statesmanlike strategy than to spend the money on the men whose ships provided Greece's only maritime power? And so the money was not distributed among the various factions but paid over to the shipowners with instructions to look to the naval strength of the country and to send a maritime force to avenge Psara.

The sudden availability of money, however, did not have the intended effect. In the early days of the war the sailors of Hydra and Spetsae had won a European-wide reputation for seamanship, daring, and bravery. Their light manoeuvrable ships had on several occasions confused and frightened the ponderous Turkish fleets and there had been a few striking successes particularly with the use of fire ships. But these vessels in no sense constituted a national navy; they remained privately owned, with either an individual owner paying his crew of the ship being owned and controlled by a kind of co-operative consisting of all the members of the crew. When everyone was poor and plunder was the main source of money, there was a clear incentive to daring. But now matters were different. Money was available simply for going to sea. The incentive for attacking the enemy had greatly diminished, and in any case, the sailors suspected with justice that the enemy was superior to the enemy they had known in 1821 and 1822. Besides, the

Pl. III A Greek Officer of Nauplia in 1825

Officier Grec de Nauplie
en 1825.

ship itself now became a far more valuable object. To possess a ship was equivalent to having a certificate on which gold would be paid regularly into the foreseeable future. Old hulks were hastily recommissioned and sent to sea in order that they might earn a share. Ships that were beyond repair were fitted out as fire-ships and the Government was sent inflated bills for compensation. A sea-going ship was now a valuable investment and there was a severe disincentive to hazard it by approaching too near the enemy.

European friends of Greece, in their moments of disenchantment with Colocotrones, Mavrocordato, and the rest, had always been able to console themselves with the belief that the Greek fleet at least was sound. Here at least—despite the unfortunate fact that they were undeniably Albanians—were the worthy descendants of Themistocles and Artemisia. Of all the ways of spending the Greek loan which had been suggested, the strengthening of the Greek fleet had always seemed the most fair and the most statesmanlike. In the event, however, the arrival of the English gold had the opposite effect. The bravery and daring of the Greek fleet was now alloyed with a fatal overcaution. During 1824 and 1825 the Greek fleet had several opportunities of engaging the Ottoman and Egyptian fleets but their success was limited. They now lost as many ships as they sunk. The enemy, despite their acknowledged inferiority in equipment and seamanship, survived several attacks by fire ships and direct actions. They began to grow in confidence and in skill.

The decision of the Government to pay huge salaries to the shipowners caused the fragile unity of Greece to break up again. Odysseus was one of the first to leave Nauplia to try to consolidate his own position in Eastern Greece by means that will be noted later. But Colocotrones and the primates of the Morea came out in open rebellion. And so, for the second time within a few months, Greece was thrown into a civil war—this time mainly of the islanders against the Moreotes. Colocotrones and the primates of the Morea, who had fought on opposite sides in the first civil war, were now allied.

During the second civil war the full political value of the English gold was demonstrated. The Government hired 3,000 armed men from Roumeli with promises of plentiful reward to crush the rebellion in the Morea. This they did in a few weeks, with unnecessary thoroughness, harrying, burning, and laying waste the last few areas of Greece that had not already been devastated. More damage to the country was done by the wars and depredations of the undisciplined Greeks than had been done since the outbreak of the Revolution by the enemy.

Casualties were slight as was usual in the Greek irregular engagements when both sides fired their crude weapons from behind cover and felt no shame at running back if danger appeared imminent. Among the dead was

Q

Colocotrones' son, foolishly killed in a skirmish near Tripolitsa. Colocotrones himself who had unconcernedly caused the deaths of so many people
was struck with grief and surrendered to the Government. He was imprisoned in Hydra where, unwashed and unshaven, he prophesied moodily
to his visitors that the day was not far distant when Greece would again be
begging for his assistance.

Gradually, more and more Greeks found ways of getting themselves on
the Government's pay roll. The money was never accounted for in detail.
A captain would simply contract to provide a number of armed men and
draw pay for that number. Needless to add, the opportunities for embezzlement were eagerly seized. Anyone who could muster any pretensions to a
military status appeared in Nauplia demanding pay. It was probably at this
time that the Albanian dress made its decisive step towards being regarded
as the national dress of Greece. The Government party, being largely
Albanians themselves, favoured the dress and a version of it was common
among the Greek *klephts* and *armatoli*. Now it seemed that anyone who
donned an Albanian dress could claim to be a soldier and share in the
bonanza.

Yet despite the spending of hundreds of thousands of pounds' worth
of fine gold and silver in Nauplia and Hydra there was remarkably little
to show. Visitors at the time were constantly surprised to discover how
few English coins were actually to be found in Greece. No sooner had the
money arrived and been spent, than it disappeared from circulation.

Various explanations were suggested at the time. Some observers were
of the opinion that the Greeks were secretly burying the gold and some of it
may have passed out of circulation in this way.[3] In fact, however, many of
the economic consequences of the Greek loan on Greece were exactly as
modern economic theory would expect when a large amount of a strong
convertible currency is injected into a backward economy.

Much of the money fell into the hands of the richest members of society
who had no need to spend it. They simply paid the money straight into
personal accounts with western bankers—a phenomenon well-known to
modern aid-giving agencies. The money was not allowed to filter down into
society.

Many poorer Greeks who found themselves the unexpected possessors
of a few gold sovereigns simply hoarded them, usually hiding them in
their belt. In the later battles the Arab soldiers were to be surprised and
delighted at the splendid booty with which the enemy corpses were laden.

The Hydriotes took a commission of one hundred per cent for convert-
ing English gold into local currency. It was estimated that in Hydra alone
there were between ten and twenty factories in which English sovereigns
were melted down to re-emerge as denominations of Turkish piastres.[4]
The new coins were then taken to Syra (which preserved a lucrative

commercial neutrality) and exchanged for Spanish dollars. False Spanish dollars were also manufactured locally at Hydra. It was explained to one curious visitor that 'The Ottomans are buying up your English gold and sending in its stead their own base coin. So we have set up a mint to manufacture coin still baser and have agents at Constantinople to dispose of it.'⁵ Whatever the truth of this complex explanation, it seems undeniable that the Greek Government was attempting to enlarge its resources by debasing the coins used in home circulation.

The sudden injection of gold stimulated such few local manufacturing industries as Greece had; it encouraged the rich to look for new ways of spending their money; and it led to a flood of imports. George Finlay, who witnessed the result of the spending of the money, described the scene at Nauplia in a vivid passage:

Every man of any consideration in his own imagination wanted to place himself at the head of a band of armed men, and hundreds of civilians paraded the streets of Nauplia with trains of kilted followers, like Scottish chieftains. Phanariots and doctors in medicine, who in the month of April 1824 were clad in ragged coats, and who lived on scanty rations, threw off that patriotic chrysalis before summer was past, and emerged in all the splendour of brigand life, fluttering about in rich Albanian habiliments, refulgent with brilliant and unused arms, and followed by diminutive pipe-bearers and tall henchmen. . . . Nauplia certainly offered a splendid spectacle to any one who could forget that it was the capital of an impoverished nation struggling through starvation to establish its liberty. The streets were for many months crowded with thousands of gallant young men in picturesque dresses and richly ornamented arms who ought to have been on the frontiers of Greece. . . . The illegal gains made by drawing pay and rations for troops who were never mustered, quite as much as the commissions of colonel given to apothecaries, and of captain to grooms and pipe-bearers, demoralised the military forces of Greece. The war with the Sultan seemed to be forgotten by the soldiers who thought only of indulging in the luxury of embroidered dresses and splendid arms. This is the dominant passion of every military class in Turkey, whether Greeks, Albanians, or Turks. The money poured into Greece by the loans suddenly created a demand for Albanian equipments. The bazaars of Tripolitza, Nauplia, Mesolonghi, and Athens were filled with gold-embroidered jackets, gilded yataghans, and silver-mounted pistols. Tailors came flocking to Greece from Joannina and Saloniki. Sabres, pistols, and long guns, richly mounted, were constantly passing through the Ionian Islands as articles of trade between Albania and the Morea. The arms and dress of an ordinary palikari, made in imitation of the garb of the Tosks of Southern Albania, often cost £50. Those of a chiliarch [Colonel] or a strategos [General] with the showy trappings for his horse, generally exceeded £300.⁶

Meanwhile Greece was threatened by the greatest menace to its existence that had yet occurred. The Arabs were on their way, gathering their strength and preparing their plans largely undisturbed by the Greeks. In February 1825 Ibrahim disembarked at Modon, the small fortress in the Southern Peloponnese which the Greeks had never managed to capture. He brought 4,000 infantry and 500 cavalry. His fleet immediately returned to Crete and brought a further 6,000 infantry, 500 cavalry, and a strong corps of artillery. With hardly any interference from the Greeks he established a strong base on shore and a secure line of communications to Egypt for supplies and reinforcements. At the end of March the Egyptian army marched out to lay siege to the important fortress of Navarino. Among their troops was a unit of Turkish Moreotes, survivors of the 1821 massacres, determined to play their part in reconquering the land of their birth.

The Egyptian camp presented a sight such as had never before been seen in Greece. The troops were clothed in a simple uniform and all had the same weapons. The army was in two watches so that one division was always on guard or exercising while the other was resting. Everywhere there was order and discipline and quiet efficiency. The troops were mainly Arab Egyptians apparently in poor physical condition. Many of them had the familiar Egyptian eye diseases. There were also units of Albanians and of negroes, although many of these had died of cold during the campaign in Crete. They were all instantly obedient to the commands of their officers, conscious that life was cheap and that they could instantly be subjected to arbitrary and cruel punishments. There could be no doubt that they were professional and experienced soldiers.

Here and there European officers could be seen instructing their men.* They were almost entirely French and Italians, veterans of the armies of the great Napoleon. The leader of the Europeans, Soleiman Bey, clearly enjoyed the confidence and respect of Ibrahim, and there can have been few men even in that violent age with more experience of war. Joseph-Anthelme Sève[7] was put in the French navy at the age of ten and had already experienced seven years of war when he was wounded at Trafalgar in 1805. Two years later he was dismissed from the navy for striking an officer, but he promptly joined the army, and gradually worked his way through the non-commissioned ranks. In 1809 he was left on the battlefield with a gun-shot wound and three sabre cuts and spent several months as a prisoner in Hungary, but in 1812 he was back with the Grand Army in Russia and was wounded yet again at Posen in 1813. In the campaigns of 1814 he distinguished himself so prominently that he was raised to officer rank and given the Cross of the Legion of Honour. Shortly after Waterloo, at which he was present as a Captain, Sève was retired from the army to join the ranks of the discontented Bonapartist unemployed. He joined Mehemet Ali's service in 1819, changed his name to Soleiman, became a Moslem, amassed a large fortune, and spent the next twenty years of his life—as he had spent the previous twenty—in almost continuous fighting. He was a coarse, drunken, cruel soldier, exulting in violence, but he played an important

* The number of Europeans in Ibrahim's army was often exaggerated, some accounts referring to hundreds. In fact, there seem to have been less than twenty.

part in building up and extending the short-lived empire of Mehemet Ali. In background, Sève and the other officers resembled the Philhellenes, against whom they were ready to fight, some of whom were their old comrades. The Europeans of Ibrahim's army were happy to declare that Greece had been their first love and some had even changed over from the Greek side. Gubernatis, the former Philhellene, commander of the Regiment Tarella after the battle of Peta, had asked to be excused and had remained in Egypt. But those with long memories might have recognized the flamboyant Bekir Aga as the Corsican Drum-Major Mari who had come to Greece from Marseilles in 1822 and had been a member of the Battalion of Philhellenes. Doctor St. André,[8] another Frenchman who had come in an early expedition from Marseilles, now enjoying 8,000 francs a year, claimed to have changed sides in disgust at Greek untrustworthiness.

In war success is the only standard. Ever since the battle of Peta in July 1822, the Greeks had despised European regular military tactics. The other events of 1822 appeared to confirm their judgement. Whereas the Regiment Tarella and the Battalion of Philhellenes, using regular tactics, had been slaughtered by the Turks at Peta, Colocotrones with the old-fashioned irregular tactics of the *klephts* had destroyed a whole Turkish army near Corinth. When the Regiment was disbanded in 1823 Greece had no regular forces. The Byron Brigade had lasted as an organized force for only a few weeks. At the beginning of 1825 few Greeks felt any sense of military inadequacy. Since the success of 1822 they had come to despise the Moslems, foolishly relying on them to be incompetent as they had been on previous occasions.

With great ceremony and much glitter the chieftains of Greece decided to lead their men against the Egyptians and so relieve Navarino. The first few skirmishing encounters shook the confidence of the Greeks who took part in them but the general view was still highly optimistic. In the middle of April 1825 sixteen Greek and Albanian chieftains with their men took up their position opposite Ibrahim's lines. They included men both from the Morea and from Roumeli who were generally regarded as the best in Greece as well as the far-famed Suliotes. The position was prepared in accordance with the usual system with small barricades and trenches to provide cover. It was probably the most effective force that Greece was capable of putting in the field, installed on ground of their own choosing, and fully prepared to fight the kind of battle they knew best.

Ibrahim quickly appreciated how events were moving and decided to seize the initiative. He led his men out to the attack. After a short halt which was spent in reconnoitring the Greek position, he ordered the first regiment of Arabs to advance. The Arabs fixed bayonets and began a steady march to the beat of drums towards the Greek position. Although many fell from the fire of the Greeks they kept their ranks and marched straight towards the Greek barricades without wavering. Then as they approached close, the officers gave the order, they lowered their bayonets, started to cheer, broke into a double and charged. The Greeks were thunderstruck—this was not the enemy they knew. They broke and ran, strewing their jewelled weapons in all directions. Ibrahim's cavalry was, according to the best regular tactics, waiting in the rear to appear round the flank and cut down the fleeing disorganized enemy.

Probably only about 600 Greeks were killed at this battle, but it was one of the most important engagements of the war. It proved dramatically and decisively a point which had always been true, that a small body of regular disciplined troops would prove superior to a large horde of individualists. The unanimous view of the Philhellenes from Baleste onwards was now vindicated. The thoughts of the Greeks again turned to the possibility of setting up a regular army.

Ibrahim went from success to success. The Greeks stiffened their resistance but time and again they proved incapable of withstanding the attacks by the Arab regulars. In May, Navarino was forced to capitulate and here again the value of regular disciplined troops was revealed. The besieged Greeks in Navarino were offered the opportunity of leaving the place in safety on specially chartered vessels. They accepted, although many must have had their doubts when they remembered how the Greeks had treated the Turks who had capitulated to them in the early years of the Revolution. The corps of Moreote Turks attached to Ibrahim's army, survivors of the massacres of 1821, were ready to take their revenge as the defenceless Greeks opened the gates but the disciplined Arab troops acted as escort and the terms of the capitulation were scrupulously honoured. Ibrahim's magnanimity was as much dictated by policy as by humanity. He hoped that his rule would be more readily accepted by the population and that other fortresses still on his path would be more willing to come to terms if he could establish a reputation for honesty and justice as well as for military effectiveness. In this respect, as in many others, Ibrahim's behaviour and outlook were more akin to the Europeans than to the Greeks. Several Philhellenes were captured at Navarino and had the opportunity of meeting Ibrahim before they were released. They were treated like gentlemen throughout their short capture and they must have felt more at home in the officers' messes than they were among the Greeks. Ibrahim was interested in his reputation in Europe. 'At least do me justice,' he explained to one Philhellene, 'when you read in your newspapers that I drink blood and eat human flesh to say what you have seen.' To another Philhellene who remarked that Ibrahim had shown the generosity that Napoleon would have shown, he declared 'Napoleon! I know that I will never be worthy to kiss his shoes.'[9] Ibrahim offered a high salary to any Philhellenes who would join his service. On this occasion the only one to accept was Lord Byron's physician, Millingen, who later settled in Constantinople where, as doctor to successive Sultans, he was a well-known figure for many years.

After his success at Navarino, Ibrahim now had a secure base in Greece from which to conquer the country. At last the Greek Government began to realize that Greece was facing its biggest challenge. The archimandrite Dikaios was given the command of a new force of 3,000 men and left Nauplia in May, but by the time he reached the vicinity of the Arab camp half his men had deserted. The battle which took place on 1 June 1825 was one of the best contested during the war. The Greeks attempted to stand their ground behind their barricades but again the Arab regulars, who greatly outnumbered them, stormed their position with the bayonet.

The cry was now raised in Nauplia that there was only one man in Greece who could save the situation. The old brigand Colocotrones, who had been imprisoned at Hydra following the second civil war, was released and appointed Commander-in-Chief, but he could do nothing. The irregular Greek troops were simply not good enough. Even on rough ground where they had won their best successes in the past they were consistently defeated. The disciplined Arabs, sometimes without the help of their cavalry and artillery, always proved superior. Throughout the summer of 1825, until the campaigning season ended in October, Ibrahim captured town after town in the Morea. Tripolitsa, Argos, and Calamata—the three largest towns—were all recaptured and sacked.

At the end of June 1825 Ibrahim's army appeared outside Nauplia, the provisional capital of Greece, and it looked as if the Greek Revolution would soon be over. Ibrahim retired since he had no equipment for a siege but no one doubted that he would be back. In their desperation the Greek Government offered to put the country under the rule of Great Britain in exchange for British protection—the so-called Act of Submission. The British Government had neither the wish nor the ability to accept responsibility for Greece and the offer was rejected. But this apparent attempt to confirm the British influence in Greece which was thought to derive from the loan was to have important repercussions later.

Ibrahim's methods became steadily more cruel. At first he had thought to reconcile the Greeks by a policy of clemency but in this he misjudged his enemy. The majority of the Greeks continued to regard the war as one of religious or racial extermination. The Hydriote ships continued to exterminate their prisoners and on one occasion in June 1825 about 250 were systematically butchered in the streets of Hydra itself. Attempts by the Greek Government to prohibit the worst barbarities had some success but they always tended to break down in emergency. It was commonly thought that Ibrahim intended to exterminate the Greeks of the Morea and settle the place with Arabs from Egypt. This rumour, although probably unfounded, made compromise unthinkable. Ibrahim, while maintaining his European military methods, reverted to Eastern military ethics. His troops were permitted and encouraged to burn all the Greek towns and villages through which they passed. Europeans who called on him now heard him declare that he 'would burn and destroy the whole Morea'.[10] Crops and beasts were seized and destroyed wherever he went, although (as if remembering the rules of warfare of Classical Greece) he took care not to destroy the olive trees. The local population of the Morea, which had already suffered from the depredations of the civil war and from the general anarchy which existed during much of the war, was now reduced to near destitution. A slave market was opened at Modon where human beings were branded, loaded with chains, and used in labour gangs. From Modon, as opportunity arose, they were shipped to Egypt to be employed as galley-slaves for the rest of their life.

Meanwhile, at the time when the Arabs were laying waste the Peloponnese, the Turks were bestirring themselves further north. In the north-west, under a vigorous new pasha, the Albanians were again persuaded to join the Turkish cause and to take part in a Turkish expedition south against Free Greece. Without difficulty the new Ottoman army crossed the Makrinoros, as its predecessor had done in 1822 after the battle of Peta, and proceeded to lay siege to Missolonghi. By the summer of 1825, Missolonghi was invested by land and sea and it was clear that this time the Ottoman forces were not going to allow themselves to be destroyed by bad organization or lack of preparedness. Throughout the second half of 1825 a long battle for Missolonghi was fought out near the town with first one side then the other appearing to have the upper hand. The Greek ships attacked the Ottoman fleet and succeeded in replenishing the town with supplies, but as winter approached Missolonghi was still under close siege. Then in November Ibrahim was invited to lead his Arabs to assist the Turks before Missolonghi and spent the winter months with his accustomed vigour in bringing up supplies and preparing for a renewed offensive in the spring.

As 1825 advanced and everywhere the Greeks were clearly losing the war it was remembered that there was another possible method of salvation. In the uncertain military situation of 1822 numerous chieftains in Roumeli had succeeded in keeping their options open, joining first the Greeks then the Turks, then the Greeks again. A broad band of Central Greece south of Thermopylae remained determinedly undecided whether it was Greece or Turkey. These chieftains were often called traitors and obviously, in a sense, so they were. But few of them felt any sense of shame or betrayal. The concept of loyalty to a 'nation' was alien, or at best novel, to most Greeks. They preferred their traditional loyalties, to their religion, to their tribe, to their district, to their leader; and since the Ottoman

Government had as yet little idea of nationality they were content to do business with local leaders on their terms—to build up their loyalties on a solid basis of self-interest reinforced, if possible, by fear.

The great Odysseus who ruled eastern Greece with a firm hand had made a pact with the Turks in 1822. Now that the Greek cause was again in danger, he once more decided to bend with the wind. He opened negotiations with his old friends, the neighbouring Turkish authorities, but his power was slipping away from him. Since the Greek Government had apparently unlimited gold at its disposal and was prepared to dispense it to anyone who could claim to be the leader of a military force, many of the armed Greeks who had previously looked to Odysseus for their leadership and support were moving to other masters. Odysseus now began to make overtures to the Turks, on the basis that he would recognize Ottoman sovereignty in exchange for a promise to be confirmed in his position of local leadership. The Turks were prepared to accept his offer, although they had already sufficient experience of the man to insist that he should openly join their army before the deal was confirmed.

The attempt of Odysseus to defect resulted in a curious episode which illustrated the difficulties with which the Philhellenes were struggling in attempting to understand the Greek political scene. Odysseus never had any higher ambition than to be an Eastern chieftain and certainly cared nothing for any notion of Hellas or regeneration or the usual Greek and philhellenic myths. In this respect he was a typical Greek of the time, but his outlook was totally incomprehensible to many Philhellenes. To them Odysseus was a colourful and powerful figure with an eminently Greek sounding name. He had to be fitted into some philhellenic preconception. To Stanhope Odysseus represented the hope of turning Greece into a constitutional republic with free and representative institutions—perhaps the most misconceived of all views of his character. But Odysseus was also the cynosure of the type of Philhellenes whom I have called the romantic Byronists, the men who, unlike Byron himself, came to Greece in search of the exoticism of Byron's Grecian and Turkish tales. Odysseus, to such men, was a true Greek, a Greek who lived among mountains and wore colourful clothes.

The most extreme of the romantic Byronists was Edward John Trelawny, who had come to Greece with Byron in 1823. To the historian or biographer, Trelawny is an intensely irritating figure because of his uncomfortable habit of telling lies about everything he did. But Trelawny's fault was simply to exaggerate for the sake of effect, to stretch truth at the edges to make a better story. As a Philhellene he had no ideas of his own. He parted from Byron because Byron was not Byronic enough for him, Byron was too cautious, too balanced, too interested in discovering the facts of the situation. Trelawny's aim was mainly to swagger about Greece in exotic dress and to enjoy the sensation of being a Byronic hero, a Lara or a Conrad. He hated the Europeanized Greeks like Mavrocordato who interfered with his image of the situation. As a rationalization of his preconceptions he seized eagerly on Colonel Stanhope's belief that Odysseus could become the Washington of Greece. After Byron's death for a time he had hopes that he might be regarded as his spiritual heir. He was surrounded by a group of volunteers, mostly British, of the same cast of mind as himself, all proclaiming how they alone had found a Greek worthy of the name. Trelawny seemed a useful ally. [11]

Odysseus charmed Trelawny as he had charmed Stanhope by appealing to his preconceptions of himself. He installed him in a huge cavern in Mount Parnassus which he had fortified as a retreat safe from Greek or Turk. The cavern could only be approached by long ladders let down from above. It was guarded by the cannon which Gordon had given to the London Greek Committee and Stanhope had foolishly transferred to Odysseus. It was capacious enough to hold a military force of some hundreds and was provisioned for a long siege. It had every comfort, even a set of Waverley novels on which the Byronists could feed their romantic imaginations. Odysseus and Trelawny became warm friends and in true Eastern style the friendship was cemented by marriage. Trelawny was married to a half-sister of Odysseus, Tersitsa, a girl with whom he had no language in common and who was then aged about thirteen or fourteen. Trelawny was immensely flattered.

The attachment to the unreliable Odysseus of Trelawny and other apparently influential Philhellenes was seen as an intolerable threat by the Greeks who realized what was really happening. It was decided to kill Odysseus as had been planned in 1822 in similar circumstances. As a first step Trelawny too was to be killed and the cave seized from Odysseus' power. The details of the scheme are not fully known but it is certain that Mavrocordato was one of the instigators along with several Philhellenes. Two of Trelawny's companions, Fenton and Whitcombe, were bribed by money and promises to try to assassinate him in the cave. The attempt was made in June 1825. Fenton fired a shot which severely wounded Trelawny, but he was at once himself shot dead by another of Trelawny's companions. Whitcombe was allowed to survive. [12]

Trelawny, after recovering from his wounds, was eventually taken down from the cave and left Greece in a British warship, apparently unaware to the end that he had chosen the least philhellenic of all Greeks as his hero. Odysseus himself had not long to live. Various attempts were made by the Greek Government to kill him and at last he was persuaded to surrender. One day in October 1825 his body was found suspended from the walls of the Acropolis of Athens, murdered by Greeks as he had himself murdered so many. And so Greece was saved the humiliation of having its most famous hero rejoin the Turks, one of the few scraps of comfort in the black year of 1825, and indirectly one of the beneficial consequences of the supply of English gold.

Early in 1826 the attack on Missolonghi was renewed. Ibrahim was anxious to show that his Arabs were superior to the Turks who had been conducting the siege before he arrived. He committed his troops to a series of murderous assaults on Missolonghi's puny defences. For the first time the bayonet failed. The desperate inhabitants of the town repulsed attack after attack from behind their mounds, but there was no relief. The Turks and their allies at great cost captured the islands in the lagoon and succeeded in cutting off Missolonghi completely by sea as well as by land. A squadron of Hydriote ships was paid a large sum by the Greek Government to attempt to break the ring but their operations were half-hearted and ineffective. It could no longer be concealed that the Greeks were losing their superiority at sea. The English gold had sapped their daring and, unlike the Turks and Egyptians, they had not improved their naval technology and tactics during the course of the war.

By April the people of Missolonghi had supplies for only a few days. They contemptuously rejected proposals for a capitulation and prepared to make a last desperate effort. It was decided to attempt a sortie *en masse* and to break through the enemy lines to the mountains beyond. The night of 22 April 1826 was set for this exodus and an arrangement was made for a body of armed Greeks to attack the besiegers' rear as a diversion. Of the total population of the besieged town of about 9,000 there were about 2,000 persons of all ages who were too weak or ill to join in the exodus: these were to be left behind to their fate along with some of their friends and relatives who could not bear to leave them. The others, including many women and children, made breaches in the mounds and prepared bridges by which to cross the great ditch that separated them from their enemies.

At nine o'clock the exodus began and at first all seemed to be well. Some thousands crossed the bridges and the vanguard had charged through the Turkish lines before they appreciated what was happening. But soon confusion broke out. The Turks began to fire on the jostling crowds and several people fell off the bridges into the ditch. There was a momentary panic and then the crowds fell back into Missolonghi. Their fate was now certain. Ibrahim immediately ordered an attack on the weakened defences and captured all the walls. The next morning at dawn, his officers gave permission to the troops to enter the town and the whole place was given over to slaughter and plunder. Several groups of Greeks blew themselves up in their powder magazines when surrounded by their enemies rather than surrender. Within a few hours the town of Missolonghi was a smoking lifeless ruin.

As usual the statistics for this ghastly event cannot be ascertained.

Ibrahim boasted that his men collected 3,000 heads, and ten barrels of salted human ears were dispatched to Constantinople to gratify the Sultan. Between 3,000 and 4,000 women and boys were taken as slaves. Even the party which had escaped through the Turkish lines was largely destroyed since they had the misfortune to fall in with a party of Albanian horsemen. Hundreds died of starvation.

Most of the Philhellenes who had taken part in the defence of Missolonghi perished among the ruins. Among the dead were von Dittmar, the Prussian officer who had struggled with Kephalas for the loyalty of the German Legion; Bellier de Launay, the impostor who had so impressed Stanhope and the members of the London Greek Committee; Adolph von Lübtow, thought to be one of the Germans who called on Byron at Genoa in April 1823 to beg money and who had subsequently returned to Greece; and Stitzelberger, the officer from Baden who had commanded the Byron Brigade for a short time after Byron's death. The Swiss Johann Jacob Meyer, who had come in one of the early expeditions from Marseilles and had later become editor of Stanhope's newspaper, the *Greek Chronicle*, managed to send a letter out of the town shortly before the sortie: 'I declare to you,' he wrote, 'that we have sworn to defend Mesolonghi foot by foot, to listen to no capitulation, and to bury ourselves in its ruins. Our last hour approaches. History will do us justice and posterity weep over our misfortunes.'[13] Meyer was cut to pieces by Turkish horsemen and his Greek wife and child taken into slavery.

By Sultan Mahmoud in Constantinople and Mehemet Ali in Cairo, the news of the fall of Missolonghi was greeted with jubilation. Here, it appeared, was yet further evidence of the success of their policy. Another important Greek town had been captured and the Greeks had been taught a salutary lesson about the folly of prolonging their resistance. In reality, the fall of Missolonghi had a far greater significance. It was one of the most decisive events of the war.

The Turks never succeeded in understanding why European public opinion moved as it did. They were vaguely aware that the Greek Revolution had some ideological content beyond the easily comprehensible motives of religious hostility and hatred of Turks. But they never had much interest in the history or culture of other peoples and their attempts to combat the ideological enemy were heavy-handed, belated, and ineffective. It was decreed about this time, for example, that the Greeks of the Ottoman Empire who were still under Turkish rule should no longer be permitted to call their sons 'Constantine' because of the political implications of that name, but there was no official concern when they changed their names to 'Pericles' or 'Miltiades'.[14] The Turks also threatened, if Athens should again fall into their hands, to destroy the Parthenon, because of its symbolic unifying effect on Greeks and Philhellenes—another lunge at the curiously elusive idea. [15] But it was totally incomprehensible that the capture of a small fishing town in Western Greece should have ideological significance. Missolonghi had no classical associations. It even had an Italian name. True, the siege had been hard fought and the Greeks in their desperation had resisted more strongly than in recent battles, but that was a normal phenomenon of war. If the Greeks of Missolonghi had perished that was their own fault for not accepting the terms of capitulation. Ibrahim had done little more than often occurred when a city was taken by assault even under European military ethics.

One of Ibrahim's European doctors remarked when he entered the ruins of Missolonghi that on the wall of one of the houses someone had written '*Hic e vita decessit Lord Byron*'. [16] Here was a clue to a factor which no Turk could have been expected to understand. In the two years since the death of Lord Byron, Missolonghi had become the most famous town in Modern Greece, the symbol of the Greek War of Independence, the focus of all philhellenic feeling. The name of Missolonghi now carried a host of associations all over Western Europe soon to be marvellously illustrated in Delacroix's huge painting of 'Greece expiring on the ruins of Missolonghi'.

The heroism of the Greeks at Missolonghi swept away years of disillusion and disappointment with Greek actions since 1821. The way was open to a resurgence of philhellenic feeling in Western Europe which was to play an important part in the outcome of the war. As one of the Turkish generals remarked, 'We are no longer fighting the Greeks but all Europe.' [17]

24. The Shade of Napoleon

In 1823 the French army, which had been 'observing' the situation in Spain from the Pyrenees, received orders to cross the frontier. It met with little resistance. The Spanish constitutionalist Government fled from Madrid and its authority vanished. A coup in Lisbon, which took place on the news of the French invasion of Spain, restored the absolutist monarchy in Portugal. In a brief, almost bloodless, campaign, the French army extinguished the last liberal revolutionary governments in Europe. It was an astonishing success and most of the chancelleries of Europe were delighted. Just as the Austrians had acted on behalf of the absolutist powers to extinguish the revolutions in Naples and Piedmont in 1821, so the French could claim to have been carrying out the collective wishes of the powers in eradicating the cancer from Spain. Only the British had opposed the move, but the French had correctly calculated that they would not go to war on the issue. France, eight years after the battle of Waterloo, was indisputably again a great power. She had been trusted with a delicate military operation by her allies, who had been so recently her enemies, and had carried it out to their satisfaction. And she had successfully defied the old enemy across the Channel.

The events in Spain had an important effect on the Greek War of Independence. The solution of the Spanish problem allowed European statesmen to turn their attention more fully to the last untidy situation in Europe, the existence of Free Greece. It also led to a new phase of philhellenism. The torch which had been taken up by the Germans and Swiss and then passed to the English was now to be carried by the French.

Even before the death of Lord Byron in April 1824 the first signs of the new movement were to be seen. When the *Ann* and her cargo sent by the London Greek Committee reached Malta in December 1823, a mysterious figure came on board and asked to be given passage to Greece. As Humphreys, one of the British Philhellenes on board the ship, wrote: 'A French gentleman who joined, who calls himself Borel but I believe he is travelling incognito, is very clever. I should think he will be very useful with the diplomatic line.'[1] Colonel Stanhope, the Committee's agent in Greece, knew more of the man and prepared to welcome him: 'The intelligent soldier, mechanic, and agriculturist', he wrote in guarded terms to Bowring, 'whom you mention as going to settle in Greece, will be a most useful character there: he may command my services.'[2]

The secret of Monsieur Borel's alias was not well kept. As one French officer who met him in Greece records, his first words were 'I travel under the name of Morel [*sic*] but I am Colonel Fabvier.'[3] No further introduction was necessary.

Charles Fabvier was a soldier of heroic proportions who seems to come straight from one of those huge canvases of Napoleonic battles so beloved by the French. He stood over six feet tall and had a stern imposing military manner. He was highly intelligent, ambitious, and determined. All his early life had been spent in the army. After graduating from the Ecole Polytechnique as an artilleryman in 1805, he joined the Grand Army. Thereafter his rise was rapid as he distinguished himself in campaign after campaign. In 1807 he was entrusted with an important military mission to Asia Minor and Persia during which he had his first experience of the East. In 1812 he was with the Grand Army in Russia. He became ADC to Marshal Marmont, a Baron of the Empire and Commandant of the Legion of Honour. Then came the first abdication, the Hundred Days, and the final defeat of Napoleon. In 1815, the humiliation of seeing the allied armies on the soil of France was almost intolerable to him but, like so many of Napoleon's officers, Fabvier was almost equally disgusted at the return of the Bourbons and their émigré friends.

There was no place in Restoration France for a successful and ambitious Napoleonic officer especially if, like Fabvier, he was temperamentally outspoken. Besides, Fabvier had emphatic liberal views which he equated with respect for Napoleon. Soon he was on the lists of the secret police. In 1820 he was involved in an ill-prepared conspiracy to attempt a Napoleonic restoration and then in 1822 the affair of the four sergeants of La Rochelle (in which Bowring was also suspected). He was obliged to go into exile, and Spain was the obvious place.

Fabvier became one of the leaders of the growing band of escaped revolutionaries and political refugees who were gradually filtering into Spain as other countries were closed to them. There were groups of Italians, victims of the upsets of 1821, French revolutionaries and Bonapartists, exiles from earlier political changes, and the usual miscellany of idealists, mercenaries, adventure-seekers (including some former

Philhellenes) who were attracted to fight in a good cause. Fabvier seems to have hoped that a Liberal Foreign Legion could be formed in Spain which would eventually be the spearhead of a renewed Napoleonic liberation of France. When the French army of the Bourbons was menacing Spain from across the frontier, Fabvier calculated that if he could assemble a little army of French old soldiers like himself under the tricolour (which was the symbol of the Revolution, of Napoleon, and of the Empire), then the French army drawn up under the white flag of the Bourbons would be unable to hold together. They would remember the great days of old and would desert to their old love.

As it turned out, no such desertions occurred. Already a new generation of French soldiers manned the ranks who cared nothing for Fabvier's ideas. Napoleon, they knew, was dead even if rumours were put around to the contrary. And if they were unwilling to fire upon Frenchmen drawn up under the tricolour, these Frenchmen were equally unwilling to fire on the famous regiments in whose ranks they had spent the proudest moments of their lives. The bands of refugees in Spain dispersed and looked around to find a new life and a new home. Some hung on with the scattered groups of Spanish constitutionalists who attempted to oppose the French army in remoter parts of Spain; others fled to Portugal hoping to find a passage to South America; others were captured and taken back to France to stand trial for having opposed the King's army. Many were scattered around Europe, mainly in England and the Netherlands, living a semi-clandestine existence, often on charity, waiting for an opportunity to renew their life.

Fabvier felt a deep sense of loyalty to the men who had followed him to disaster, some of whom had been with him for years. What could he now offer them? Like so many of the characters mentioned in this book he surveyed the world's trouble spots—now only South America and Greece remained. To a man of liberal principles Greece was the obvious choice. During the second half of 1823 he darted about Western Europe in various disguises apparently organizing his sources of support. He visited England where he had discussions with the liberals of the Spanish Committee, who were largely the same small group that inspired the Greek Committee. He also visited Belgium, apparently as a convenient rendezvous to communicate with his friends and supporters within France. The French secret police followed his movements tirelessly. In August he was reported to be back in France itself under the alias of Cabillo Tores. Later in the year, instructions were given to the prefects of half a dozen provinces to look out for him but they lost track. The next news they had was from an intercepted letter posted in Malta in which Fabvier announced that he and several French officers intended to join Lord Byron and fight alongside him for the cause of Greek independence.

Fabvier's first visit to Greece was in the nature of a reconnaissance.

He travelled unnoticed through the Peloponnese and, while the Byron Brigade was wasting uselessly at Missolonghi, he was putting new proposals to the Greek leaders. Within a few months he was back in England and again in Belgium. In his pocket he carried a contract signed by the Greek Government for the establishment on Greek soil of an 'agricultural and industrial colony' of which he was to be the chief. Fabvier was to be given a concession of between 3,000 and 4,000 acres of land for which he undertook to pay as from 1 January 1826. In return he undertook to institute an training programme for the Greeks, helping them to introduce more modern agricultural techniques and to establish manufacturing industries to produce the goods which Greece had to import from abroad. In addition he undertook to provide a full range of military assistance, construction of arsenals, fortification of towns, instruction in the art of defence and of attack, establishment of military academies.

Fabvier's return to Western Europe in 1824 was to arrange for his old comrades to go to Greece to establish the colony; to provide them with passports; to obtain money from his supporters in France; and to liaise with the philhellenic societies. The French secret police, still trying to keep track of him as he moved from one mysterious assignation to another, were baffled to read letters referring to the obtaining of passports in Belgium for his 'Greek workers'. The Greek workers were of course the French and other soldiers who had been involved with Fabvier in his eventful life since 1820 and were now being rounded up to sail to a new life in Greece.

And so through 1824 and 1825 a new wave of Philhellenes began to make their way to Greece. The revolutionaries and refugees who had been concentrated in Spain and then scattered by the French invasion began to reassemble again, this time in Greece. Individuals and small groups made their way to the last corner of Europe where the flag of liberty was still flying and where a soldier could lend a hand. Some came direct from Spain, others from their temporary refuges in the Netherlands, Britain, and elsewhere. Most were Italians or French, but there was a sprinkling of other nationalities. The French were mainly Bonapartists. From France itself former Napoleonic officers, who had been purged from the army, decided to join their old comrades on their way to Greece. Even if they had been careful to keep clear of politics, they could not escape the ever-present police suspiciously recording the details of their lives. For a compulsorily retired Napoleonic officer, life in Restoration France could be irksome and claustrophobic. The secret police dutifully reported as old Bonapartists disappeared from their homes on their way to the ports. Gibassier,[4] a former Captain, left for Leghorn against the wishes of his family after receiving letters from Fabvier. Bourbaki,[5] once a Colonel in the Imperial army who had been under constant watch, left to join his old comrades. Berton,[6] the son of the General executed in 1820 for opposition to the régime, hoped to vindicate his father's memory. Regnault de St. Jean d'Angely, later a Marshal of France, who had been promoted for valour by the Emperor on the battlefield of Waterloo, left to look for an opportunity of fighting under the famous Colonel Fabvier.

In one important respect this latest wave of Philhellenes stood out from their predecessors. Almost every one was a professional soldier with long years of active experience behind him on dozens of the battlefields of Europe. These were no runaway students or beardless subalterns; they were no romantics trying to make a reality of Byronic dreams; but men on the verge of middle age, men already set in their ways and set in their beliefs, men who had no illusions about the nature of war.

Among these grizzled Bonapartists one exception is worth a mention. In 1827 Paul-Marie Bonaparte, the son of Lucien and nephew of Napoleon, was a student at the University of Bologna. He was then aged eighteen and was said to bear a remarkable resemblance to his uncle, the late Emperor. In March he left Italy secretly under an assumed name and made his way to the Ionian Islands with the intention of joining the Greeks. But while still on board ship at Nauplia he accidentally shot himself when cleaning a pistol and died soon afterwards.[7] His body was embalmed and eventually buried in 1832 on the island of Sphacteria alongside the French sailors who died in the Battle of Navarino.

Fabvier himself was typical of many of the French who came to Greece at this time. Most European liberals looked with envy and admiration at the free institutions of Britain which had survived a period of repression after Waterloo. In their struggles against the absolutist monarchies most would have settled for far less. But for men like Fabvier the fact that England enjoyed a liberal political system was a constant shame. To them their late leader, the Emperor Napoleon, was the embodiment of everything they held dear and the memory grew ever more tender with the passage of time. As the stories of the Empire faded into myth, Napoleon came to be thought of as the great liberator. England might be the most enlightened country in Europe, but for Waterloo and the downfall of Napoleon the English could never be forgiven. Men like Fabvier combined a fierce devotion to the cause of liberalism with a deep-seated hatred of the British. They were liberals, some of them prepared to go to war against their former comrades in arms in the French army in their fight to establish a more liberal régime in France, but they were also heirs of a long tradition of anti-British feeling. The fact that, after the collapse of the constitutionalist Government in Spain, the British Government was the only government to show them any sympathy and Britain almost the only country which would accept them as exiles, merely intensified their mortification. Hatred of the British was one of their most powerful motivating forces.

Fabvier arrived back in Greece in May 1825 with a few of his followers. The country had changed drastically in the year or so since he had left. In February 1825 Ibrahim and his Arab army had landed in Greece and they were already in control of much of the Peloponnese. There could be no question now of establishing the proposed agricultural and industrial colony. The very existence of Free Greece was at stake. If Fabvier and his followers were to find a permanent home in Greece, they first would have to fight for it.

Fabvier's return to Greece coincided with the belated realization on the part of the Greek Government that the armed bands of the captains were simply not good enough to defend the country against Ibrahim's Arab troops. In the middle of June 1825 the Greek Government decided to attempt again to establish a disciplined regular force which might have some chance of withstanding the invaders. The situation was desperate. Ibrahim's army was only a few hours' from the seat of government at Nauplia. The Greeks turned to the only group of Philhellenes who might help them with a crash programme of military training. Fabvier was asked if he would undertake the task of raising, training, and commanding a regular force.

It was a formidable task. Greece had no regular troops at all, except for a small ceremonial guard that had been maintained at Nauplia after the disbandment of the Regiment in 1823. Fabvier accepted, but on certain conditions. He was promised virtually absolute control over all aspects of the life and use of the force; also the full support of the Government in enforcing a strict law of conscription and in using the gold of the British loan to pay the men.

It was just at this time that the Greeks were sending desperate appeals to the representatives of the British Government in the area begging that Britain would take Greece under her protection. The suggestion was being canvassed that Leopold of Saxe Coburg (later to be King of Belgium) or the Duke of Sussex should be appointed King of Greece. When Ibrahim was outside Nauplia there was talk of raising the Union Jack over the fortress in the hope that the British warships in the harbour would come to their rescue. For Fabvier, the prospect of Britain establishing a protectorate over Greece was intolerable. He declared to the Greek Government that he would only accept the command if they promised to fight to the last extremity. If, however, they intended to raise the flag of another country he would not help them—not even if it was the flag of France. The conditions were accepted, although the Greek Government was hardly in a position to ensure that it would keep its promises.

On 4 July 1825, in a little ceremony in Nauplia, Fabvier was presented to the men who were to form the new regular force. The standards which had once belonged to the Regiment Tarella were brought out and re-presented. Fabvier himself appeared with all his medals in the uniform of an officer of France. In his speech he declared his readiness to die for his new country. Today, he said, he was a Frenchman but tomorrow they would see that he was a Greek. The next day he appeared wearing the magnificent dress of a Greek *palikar* and thereafter he never wore anything else. It was more than a colourful philhellenic gesture. The Greeks could see that he meant it. Fabvier and his little band of followers, for whom life since Waterloo had been a series of retreats and defeats, were now at the end of the road. Their fate was inextricably tied to Greece. They had no other home.

25. 'No freedom to fight for at home'

At the beginning of 1823, the Italian Philhellene Brengeri, one of the survivors of the Battle of Peta, was surprised to meet at Tripolitsa a Colonel in the Neapolitan service whom he had believed to be in Spain. The Colonel, whose name was Poerio, took great care to keep his identity secret, being referred to in correspondence simply as 'a Calabrian'. He had come to Greece from Spain with a message from General Pepe, the leader of the unsuccessful revolution in Naples, who had now gone with a large number of his followers to help the constitutionalist Government in Spain.

In Greece no secret was safe for long and soon it was known that General Pepe had made a proposal to Mavrocordato. Brengeri believed that Pepe had offered to bring a regiment of Italian refugee officers to fight for Greek independence.[1] In fact, from Pepe's own version,[2] it appears that he was asking for help, not offering it. He suggested that Mavrocordato should give him the command of a thousand Greeks so that he could attempt a constitutionalist counter-revolution in Naples by landing a force in Calabria. He apparently had no idea that Mavrocordato, then nominally President of Greece, could not at that time command a hundred Greeks in Greece itself, let alone send a thousand abroad.

The idea was, however, an interesting one and it was to reappear. Brengeri himself had come to the Morea as a political exile from Rome, hoping to liberate Greece 'and some day my own country which groans under the sacerdotal yoke'.[3] Many other Italians were to dream that the struggle for Italian independence and for an Italian constitution could somehow be carried on from abroad.

The number of Italians who were compelled to leave their country by the upheavals of 1820 and 1821 is unknown, but there were many hundreds. Their history is a sad one. They had in many cases to leave home in a hurry without family or belongings or money and to find a refuge in any country that would take them. Dozens had crossed to Greece in 1821 only to die at Peta or to succumb to disease. Many had tried to find a home in the West, in England, France, Switzerland, or the Netherlands, but it was a hard life. In France they were harried by the police and the ambassadors of the absolutist powers complained to the smaller countries if they took too many exiles and appeared to be 'harbouring revolution'. Some found a new life in the New World, but there were very few who could afford the fare. The luckier exiles managed to cross to England where they were greeted with sympathy. Brengeri, who had been on the round of temporary refugees, spoke for many when he said of England 'Here unmolested I breathe the air of liberty and here, unless any unforeseen event should disappoint my expectation, I hope to end my days.'4

But the refugee's life is always hard. They had to learn to speak a foreign language and to try to earn a living. Soldiering was the only trade they knew. Even in England there is a limit to the number of people who want Italian lessons. The bread of charity soon turns sour. In a hundred ways they suffered the humiliations of poverty and the frustrations of being outsiders. In Italy they had been the leaders, both politically and intellectually, but now they had nothing to look forward to.

In the first years after their expulsion from Italy there was still one hope to cling to. As long as there existed a constitutionalist Government in Spain with a need for officers of reliable political opinions, they might find employment. Many Italian refugees made their way direct to Spain and many others drifted there from their exiles elsewhere. In Spain, where they were enrolled, like Fabvier's exiled Frenchmen, in the Liberal Foreign Legion, they felt at least that they were making a contribution. In particular they were keeping together, preserving some kind of organization and military structure against the day when they might return to their homeland. But with the collapse of the constitutionalist Government in Spain in 1823 they were obliged to move again.

And so, just as Fabvier's thoughts were turned to Greece because there was nowhere else in Europe to go, the Italian revolutionaries began to consider whether they too could not use Greece as a base from which to pursue their own policies; to set up in Greece the skeleton organization which had existed in Spain; and to continue their preparations for a new liberal revolution in Italy.

In late 1824 a certain General Rossaroll arrived at Zante on his way to Greece from Spain. In the Ionian Islands he was a well-known figure since he had commanded the garrison during the French occupation of some of the islands during the Napoleonic War. A Neapolitan by birth,

Rossaroll, like so many of his countrymen, had risen to high military rank in the service of Napoleon. When the peace came and the stupid Bourbons were restored in the Kingdom of Naples, he joined the Carbonari and took part in the abortive revolution of 1821. He had been condemned to death but had escaped to Spain.

Rossaroll's plan was for the restoration of the family of Murat to the throne of Naples in exchange for the promise of a constitution. Murat, one of Napoleon's marshals, who had been made King of Naples by the Emperor, was shot by firing squad after the Restoration in 1815. Rossaroll claimed that he could raise money from Murat's widow to pay the Italian exiles in Greece. As he proclaimed, according to the curious translation sent to London by the interception authorities in the Ionian Islands: 'Many Italian Patriots would unite themselves to me as also here at Zante, besides the Moreotes who know me since seventeen years ago. Dissembling to fight the Turks we would not cause suspicion, keeping thus out enterprize.' When the little army was ready, an attempt would be made to invade Naples and put the young Napoleon-Achille Murat on the throne. 5

Rossaroll died of disease in 1825, but even in his few months in Greece his scheme made some progress. Meanwhile, it was natural that London should become the centre for the movement. The Greek deputies, Orlandos and Louriottis, were the only official representatives of the Greeks in Western Europe. They had at their disposal the proceeds of the two loans. In any scheme to keep the cause of Italian liberalism afloat that money would clearly be useful.

During 1824 and 1825 a succession of prominent Italian revolutionaries made their way from England to Greece, most of them apparently on business connected with this plan. Count Palma, who had been a member of the short-lived liberal Government in Piedmont in 1821, paid a short visit to Greece in 1824 on a 'mission' unspecified. 6 Like Rossaroll he had been a successful Napoleonic officer, had been condemned to death in his absence, and had served in Spain until the collapse of the constitutionalists. Count Pecchio, another condemned Italian revolutionary, who had been in Spain, left his exile in England to go to Greece for a few weeks in 1825 because he was 'desirous of paying a visit to the members of the Government'. 7 The Ionian Islands buzzed with intrigues and rumours connected with the same consultations.

Whether the missions resulted in any concrete agreements between the Italians and the Greeks is doubtful. The Greek deputies in London had notoriously little authority to speak for the Greek Government at home, whose policies and membership were in any case always changing. Until the decision to establish a regular force under Fabvier was taken in June 1825, the Greeks had no apparent need for foreign officers. But the Italians were insistent—they declared that they had no other theatre for their energies; that they would steer clear of politics; that the cost of living would be less in Greece than in England. The deputies were weak men, inclined to save themselves inconvenience in the traditional oriental way, by making unfulfillable promises. It was said,[8] too, that they calculated that the announcement that famous men were on their way to fight for Greece would give a puff to the Greek bonds. The members of the London Greek Committee, while they still had influence with the deputies, advised them against entangling themselves with the Italians.[9] To send to Greece the condemned Italian revolutionaries who had been expelled from Spain, Bowring argued, was merely to provide evidence to the hostile absolutist powers that the revolutions of Italy, Spain, and Greece were all instigated by the same elements.

Certainly it did all look suspicious. The Italian revolutionaries whether from Naples, Piedmont or elsewhere, were clearly acting together and had close ties with the Spanish. They now seemed to be concentrating in London. The members of the London Greek Committee were, by and large, the same men as composed the Committees which favoured the Italian and Spanish Revolutions and harboured their refugees. A glance at the collected works of Edward Blaquiere would have dispelled any lingering doubts about their political unreliability. Bowring had been instrumental in setting up a philhellenic committee in Madrid in 1821 along with the condemned Italian Count Palma. And then there was Fabvier who had attempted revolution in France and Spain and was now off to Greece. Had not Bowring been involved with him, too, in the affair of the four sergeants of La Rochelle and expelled from France as a result? Wherever you looked, everybody involved in the revolution business was connected with everybody else. Those inclined to the conspiracy theory of politics— a definition which includes most secret services—could be excused if they congratulated themselves on the astuteness of their perception.

In November 1824, the most famous of all Italian Philhellenes set sail from London in the *Little Sally*, which was conveying an instalment of gold to Greece. Count Santa Rosa or, to give him his full style, Santorre Annibale di Rossi di Pomarolo Conte di Santa Rosa, one of the leaders of the revolution in Piedmont, had served, like Palma, as a minister in the short-lived Government. When the Austrians arrived in 1821 he fled to France, under sentence of death, and tried to go to ground as Paul Conty, a Piedmontese merchant. But when the French Government decided to expel all refugees the police soon tracked him down. His stammer gave him away. He was told that he could leave France for any country except Spain or Portugal, and he chose England.[10] For a few months he lived quietly in Nottingham with his wife and eight children. Count Santa Rosa was accompanied to Greece by another prominent Piedmontese refugee, Count Giacinto Provana di Collegno who had also been an officer in

Napoleon's army. He had taken part in the disastrous Russian campaign of 1812 and the Waterloo campaign of 1815. Compelled to flee from Piedmont under sentence of death in 1821, he had gone to Spain and, on the collapse of the constitutionalists there, he had followed the usual path to England.

About the same time, another Piedmontese revolutionary who had been in Spain, Count Porro, made his way to Greece. Count Pecorara, yet another Piedmontese who had been in Spain, followed in 1826. Count Gamba, who had been Lord Byron's secretary and had returned with his body to England, decided to return to Greece in 1825: he had been closely involved with Byron's revolutionary activities in Italy. Observers of the Greek scene at this time felt that the country was being overrun by Carbonari Counts.[11]

Santa Rosa wrote to a friend the day before he set sail: 'Tomorrow I leave for Greece with Collegno. I must burst out. I do not know if I can be useful but I am prepared for all sorts of difficulties. Bowring and the others disapprove. But throughout history the destinies of Greece and Italy have been interwoven.'[12]

Here was a new aspect of philhellenism, the link between Greece and Rome. If Greece was being regenerated, was it not fitting that she should assist the men who were trying to regenerate Italy? Count Palma declared that he was motivated by 'the desire that I entertained to contribute to the welfare of Greece which we Italians must look upon as our mother country'.[13] Count Pecchio wrote enthusiastically about Greece, 'the ancient sister of Italy', and composed a historical appendix to his book to justify the phrase. He traced the links between Ancient Greece and Ancient Rome and the numerous occasions since ancient times when the Italians and Greeks had come into contact; Italy 'stretching out her arms' to receive the exiles from the fall of Constantinople, the Renaissance in Italy, the campaigns of the Venetians against the Turks, and so on. These considerations, Pecchio declared, were 'not less dictated from the recollection of the past, than from the present feelings of the heart'. During two thousand years, he affirmed, there had been 'sympathy and fraternal affection' between the two peoples.[14]

This profession by the Italians of a special regard for Greece was to some extent merely a disguise intended to conceal their true motive which was to hold together in Greece some kind of Italian liberal organization in exile, but it was not entirely disingenuous. Santa Rosa, in particular (who took a copy of Plato with him to Greece), felt in some vague way that he had a duty to go to Greece, to repay some ancient debt; that simply to continue in his relatively comfortable exile in England would be a betrayal.

The Carbonari Counts suffered from a worse delusion. They had a greatly exaggerated opinion of the welcome to be expected in Greece. They declared that they were ready for all sorts of difficulties but they had no idea of what conditions were really like. They naïvely imagined that the Greeks would want to make use of their experience. Santa Rosa thought, for example, that he might make his contribution by commanding a battalion or by reorganizing the finances. Porro talked hopefully about becoming a Privy Councillor. Others suggested that they had experience of this or that branch of administration or law which could be made use of.

The reality of Greek conditions came as a shock. Count Pecchio declared honestly that 'as soon as the stranger puts his foot on shore, his enthusiasm ceases, the enchantment disappears'.[15] It was the fetid smell of Nauplia which disgusted him, especially as he realized at once that it was the 'nuisances' littering the narrow streets which were mainly responsible for the endemic killing fevers which were sweeping the country. Then came the realization that there were no battalions to be commanded, no ministries in need of permanent secretaries; that men, however experienced, with no knowledge of Greek and no money, were unlikely to be able to contribute much to the Greek political scene. The Carbonari Counts forgot that, because a country is backward and its people poor, its politics are not necessarily simple.

Most of the Counts gulped down their disappointment and adjusted their ideas to the situation. Porro took on the thankless task of trying to organize the commissariat for Fabvier's little force—a job lacking in glamour but one of the most important and difficult in Greece. Collegno offered his skill as an artillery officer. But for Santa Rosa the shock was too severe. Far from welcoming the leader of the Piedmontese Revolution as a trusted adviser—as Santa Rosa had been led to expect in London—the Greek Government were frankly horrified at the arrival of this most famous carbonaro. He was asked to change his name, and Count Derossi hung around Nauplia waiting for the Government to decide what to do with him. He bitterly regretted his decision to come to Greece which he saw as a terrible mistake and talked about returning to England. To look at the miniature of his wife and children which he carried sent him into floods of tears.

In April 1825, when the future of Greece seemed to depend upon the outcome of the siege of Navarino, Santa Rosa bought an Albanian dress and set off with the Greek forces to play his part in the wars as a simple soldier. It was a gesture only. The *palikars* themselves were incapable of resisting the bayonets of the Arab regulars. What hope had a middle-aged Italian who differed from the Greeks in every respect except their dress? Santa Rosa was duly killed on 8 May when he was caught in a cave on the island of Sphacteria and refused to surrender. It was a needless sacrifice. Ibrahim, at this time anxious to impress European opinion by his clemency, set free his prisoners including Collegno after offering them handsome salaries to change sides. Ibrahim even permitted Collegno to conduct a search for Santa Rosa's body but it was never found. If the occasion had demanded a useless gesture, Santa Rosa's death would have been magnificent. As it was, no one in Greece, apart from his sorrowing friends, paid much attention.

Meanwhile the lesser Italian revolutionaries were gathering in Greece. In the summer of 1825 two expeditions set sail from London, consisting in all of about forty men. Antonio Morandi, who came in one of them, described how one day in late 1824 he was invited to a meeting of Italian exiles in London at which Louriottis, the Greek deputy, was present.[16] The news of the destruction of Psara had recently arrived and two exiled poets, Rossetti* and Pistrucci, were invited to recite verses in honour of the Greek Revolution. According to Morandi it was a sublime performance, the two poets reciting alternate passages of a long poem which sent the whole company into ecstasies of emotion. At the end Louriottis came up to Morandi and said, 'You too, my dear Morandi, who are an exile from your country for the cause of liberty, and have fought in Spain for the defence of liberty, will you not go to Greece to help the cause of liberty against the Ottoman?' There and then several Italians clasped hands with Louriottis and decided to go.

The Italian expeditions were well supplied with arms of all types and with money provided by the Greek deputies from the loan. They carried a letter of introduction from Orlandos and Louriottis addressed to the Greek Government. 'These gentlemen have all served in Europe and are desirous of a military career in our country; on their arrival they will put themselves at once under the orders of the Government, but they desire to be commanded by their compatriot Colonel Collegno who is in Greece.'[17] A few months later, an expedition of sixteen Italian refugees who had been collected in France set sail from Marseilles under the command of the Neapolitan exile, Colonel Vincenzo Pisa. Numerous other Italians made their way to Greece independently from their places of exile all over Europe.

Altogether, probably sixty or seventy Italian refugees arrived in Greece in 1825 and 1826 determined there to continue the struggle for liberty. They were a remarkable body of men from all over Italy, Colonels and Corporals thrown together by a common fate. For the majority of them only three facts are known about their careers before they reached Greece: that they had served in the armies of Napoleon; that they had taken part in the military revolts in Piedmont or Naples in 1820–1; and that they had subsequently served in Spain. Like the Bonapartists, they were already three-time losers. Approaching middle age, they were professional soldiers by upbringing but by now professional revolutionaries as well. They paraded their revolutionary experiences like battle honours. At least a

* The father of Dante Gabriel.

dozen of them enjoyed that ultimate cachet of the international revolutionary, a sentence of death *in absentia.*[18]

Some of these men, one might imagine, would already have had enough of the military life. Vincenzo Aimino had been decorated for his part in twelve years of active service prior to Waterloo before his condemnation to death in 1821 and subsequent service in Spain. Giacomuzzi Pasquale, grey from thirty years' active service, had spent a period in a French prison after being captured in Spain. He took command of one of the outer batteries at the siege of Missolonghi and spent four and a half hours in the water swimming back when it was overcome. Antonio Forsano, an Under-Officer of Napoleon's army, exiled from Piedmont in 1821, had lost an eye in the fighting in Spain.

Count Collegno, who was to have taken command of the exiles, had already left Greece before most of them arrived. Like Santa Rosa he was disgusted at the welcome he received and the low opinion of his talents which the Greeks seemed to hold. He did his best to serve them during the siege of Navarino, but left Greece soon afterwards to return to England. The leadership of the Italian exiles was taken up by Colonel Vincenzo Pisa. His military career dated back to the Battle of Marengo in 1800 at which he had been wounded. After the collapse of the Revolution in Naples in 1821 he went on the usual circuit of Spain, capture, imprisonment in France, then to England, and finally to Greece. He was now weak from encroaching age and from the effects of innumerable wounds and, it was said cryptically,[19] from time to time he suffered bouts of physical and moral disintegration.

There was another class of Italian refugees. In their search for employment the victims of the 1821 diaspora had wandered through the Mediterranean region and beyond. Italian officers of good family were to be found all over the Levant, sometimes posing as doctors, sometimes acting as advisers (more properly as status-symbols) to some pasha. In particular, Mehemet Ali in Egypt was always on the look out for suitable men to act as instructors. At the end of 1824, that is before the Egyptian invasion of the Morea, there were in Mehemet's service five Neapolitans and sixteen Piedmontese, all refugees, as well as a few French and four Spaniards.[20] Some of these men accompanied Ibrahim's army to Greece.

Giovanni Romei was now a Colonel of Engineers in the Egyptian service.[21] He had been condemned for his part in the Revolution in Piedmont and had drifted to Egypt. From the first day he set foot in Greece he felt that he was on the wrong side. One of his lieutenants, Scarpa, an exile from Venice, shared his view.

It was just at this time that General Rossaroll had established himself at Zante to act as a rallying point for the Italian refugees who were arriving from their scattered exiles in Europe. Shortly after the Egyptian invaders arrived, Rossaroll was surprised to receive a letter from Romei, whom he had known in Spain, intimating that he wanted to change sides. By the hand of the same messenger (a French merchant who was supplying the Egyptian army) he received another letter from another Italian refugee in Ibrahim's service suggesting that Rossaroll should join the Egyptians!

Romei was at once recruited to the 'Army of the Liberals', as Rossaroll called his little force of exiles, but he was not permitted to change sides at once. Rossaroll wanted to exploit the opportunity to the full. And so, while Ibrahim's army was besieging Navarino, an extremely dangerous correspondence was conducted between the Italian refugees in the opposing armies. At Rossaroll's request, Romei supplied intelligence about the strength, disposition, and intentions of Ibrahim's forces. With this information Rossaroll was able to build up his own influence with the Greek Government and the other Philhellenes, at this time mainly French, who were intensely suspicious of his intentions. Rossaroll claimed that if he were allowed to handle the situation in his own way he could arrange for a wholesale desertion of Ibrahim's officers or, at worst, destroy completely his confidence in their loyalty.

The operation involved extreme danger for Romei and Scarpa. They must have realized that their line of communication to Rossaroll was insecure, although they could hardly have guessed that their letters were being intercepted by the British authorities *en route* and copies sent to London.

One of the most surprising features of the correspondence is the unquestioning assumption on the part of General Rossaroll that, because he was Romei's superior in the masonic hierarchy, he was entitled to demand total obedience even to the extent of ordering Romei to perform tasks of extreme danger. It is a measure of the intense loyalty which the Italian refugees felt for one another, a result of years of practice in secret societies, freemasonry, and carbonarism, that Romei seems never to have doubted that his duty was to give instant obedience.

The following extracts from one of Rossaroll's letters to Romei give an indication of the relationship:

Dearest Confrere Romei
  Your honour is saved in spite of the horrific crime you have committed by selling yourself to the sacrilegious enemies of Greek and universal liberty. I, as you know, am 33 [apparently a masonic rank] and my friend Count Dionisio Roma [an Ionian nobleman] is a 31 [apparently another masonic rank]. Touched with pity by the phrases you have used in your letter to me, we assembled a lodge and after giving an assurance that you were commissioned by us to join the cursed people, we passed an unanimous resolution, that the Grand Inquisitor, the S. Roma, should give you an attestation of your masonic virtues, and should declare the services you have rendered to the liberty of Greece, under the guise of the turban. . . .

In virtue of the project and plan of campaign, I shall proceed to join Conduriotti, the present head of the Greek Government, in order to direct the movements of the Army of the Liberals, and Roma will remain at Zante and be the medium of our correspondence.

In the meantime we being old soldiers and wretchedly poor, having lost all we possessed at home in the sacred cause of liberty, it is not right we should find ourselves at the close of the war without reward for our operations, and therefore Roma and the F.F. [Fratelli] will stipulate with the Greek Government for a grant of as much landed property as shall ensure to ourselves and families a decent and easy subsistence and a compensation for our heavy losses in Italy. We will arrange then when the moment arrives for your leaving those brutes, you shall, on joining me, be at the head of the *état major*, or commanding officer of the Corps of Engineers and Artillery. . . .

I will open to you the road to honour under the Ensign of true Glory, and you will fly to our beloved Mother, Liberty, who holds out her arms to receive you, once the most undutiful of her sons, into her bosom. . . . .

Send me the cross of the Eagle of the two Sicilies and the large medal of honour of Giachino, which you promised me at Barcelona: they will be useful to me at this moment and can be of service to you.[22]

Romei supplied Rossaroll with a steady stream of military intelligence which would have been extremely valuable if the Greeks had been in any position to take advantage of it. He deliberately arranged Ibrahim's siege artillery at Navarino so far back from the defences that they did little damage. It is said too that he directed the artillery fire of the Greeks— which was commanded by Count Collegno—to try to hit Ibrahim's headquarters.[23]

Scarpa succeeded in changing sides and joined Colonel Fabvier. He took part in the campaigns of 1826 and 1827, but died of disease before the end of the war. Albertini, another Philhellene, who is recorded as having died at Nauplia, is probably the same as the Piedmontese revolutionary Albertini who came with Ibrahim's army. Romei himself was detected before he could make the move. He was arrested and sent to Egypt in chains, but is said to have suffered no other punishment than dismissal from Mehemet's service.[24]

A soldier must sell his labour where he can. Service in Greece might give a warm feeling of moral righteousness but few other rewards. As one of Ibrahim's officers remarked sadly to Collegno during his capture after the fall of Navarino, 'The liberty for which I fought for thirty years in every country left me without bread. At my age I cannot do anything else. I am a soldier.' This man, a Polish Colonel, had known Collegno in Turin in 1821 during the brief ecstatic days of the Piedmontese Revolution.[25] Increasingly, the Italians felt that the cost of their principles was too high, that they could not afford to join a losing side for a fourth time. Eight men from one of the expeditions of Italians sent from London left immediately for Smyrna after they had taken a quick look at the pitiful little army they were to join in Greece. [26]

Monteverde, a refugee from the Austrian part of Italy, who had been in Greece since the early days of the Revolution, was described by a fellow Philhellene in 1825 as among the few men of 'great bravery and leading a life of unrewarded hardship, danger, and unceasing privation that does honour to their constancy and courage'. [27] During the battles near Missolonghi in March 1826 the Suliotes brought in the head of a European who was directing the Turkish artillery which was recognized to be that of the former Philhellene. [28]

The Piedmontese Calosso had the classic background of an Italian Philhellene. [29] Captain of hussars in Napoleon's Grand Army, he took part in the Revolution in Piedmont, was exiled, drifted to France, Spain, England, and then on to Greece when the Italian revolutionaries began to reassemble there. He joined Fabvier and took part in one of the Greek campaigns but quarrelled with him and left Greece in 1826. He turned up in Constantinople in a miserable state, with hardly a pair of shoes, hoping for help from the large Italian merchant colony. The Italians, fearing to involve themselves with an acknowledged carbonaro, treated him as an outcast. For a while he was employed by a Swiss businessman who had the idea of establishing a brewery at Constantinople, but the sherbert-loving Turks were disgusted by their first taste of beer and the enterprise was a failure. Calosso again joined the ranks of impoverished Italian exiles who were to be found all over the Ottoman Empire. Suddenly an unexpected opportunity for employment appeared.

It had been obvious for generations that the Corps of Janissaries on whose strength the Ottoman Empire had been built centuries before was now a dangerous anachronism. Not only were their traditional fighting methods repeatedly proved useless against European armies, but they had turned themselves into a dangerous internal political force. Sultan Selim III had been put to death in 1807 mainly as a result of his attempt to impose reforms on the Janissaries. Ever since Mahmoud's accession in 1808 he had been preparing for the day when he too could make the attempt. In 1826 the moment seemed right.

In June, with scrupulous attention to the exact letter of the law, Mahmoud published a decree requiring some of the Janissaries to begin new military exercises, according to the European style. The effect was as expected. The Janissaries of the capital refused to obey and began to march on the Seraglio demanding that the Sultan's ministers should be beheaded. Mahmoud was ready. He unfurled the Sacred Standard of the Prophet and called on all True Believers to rally to their Padishah and their Caliph. As the Janissaries surged through the narrow streets, Mahmoud's artillery-men whom he had for years been building up as a specially loyal force, opened fire on them. The Janissaries lost many men but the remnant retired in good order to their barracks. Now Mahmoud showed the full extent of his ruthlessness. His artillery was drawn up before the barracks and blasted it ceaselessly until the last of the Janissaries of Constantinople had perished among the blazing bloodstained ruins. Four thousand men are said to have been killed on this day in Constantinople. Many thousands more were put to death in cities throughout the Empire as the ancient corps of Janissaries was systematically exterminated.

Having destroyed the old system, Mahmoud immediately began to build a new one. An army of 40,000 was formed to be trained in European tactics. If the Egyptians had been taught European methods and the Greeks were belatedly learning them, now it was the turn of the Turks.

Calosso now came into his own. It was known in Constantinople that he was a superb horseman. Mahmoud was determined to have European cavalry. On the recommendation of the French Ambassador, who saw it as in the interest of France to resettle distressed Philhellenes in the Turkish service, Calosso was engaged to run the military riding school and then, when he had made a success of that, to train the new cavalry. Mahmoud, who did nothing by halves, was determined to be the best horseman in his own new army. He put himself under Calosso's instruction and quickly became an expert. Calosso grew in influence—he was handsomely paid, wore the uniform of the new guard distinguished by a diamond crescent, and was given one of the best houses in Pera. It was even said that he once received the unprecedented honour of being permitted to kiss the imperial feet.

But it would be wrong to leave the Italians with such an exceptional case as Calosso. The contingents of the little Italian revolutionary army in exile, as they arrived in 1825 and 1826, joined Fabvier and his Frenchmen and played a major part in helping the Greeks, at last, to build up a regular force. Many were to be killed or to die of disease in the closing years of the war. Others later found a way of breaking out of the international revolutionary circuit, on which so much of their lives had been spent, and of returning home. But whereas the Bonapartists were reabsorbed into the main stream of French life after the July Revolution of 1830, if not before, the Italians for the most part had no such good fortune. The longed-for day when a new liberal revolution would break out in Italy, the day for which they had been organizing since 1821, did not come until 1848. By then Greek independence had long since been won and there was little room there for professional foreign officers, but a few remained. In 1848 Antonio Morandi, who had been condemned to death in 1821 and then gone on to Spain and England, set off from Greece to attempt again the liberation of his own country.

Pl. IV Greece Expiring on the Ruins of Missolonghi, by Delacroix

26. *French Idealism and French Cynicism*

At the time when Colonel Fabvier was given the task of organizing a regular force in the summer of 1825, another French soldier appeared at Nauplia. He was General Roche, a very different type of Frenchman. Although Roche's military career, like Fabvier's, had been spent in the service of Napoleon, he had accommodated himself to the restoration of the Bourbons in 1815. To Roche, the notion that there was a future in Bonapartism ten years after Waterloo and four years after the death of the Emperor was dangerous rubbish. He shared many of Fabvier's liberal political principles and his hatred of the English, but at the same time regarded such men as Fabvier who had dared to take up arms against France as little better than traitors. Roche was the official agent in Greece of the Paris Greek Committee, a philhellenic organization not so far mentioned in the story. His presence at Nauplia was the result of a complex interaction of circumstances, and his brand of philhellenism had very different roots from Fabvier's. As usual, concern for Greece was only part of his motivation.

The French Government until 1823 was mainly preoccupied with the situation in Spain. When that problem was neatly solved by invasion they were able to devote more attention to other foreign policy issues. And the success gave them a new confidence. Viewed from Paris, the Greek Revolution had taken a disturbing turn. From all points of view the British seemed to be in the ascendant. First there was the sensational expedition of Lord Byron and then the two loans on the London Stock Exchange. The appeals of the Greeks in the summer of 1825 to put their country under the protection of Great Britain seemed merely to confirm a tendency which was already plain—that Greece was going to be virtually a British satellite; that in yet another part of the world the French had been beaten to the post by their hated rivals across the Channel. In fact, as the reader will have seen, the impact of the British Philhellenes, even including Lord Byron, on the situation in Greece was extremely limited and certainly the influence gained was disproportionate to the resources and energy expended. But, as ever, by the time the news from Greece had been passed to European ears through the filter of distortion and preconception, the situation seemed otherwise. The French Government had also heard of another plan which was circulating in Greece at this time, to invite Count Capodistria from his retirement in Switzerland, to become President of Greece. On the face of it, this plan too was abhorrent since it was assumed (again wrongly) that Capodistria, who had earlier been the Czar's foreign minister, must necessarily be the agent of some scheme to establish Russian domination in Greece. In any case, it was clear that both the British and the Russians had their supporters in Greece, and France appeared to be out in the cold. Something must be done to reassert the interest of France. With the failure of the schemes to establish French influence through the Knights of Malta, other policies had to be attempted.

At the beginning of July 1825 the British authorities in the Ionian Islands intercepted a letter which revealed that a French Philhellene recently arrived in Greece, Théobald Piscatory, was in fact a secret agent of the French foreign office. He had attempted to suborn Mavrocordato's secretary, a Frenchman called Grasset, by offering him an important government post in France in exchange for information. Grasset had declined.[1] It was also known that Piscatory had arranged to have a long conference on his way out with Capodistria in Switzerland and with a known Russian agent in Greece.

Piscatory's mission was to explore an idea that had originally come from the Russian Government, that France and Russia should co-operate to settle the affairs of Greece to the exclusion of the British. The initiative failed mainly because Russia felt that she was entitled to what would later have been called 'a free hand in Greece'. The Russians felt that since Austria had been given a free hand to solve the situation in Italy, and France had been given a free hand to solve the situation in Spain, it was now their turn to solve the Greek question by a military attack on Turkey. Besides disliking this idea, the French were aware, like the British, that the Russian Government's intelligence about events in Greece itself was poor. For France the real rival was always Britain.

At the same time the British authorities were intercepting letters which gave evidence of a far more important French intrigue, a scheme to provide Greece with a French king. The princes of the French royal family featured prominently in French foreign policy at the time. The unfortunate boys were being hawked round the newly independent states of South America to any country that seemed inclined to accept French help. An extract from one of the early letters gives something of the flavour of how the Greek intrigue was planned. The writer of the (translated) letter was a Greek called Vitales whose imprudent correspondence had also revealed to the British much about the Knights of Malta. The numbers were intended to be a code but the British had little difficulty in identifying the chief characters.

You say that 50 [Villévêque leader of the Orleanists in the French chamber] and 52 [Roche] will come from the friend's brother [reference unknown] to fetch him bringing the necessary funds for the purchase, and that if this had taken place when the friend proposed, the operation would by this time have been terminated, and thus 39 [Russia] 36 [Austria], and 35 [France] would have remained *dalla provista* of 29 [Duke of Nemours]. But now we must of necessity have patience, [and] I continue to hope that my offers will have the preference. . . . The concurrents are already at work and it behoves me to be secret. When it is made known, everything will be concluded or at least the plan will be adopted. Up to the present time it seems that my offers and proposals seem to be well regarded and listened to by those charged with the affairs who are 5 [Constantine Botsaris] and 6 [Colocotrones] and they ordered two persons only, 53 [Ainian] and 57 [Tricoupes] to speak with me. They afterwards will speak with the above-mentioned 5 [Botsaris] and 6 [Colocotrones] who will fix what is best to be done. What this is I cannot say as yet, but the idea was up to the day before yesterday that two persons should go to verify what has been written by 50 [Villévêque] and offered by me and that 30 [Duke of Orleans] should accept for 29 [Duke of Nemours] without opposition on the part of 35 [King of France]. I must now repeat to you how much I am embarrassed by 52's [Roche's] proceedings but that I shall do as well as I can for our interests. Let us now see what is to be done if 50 [Villévêque] or 52 [Roche] should arrive here with the earnest money. . . .[2]

The British watched the development of this scheme for over a year, piecing it together from such obscure fragments as the extract quoted. To recount its vicissitudes in detail and explore the motives and inter-actions of the main participants would fill a volume. The chief features can however be briefly stated. The Duke of Orleans (later to be King Louis-Philippe of France) formed a focus of opposition in Restoration France for various groups who were opposed to the policies of the King. The Duke of Orleans was not at this time actively plotting to usurp the throne from the senior branch of the House of Bourbon, but naturally the King kept a watchful eye on him. The Duke of Nemours was one of Orleans' sons, then aged eleven. Under the plan this unlucky boy was to be made King of Greece in exchange for active French help in one form or another but, since a regency would be necessary, control of the country would lie effectively in the hands of the French royal family. The various Greek leaders, especially Mavrocordato, gave indications from time to time that they were in favour of the scheme, but their main motive was simply to encourage as many ties as possible with Western European interests in the hope that the powers would eventually come to Greece's rescue.

At the time when the Orleanist party, including General Roche, were active in France and in Greece, trying to gather support for their plans, an astonishing change was occurring in French public opinion. During 1825 when public opinion in England was growing weary of philhellenism, a new movement was on the march in France. And the French philhellenic movement was to reach its greatest strength in 1826 at the very time when the English Philhellenes—following the scandal of the loans—were at their lowest point. The French movement was the last and greatest manifestation of militant philhellenism during the Greek War of Independence.

Apart from localized efforts by the professors and churchmen in 1821 and 1822, the first philhellenic organization in France was founded in 1823. It was a sub-committee of the *Société de la Morale Chrétienne*,[3] a philanthropic organization devoted to charitable purposes and social reform, such as the abolition of slavery, improving the conditions in prisons, aiding orphans, the abolition of the death penalty, and the abolition of gambling. Like their colleagues in the London Greek Committee, the first French Philhellenes were men of liberal ideas not particularly interested in the Greeks as Greeks but drawn to take an interest because of their general political outlook.

The Society confined itself entirely to charitable works. In particular it played an important part, along with the Swiss and South German Societies, in sending to Greece the refugees from Russia who had been herded across Europe in great misery in 1822. Sending these wretched victims of distant upheavals to Greece was to do them no service, since in a land thousands of miles from their homeland they had no friends and no means of earning a livelihood. But the charitable work was done in good faith and no one doubted at the time that they would be better off in Greece. Although the Society made no secret of its sympathy with the cause of the Greek Revolution, it was scrupulously careful to do nothing which could be interpreted as giving active support to the revolutionaries. As one of the reports declared:

> The philhellenic committees of England, Germany etc. send to the Hellenes officers, armaments, ships, munitions of war etc. Our committee, which is purely philanthropic, will send them (or at least solicit for them) books for their libraries, schoolmasters for their schools, ploughs for their devastated fields, machines and patterns for their factories, directions and advice for all their establishments of public utility.[4]

The Christian Moral Society collected in all about £300. But already by the end of 1824 it had passed its peak. Public opinion was now demanding more active, warlike measures in favour of the Greeks. In February 1825 was founded the *Société philanthropique en faveur des Grecs,*[5] usually known as the Paris Greek Committee. Many members of the old Christian Moral Society who had been engaged in the relief work came over to join the new committee and it soon outstripped its parent. During the next three years the Paris Greek Committee collected over one and a half million francs, about £65,000 at the current rate of exchange, nearly six times the amount collected by the London Greek Committee during its period of pre-eminence. The Committee became the centre for renewed philhellenic activity all over Western Europe. It sent men, equipment, and money to Greece in quantities which had an important effect on the outcome of the war, and was undoubtedly the best organized and most effective of all the militant philhellenic movements to arise during the war.

It is strange that philhellenism in France should not have begun to make a major impact until 1825, four full years after the outbreak of the Greek Revolution. No explanation is fully satisfactory. Part of the reason lay in the attitude of the French Government, which turned increasingly to Greece after the invasion of Spain, and in particular in the efforts of the Orleanists and others to promote their schemes for a French King of Greece. Yet while the shift of emphasis on the part of the French Government from tolerance of philhellenism to more active encouragement was no doubt important, the Government never departed from its sister policy of support for Mehemet Ali. Other causes must be looked for and, as with so many episodes in the history of philhellenism, the influence of Lord Byron is never far away. Much of the stimulus for the upsurge of philhellenism in France in 1824 and 1825 can be attributed to the story and mythology of Lord Byron's pilgrimage to Greece and his death at Missolonghi.[6]

French literature in the early nineteenth century was perhaps more influenced by the poetry and the life of Lord Byron than by any other foreigner. Byron's influence in France was greater even than in England and if much of his poetry was misunderstood and the popular view of his character was hopelessly distorted, that is the fate (and the mark) of great men. The depth of the impression which Byron was making in France was not realized until his death was announced on 18 May 1824. A flood of books of poetry on the death of Byron were hurriedly printed—no less than fourteen separate works in 1824 alone. The Opéra immediately arranged for a new tragedy to be prepared on the theme. The students of Paris are said to have spontaneously put on mourning and spent the rest of the fateful day tearfully reading aloud passages from the poems of the great hero. Reprints of his works and reproductions of his (long-since romanticized) portrait were rushed through the presses. Commemorative medals were struck. An exhibition of a picture of the death of Lord Byron by a Greek artist drew large crowds. It is said to have shown the body of the poet stretched out on a bed. An observer records that 'The sword which Childe Harold had drawn for the cause of the Greeks is hanging on the base of a statue of Liberty. The lyre whose sounds had sustained the sacred fire of independence is thrown near the coffin of the modern Tyrtaeus: its strings are broken. The shadows of some kneeling Greeks surround the death-bed of their noble defender.'[7]

The sensation caused by Byron's death drew French attention to the situation in Greece, but quickly a romantic philhellenic movement took off on wings of its own. The books of verse on Greek themes published at this time are numerous. As ever, many were by authors who never again attempted to write poetry. All the old themes were there, comparisons between Ancient and Modern Greeks, the war of the Christians against the infidel barbarians, the call to fight a new crusade. The name of the great romantic poet itself entered the convention of romantic philhellenism. Poets began to call Greece the land of Homer and Byron. The name of Missolonghi which had been virtually unknown in Western Europe before 1824 now carried more exciting associations than Athens or Sparta or Corinth. The Battle of Peta was similarly transmogrified. Poems on the theme 'The Strangers in Greece' or 'The Philhellenes' made it appear that the events of 1822 had been a great adventure.[8]

The uniformity of sentiment in these poems is their most surprising characteristic. There must still have been large sections of the population to whom philhellenic themes were not yet banal. Nothing is lost in the translation of this typical extract from a poem on the volunteers setting sail from France to fight for Greece, Liberty, and Religion:

> Arise, Parthenon receive your heroes,
> Your sacred ruins serve them as a tomb,
> Take up your chisels, O Daughters of Memory,
> Engrave their obscure names in the temple of glory!
> For to die for the cross and for liberty
>   Is the supreme glory,
>   It is to die for humanity,
>   It is to die for God himself!!![9]

In a few of the poems the authors convey something of the attempts of frustrated Bonapartists to stage a revival of their cause by their exploits in Greece. Fabvier and his followers were of course the heroes to be compared with the great men of antiquity. The shade of Leonidas was commonly introduced to give advice to his latter-day imitators. Théophile Féburier, who visited Greece as a volunteer, published a poem 'Corsica, the Isle of Elba, the Greeks, and Saint Helena'[10] in praise of Napoleon and the Napoleonic officers who gave their help to Greece when the sovereigns of Europe refused to do so. Byron's sympathy with Napoleon was not overlooked and the names of the two men were frequently linked. As another poet wrote:

Two heroes, of their time, the light and the flame,
Came, sang, conquered, reigned, languished!
Far from their native land they took their soul.
Saint Helena! . . . Missolonghi.[11]

The news of the destruction of Missolonghi in April 1826 sent a thrill
of horror all over Europe. But whereas in England the main result was
to deliver a virtual *coup de grâce* to the flagging Greek bonds, in France it
led to a further immense intensification of philhellenic feeling. The name of
Missolonghi became one of the great rallying cries of the nineteenth
century and not a few who responded to it believed that Lord Byron had
died in the destruction of the town. It was at this time that Victor Hugo
wrote his famous ode 'The Heads of the Seraglio', in which he imagines
the heads of the heroes of Modern Greece exposed at Constantinople. The
name of Missolonghi resounds through the poem until the fateful message
arrives 'Missolonghi n'est plus'. On this occasion too the unknown
Alexandre Dumas began his long career with a philhellenic dithyramb sold
for the benefit of the Greeks.

In the Paris of 1825 and 1826 it must have been difficult to escape the
influence of the friends of the Greeks. In October 1825 there opened at
the *Académie Royale de Musique* a lyrical tragedy *The Siege of Corinth* with
music by Rossini. In November, at the *Théâtre Français*, was the first performance of Pichald's tragedy *Leonidas*. In the box of the Duke of Orleans
were two young Greeks, the sons of the Greek Admirals Canaris and
Miaulis, sent to France for education at the expense of the Greek Committee,
and taken to the theatre to promote the cause in the same way that Blaquiere
had taken his Greek boys to the Stock Exchange in London. The author,
when his play was printed shortly afterwards, admitted that his huge success
was due to the wave of feeling on behalf of the Greeks. For the French,
he said, Greece was a second fatherland and the audience was not so much
applauding the exploits of the ancient Leonidas as the modern Leonidas,
Marco Botsaris.

Exhibitions of pictures were held for the benefit of the Greeks. A
charge was made for admission and sometimes pictures were sold. Delacroix's famous 'Scenes from the Massacres of Scio', inspired by the Chios
massacre of 1822, was exhibited at the Salon in 1824 where it was bought
by the King for the Louvre. Several of Delacroix's pictures were shown
in the exhibitions arranged for the Greeks in May 1826, mostly from
Byronic themes, such as 'The Combat of the Giaour and the Pasha', 'A
Turkish officer killed in the mountains'. The magnificent 'Greece expiring
on the Ruins of Missolonghi' came later. At the exhibition arranged for
the Greeks in September 1826 Scheffer's 'Taking of Missolonghi' and
Colin's 'Massacre of the Greeks' could be seen. The print shops were full
of portraits of Fabvier and the usual patriotic handbills adapted to Grecian

themes—tearful mothers and beautiful maidens bidding farewell to soldiers off to the wars, returning heroes being decked with wreaths, usually with a few ruined columns and a turban or ataghan worked into the composition to point up the context.

Concerts were held in various towns in France to raise money for the cause. We hear too of balls, raffles, and amateur theatricals. A lemonade dealer gave a day's profits. In Paris a fashionable jeweller put on sale, for the benefit of the Greeks, brooches in the shape and colours of the Greek flag. The ladies of Paris are said to have divided out the city and made a door-to-door collection.

Books on Greece tumbled from the presses. Over one hundred and twelve new titles in French can be counted for 1825 and 1826—histories, memoirs, verses, pamphlets, brochures, appeals. At least three different works were published under the title *Histoire de la Régénération de la Grèce*. Increasingly there could be seen on the title pages of new publications the words *Vendu au profit des Grecs*, 'Sold for the benefit of the Greeks'.

All the usual philhellenic themes appear in these books as well as the peculiarly French accretions, nostalgia for Napoleon and the ill-concealed dislike of the English. The most influential was probably the short pamphlet by Chateaubriand, *Note on Greece*, first published in 1825.

'Will our century,' he demanded, 'watch hordes of savages extinguish civilization at its rebirth on the tomb of a people who civilized the world? Will Christendom calmly allow Turks to strangle Christians? And will the Legitimate Monarchs of Europe shamelessly permit their sacred name to be given to a tyranny which could have reddened the Tiber?'[12]

Chateaubriand had, like Byron, visited Greece in his younger days before the Revolution. Like Byron his book of travel experiences had reflected the literary philhellenic ideas of the time, but unlike Byron Chateaubriand was a major politician in his own right as well as a man of letters.

This huge enthusiasm in favour of the Greeks which swept France in 1825 and 1826 was surveyed with satisfaction by the illustrious men of the Paris Greek Committee. The movement which they had encouraged and nurtured had grown beyond their most ambitious hopes. And despite the vast extension of activity all over France, the Paris Committee remained indisputably in control. In contrast with the London Greek Committee, which always rested on a narrow political base, the Paris Committee gradually extended its membership and influence to an ever wider spectrum of opinion.[13] The Committee was brilliant with famous names. The Duc de Choiseul, the Duc de Broglie, the Duc de Dalberg, the Duc de Fitzjames, the Comte d'Harcourt, the Comte de Laborde, Generals Sébastiani and Gérard, the banker Lafitte, the publisher Didot, Benjamin Constant. The Marquis de Lafayette had fought alongside George Washington in the

War of American Independence and had proposed the design of the tri-colour in 1789 on the outbreak of the French Revolution. Originally the Committee seems to have been largely composed of Liberals and Orleanists, but with the accession of Chateaubriand, who had served as Foreign Minister to the restored Bourbons, it became a national movement. Napoleonic Generals and lifelong Republicans joined their names with devoted supporters of the Restoration. Not the least of the effects of the Greek War of Independence was the part it played in bringing about a reconciliation between the bitter political divisions of Restoration France.

The Committee was at first very circumspect in its activities, declaring that 'it had no other object but to serve the cause of humanity and religion'. Much emphasis was put on the educating of Greek children and the redeeming of captive Greeks from the slave markets. By the beginning of 1825, however, it was preparing to send volunteers and military supplies to Greece. General Roche was sent ahead to prepare the way for their arrival. These military expeditions, which represent the main achievement of French philhellenism, will be described later. At the beginning of 1826 the Committee began to publish a regular bulletin on its activities and this was a skilful vehicle of propaganda. News from Greece was printed and details were given of the expenditure of the Committee's funds. The Committee took to publishing lists of subscribers to the cause and recording the various activities in support of the cause going on all over France. There are few better stimulants to benevolence than the sight of other people's names lauded in print for their charitable donations. Soon, long lists were appearing of subscriptions from all walks of life all over France: a tailor giving ten francs, a tanner three francs, a hairdresser contributing 160 francs from a collection made during a hairdressing course, a printer giving his services free for the printing of appeals. General Lafayette subscribed 5,000 francs, Casimir Périer 6,000, the House of Orleans 16,000, the Masonic Lodges 7,927.50. 'An illustrious traveller in Florence' gave 20,000 francs. The bulletin carefully recorded the establishment of subsidiary committees, at first only in France but soon elsewhere in Europe. The Paris Greek Committee found itself at the head of a vast movement which by mid-1826 had spread over much of Continental Europe. Russia, Austria and Italy remained obstinately closed apart from a few donations sent out, but philhellenism revived in several cities where it had died out or been stamped out in 1822 or 1823. In parts of Germany previously intolerant governments now turned a blind eye. Philhellenism suddenly became fashionable. If the great noblemen of Restoration France were encouraging the cause, could it really be a danger to minor German states? In Sweden the King's sister donated a large sum and set up an association of Swedish women to campaign for the Greeks. In the Netherlands there was a notable revival. Even in Prussia, whose Government had been among the most hostile in 1821 and 1822, the mood changed. The subscription list for Berlin was headed by the name of the Queen.

The Swiss Greek Societies, some of which had continued to exist since the early days of the war, played their part in the general revival. In the first years they had happily taken their lead from the South Germans. They then transferred their support to the British. It was only logical to continue their quiet good work under the guidance of the new giant in Paris. The Swiss Societies now had a dynamic leader, the banker Eynard, who journeyed all over Western Europe collecting money for the cause.

The Paris Greek Committee was not all that it appeared. Colonel Stanhope, who attended one of their meetings in April 1825, was solemnly assured by General Sébastiani that there was no question of any rivalry with Britain. The agent of the Paris Committee, General Roche, had, he explained, been specifically instructed on the point. 'This sentiment', declared Stanhope, 'was worthy of a lofty-minded Frenchman.'[14]

In fact the prime purpose of General Roche's visit to Greece was to promote the Orleanist intrigue. Although nominally the agent of the Paris Greek Committee, his real master was the Duke of Orleans. The open instructions which he carried specifically prohibited him from indulging in political activities, but he also had secret instructions from the Duke of Orleans. These had been approved by the French Government and were known to only a few members of the Committee (including, incidentally, General Sébastiani). The Paris Committee, like any organization built on contributions from the simple, the honest, and the inexperienced, was an easy prey to unscrupulous leaders.

More than any other philhellenic organization, it was used by the Governmen as an instrument of its foreign policy. The London Committee had been unashamedly nationalistic and some of its members discussed policies from time to time with members of the British Government. But with the Paris Committee a deliberate attempt was made to take over the direction of the whole movement. The majority of members remained in ignorance that the Committee was under the control of the Government. Certainly the thousands of Frenchmen who donated money did not suspect that the allegedly charitable organization composed largely of opposition statesmen was being used as a front by the French foreign office.

It would be interesting to know whether the French Government gave funds. In 1825 it began to give other forms of suppport. The restrictions at Marseilles, from which no philhellenic expedition had been allowed to sail since the ill-fated German Legion in December 1822, were quietly lifted. No restrictions were put on the purchase and export of arms intended for the Greeks. The recruitment of volunteers went on undisturbed. Returning Philhellenes were no longer watched by the secret police as suspect revolutionaries, but permitted to give public accounts of their experience in order to boost the cause. Although the intimate nature of the connection between the Committee and the French Government was not known, the Government was not averse to swimming with the current of public opinion and making it appear that it was sympathetic to the cause of the Greeks.

However, at the same time as it was actively encouraging the French Philhellenes, the French Government was faced with the decision what to do with its older policy of support for Mehemet Ali. The consolidation of French influence in Egypt had been pursued as occasion offered ever since Bonaparte's expedition in 1798. It was connected with the deep-rooted French dream of building a position in the Middle East to match the British in India. In the 1820s the fruits of the policy had at last begun to appear. Mehemet Ali, in return for French technical and economic help, seemed quite ready to listen to the advice of the French Government. Everyone knew that Drovetti, the French consul in Cairo, was not there to look after French citizens in distress or to help exporters with the customs formalities. He was one of the most powerful men in the land.

The trouble with this kind of exclusive relationship is that the client government tends to make increasing demands on its patron. In particular, the clients usually develop an insatiable appetite for military equipment and for military assistance.[15] Only foolish governments believe that questions of arms exports can be insulated from wider issues. A willingness to arm a client state is the ultimate test of international friendship, and to arm a state openly is the ultimate kiss of approval. Mehemet Ali understood these matters.

The European officers who had first brought Mehemet's army up to a European standard had been recruited privately without active French Government participation. Colonel Sève, the most famous, went to Egypt long before the Greek Revolution; Mari and Gubernatis were former Philhellenes, the rest were Italian refugees. Then in the summer of 1824, when it was already known that the Egyptians were going to invade Greece, Mehemet Ali made a formal proposal to the French Government that they should send a military mission to help complete the training of his new armies.

It was an extremely embarrassing request. As long as Mehemet's armies were devastating Arabia or the Sudan, no one in Europe was likely to care very much, but Greece! The French tried to warn Mehemet not to involve himself in Europe—Crete possibly but not the Morea, where he was bound to meet all sorts of obstacles from the great powers. But this was a point on which French advice was definitely not going to be taken. What then should the French do? They found themselves in a common foreign policy dilemma. They were conscious of the strong position they had built up in Egypt and of the strong influence which they exercised over

Mehemet Ali. Was it worth putting their huge investment at risk by refusing Mehemet's request for a military mission? Or should they continue to help him in the hope that they would continue to exercise influence, perhaps restraining influence?

They chose the latter. In November 1824 the mission which Mehemet Ali had requested set sail from Marseilles. It consisted of two Generals, Boyer and de Livron, and six other officers. They were recruited secretly by a French General acting on behalf of the Government and their names were cleared in advance with the French foreign office. The French Consul in Egypt was given detailed instructions about the purpose of their mission. In a memorable example of diplomatic disingenuousness General Boyer was told that 'the interests of Egypt are so linked to those of France that to serve one is to serve them both'.[16] When they arrived in Egypt, the French officers were careful to confine their activities to the training of the Egyptian armies and to refuse absolutely to follow them to Greece.

The fact that the French Government had approved the mission to Egypt was, of course, not for publication. To the French public, borne along by the gathering tide of philhellenism and congratulating the Government for its belated recognition of their cause, these men were simply renegades, traitors, unspeakable mercenaries. Some of the officers felt a sense of disquiet at the strange mission to which their patriotic duty had led them and took these charges to heart. They argued unconvincingly to themselves that, since they were only instructors, they had no responsibility for the subsequent actions of the army which they were instructing. The French Government felt that the only thing to do when one has gone too far is to go further. Through 1825 when Ibrahim was devastating Greece, they continued to allow arms and men to go to Mehemet Ali. A list of new officers to join Boyer was under consideration in the French foreign office at the time of the fall of Missolonghi and the Government was still apparently happy to continue the policy right up until the autumn of 1826 when Mehemet Ali himself dismissed General Boyer and brought the mission to an end.

The fact that French officers were actively supporting Mehemet Ali could be concealed or explained away. The officers were expected to carry the ignominy of the Government's policy personally as part of their duty to France. No doubt the French Government felt that sending a clandestine mission to Egypt was a neat solution to their problem, at the same time preserving their influence and avoiding political embarrassment at home. But no sooner had the mission arrived in Egypt than Mehemet Ali began to make other, even more embarrassing requests. He had decided, he said, that if he was going to conquer Greece then he would have to wrest naval superiority from the hardy sailors of Hydra and Spetsae and destroy them as he had destroyed Psara. What he needed was a fleet. Several modern French warships had recently visited Egypt and their captains had been delighted to show them off to the admiring pasha. In December 1824 Mehemet proposed formally to General de Livron that he should be supplied with two frigates and a brig of war of an exactly similar type to the most modern vessels in service with the French Navy.[17]

Again the French Government was faced with the dilemma whether to go on with their policy of support or to draw back. The French Admiralty advised that the construction of the vessels requested by Mehemet Ali could not be disguised as merchant-ship building, that only the French navy could supply the requisite skills and materials, and that to accept the contract was bound to be seen as a pro-Turkish gesture, but the Government decided to take the risk. It seemed such a big step to risk breaking with Mehemet and such a small step to provide just a little more help. After all, smaller vessels had already been built for him in France without attracting much notice beyond some fist-waving by the German Phil-hellenes of 1822. That, admittedly, was before the Egyptian entry into the war, before the destruction of Crete, and of Psara, but by now the French Government was firmly committed to the policy of supporting both sides. At the end of April 1825, that is after news had arrived of Ibrahim's successful landing in the Peloponnese, the decision was taken to build Mehemet the three warships he had requested. Work began at once in a commercial shipyard at Marseilles and secret instructions were sent to the naval authorities at Toulon to give all the help that was needed.

As the French Admiralty had expected, despite all precautions, the destination of the warships building at Marseilles could not be kept secret. Throughout 1826 the contradictions in French Government policy towards the war in Greece could be more clearly seen at Marseilles than anywhere else. Two ships flying the Greek flag, the *Spartiate* and the *Epaminondas*, were received with enthusiasm by the crowds as the *Amphitrite* had been in England. Expedition after expedition of Philhellenes, French and Italians, left to the sound of cheers and stirring military music. The Marseilles philhellenic committee arranged a ceremony to mark their dispatch of a ceremonial sabre to Fabvier and of a silk banner to Notho Botsaris and the Suliotes, the brave defenders of Missolonghi. Yet all the while everyone knew that behind the walls of the dockyard warships were being built to enable Ibrahim and his Arabs to conquer (and, it was generally believed, exterminate) the Greeks.

Feelings ran high. In the middle of July, when indignation was at its highest following the news of the fall of Missolonghi, an attempt was made to set fire to one of the frigates in the yard. It was a feeble, amateurish effort and little damage was done, but it caused the Government a momentary scare. Rumours of conspiracies flew about. Perhaps the Philhellenes were revolutionaries in disguise—carbonari, Bonapartists, or liberals devoted to violence? The city authorities fatuously reminded the citizens of Marseilles that the prosperity of their city depended upon the Levant trade and on shipbuilding—arson against Egyptian ships was bad for business. An investigation was launched but no plot could be discovered. The attempt appeared to have been made by one man, Charles Beaufillot, a Philhellene who had already left for Greece.

On the date set for the launching of the second frigate, 12 August 1826, the authorities prepared themselves for expected trouble. Troops and extra gendarmerie were brought in to guard the yard. The situation remained ominously quiet but, when the moment of launch came, the ship did not enter the water but stuck fast in the mud. Sabotage was at once suspected and the police received word that there was another plot to set fire to the ship, but nothing untoward occurred. A week later a second attempt was made to launch her, but this time the vessel keeled over completely and came to an undignified and helpless halt lying on her side half in and half out of the water.

Whether this was an act of sabotage, an act of incompetence, or an act of God was never established, but it had the effect of delaying the completion of the vessel by many months and adding greatly to her cost. She eventually set sail in April 1827 to join the Egyptian fleet. Fourteen French naval officers were on board to act as instructors. Other vessels and naval officers went later. These officers, like General Boyer and his colleagues in Egypt, loyally played their part in carrying out the policy of France, even though this meant going to war against other French officers who were loyally carrying out the policy of France on the other side.

27. *Regulars Again*

When Colonel Fabvier was appointed to the command of the
new Greek regular forces in July 1825, the military situation seemed
desperate. Ibrahim's forces had shown their complete superiority and were
in control of much of the Morea. Advanced parties of his army had
appeared within sight of Nauplia, the capital of Greece.

The task which Fabvier had undertaken was daunting in the extreme.
The Regiment which had been raised by Baleste and by Tarella in 1821 and
1822 had achieved a tolerable level of discipline and skill but, even at its
best, it could never be relied upon to hold ranks at the crucial moment of
a battle. The Regiment had never had to face an enemy using regular
tactics. How much more difficult would it be for an entirely new force to
face the experienced Arabs and Albanians of Ibrahim's army. It is difficult
now to comprehend the qualities which were needed to win a battle fought
according to European methods at this time. Some of the success which
the French armies had won during the campaigns of Napoleon was due to
their famous *élan* and to a sense of taking part in a great and glorious
enterprise. But for most of the time and for most of the armies the military
qualities which decided battles were very different. Large bodies of men
had to be persuaded to stand in lines for long periods within sight and often
within range of the enemy. They had to be persuaded to keep their line
even when they saw gaps being torn in their own ranks by cannon fire,
and their comrades lying wounded and groaning by their side, and when
they could see heavy cavalry or columns of infantry about to rush upon them
with lance or bayonet. They had to be able to perform in close order and
on the march the various technically complicated operations required
for loading and discharging muskets, whose rate of fire was seldom more
than one volley a minute.

To win battles more was needed than skill in handling the weapons and a courageous disposition. There was always the thought which would arise disconcertingly at the time when a man's resources of courage seemed near exhaustion, that further along the line his comrades might already have reached that point. Men had to be habituated to a special kind of fearlessness, and to instant, unquestioning obedience. Too much imagination might be fatal. If they showed a disposition to query their orders or to take any kind of initiative, this must be stamped out of them by hours of unvarying and brutalizing drill. Old soldiers would come to appreciate that in battle their best hope of safety really did consist in holding their ranks, but most armies had a code of harsh punishments to discourage any recurring doubts. Stolidity was perhaps the most important of the military virtues.

The poor wretches who had the misfortune to man the ranks of the armies of Europe had little or no experience of other methods of waging war. They took their chance of surviving or not in much the same way as their fathers and grandfathers had done. Weapon technology and military methods had not altered substantially for generations, and the military ethos which accompanied them was traditional and institutionalized. But how were the Greeks to become regular soldiers? How could they suddenly shake off their own traditional methods and their own military ethos? They were being asked to adopt European methods which they had come to despise, to assume a kind of behaviour which was alien to them, to be followers instead of leaders, with no opportunity to show their individuality.

Fabvier seems to have understood all this more than most. He and his men had been soldiers too long to have illusions about war or to fall for the easy solutions of less experienced Philhellenes. They realized that, if they were to have any hope of success, they must give the Greeks training and discipline and more training and more discipline. Only a man who could win their respect could hope to impose such a programme and Fabvier worked ceaselessly. He learned the language, he lived simply, it was clear for all to see that he was a brave and conscientious soldier, and he had made Greece his home. The Greeks wanted to respect him. For the first time in the war they positively wanted to learn European tactics: it was no longer a case of the foreigners peddling a superior product to an uninterested customer.

Fabvier exploited these advantages to the full. From the first day he subjected his force to a training programme of unrelieved ferocity. The men were fed and provided with arms and quarters but in return they were expected to surrender their freedom completely. Recruiting was of course difficult on these conditions and Fabvier's officers had to scour the last corners of Free Greece acting as a virtual press gang.

The decision of the Greek Government to entrust him with the responsibility for the new force was a wise one. It was, however, a serious set-back to the plans of General Roche who had arrived in Greece in April 1825 as agent of the Paris Greek Committee. As we have seen, Roche's prime purpose was to persuade the Greek leaders to select a French prince as their King in exchange for promises of money and military assistance. How could Roche, an agent (although unavowed) of the French Government, co-operate with a man who had taken up arms against France and who was reputed to be deeply involved in plots to overthrow the Bourbons, and bring back a new Napoleon? Fabvier's little force at this time was almost entirely officered with disaffected Frenchmen and condemned Italians, Bonapartists, revolutionaries, carbonari. To such men, the idea that they should assist in thrusting a puppet Bourbon prince on a reluctant Greece was ludicrous. Almost every one had spent his life since Waterloo fighting members of the House of Bourbon in France, Naples and Spain. Co-operation between Fabvier and Roche was out of the question.

Whatever his other qualities it is clear that General Roche was no diplomat. It had been intended that the proposal to establish an Orleanist kingdom, on which so many months of careful preparation had been expended, should be formally put and accepted in the summer of 1825. General Roche's part in the operation was merely to spring the trap, but when he reached Greece the task did not look so straightforward. Not only was there the embarrassment of Fabvier's presence but the whole secret of the plan seemed to be known to everyone. The leading Greeks whose encouraging statements had been carefully transmitted to the Duke of Orleans in Paris (via the British interception office) now seemed unaccountably indifferent to his protestations.

They were frankly sceptical of his promised ability to send enough troops (to be raised in Ireland or Switzerland) to turn the war against Ibrahim. They were sceptical whether the French Government itself was strong enough and they were rightly suspicious of France's involvement with Egypt. It had become increasingly clear to them that the only country with the strength and influence to make a decisive difference was Great Britain.

The Petition of July 1825 in which the Greek Government and numerous leading Greeks begged the British Government to take Greece under British protection came as a shock to Roche. Whereas all the details of the French intrigues were known to the British, the French had only a general appreciation of the activities of the pro-English group in Greece. The Petition was an unequivocal document entrusting to His Britannic Majesty 'the sacred deposit of the liberty of Greece, her independence and her political existence'. Most Greeks and foreigners thought it had been secretly invited by Captain Hamilton of H.M.S. *Cambrian* and by the British High Commissioner in the Ionian Islands.

T

Roche did not know what to do but, as he saw his plans dissolving into ruins, he felt he must do something. He decided to address a letter of protest to the Greek Government in the name of the Paris Greek Committee. But what to say? He could not complain too violently about the iniquities of submitting to the protection of a foreign power when his own mission had been to arrange precisely that. The letter took the form therefore of querying the legality of the decision. Even so, such a protest would give the appearance of being merely an outburst from a disappointed rival. Something was needed to give the protest an air of authority, to make it appear that its sentiments were widely shared.

Just then there arrived at Nauplia a striking young man calling himself Lieutenant Washington,[1] the nephew of George Washington, first President of the United States. Who better to sign an international protest against the British? Washington agreed to co-operate with Roche, and the two men duly presented their protest claiming in the preamble to be representatives (*députés*) of the Philhellenes of France and of the United States. 'It had been very painful for the undersigned', the document declared at one point, 'to see the lack of confidence which the Greek Senate has put, in these grave circumstances, in the French and American Nations.'[2]

The lettter of protest was a fiasco. By this time everybody knew the story of the Orleans intrigue or some more alarming variant of it. Roche's credibility fell sharply. Similarly, when it began to be asked who was this man Washington who spoke so confidently on behalf of the American people, the answers were not reassuring.

William Townsend Washington, like so many Philhellenes, seems consciously to have tried to act out in practice his own vision of himself. Washington saw himself as that familiar figure of later American military tradition, the hero as tough guy. His kinship to George Washington, if genuine at all, was distant, but he persuaded people to believe that deference was due to one who bore such an illustrious name. He had spent a short time at West Point in 1823 and then received a lieutenant's commission in the United States Army, but he resigned in 1825 in order to go to Greece. His name and his easy assumption of superiority opened all doors and he was given a letter of introduction by the Boston Greek Committee. He also carried similar letters from the Vice President of the United States, the Secretary of State, and the Secretary of War.

The Boston Committee had provided him with $300 for his passage to Greece and asked him to carry $200 to deliver to another American Philhellene in Greece, Jonathan Peckham Miller. He travelled to Greece in style and, when he met Miller, he calmly told him that he had already spent all but $84 of the money for his own use. Washington felt that it was part of the character of a strong man to be shocking, offensive, and violent. He took pleasure in taunting the other Americans in the hope that he would have a chance to show his skill as a duellist. He was dissipated and unashamedly dishonest.

The other Americans in Greece hated and despised him and quickly made it clear that Washington had no authority to sign the protest on their behalf and that he was not the agent of the American Greek Committees, and letters of complaint were sent to Boston about the wasted money. There followed his decline and fall. He left Greece in a huff and tried ostentatiously to renounce his American citizenship on board an American warship in Smyrna. Later, he turned up in Paris wearing a magnificent Greek costume—in which Delacroix painted his portrait—and was lionized by society. But his character was unchanged. He succeeded in swindling a few tradesmen and seducing at least one lady before Lafayette was told to beware of this young man so unlike his uncle who never told a lie. In 1827 Washington returned to Greece and was killed by a Greek cannon at Nauplia during an outbreak of civil violence. The career of the Philhellene with the famous name had been followed with fascinated interest in the United States and it was reported with suitable repugnance that he died cursing his native land and muttering something about Amelia and a lock of hair.

Meanwhile, throughout the summer of 1825 preparations had been going on in France to send the first French philhellenic expedition to Greece where it was expected to act under the direction of General Roche and to help promote the success of his policies. The expedition set sail from Marseilles in September under the command of a former French officer, Maxime Raybaud. Another phase of philhellenism was about to begin. A new group of Philhellenes were about to learn some old lessons.

Raybaud had been in Greece before. He had been one of the handful of officers picked up by Mavrocordato at Marseilles in July 1821 and was typical of many of the Philhellenes of the first period. He had joined the French army in 1813 but had not seen any active service. In 1820 he was compulsorily retired and one of his reasons for going to Greece was to look for employment. He had seen the aftermath of the fall of Tripolitsa in October 1821 and had been on Mavrocordato's staff at Peta. It was Raybaud who took command of the twenty-five survivors of the Battalion of Philhellenes when they stood to arms for the last time at Missolonghi in July 1822 in memory of their fallen comrades. On his return to France he wrote a book about his experiences in Greece, not a hasty indignant outburst of disappointment like those of so many returning Philhellenes but a sober, thoughtful, accurate account. It remains one of the best books about the Greek Revolution.

However, although Raybaud probably understood as much about the situation in Greece as anyone in France, his ideas were a good deal out of date. His thinking was at the same stage as Gordon's had been in early

1823 when the London Greek Committee was preparing to send their first expedition to Greece. Like Gordon—with whom he was in correspondence—Raybaud believed that Greece needed principally mountain artillery and repair facilities. And so the first expedition sent by the Paris Greek Committee in September 1825 turned out to be remarkably similar to the disastrous expedition sent with William Parry in the *Ann* by the London Greek Committee in November 1823. It consisted of a few officers, a squad of artificers led by an engineer called Arnaud, mountain guns, and a huge miscellaneous collection of military stores and equipment sufficient to establish a small arsenal and repair facility. Arnaud was given the job because he was related to Roche by marriage.

Before the expedition sailed a further example was provided of the contradictions in French Government policy. General de Livron, one of the officers who had been sent to Egypt in the French military mission, was back in France purchasing arms and equipment for Mehemet Ali. He suggested to the artificers that, instead of sailing to the aid of the Greeks, they should join their enemies, the Egyptians. Arnaud declared roundly that he would not serve the Pasha for 100,000 francs and would serve the Greeks for nothing, but the thought had been implanted nevertheless. [3]

After this inauspicious start the expedition soon degenerated into chaos. Before the ship had even reached Greece there was a mutiny among the workmen and one of the officers threatened to join the Egyptians after all. Disease broke out on board and by the time they reached Nauplia most of the workmen wanted to go straight home. [4]

When they reached Greece there was another shock. It was intended that the expedition should put itself under the command of General Roche, who should by now have sprung the Orleanist trap. Roche, however, was thoroughly discredited and isolated and clearly no longer in an influential position at the centre. That position was occupied by Fabvier who had been gathering round him all summer an increasing number of experienced officers, French and Italian, from Spain and elsewhere. The obvious solution was, of course, for Raybaud to put his expedition under the command of Colonel Fabvier but Roche did his best to put him off. Raybaud hesitated but, in the end, he and several other officers refused to subordinate themselves to Fabvier. Apart from the fact that Fabvier was politically not respectable in France, Raybaud had been promised the command, and the rank of colonel. How could he, after his service in Greece in 1821 and 1822, go back to playing a minor role? Fabvier, conscious of the growing strength of his little force, affected not to care. He declared sarcastically that the Committee would have done better to send shoes rather than comedians, since they already had enough of these in Greece. An attempt was made to set up the arsenal but it had no more success than Lord Byron and William Parry had achieved in 1824. The Arab prisoners detailed for the work died. It was said that the arsenal throughout its existence produced three cannon balls at a cost of 80,000 francs. Soon Arnaud and Raybaud returned to France.

Through the second half of 1825 Fabvier calmly continued the work of training the new regular corps. By the end of the year he had about 3,500 men under command: infantry, cavalry, and artillery. It was virtually an independent little army paid for by the gold of the English loan. Fabvier also acquired a small warship for his own use which was put under the command of a former French naval officer, Hippolyte de Croze.

At the beginning of 1826 he decided that the new corps was ready to face the enemy. Greece's new army on which so much depended was ready to take the field. Where should they go? It was suggested that they should attempt to relieve Missolonghi, which was still withstanding the siege, but that seemed altogether too ambitious an undertaking to be seriously contemplated. Similarly, an expedition into the Morea looked too dangerous for a totally inexperienced force. Instead it was decided that an expedition should march against the island of Euboea where there was no chance of encountering Ibrahim's troops. Euboea had remained in the hands of the Turks since the beginning of the war owing to their possession of a few fortresses. If Euboea could be conquered, so it was argued, not only would this show that the Greeks were capable of counterattacking, but a useful source of new supplies would be opened up. And Fabvier knew Philip of Macedon's dictum that the master of Euboea is the master of Greece. At the end of February he marched out of Athens at the head of about 2,500 men, two battalions of regular infantry, three troops of light cavalry, a contingent of gunners with four guns and 700 irregulars. The rest of the regulars, who had not yet reached a high enough standard of training, were left at Athens.

He shipped his little force across the narrow strait from Attica and approached the Turkish fortress of Carysto. His men were burning with eagerness to put their newly acquired skills to the test and demanded to be given the order to assault the place. As a disciple of Napoleon, Fabvier felt that he must encourage this spirit and give his men the taste of victory. He decided to attack a walled suburb of the town. His artillery was brought up, and under cover of their fire the troops bayoneted their way into some of the outer houses. Everything seemed to be going well, when suddenly the Greek artillery fire ceased—the axles of the cannon had snapped.* It was one of those moments in which the fate of battles is decided. A more experienced army would probably have retired in good order. As it was, the Greeks in their panic momentarily reverted to their old habits. One or two Greek officers were seen to be running away and their men followed them back in confusion. It was a temporary relapse only and Fabvier had

* They were said to have been made in London of defective materials.

Free Greece in 1826-1828

Negropont (Chalcis)

Oropos

EUBO

CORINTHIAN GULF

Mt Parnes

Eleusis

Megara

Piraeus

Mt Pentelicus

Corinth

Hexamilia
Washingtonia

SALAMIS

Athens

Phaleron

ATTICA

PELOPONNESE
or MOREA

SARONIC GULF

Aegina

AEGINA

ARGOLID

Nauplia

METHANA

Tacticopolis

POROS

Troezen

Hermione (Castri)

HYDRA

SPETSAE

little difficulty in reforming his men. But before they had recovered their poise the Turks made a sortie from the fortress and killed or wounded about fifty of them.

Fabvier decided to withdraw and obtain new guns, but the expedition's luck had run out. He was obliged to draw up his little army to await the onslaught of a detachment of Turkish cavalry who were in the vicinity. Old fears came flooding back. The cavalry had been the only branch of the Turkish army which had been successful against the Greeks during the early years of the war before the Egyptians came. The Greek regulars were determined to try out their new methods on which they were at last convinced that safety and victory depended, and in fact the situation in which they found themselves favoured regular tactics. Success seemed near if again an accident due to inexperience had not intervened. The Greek cavalry was drawn up according to the best European practice in the rear. Their commander, Regnault, went to confer with Fabvier when the Greek irregulars began to taunt them with skulking in the background. The cavalry stupidly took offence at the insults from their countrymen, mistook rashness for *élan*, and without orders charged headlong at the enemy position. The more experienced Turkish horsemen quickly outmanoeuvred them, and soon the field was covered with their headless bodies. The infantry watching this horrible spectacle kept their lines and fired successive volleys and it was largely because they did so that a remnant of the Greek cavalry was saved, but the experience destroyed their morale. Further operations in Euboea were now out of the question. Fabvier retired to the coast and awaited the arrival of vessels to take the army back to Greece. It was a Dunkirk in miniature. The Greek forces were confined for a week on a tiny beachhead, cold and hungry under continuous fire from the Turks before being taken off in small vessels. The men, blind with terror, were finally persuaded to swim out to sea to the awaiting ships. Fabvier, cool and in control throughout, was the last to leave the beach.

The expedition lost about 200 men, including some of its French and Italian officers, having achieved nothing. A staff college investigation would probably have concluded that the regulars had justified their training and only needed a little more experience, but the Greeks could not be expected to see this. The story went around that Fabvier had deliberately wasted lives in order to show the Greeks how textbook war should be fought. As soon as the expedition returned home desertions began. The battalions who had been on the expedition were depleted by about half their strength as disillusioned regulars disappeared back to their villages or rejoined their old comrades, the *palikars*. A severe crisis of confidence in the whole idea of regular troops was the result. And, as luck would have it, this coincided with the realization that the supply of English gold had finally run out. The Greek troops were broken in morale and could not even be paid. Mutinies followed, and a Greek officer was assassinated by his own men. Fabvier only succeeded in keeping the troops together by a mixture of fearlessness and ferocity. On one occasion when the men were clamouring for their arrears of pay he made a speech saying that he would pay them for eight days but nothing more. When the troops continued to shout that they wanted all or nothing, he drew his sword and demanded 'Who wants to be paid?' When the first man stepped forward Fabvier instantly struck him with his sword, shouting 'That is what is owed to you.' The man fell and Fabvier marched up and down the silenced ranks demanding whether there was anyone else. He then quietly returned and gave orders for the wounded man to be removed to the hospital.[5]

It looked as if Fabvier's experiment in raising a regular corps was doomed to failure like all the others, for the want of a little money. It was touch and go. The Swiss banker Eynard sent two agents racing across Europe with a contribution of 26,000 piastres.[6] At the same time Colonel Gordon arrived from London with £14,000, the sweepings of the second loan as he called it.[7] The Greeks had been begging Gordon to return to their country ever since he had been Hypsilantes's Chief of Staff in 1821. He had been about to go in 1823 in command of the London Committee's expedition, and then again in 1824 after the death of Byron, but after his first painful experience of Greece he was chary about involving himself in her complex problems. In the spring of 1826 he finally consented to go, on condition that he was given complete discretion about the spending of the pitiful sum remaining from the two loans. These contributions from Europe were used to pay the men. The regular corps was saved.

News of the fiasco of the Orleanist plot gradually reached Paris. Then came the news of Roche's ill-judged protest and of his association with the disreputable Washington. Those members of the Paris Greek Committee who had not been privy to Roche's secret mission were mortified. Everybody in Greece and in France, it seemed, knew more about Roche and his mission than the men who had sent him, whose agent he was supposed to be. To add to their humiliation they realized that they had been used by their political opponents for purposes of which they disapproved. They had been outmanoeuvred, their names had been exploited, and their reputations had been damaged for a reckless foreign policy gamble. It was decided to recall General Roche, allegedly for disobeying his instructions, and to send out to Greece instead Count Emanuel d'Harcourt.

At the same time the leaders of the Committee decided to give their support to Colonel Fabvier. This was not the result of spite. We may be sure that the Government consented. The decision arose from the consideration that Fabvier was the only influential Frenchman left in Greece and, if he was less malleable than they would have liked and not at all inclined to take orders from Paris, he was at least a Frenchman. The only hope of preserving some French influence to counteract the apparent British predominance was to back Fabvier even if he was more than half a traitor. A remarkable political change, which has been touched upon earlier, resulted from this decision. The leaders of Restoration France, reading of Fabvier's exploits in Greece, could not help sharing in the general pride of the French people that a Frenchman should be at the head of such a remarkable enterprise. Fabvier's Frenchness seemed more important than his Bonapartism, and indeed the whole phobia of Bonapartism seemed to be sinking into increasing irrelevance. In contrast to the Italians, the French outsiders, by their service in Greece, found it easier to re-enter the main stream of French life. In a remarkable way the desires of some of the pamphleteers of 1821 had become a reality.* The shared experience of philhellenism helped to bind up the deep wounds of Waterloo and the White Terror.

In the course of 1826, the Paris Greek Committee sent three further expeditions to Greece containing in all over a hundred men. They also sent guns, powder, uniforms, food, money, everything an army could need. Recalling Fabvier's comment on the first expedition that shoes were more useful than comedians,[8] they included a thousand pairs of shoes. Innumerable other volunteers set out on their own initiative to join the cause. Marseilles in 1826 again became a city bustling with Philhellenes as it had been in 1822. Piscatory, who has already been mentioned as a secret agent of the French Government, was in command of one of the expeditions. Raybaud on his third visit to Greece commanded another.

Unlike earlier philhellenic expeditions—with the solitary exception of the German Legion—these men were supposed to be under discipline from the start. They were not individuals being assisted with a passage to Greece, but formed troops under command. As they arrived in Greece they were formally presented to the Government and assigned to their respective duties. Raybaud, whose experience of philhellenic fiascos was unsurpassed, tried to use the time of the voyage of the fourth expedition to give lectures about conditions in Greece, but he remarked despairingly that most of his men had never seen service, were ignorant of the language, and had no concept of what they were going to.

Efforts were made to find men who had some experience of Greece. Justin, one of the generation of 1821, was persuaded to return. He had come back to France in 1822 in disgust at the Greeks and, like Persat, had been dissuaded from publishing his diary by Gordon.[9] He gave as his reason for returning to Greece a desire to avenge his old friend Baleste, first of the Philhellenes, whom he had seen killed in Crete.[10] The Prussian cavalry officer Eugen von Byern, who had taken part in the abortive attack on Athens in 1822 'dressed like a chamberlain with seven orders on his

* See page 57.

breast including the Iron Cross',[11] decided to give the Greeks a second chance in the new conditions. The French Count Jourdain who had first involved the Greeks with the Knights of Malta in 1822, reappeared in Greece, but was arrested and bundled out of the country after an intemperate protest against the Act of Submission to England.[12] Garel, a survivor of Peta, returned to Greece accompanied by his nineteen-year-old son.[13]

The irrepressible Olivier Voutier returned to Greece in 1826. He had been a cadet in the French Navy and been present when the Aphrodite of Melos (Venus de Milo) was acquired in 1820. In 1821 he had gone to Greece with Gordon and remained for a few months. He acted as ADC to Mavrocordato, along with Raybaud on the Peta campaign. In December 1823, on his return to France, he published a book of memoirs on his experiences in Greece.[14] It is a remarkable work. The best that can be said is that it is an account of what Voutier's philhellenic career ought to have been, rather than what it was. It is written in a high-flown style with proper obeisance to all the philhellenic myths. Voutier himself darts about from crisis spot to crisis spot, advising, encouraging, restraining, the friend and confidant of the great, ever present where the need is most urgent. His adventures have a story-book perfection. Before Peta, for example, he describes how he killed in single combat on horseback a famous Turk 'Cassim Bey', in front of the admiring ranks of both armies, and won as his reward a magnificent horse which belonged to a Pasha called 'Baboun'— all, alas, imaginary.

At the time when the German Greek Societies were trying to suppress the memoirs of their own Philhellenes they had eagerly seized upon Voutier's book as the one true version, and it was translated twice into German. Voutier enjoyed being a pundit on Greece. Delacroix consulted him about the detail of his Grecian pictures, and he began to put together the unused oddments from his notes to publish another book. But Nemesis was at hand. Raybaud, who had been with him during most of his time in Greece, published his own book of memoirs in 1824. Voutier's pretensions were exploded in a series of good-humoured but devastating footnotes.[15]

On Voutier's first return to Greece in 1824, Mavrocordato asked him for a copy of his book. Voutier reluctantly consented but the copy he handed over had a chapter torn out. His philhellenism had got the better of his veracity he explained. Mavrocordato commented sourly after looking through the remainder that the lost pages could not have contained more lies than the rest.[16] The more prosaic Raybaud continued to be fascinated by the flamboyance of Voutier, despising him and yet fearing him as a rival. The two men always seemed to be together pouring out accusations about one another to anybody who would listen. At last in 1826 they fought a duel in Greece in which both were hurt and Raybaud was severely wounded in the arm.[17]

Most of the men sent by the Paris Greek Committee in 1826 had, of course, never been in Greece before. Nearly all claimed to be officers and to have some military experience and they came from all over France. Every age and class were represented, boys in their teens and hardened soldiers. One man had already served in twenty-seven campaigns and carried nine wounds on his body.[18] Old Bonapartists were joined by officers of the Bourbon Guards. A former General gave as his reason for going to Greece that he preferred fighting to vegetating in a garrison.[19] A party of officers was said to have come from the King's household.[20] There were numerous Corsicans perhaps more interested in the opportunities for pay than in promoting the Bonapartist cause. When one of the Corsicans killed a comrade by hiding on the roof of a house and shooting as he came round the corner, a court-martial of Philhellenes ruled that this was not murder but a duel fought honourably according to Corsican rules.[21]

As ever there were men who had no military experience at all. A journalist who had spent his career writing about the cause of Greece decided to give more active help.[22] A student who had won a prize for a discourse on Ancient Greece which he had performed at his rhetoric class, applied to the Duc de Choiseul for money to enable him to go.[23] An author who had originally written pro-Turkish articles for the *Oriental Spectator* and then published one of the first full-length histories of the Greek Revolution enlisted as a volunteer.[24] A boy known only as Etienne claimed to have spent five years as a slave in Constantinople after being captured in 1821 when he had been one of the first Philhellenes.[25] Several seamen deserted from the French naval squadron in the Mediterranean preferring service on land under Fabvier to the barbaric conditions of the lower deck.[26]

The majority of the volunteers were French but there was a sprinkling of other nationalities: Swiss, German, and Scandinavian. Two Germans who were always together were known both to be sons of Generals and to be living under assumed names.[27] A dandy from Pomerania was said by his exasperated companion to have taken two hours to dress.[28] In the Netherlands,[29] at the instigation of the Swiss banker Eynard, plans were made to raise a Liberal Legion of fifty men but this idea was vetoed by the Dutch Government. The money was devoted to Greek education and charity but a few men had already set off.

As usual some of the volunteers regretted their decision as soon as they reached Greece, and began the long trek home. As usual the brutality of Greek conditions shocked even the most hardened. They were disgusted at the practice of killing prisoners, of mutilating bodies, of cutting off heads, and all the other characteristics of irregular warfare. In five years of fighting, Western morals had made little headway. A young French officer who had brought his wife with him to Greece was wounded in a skirmish. Caraiskakis, one of the most famous Greek captains, invited the couple to his house and suggested a shooting competition for their amusement. To their horror the target turned out to be an Albanian prisoner.[30]

Fabvier himself, despite the growing attention and respect paid to him by the Paris Greek Committee and by the volunteers, remained as always unimpressed. General Roche, who in his early months in Greece had begged Philhellenes not to go near Fabvier, spent the last months before his departure in exhorting them to join him. Fabvier gave no sign of satisfaction. Contempt came easily to his lips and attempts at flattery merely exaggerated his apparent harshness. He never had a good word for the Committee. They had sent a thousand useless things, he declared;* the men they sent were, with one or two exceptions, useless or wretched or disloyal; the only men whom he could trust were those 'thrown here by political tempests'[31]— in other words his old comrades the French Bonapartists and the Italian revolutionary refugees. Nevertheless, it was the support of the Paris Committee and its sister organizations elsewhere in Europe that kept Fabvier's force in being in 1826. He was still nominally the employee of the Greek Government, but in fact he was the commander of a little army of Greeks and Philhellenes which was operating largely independently, drawing all its supplies and its strength from abroad.

Many of the Greek officers were dismissed not without much rancour. Their lack of experience had proved a severe liability in Euboea, and Fabvier could not risk failure a second time. The regulars were officered almost entirely by Frenchmen and Italians. Fabvier now had ninety-three Philhellenes under his command, far too many to give everyone a position of responsibility with the regulars. It was decided, therefore, to set up a special unit composed entirely of Philhellenes. The command of this unit, known simply as the Company of Philhellenes, was entrusted to the grizzled and vastly experienced Italian exile, Colonel Vincenzo Pisa. The situation had an uncanny resemblance to the situation in 1822 before the Battle of Peta. Then Greece's regular forces had consisted of one regiment of Greeks and two companies of Philhellenes; now four years later she had two battalions of Greeks and one company of Philhellenes. There were few to point out the sad comparison. Only two or three of Fabvier's hundred or so Europeans had been in Greece during that earlier phase.

There were none of the scenes of earlier years when bands of Europeans were to be found begging their way from village to village, but life was

---

* Fabvier may have had in mind especially the musical instruments which every philhellenic society had an irresistible longing to send to Greece and which must by now have been piling up alarmingly in Nauplia. They were put to some use. The ships bringing the English gold were greeted at the quay by renderings of airs from the latest hit, *Der Freischütz*.[32] The Sultan's new regular troops also had a military band which was said to give spirited performances of Rossini overtures,[33] surely a less terrifying sound to potential enemies than the drums, kettles, and howls of the Janissaries which it replaced.

almost as dangerous. The dreadful diseases of the East still swept the country and few Philhellenes who remained any time in Greece escaped them. William Humphreys, the young unemployed British officer who had gone to Greece in 1821, and returned in 1823 to serve with Byron, finally succumbed in 1826.[34] Count Gamba, the young brother of Byron's last mistress who had accompanied his body back to England and then returned to Greece with a party of Italian revolutionaries, died in 1827.[35] Bruno, one of Byron's doctors, also returned to Greece with the Italian exiles: he is said to have been murdered by a Greek surgeon who coveted his instruments.[36] Nine Germans are reported to have died in October 1826 through eating pork.[37]

The failure of the expedition to Euboea had shown that the regulars were not yet ready to face Turks let alone Ibrahim's army. Further training was necessary. Fabvier decided that his best plan was to take his men right away from the intrigue-filled atmosphere of Nauplia and Hydra so that they could concentrate on their training. His military eye chose the peninsula of Methana.

A huge volcanic peak on the north coast of the Argolid, Methana is entirely surrounded by water except where a narrow isthmus, a few hundred yards wide, joins it to the mainland. When Fabvier arrived the penninsula was largely uninhabited but there was enough land and water to provide a livelihood. During the summer of 1826 he transformed it into a military base. The isthmus had been fortified in ancient times and Fabvier rebuilt and strengthened the walls. The cannon sent by the Paris Committee and by the deputies in London were taken straight to Methana. Two forts were built. A vast quantity of arms, ammunition, and military equipment was stored in specially constructed magazines. A hospital was established and an artillery park. The villagers were encouraged to cultivate as much of the area of the peninsula as possible to provide a reliable local supply of food. Methana was a European military stronghold in miniature. Fabvier gave it a new name, Tacticopolis, the city of the regulars.

He justified his choice of Methana on the grounds that it was conveniently central, within easy reach of all the important places that remained in the hands of the Greeks. There may have been something in this consideration, but another was uppermost in his mind. Fabvier was thinking ahead to the ultimate catastrophe. Methana would be the Cadiz of Greece,[38] he declared, Cadiz the town in Spain where the constitutionalists had held out longest against the French invaders in 1823. Fabvier seems to have believed that, even if Greece was entirely reconquered by Ibrahim and the Turks, his little army could still defend themselves on the peninsula. Methana might have to be the scene of the last stand of the liberals, the Bonapartists, the carbonari and all the other followers of lost causes to whom Greece was the last and only remaining refuge.

In the summer of 1826 Greece was approaching the lowest point of her fortunes. The fall of Missolonghi in April had been the signal for another enemy advance. Ibrahim and his Egyptians retired to the Morea and spent the summer in consolidating their position there. Mehemet Ali had no wish to fight the war of the Turks on their behalf outside the province over which he had been given control. The Turks themselves, however, now resumed their advance. The whole of Western Greece was quickly reconquered and, as usual, a long list of Greek captains and their followers changed sides and actively served the Turks. Several bands of Greek *armatoli* reverted to their pre-Revolutionary role of guarding the important roads and passes on contract to the Turkish authorities.

Free Greece was now confined to a small area round the isthmus, mainly Attica and the Argolid and some of the islands. Since Ibrahim for the time being seemed content to remain relatively inactive, the main threat came from the north. The Acropolis of Athens, the only fortress in Greek hands between the Turks and the isthmus, began to assume an increasing strategic importance. Since the spring of 1825 it had been in the hands of one of the most unscrupulous of the warlords, Ghouras, who had been a follower of Odysseus but had turned on his master at his moment of weakness, had arranged for Odysseus to be hanged from the Acropolis battlements, and had succeeded to the remnants of his little empire in Eastern Greece. His rule was so arbitrary, violent, and extortionate that the people grew to hate him and his band of armed bullies, and as soon as the the Turks appeared again, the miserable peasants of Attica welcomed them as deliverers. The massacres of the Turkish minority and of the Turkish garrison in 1821 and 1822 were forgotten. Soon the Turks re-entered Athens itself leaving only the Acropolis in the hands of the Greeks.

The Greek Government reverted to the position of impotence which had existed before the arrival of the English gold. The Greeks who had enjoyed a brief sensation of riches in 1825 saw their standard of living slipping away from them. The Hydriote ships which in the early years of the war had terrified the Aegean with their daring and ferocity, now refused to go to sea unless they were paid. The irregular troops who had flocked to Nauplia in 1825 to share in the bonanza suffered what is now politely called a crisis of rising expectations. They wanted money. They began to threaten and bully the people of the towns. Fighting broke out, too localized to be dignified with the name of civil war, more a series of armed brawls. Some of the Greek leaders tried to leave for the Ionian Islands but the authorities there refused to admit them.

The treasury was empty. The only income which the Greek Government had at its disposal was a trickle of contributions from the philhellenic organizations of Europe. Nauplia was crowded with refugees and beggars including Missolonghiotes who had been bought from Turkish slave markets and released with the aid of money from Western Europe. Typhus, never far away, broke out again. It became increasingly clear that many Greeks were not merely suffering extreme hardship but were on the road to actual starvation.

The days of the Greek Revolution seemed to be numbered. Greece seemed about to slide to an undignified end, torn apart by internal violence and sectional greed.

There was one ray of hope on the horizon. An English admiral was said to be on the way with a fleet of new ships which were going to blast the Ottoman fleet out of the water and drive the Arabs back to Egypt. The Greeks had been hearing this story for so long that it had begun to take on the characteristics of a myth with which the doomed console themselves. Then in the middle of July an English merchant ship arrived at Nauplia with a strange cargo. Most Greeks had never seen coal, but they were assured that it was necessary for the new fleet. Perhaps the fabulous admiral was really coming after all.

The loans of £2,800,000 which the foolish investors of Great Britain made to the Greeks in 1824 and 1825 probably had a decisive influence on the outcome of the war. The gold gave the Greek Government an economic hold over the captains for a few crucial months in 1824 and 1825 and was, for example, a factor in neutralizing the effect of the change of loyalty of Odysseus. But this was an unlooked for result, a by-product of other policies. The dramatic increase in military strength which the loan money was intended to purchase never materialized. Schemes to raise an army of mercenaries never progressed beyond the planning stage.

Apart from a few guns and other supplies the only material benefits which the Greeks obtained from the loan money were a few ships built in England and the United States. The story of this fleet is more complex than any other episode of philhellenism. To give the main outlines and to give them some coherence it is necessary to depart from a chronological order and to pursue several themes at once.

Frank Abney Hastings[1] has been mentioned only incidentally so far. He was one of the few Philhellenes for whom all Greeks and all foreigners had nothing but admiration. He was also responsible for the most imaginative idea for helping Greece that emerged during the war. Hastings was the younger son of a General in the British army, a man of wealth and influence. He was commissioned into the British Navy in 1805 when he was eleven and was present at the Battle of Trafalgar. During the next fifteen years he had a distinguished naval career in war and peace all over the world. He seemed set to rise to the top of his profession until in 1820, when he was in command of H.M.S. *Kangaroo* in the West Indies, an incident occurred which transformed his life. As he was bringing his vessel into Port Royal in Jamaica in view of the fleet, the Flag Captain of the Admiral's

12 French Workers Contributing Money for the Greek Cause. The inscription reads 'The Greeks are French! Misery speaks! Let us do one more good thing and drink one bottle less'

13a Frank Abney Hastings

b The *Hellas* frigate and the *Karteria* steamship

ship shouted at him in a voice that rang through the harbour: 'You have overlayed your anchor—you ought to be ashamed of yourself—you damned lubber, you—who are you?'

The etiquette of the Royal Navy is strict, and in 1820 it was stricter. But by any standards, Hastings' reaction to the apparent insult to his seamanship was surely disproportionate. He waited until he had handed over the command of his ship and was technically a civilian on half-pay, and then challenged the Flag Captain to a duel. It never took place but news of the affair came to the ears of the Admiral; Hastings was reported to the Admiralty; and he was promptly dismissed. Duelling had long been illegal in Britain and the authorities were rightly concerned to prevent the stupid custom from regaining a grip. Hastings wrote pleading letters to the Admiralty protesting that he had suffered an intolerable humiliation which no naval officer could possibly have submitted to. If any such officers existed, he declared, 'I do not envy them their dearly purchased rank; and God forbid that the British navy should have no better supporters of its character than such spiritless creatures.' Government departments sometimes bend to expressions of contrition or to flattery but rarely to petulance or abuse. The Admiralty refused to reinstate him.

His career ruined, Hastings consoled himself with the thought that, if he could distinguish himself in some foreign naval service, he might one day be reinstated. He set about fitting himself for such a role by going to France to learn the language. It was while he was there in 1822 that the call went out for volunteers for Greece and he followed the trail of the German soldiers and students to Marseilles. Unlike most of that generation of Philhellenes he was wealthy and he subsidized the passage of his friends to Greece.

As with so many of the early Philhellenes, Hastings found that the Greeks were suspicious of his motives in coming to Greece and the rumour was put around that he was an English spy. Hastings scotched this story by sending a letter to Mavrocordato. His explanation, totally convincing, has the forthrightness permissible only to the rich and the aristocratic.

If the English Government required a spy in Greece it would not address itself to a person in my condition. I am the younger son of Charles Hastings, Baronet, a General in the Army, who was educated with the Marquis of Hastings, Governor-General of India; so that I could surely find a more lucrative, less dangerous, and more respectable employment in India than that of a spy in Greece.

Hastings joined the crew of a Hydriote ship, the *Themistocles*, and took part in several engagements. When the great Turkish land invasion reached the isthmus, he spent part of his fortune to take into his service a force of fifty armed Greeks. Hastings shared the frustrations and the disgust at the atrocities which affected so many of his companions but, unlike them, he succeeded in winning the respect of the Greeks. This was partly due to the

U

open-handedness with which he spent his money, but mainly to a reputation which he developed for bravery and seamanship. One particular incident made a great impression. The *Themistocles* was pursuing a Turkish coastal vessel off the north of Mitylene when suddenly the wind dropped. The ship found itself becalmed within range of the shore and drifting nearer on a tidal current. Two hundred and fifty Turks were rapidly brought up and began to fire on the ship with their muskets. The crew lay down behind the bulwarks and refused to move, when suddenly Hastings, sensing a light breeze, sprang on to the bowsprit and succeeded in getting the ship's head round. Her sails filled and she moved out of range.

During his time with the Hydriotes Hastings was thinking deeply about the strategic situation of Greece and how best her limited resources could be deployed. He had a profound understanding of the potentialities of sea power which went far beyond the normal education of a naval officer. He also appreciated that naval warfare was not a static art but could be developed in the light of technological change. In these respects he differed sharply from most of his contemporaries.

During the twenty-five or so years of the wars with Revolutionary and Napoleonic France the techniques of war remained remarkably unchanged. Wars altered in scale, in organization, in aims, but the weapons and tactics showed only minor modifications. As far as land warfare was concerned, virtually the only innovation in weaponry was the Congreve rocket and this gave a very mixed performance. This astonishing conservatism persisted partly because the effort required to train up huge masses of men to fight the normal tactics was so immense and the necessary skills and attitudes took so long to inculcate that there was no energy left to contemplate experiments, but mainly because military men simply did not think in terms of experiment. The notions that military methods should develop in parallel with changes in technology, and that military success might depend upon being more technologically up-to-date than the enemy were still novel. And in fact there were as yet few improvements in technology which could be directly applied to the battlefield.

As far as naval warfare was concerned, on the other hand, the biggest technical innovation for at least three hundred years was about to begin. In 1801 the *Charlotte Dundas*, a sturdy vessel fitted with a steam engine and paddle wheels, towed two seventy-ton barges along the Forth and Clyde Canal against the wind. Thereafter the progress of steam was rapid. In 1812 the *Thames* sailed from Greenock to London; in 1819 the *Savannah* crossed the Atlantic; in 1824 the *Falcon* sailed from London to India. These were all sailing vessels, merchant vessels with engines only for subsidiary use, but for those that had eyes to see it was clear that an important change was occurring. Now there was a prospect of overcoming the one terrible weakness of the sailing ship, its inability to move in a calm.

When Frank Abney Hastings learnt of the arrival of Lord Byron at Cephalonia in 1823 he put his thoughts on Greek defence policy on paper and submitted them for his consideration.[2] The memorandum could serve as a model to naval staffs in any country. It is clear, sensible, and imaginative and yet the lessons of Hastings' practical experience at sea are given their due weight.

Hastings argued that since the Greeks had no regular forces, no artillery and no engineers they could never capture the Turkish fortresses except by starving them out. Since the remaining fortresses were all supplied by sea, naval superiority was required. It was more sensible to concentrate resources on achieving this naval superiority than to attempt to reform the land forces on regular lines. In addition, no Turkish invasion of Greece could be successful unless it was continually supplied by sea. If the Greeks could achieve naval superiority they were free from the threat of invasion.

Hastings reasoned that naval superiority could be achieved by the possession of one steam vessel. In action, such a vessel could be manoeuvred to produce a higher rate of fire than the enemy. Furthermore, instead of firing cold cannon balls, she could, with certain precautions, fire red-hot shot, heated in the ship's boilers, which would have a far greater destructive effect. Hastings also suggested numerous other technical and tactical improvements and sketched out the chief characteristics of the type of vessel he had in mind. He suggested that its construction could be financed from the funds at the disposal of the London Greek Committee and that it might even make a profit from the sale of Turkish ships which she would capture. He himself offered to make a contribution of £1,000 if he were promised the command.

Hastings seems to have made little impression either on Lord Byron or on Colonel Stanhope but he continued to press his ideas, and when Edward Blaquiere was in Greece in 1824 he made a valuable convert. Enthusiasm is infectious and Hastings decided it was worthwhile to return to England with Blaquiere in the *Amphitrite* to promote the scheme. The plan to build a steamship was as a result duly picked out for special praise in Blaquiere's book on Greece which came out in 1825. Hastings, Blaquiere mentioned, was now ready to spend £5,000 out of his own pocket on the ship.

The Greek Government and their deputies in London needed no convincing that it would be sensible to spend some of the loan money on improving their naval power. They felt, however, that their purpose would be as well served by purchasing conventional ships as by risking something as new-fangled and uncertain as a steam ship. Recalling perhaps the fiasco of William Parry and his Congreve rockets, they were becoming suspicious of the advanced notions, military and political, of the pundits of the London Greek Committee.

The deputies were under instructions from the Greek Government to purchase conventional sailing frigates and they began to make preparations to do this in 1824 with some of the money from the first loan. Their original idea was to obtain eight small vessels but in December 1824 they were persuaded that it would be preferable if instead they bought two larger vessels mounting fifty guns each instead of fifteen. It was decided that these ships should be built in the United States; a decision that warrants a brief digression.

The United States, like most of the Western world, had been touched by the philhellenic enthusiasm of 1821 and 1822.[3] As elsewhere the main promoters were professors and churchmen and the movement was short-lived. But when the news arrived in 1823 of Lord Byron's 'pilgrimage' to Greece, interest revived, and during 1823 and 1824 it was at its height. Committees were established in New York, Philadelphia, Boston, and numerous other towns. Subscriptions were raised, pamphlets published, charity balls organized, and all the usual means of raising money were tried. In New York a huge cross was erected on Brooklyn Heights with the inscription 'Sacred to the Greek Cause'. As it was set in place the toast was given which unwittingly recalled the original aims of the Greek Revolution, 'May the Grecian Cross be planted from village to village and from steeple to steeple until it rests on the Dome of St. Sophia'.

Americans saw the Greek Revolution in terms of their own recent revolution against the British. The American volunteers saw themselves as so many Lafayettes, and the old general himself did not discourage the comparison on his visit to America in 1824 to receive his mead of homage. Thomas Jefferson suggested that the Greeks might like to examine the constitutions of the United States to find a possible model for their own. If the suggestion proved useful, the Greeks should consider it 'a tribute rendered to the names [manes?] of your Homer, your Demosthenes whose blood is still flowing in your veins'.

A certain smugness pervades many American philhellenic pronouncements, an assumption that the United States had a nearly perfect political system and a peaceful and benevolent government which had no need or desire to embroil itself in the sordid rivalries of Europe. American Philhellenes adopted a high moral tone, high even by philhellenic standards. This attitude was encouraged by the Benthamites of the London Greek Committee—especially Stanhope*—for whom the United States, combining a free constitution with puritanical Christianity, represented the best political system yet in operation.

In many ways, however, the American philhellenic movement was a cultural colony of the movement in Britain. Although the United States Committees collected in 1823 and 1824 a sum estimated at $80,000 for the benefit

---

* Stanhope, when warned not to try to Anglicize Greece, declared roundly that he preferred to Americanize her.

of the Greeks,⁴ nearly four times as much as the London Committee, they still looked to London for their lead. Distance seems to have lent enchantment or, at worst, credibility to the activities of Hobhouse, Hume, Bowring, Stanhope, and Blaquiere whose efforts on behalf of the cause had such moderate success in their own country. The money collected in the United States was sent to London to be handed over to the Greek deputies where it disappeared along with the loan money down the drain of waste and corruption. American Philhellenes who went to Greece soon tired of explaining that they were not English and reluctantly accepted the status of honorary Englishmen and the considerable advantages which the status conferred.

The United States Government, like so many in Europe, found itself perplexed by the Greek situation. At the end of 1822 President Monroe made an enthusiastic declaration in favour of the Greeks, ending with the categorical statement: 'A strong hope is entertained that these people will recover their independence and resume their equal station among the nations of the earth.' The Greeks saw a chance of securing a diplomatic recognition from a country more significant than the Sovereign Knights of Malta, their only success so far. Mavrocordato wrote to Secretary of State John Quincy Adams in terms which diplomats use when they are being polite about countries which have no shared interest or experience. He fastened on the only point the two countries had in common, the fact that neither had a king, and eked out the rest of the letter with flattering generalities.

If an immense distance separates America from Greece, their constitutions and their reciprocal interests bring them so close together that we cannot possibly omit to look forward to the establishment of relations whose happy results cannot possibly be doubted.

Adams, while firmly rejecting the proposal, showed that he too was a master of the *genre*:

The people of the United States . . . sympathizing with the cause of freedom and independence wherever its standard is unfurled, behold with peculiar interest the display of Grecian energy in defence of Grecian liberties, and the association of heroic exertions, at the present time, with the proudest glories of former ages, in the land of Epaminondas and of Philopoemen. . . . If in the progress of events, the Greeks should be enabled to establish and organize themselves into an independent nation, the United States will be among the first to welcome them, in that capacity, into the general family, to establish diplomatic and commercial relations with them, suited to the mutual interests of the two countries, and to recognize, with special satisfaction, their constituted state in the character of a sister Republic.

Meanwhile Adams, like any good Foreign Minister, had his eye firmly on the national interest.⁵ For all his talk about liberty and Epaminondas, it was clear to him that Turkey was a far more promising partner for the United States than poor struggling Greece. In April 1823, four months before he sent the reply to Mavrocordato, Adams had dispatched an agent to Constantinople to open secret negotiations with the Turks. George Bethune English, a gifted Harvard graduate with a flair for languages, sampled several careers, the law, the press, the church, before becoming a Lieutenant in the Marines. His voyage to the Mediterranean gave him a taste for the East. In 1820 he went to Egypt, became a Moslem, and accompanied one of Mehemet Ali's conquering expeditions into Africa as an artillery officer. When he arrived at Constantinople in 1823 on his secret mission he ostentatiously sported Eastern dress and the Turks apparently accepted the unlikely tale that he was 'an American musselman who has come from a far distant country to visit the Capital of Islam'. The European diplomatic missions regarded him as simply another eccentric Middle Eastern traveller of a type that was already becoming common. It was a perfect disguise. English was remarkably successful in his overtures to the Turks. His purpose was to obtain a commercial treaty which would secure the American trade in the Levant, an object which successive American administrations had set their heart on since the time of George Washington. The American Levant trade was now very valuable but, in the absence of a commercial treaty, the Americans were obliged to rely on consular facilities provided—on repayment—by the British. This was humiliating but there was a more important consideration. The most lucrative commodity of the American trade now had to be handled with discretion. The purchasing and adulterating of the opium produced near Smyrna was a delicate business, if only because many people at home were already questioning whether it was right to make fortunes out of befuddling and poisoning the Chinese. The opium trade from Smyrna was now virtually an American monopoly which a few merchants had built up during the period of American neutrality at the beginning of the century.

In the autumn of 1824 a large American naval squadron, including the largest American warship ever to cross the Atlantic, the U.S.S. *North Carolina*, appeared in the Eastern Mediterranean. The main object of this expedition was to impress the Turks and follow up, at a higher level, the negotiations begun by English at Constantinople. The Commander of the squadron duly met the Turkish naval Commander-in-Chief, succesfully impressed him with American naval power and continued the negotiation for the treaty taking care to heed the warning from Washington to be 'especially careful that neither the meeting nor any movement contingent upon it shall be made susceptible of any unfavourable operation upon the cause of the Greeks'. The Americans did not obtain their coveted commercial treaty until 1830 and then they were manoeuvred into signing a secret clause which gave the Turks the right to buy warships in the United States.

Meanwhile the United States Government was studiously cultivating the Greeks, competing with the European powers in the business of conferring favours which might later be converted into commercial advantages. At the time when George English was conducting his secret negotiations with the Turks in Constantinople, Richard Rush, the American Minister in London, was paying assiduous attention to Orlandos and Louriottis.

Through Rush's agency, the Greek and American Governments continued to exchange letters of mutual esteem. The Americans professed themselves deeply interested in the outcome of Greece's struggle for liberty but carefully refused to concede the one point which the Greeks wanted, diplomatic recognition. The Greeks returned the flattery, skilfully drafting their messages to appeal to American preconceptions. Rush, by making himself the agency by which the money collected by the United States Greek Committees was forwarded, ensured that he was privy to the dealings between the Greeks and the United States' Committees. Soon his lobbying began to pay off. At the end of 1824 the Greek deputies approached him to inquire whether they could obtain in the United States the frigates which they had been instructed to order from the proceeds of the loan. Here was a chance for the United States and Rush eagerly seized it. Diplomatic recognition the United States could not give, but export contracts—that was another matter. As Rush reported, he was 'desirous to see money expended in the United States by foreigners, whenever it may be done in a way of lawful traffick'. Although it was out of the question that the United States Government should compromise its valuable neutrality by openly supplying naval material to the Greeks, 'it might perhaps be competent to individual citizens or shipwrights of the United States to receive proposals, consistently with the duties of neutrality'.

By an apparently happy coincidence, the president of the New York Greek Committee, William Bayard, was also a partner in the merchant house of LeRoy, Bayard and Company which was ready to undertake the supervision of the construction. After some discussion, arrangements were made for Bayard's company, in association with another merchant house, to build two frigates in the United States at an expected cost of about $250,000 each, 'built of live oak, sheathed with copper and including guns and carriages'. This seemed expensive but money was still plentiful. The deputies had set aside £150,000 from the loan money which was more than enough.* The two ships were provisionally named the *Hope* and the *Liberator*.[6]

William Bayard, as part of the arrangement, made discreet inquiries

---

* Hastings advised that second-hand East Indiamen, which were generally reckoned to be as good as warships, would be a better buy. The current price for them was about £25,000 or about $100,000 at the current rate of exchange.

among his friends at Washington, and was able to ascertain that the United States Government would not invoke the law but was prepared to turn a blind eye. The Government was so anxious to see the contract placed in the United States that it gave leave to Captain Chauncey, an officer of the U.S. Navy, to allow him to accept appointment as supervisor of the construction. The deputies in London sent as their agent on the spot a French General named Lallemand, but he was more at home on the back of a horse than among the bankers of downtown New York. He was happy to leave all the shipbuilding arrangements to Bayard.

Meanwhile at the beginning of 1825, after the second loan had been successfully floated in London, the Greek deputies seemed to have virtually unlimited money to spend on any project that took their fancy. The old idea of recruiting a mercenary army was an obvious candidate for revival. This had been the favourite philhellenic solution to Greece's problems since 1821, the idea of Hypsilantes and of Baleste, of General Normann, of the promoters of the German Legion, of the Knights of Malta, of Colonel Gordon, of General Roche and the Orleanists, and no doubt of many others.

With the help of those members of the London Greek Committee with whom they were still on reasonable terms, the Greek deputies approached various candidates with the right military experience to see whether a military expedition could be mounted. Colonel Gordon was the obvious choice but he knew too much about Greek politics to accept their promises. Unsuccessful overtures were also made to Sir Robert Wilson, a British General who, after a lifetime fighting the French, discovered that he was sympathetic to Bonapartism, and whose most recent exploit had been to raise a force of British volunteers to fight for the Constitutionalists in Spain. Discussions were continued with Sir Richard Church, who had commanded Greek troops in the Ionian Islands.

The man whom the Greeks thought they wanted most was Charles James Napier who was already been mentioned as entertaining Byron in Cephalonia in 1823. Napier went to England in 1824 to offer his services and then again in 1825, but no agreement could be reached. He demanded a sum of £12,000 for himself in compensation for giving up his career in the British army; £100,000 or £150,000 to pay his troops; 15,000 muskets; and at least 500 Englishmen, Irishmen, or Scotsmen. Napier's terms look excessive for a man whose pay was about £300 a year and who had already been given clear hints that he had been passed over, but the Greek deputies agreed in principle.

When, soon afterwards, they decided that they did not want the army after all, they still wanted Napier as a commander but he refused to accept. He had an intense, fanatical craving for military glory and the decision cost him dear, but it was inevitable. For Napier it was not the trappings of war that attracted him, not the uniforms, the ceremonial, the adulation and obedience of subordinates, not even the sensation of leading a victorious army through a conquered territory. Napier loved the violence itself and he loved the power. When not actually fighting, his greatest love was to tidy up ruthlessly any situation in which he found himself, to establish law and order, his law and his order. Soon he was to find a suitable theatre for his talents in India. Greece was fortunate to escape him.

In the spring of 1825 the Greek deputies finally accepted the persuasion of Hastings and Blaquiere and decided to build a steam vessel. There seemed to be plenty of money available for new ideas now that the second loan had been so successfully launched. In March the deputies authorized Ricardos, their bankers, to pay £10,000 to Edward Ellice M.P., a member of the London Greek Committee who had undertaken to make the arrangements. The ship itself, a corvette of 400 tons, was to be built at Deptford on the Thames; the steam engines to be provided by Alexander Galloway of Smithfield, London. Hastings undertook to provide the armament. The ship was provisionally named the *Perseverance*, a quality which her creators were to need in large measure.

With the decision to build the frigates in America and the steamship in England, the Greeks became gradually committed to spending the loan money on a naval policy. All that was needed was an Admiral. Then in June 1825 one of the most famous naval heroes of the age arrived in England and declared himself ready to take command of a naval expedition to fight for Greek independence.

Thomas Cochrane, Tenth Earl of Dundonald, Baron Cochrane of Dundonald, of Paisley, and of Ochiltree in the Peerage of Scotland, Marquess of Maranham in the Empire of Brazil, G.C.B., and Admiral of the Fleet, lies among the great men of England in Westminster Abbey.7 Four other nations lay wreaths on his tomb. The eulogistic inscription placed there in 1860 when he died in his eighty-fifth year exaggerates only a little the reputation which he enjoyed at the end of his life. Thomas Cochrane, it declares,

> Who by the Confidence which his Genius,
>   His Science and Extraordinary Daring
> Inspired, by his Heroic Exertions in the
>   Cause of Freedom, and his Splendid
> Services alike to his own Country,
>   Greece, Brazil, Chili, and Peru,
> Achieved a Name Illustrious throughout
>   The World for Courage, Patriotism,
>   And Chivalry.

In 1825 Cochrane's own generation took, on the whole, a different view. During the long French wars he had built up a huge reputation as a daring and flamboyant officer. By instinct he always seemed to do the unconventional and the unexpected and he was always drawing attention to himself. He treated his superior officers with undisguised contempt. He was also extremely successful. In particular, he applied his talents to capturing enemy vessels and so earned more prize money than any other man in the history of the British Navy. In 1805 alone he won £75,000.

Cochrane was court-martialled in 1798, when he was twenty-three, for indiscipline. In 1808 he provoked a court martial for his Commander-in-Chief, Lord Gambier, but the move backfired and Cochrane was put on half pay. No doubt the authorities felt they were well rid of an undisciplined ambitious exhibitionist. His civilian career was just as tempestuous. He became a Member of Parliament and gave vehement support to all the liberal causes of the hour. Along with several of the men who were later to be associated with the London Greek Committee, he threw himself with gusto into the delightful and ever-praiseworthy business of exposing the incompetence and extravagance of the Government.

An arrest and escape from prison at Malta, an attempt to resist an armed military force for two days in a barricaded house in Westminster, a runaway marriage to Gretna Green—incidents such as these were all part of Cochrane's daily life. Then in 1814, for a second time, he seemed to have overreached himself. In February of that year a breathless young man arrived at Dover in a scarlet uniform and, on his way to London, ostentatiously put it about that he was bearing news of a great allied victory and of the death of Napoleon. The price of shares on the London Stock Exchange immediately soared and when the hoax was uncovered, it was noticed that Lord Cochrane was one of a handful of people who had made a fortune. Justly or unjustly he was tried, found guilty, fined, and imprisoned. He was expelled from the House of Commons, deprived of his K.C.B., and cashiered from the Navy. As a small mercy, the sentence to sit publicly in the stocks was commuted.

In 1818 Cochrane accepted an invitation to go to Chile where the revolutionaries were in the process of expelling the last Spanish garrisons. His fleet consisted of a few small second-hand vessels and one frigate captured from the Spanish. For the first two years he achieved little except the usual huge reputation for exhibitionism, wilfulness, disobedience, and quarrelsomeness. Then in January 1820, apparently on a sudden impulse and without proper preparation or orders from the Government, he attacked the main naval base still in Spanish hands. The sheer effrontery of the move caught the Spanish by surprise and the place was taken. Soon afterwards he led a force against the Spanish in Peru and, by a similar combination of enterprise and daring, succeeded in capturing the Spanish flagship.

Cochrane had intended to settle in Chile and built himself a handsome house there, but he quarrelled incessantly with the Chilean leaders particularly about money both for himself and for the European volunteers who followed him. And, although he had done more than most of the local leaders to ensure that independence was safe, he became increasingly aware that the struggle in which he was engaged, allegedly for liberty, was merely transferring the poor South Americans from one unscrupulous government to another. Chile was racked with civil war and some of the important towns had fallen again to the Spanish when Cochrane received an invitation to join the service of Brazil where the young Don Pedro had proclaimed himself Constitutional Emperor in defiance of Portugal. His success there, too, was almost incredible. On one occasion with only two ships he attacked a Portuguese convoy of thirteen warships and over sixty merchant ships and captured or destroyed all but thirteen. On another occasion, with only one ship, Cochrane persuaded the garrison of an important fortress to surrender by pretending that he had a huge force coming up behind. By such enterprising bluff he secured the independence of all the northern provinces of Brazil. There soon followed, however, the usual quarrels and swift disillusionment with the way in which constitutionalist liberty worked in practice. In the summer of 1825 he wrote a series of letters of resignation to the Brazilian Government—his usual method of applying pressure—and when he received no reply, sailed off in one of the frigates. On 25 June he arrived unannounced at Portsmouth and went off for a holiday in Scotland.

Cochrane's legal status at this point would have been difficult to define. He had so openly defied the Foreign Enlistment Act of 1819 that he was virtually asking the British Government to prosecute him; unless, of course, he should be regarded as a Brazilian, but in that case his action in sailing without orders across the Atlantic with half the Brazilian fleet was desertion or mutiny. Cochrane, the great fighter for constitutional liberty, cared nothing for these matters.

At the court martial in 1798, Admiral St. Vincent had described Cochrane as 'mad, romantic, money-getting, and not truth-telling', and seldom has a personal file contained such an accurate description. In 1825, twenty-seven years later, he was the same man. In particular, despite the numerous vast fortunes which he had already accumulated, Cochrane's appetite for money was as sharp as ever. His quarrels with Chile and Brazil had been as much about money as politics and he never received everything that he was promised. Chile had given him a draft for $120,000 drawn on the Peruvian Government which they refused to pay. The Brazilian Government, Cochrane reckoned, owed him £100,000 and it did eventually pay £40,000 to his family after his death.

To serve the Greeks he demanded payment in advance and at a rate which would compensate him for giving up his career in the Brazilian

Navy from which he had just deserted. After negotiations with the Greek
deputies a contract was settled. They were to provide him with a fleet out
of the loan money. He himself was to receive £37,000 in advance and a
further £20,000 was set aside to be paid to him when Greek independence
had been secured. Prudently, he insisted that the money should be physically
set aside by being paid to one of his friends in trust and not left with the
deputies.

£57,000 is a large fee by anyone's standard. To give a measure of its
value in 1825 it is worth recalling that the total resources of the Paris Greek
Committee collected over three years from all over Europe amounted to
about £65,000. With this they financed four philhellenic military expeditions, a large programme of education for Greeks in France, the redeeming
of hundreds of slaves after the fall of Missolonghi, the purchase of a warship for Lord Cochrane, and much else besides. The total revenues of the
Greek Government in 1825 (which was reckoned to be the year in which it
authority was widest and its income was greatest) came to the equivalent
of about £90,000.

Cochrane did not ignore the perquisites of the appointment. Remembering his fortune from prize money in the British Navy, he insisted that,
apart from his fee, he should have the right to the proceeds of the sale
of any ships captured from the enemy 'as is customary in such cases
amongst civilized nations'. In addition, he is said to have made a further
£100,000 out of judicious speculating in Greek bonds when his decision
to join the Greeks was made public. Lord Cochrane's philhellenism rested
on solid financial foundations.

Nevertheless, the Greeks' decision was perhaps right. They had hired
probably the most famous and most successful fighter in the world. Not
only had he never known failure: his success had without exception been
brilliant. For their £57,000 they were buying a reputation which might
do more for the Greek cause than all the ships. When news arrived that the
great liberator was on his way, a sudden relapse of morale was felt on the
Ottoman side. One traveller remarked that the Turkish fleet was so terrified
that it would never venture out of port even if Lord Cochrane had only
one small schooner.[8] Another traveller, more familiar with Turkish
psychology, declared that 'the Turks imagined him to be a sort of half man,
half devil—a sorcerer who needed not the agency of winds and currents,
but who could rush to his object in spite of them. I really believe some of
them thought he could sail his ships on land.'[9]

One of the reasons for Cochrane's successes in the past had been his
willingness to improvise, and to experiment with new methods and to look
for new military technologies. He was one of the first naval officers to
recognize the potential of the steam engine and in 1818 he had arranged
for an old sailing vessel to be fitted with steam engines for the Chilean

navy. The *Rising Star* did not reach South America until the fighting in Chile was over, but she was probably the second steamship to cross the Atlantic—she was certainly the first steamship to reach the Pacific. When, many years later, Lord Cochrane was received back into the forgiving bosom of the Royal Navy, he was to play a decisive part in introducing a new generation of steam warships and so prolonging British naval superiority for another hundred years.

It was natural that his mind should turn to steamships in accepting the invitation to fight for Greece. Not only was this the kind of bold innovation which appealed to him but a circle of Philhellenes in favour of steamships already existed in London, led by Hastings and Blaquiere, ready to press the idea on the deputies. And the *Perseverance* was already under construction.

Lord Cochrane submitted a list of his demands. In no circumstances he declared, would he enter the Greek service with their present inefficient naval force. He required:

Six steam vessels having each two guns in the bow and perhaps two in the stern not less than 68-pounder long guns. The bottoms of two old 74-gun ships, upper decks cut off and heavy cannon mounted on the lower deck. These vessels well manned appear to be sufficient to destroy the whole Turkish naval power.

Admiral Lord Exmouth is reported to have declared when he heard of the scheme, 'Why, it's not only the Turkish fleet but all the navies in the world you will be able to conquer with such craft as these', and it is easy, in the knowledge of the subsequent development of naval warfare, to congratulate both Cochrane and Exmouth on their strategic vision. It is more difficult to appreciate the imagination of Cochrane's plan, the total self-confidence and the boldness verging on rashness which it implied.

The steamship had far from proved itself as a naval weapon although well enough tested for civil purposes. The East India Company had made use of one in the Burma River War with some success, but that was hardly decisive evidence. No major navy had yet adopted steam in any of its main ships and this was not entirely due to neophobia or obscurantism. War is risky enough without gratuitously introducing new opportunities for failure. As has been shown again and again at the cost of innumerable lives, there is many a long step between the conceiving of a brilliant technological idea and the building of a practical, efficient, and reliable machine.*

Lord Cochrane had no doubts, and he did not attempt to hedge his bets

---

* French friends of the Greeks were at this time advocating the adoption of another type of secret naval weapon, a ship which could sail under water.[10] The submarine in 1825 was at about the same stage of development as the steamship and, in other circumstances, might have been chosen instead. The idea of a steam warship was not much more revolutionary.

by asking for conventional warships as well. Six steamships was what he wanted, nothing more, nothing less, although he would, of course, also take under command the two frigates building in America. Edward Ellice assured the Greek deputies that 'Within a few weeks Lord Cochrane will be at Constantinople and will burn the Turkish vessels in the port'. Cochrane added that he would burn Constantinople itself to the ground.

The deputies were persuaded to set aside £150,000 from the loan money to build a steam fleet (including the £57,000 fee to Cochrane). In August they placed orders for five more steamships of much the same size as the *Perseverance*. They were to be completed by November 1825, that is less than three months from the date of the order. It was also the date on which the two frigates building in the United States were expected to be ready. The Greek deputies and their friends on the London Greek Committee were able to congratulate themselves, for a few short weeks, that they had laid the preparations for an expedition which would at last ensure the freedom of Greece. It was a precious moment, duly savoured.

Cochrane arrived in London in November 1825 ready to take command of his new fleet, and the trouble began. Shipbuilding contracts are notoriously liable to slippage, especially when the designs incorporate new technology: some delay might therefore be expected. Three of the ships had to be lengthened in the hull when it was discovered that the full pay-load of engines, armament, and fuel made them unseaworthy—setbacks known affectionately in the business as 'teething troubles'. But that was not all. As a result of the antics of Bowring and the other speculators, the relationship between the Greek deputies and the members of the London Greek Committee was now near breaking point. The bondholders were becoming restive and the first suspicions about the fate of their money were being voiced. The British Government also began to take fright. They were anxious to help the British Philhellenes if this could be done discreetly but discretion was not the most prominent of Cochrane's qualities. The bondholders, anxious to inflate their credit on the Stock Exchange, trumpeted Cochrane's accession to their cause on every occasion, but this merely added to the embarrassment of the Government. How could the Government insist to the Turks that Britain was neutral in the war if one of her most famous admirals was supervising the construction of a hostile fleet in England? If the Foreign Enlistment Act meant anything, then surely Cochrane who had enlisted in at least three foreign navies deserved to be prosecuted? A decision to prosecute was in fact taken by the Cabinet, but it was not necessary to put it into effect. Cochrane took the hint and prudently slipped over to France leaving the task of preparing the fleet to his friends.

Six months passed and still there was no sign of the ships being ready. Cochrane, to whom inaction was torture, occupied himself in reading fifty books on Greece specially sent to him in France. Then in May 1826 he paid a secret visit to the yard of Alexander Galloway, the London engineers who were building the steam engines, and discussed progress with the deputies. He threatened to give up the whole idea but agreed to continue on receiving promises that three of the ships were almost finished.

The delays were not entirely due to technical factors. Mehemet Ali, learning that steamships were coming into fashion in Europe, decided characteristically to have one for himself. He bought a Margate packet steamer and mounted three guns on her. When it appeared that more modern machinery was required, who more appropriate to supply it than Alexander Galloway of Smithfield, London? Galloway's son was sent to Egypt where he had hopes of being appointed resident engineer to the Pasha at a salary at £1,500.

It is always said to be difficult to serve two masters and the difficulty is presumably increased when they are engaged in a war of mutual extermination. Galloway, while willing to provide engines for warships for the Greeks, had to consider the likely reaction of his other customer, the Pasha of Egypt. If the company appeared to be unnecessarily philhellenic, the Pasha would certainly withdraw the offer to young Galloway and perhaps have him bastinadoed to death to emphasize the point. A policy of procrastination on the Greek steamships was only common prudence, at least until young Galloway had a chance to leave Egypt. In 1826 the Greeks intercepted a ship carrying machinery from Galloways to Egypt and several compromising letters. It appeared that Galloway was cheating Mehemet Ali as well as the Greek deputies.

At last on 18 May 1826, nearly a year behind schedule, the trials of the *Perseverance* seemed to pass off satisfactorily. News had recently arrived of the fall of Missolonghi and it was decided that Hastings should sail at once to Greece, leaving Cochrane to come on later with the rest of the fleet. Cochrane took up position off the coast of Ireland with his staff in two yachts that had been bought for him out of the loan money. He expected to receive word to set sail at any moment.

To the great delight of the bondholders the *Perseverance* left the Thames in May. At last Hastings had the ship about which he had dreamed for four years and longer. Her crew consisted mostly of British seamen whose recruitment was not interfered with since the ship's papers declared she was bound for Holland. Under canvas she seemed satisfactory if slow, but it soon became clear that her engines were not powerful enough for her weight and the paddles were too high in the water. Almost as soon as Hastings reached the Mediterranean her boilers burst and she was delayed for three months at Cagliari repairing the damage. It also emerged that she could not raise enough steam by burning wood but needed coal. This had to be sent out in a specially chartered vessel from England. The *Perseverance*

did not reach Nauplia until September 1826. As yet she had no armament. Hastings had ordered the guns and supervised their construction
in England, but in order not to run foul of the law, it was decided to send
them to the United States and from there to Greece. While in the United
States they were lost for a while, but eventually they were dispatched to
Greece and arrived in Nauplia in December 1826.

Meanwhile in June Lord Cochrane, who had been waiting off Ireland
in his yacht, received news that the next two steamships the *Enterprize* and
the *Irresistible* were ready and, as arranged, he immediately set sail for the
Mediterranean. It was not until he reached Messina, where he had hoped
to rendezvous with his fleet, that he discovered that the news was false.
The ships had not yet set sail. Galloway need not have bothered to pro-
crastinate; the technical difficulties were quite sufficient by themselves to
impose the necessary delays. The design fault in these two ships was more
than 'teething troubles'; it turned out that steam could not be raised of
sufficient power to propel the vessels without blowing up the boilers. Lord
Cochrane was therefore consigned to another period of waiting, his third
since the date on which his fleet was supposed to be ready.

It was just at this time, the summer of 1826, that the scandal of the loans
was being enjoyed throughout Britain as one by one the leaders of the
London Greek Committee were held up to public mockery. Now the scandal
of the steamships added to the general delight. More was soon to come.
The deputies, who had left all the details of supervising the work to Ricardos,
their bankers, were surprised to learn that work on three of the steamships,
the *Mercury*, *Alert* and *Lasher*, had been suspended. The explanation which
Ricardos eventually provided in August 1826 caused even more surprise.
Out of the £150,000 which had been set aside for Cochrane's fee and the
building of the six steamships, £123,109 had already been spent. All the
Greeks had to show for this money was one defective vessel limping to
Greece without armament and one angry Admiral cruising aimlessly
about the Western Mediterranean searching for his phantom fleet.

Meanwhile, alarming news had arrived from the United States from
where the deputies believed they were soon to receive two fine new
frigates, the *Hope* and the *Liberator*, for $250,000 each. Another scandal
was bursting out.

The negotiation of naval contracts is no work for amateurs and even
the experts whom governments employ on this task are well accustomed
to having to answer for the results of faulty estimating. Generally speaking,
when shipbuilding business is slack, the contractors are often driven by
over-optimism to the verge of bankruptcy; when on the other hand shipbuilding business is brisk, they make handsome profits from government
money. There are innumerable variations of types of contract which reflect
the balance of negotiating strength, ranging from 'fixed price', where the

14 'Regeneration
of the Greek
Parnassus'

15 A French
View of the
Battle of Athens,
1827

16 Athens as it really looked at about this time

17 The Port and Temple at Aegina where Howe built the American Mole

contractor is obliged to tender in advance and is therefore under strong incentive to perform the work as economically as possible, to 'cost plus' where the purchaser agrees to pay the cost of the work plus a certain sum for profit. The incentive here to economy is much less but it still has some force.

In 1825, despite the American Government's eagerness for more export orders, the shipyards of the United States were already committed almost to capacity. Naval vessels were under construction for Brazil, Mexico, Peru, and Colombia as well as for the United States Government. Labour and materials were short and costs were rising rapidly. The deputies should therefore have been on guard to look carefully at the details of the contract.

As it was, Bayards persuaded Lallemand, the agent of the Greeks in New York, and the Greek deputies in London that no formal contract at all was necessary; instead, the ships should be built by 'day's work'. Two New York shipbuilders were told to begin work at once; to devote all their resources to ensuring the speedy completion of the vessels to the highest standard; and to make any contracts they needed to obtain labour or materials. It was a virtual invitation to extravagance. Furthermore, Bayards and the other 'supervising' house Howlands, so far from having a financial incentive to impose economy, were on the contrary themselves under a strong temptation to push up the costs. They paid themselves a commission of 10 per cent* on every transaction and charged a 2½ per cent fee for bills on Ricardos in London.

In October 1825 the Greek deputies in London learnt to their dismay that $750,000 had already been paid out by Ricardos, that is $250,000 more than had been bargained for, and that the ships would not be ready for another four months. The estimate of the final cost was put at $1,100,000. Ricardos refused to advance any further money and bills from New York were not honoured.

At this moment the Greek deputies had eight warships under construction on their account in England and America, and it looked as if they would never acquire any of them. When they protested that they should not have to pay any more for the frigates, they were reminded that the whole transaction of building warships for an unrecognized foreign customer was illegal and that the uncompleted vessels might be seized for that reason. The Greek deputies, unscrupulous as they were, had met their match.

Early in 1826 they sent a new agent called Contostavlos to New York to try to straighten matters out. He found a muddle of unpaid bills and outstanding claims and it was obvious that the loan money (most of the

---

* The normal rate at the time was 2½ per cent but some experts argued that, in cases of exceptional risk, 5 per cent might be admissible. Bayards declared blandly in their defence that Colombia was charged 12½ per cent.

remainder of which had already been wasted elsewhere) would never stretch to completing both vessels. Arbitrators were engaged and, through the help of several prominent Americans who favoured the Greek cause, including Edward Everett and Daniel Webster, a solution was arrived at. After a valuation by experts, the United States Navy agreed to buy one of the frigates, the *Liberator*, for $233,570.97: she had already cost $440,606.41. With this money, work on the other frigate, the *Hope*, was completed. She was renamed the *Hellas* and eventually reached Nauplia in November 1826. She was a magnificent vessel, according to many observers, one of the most beautiful ships of her day, but she was not worth £155,000.

In October 1826 Lord Cochrane, exasperated to fury by his months of waiting, sailed to Marseilles to try to obtain news from England. Hobhouse went out to meet him there. During Cochrane's enforced wait a new proposal had been made to him. The Knights of Malta, hearing of the difficulties with the steam fleet, now offered to employ Cochrane instead if he would fly their flag. A French businessman, who was looking for commercial advantages in Crete, was behind the idea but it never came to anything. Blaquiere knew all about it and several others warned the Greek Government not to countenance it.

As it turned out, the French were now anxious to make Cochrane's expedition a success. Hobhouse had had discussions with the Paris Committee on his way and Eynard from Switzerland had also promised support. The apparent *volte-face* of the French Philhellenes from overt rivalry with the English to active co-operation was partly due to the developing diplomatic situation, but mainly because it was now clear to all Philhellenes that Greece was on the verge of extinction. Since the fall of Missolonghi in April 1826, Greece had been kept in existence largely by the donations of European Philhellenes. If the country was to survive, then Cochrane's expedition had to be a success; there would be plenty of time for resuming national rivalries once Greek independence had been secured. The main thing was for Cochrane to go to Greece at once.

The Paris and Marseilles Greek Committee agreed to spend virtually all their remaining money in buying a warship so that Cochrane could arrive with at least some appearance of having a naval force at his command, even if in fact his reputation was now to be his chief weapon. Gazing ruefully at the warships building for Mehemet Ali in the Marseilles dockyard, the French Philhellenes bought a brig of war, the *Sauveur*, and arranged to have her fitted out in the same port.

At last, at the end of February 1827, Cochrane set sail from Marseilles for Greece. Instead of a steam fleet he had only three small sailing vessels, the *Sauveur* and the two yachts. He was fifteen months behind schedule, but, if anything, the delay had served to increase the terror in which his name was held by the Turks. With typical panache and sound military psychology he wrote a letter to Mehemet Ali telling him that at last he was on his way. Perhaps, he suggested ironically, instead of molesting the poor Greeks, His Highness should consider using his energies to cut a canal through from the Mediterranean to Suez. In another letter intended to soften up the opposition he simply referred Mehemet to the thirty-first chapter of Isaiah: 'Now the Egyptians are men and not God; and their horses flesh, and not spirit. When the Lord shall stretch out his hand, both he that helpeth shall fall, and he that is holpen shall fall down, and they all shall fall together.' Lord Cochrane often saw himself as the instrument of the Lord of Hosts.

The story of the five steamships which Cochrane left behind can be briefly told. Trials of the *Enterprize** were held in October and December 1826 without success, but in April 1827 she finally left the Thames. In the English Channel her engines stopped three times, then she burst a boiler and had to be ignominiously towed into Plymouth for repairs, She eventually reached Greece in September 1827. The *Irresistible*,† which also proved next to useless as a steamship, did not arrive until September 1828 by which time most of the fighting was over. Of the other vessels, one, the *Mercury*, was eventually completed with the help of an advance of £2,000 from Cochrane. Edward Blaquiere took her to Greece at the end of 1828. No money was ever forthcoming to complete the other two, the *Alert* and the *Lasher*, and they were abandoned to rot in the Thames.

For the expenditure of over £300,000 of the loan money the Greeks had expected to obtain, by the end of 1825, a fleet of two frigates and six steamships, to say nothing of the two yachts. When the decisive battles for Greece seemed to be imminent in the winter of 1826 all they had achieved was one excellent frigate, one defective steamship, the two yachts, and the old brig provided by the French Philhellenes. But Lord Cochrane had liberated half of South America with less. An Admiral who was reputedly able to sail his ships across land might still accomplish some surprises.

* Renamed *Epicheiresis* in Greece.
† Renamed *Hermes* in Greece.

The Princess Lieven, wife of the Russian Ambassador to the Court of St. James, was not a beautiful woman, but she charmed many of the great men of the age. This was partly due to her personal talents and partly because she had more influence over Russian foreign policy than her husband the Ambassador. The princess's diplomatic qualifications were formidable. She had been the mistress of Metternich the Austrian Chancellor and was now one of the small set that shared the social life and the state secrets of George IV; she was a friend of Castlereagh and of Canning; and 'more than a friend' to Lord Grey.

In the summer of 1825 Princess Lieven paid a visit to Russia. On the night she was due to return to England she was hastily summoned to see Czar Alexander who was now living the life of a religious hermit away from St. Petersburg. The Princess was asked to see that a message about Greece, too delicate to be entrusted to any of the usual channels, was passed to Canning. The Czar said:

My people demand war; my armies are full of ardour to make it, perhaps I could not long resist them. My Allies have abandoned me. Compare my conduct to theirs. Everybody has intrigued in Greece. I alone have remained pure. I have pushed scruples so far as not to have a single wretched agent in Greece, not an intelligence agent even, and I have to be content with the scraps that fall from the table of my Allies. Let England think of that. If they grasp hands with us, we are sure of controlling events and of establishing in the East an order of things conformable to the interest of Europe and to the laws of religion and humanity.[1]

Alexander insisted that Russia would never make advances to England, but the British Government should understand that, if they made the first move, it would not be repulsed.

Princess Lieven duly passed the hint to Canning and he immediately realized that the long international deadlock was broken. Formal discussions were begun with the Russians about the settlement of the Greek question and were soon making progress. The death of the old Czar did not interrupt the work; in early 1826 the Duke of Wellington set sail for Russia to agree the final points; and on 4 April 1826 an Anglo-Russian protocol on the affairs of Greece was signed at St. Petersburg.

It consisted of only six short articles, but it was the most important move towards a settlement that had occurred during the five years of the Greek war. The two powers had at last recognized that they were well placed to take the initiative; Britain because of the repeated requests of the Greeks to take their country under her protection, Russia because she had an army on the Turkish frontier. They agreed that they would act together to seek a settlement by offering 'mediation' between the Greeks and Turks.

The foundation of the agreement was clause five, which declared that neither His Imperial Majesty nor His Britannic Majesty would look for for 'any increase in territory, any exclusive influence, or any commercial advantage for their subjects not open to those of other nations'. This article, provided always that His Imperial Majesty could be trusted, removed the danger that the Russians would invade Turkey and compel the Sultan to cede the Danubian Provinces and Greece or to make some arrangement which would be tantamount to the same thing. The protocol ended with an invitation to the other great powers to join in the arrangement. News now began to arrive that the Russian army on the Danube was being reinforced. Canning responded by strengthening the British naval squadron in the Eastern Mediterranean.

The protocol represented a considerable realignment in the politics of Europe. Russia had for the first time broken away from her alliance with the other absolutist powers, Austria and Prussia, and Metternich was furious. France, too, quickly recognized the fundamental change that had occurred. It was now obvious that, in the face of an Anglo-Russian alliance in the Levant, France could do little on her own. When therefore during the summer of 1826 the suggestion was made that France also might like to join the protocol in accordance with the sixth article, the overture was received sympathetically in Paris. Austria and Prussia remained obstinately aloof, but during the next year a long round of diplomatic negotiations converted the principles of the protocol into the Treaty of London signed by Britain, Russia, and France. The three great powers on whom the Greeks most depended were now united.

It is one thing to offer mediation, quite another to persuade the warring parties to accept it. The Greeks, who were still regarded internationally as rebels, seemed ready to settle on the basis of continuing to acknowledge Ottoman suzerainty provided all Turkish troops were removed from

Greece and in any case they were in no position to argue; but for the Turks, the very existence of the protocol was anathema. When a government is putting down a rebellious province it has no need of 'mediation' from foreigners. Would the British Government accept Turkish 'mediation' in dealing with the ever-troublesome Irish? Some excuse was necessary if the great powers were to intervene in matters which they had hitherto acknowledged as the exclusive concern of the Ottoman Government.

It was decided to hang the approach to the Turks on the stories that were circulating about Ibrahim's declared intention to exterminate the inhabitants of the Morea and to repopulate the area with Egyptians. If the stories were true, Ibrahim's methods seemed to be sufficiently different from the recognized usage of civilized powers as to make pressure from foreigners seem less improper. The 'barbarization' of Greece, as the alleged policy was called, could be said to be of general international interest even if the powers claimed no right to speak on behalf of the unfortunate Greeks who were to be barbarized. Canning was delighted with this suggested lead-in, since it was different from the type of approach which had been urged on the Government since the beginning of the war. There was to be no mention of the clichés of philhellenism, no claim to intervene on behalf of the Christians in the Ottoman Empire. As Canning himself wrote, he liked it the better 'because it has nothing to do with Epaminondas nor (with reverence be it spoken) with St. Paul'. [2] The powers were more likely to impress the Turks if they spoke with the familiar voice of self-interest than if they claimed some special virtue or consideration for the Greeks which Turks especially were unlikely to find convincing.

The three powers had a variety of means by which to put pressure on the Turks to accept 'mediation', but it soon became clear that they were not going to yield. Both the Ottoman Government in Constantinople and Mehemet Ali in Cairo denied categorically the stories about the intended 'barbarization' of the Morea, although making plain that they intended to settle the Greek Revolution in the traditional Ottoman way. The powers were therefore driven along a course of action which was vaguely implicit in the protocol and gradually became explicit. If the warring parties refused 'mediation', then they would have to be compelled to accept it. A hint of the possibility of violence began to appear and this bound the allies more closely together. If they did not act together, then Russia might decide to act alone, and this was something the two others could not accept. Russia insisted that, if the Turks did not accept mediation within a reasonable time, then the powers should instruct their naval forces in the Mediterranean to interpose themselves physically between the combatants and prevent any new reinforcements, Turkish or Egyptian, from being sent to Greece. These thoughts were gradually brought together and were finally made explicit in the Treaty of London of July 1827. A secret article, which was soon made public, committed the three powers, if necessary, to compulsion.

Meanwhile the situation of the Greeks continued to deteriorate. After the fall of Missolonghi in April 1826, most of Roumeli, the area north of the gulf of Corinth, reverted to allegiance to the Turks, and a Turkish army advanced into Attica. The area held by the Greeks gradually contracted as they were pressed from the north by the Turks and from the south by the Egyptians. Then in August 1826 the town of Athens was retaken by the Turks although the Acropolis still held out. The Acropolis of Athens was now the last fortress in Greek hands in the way of a final Turkish advance towards the isthmus. To the leaders of the Greek Government it seemed vital that it should be held.

The eyes of the world at this moment of supreme crisis were therefore fastened on the most famous spot in all Greece. The Acropolis of Athens which contained the most impressive visible remains of the classical age* was now an island in a barbarian sea. The Greeks seemed to be defending not so much a fortress as a talisman of civilization itself, the hope of regeneration, and the symbol of the identity of the Ancient and Modern Greeks. The situation in 1826 had an uncanny superficial resemblance to the other supreme crisis of the Greeks in 480 B.C. when the Persians had sacked the city. The oriental barbarians were again in Athens. As in 480, the citizens took refuge on the island of Salamis. As in 480, their hopes lay mainly in their wooden walls.

The Greek Government decided to use the last forces at its command in an attempt to relieve the beseiged Acropolis, and the military history of Greece from the autumn of 1826 to the spring of 1827 is mainly concerned with operations designed to achieve this purpose.† In late August 1826 Colonel Fabvier felt that he must again entrust his regulars to battle even although he was still dissatisfied with their state of training. It was decided that he should attempt to fight his way to Athens from Eleusis in company with a large body of irregular *palikars*. This route was chosen in preference to the more direct road from the Piraeus because the rocky terrain afforded more protection against the Turkish cavalry.

The result was the same as in every operation during the five years of the war in which the Greeks had attempted to combine the two methods of fighting. As soon as the enemy appeared, the irregulars hurriedly took cover leaving the regulars in the lurch to defend themselves as best they could. Only Fabvier's skill and the sound training which he had

---

* The British obtained a firman from the Porte requiring that the monuments of Athens should not be damaged in the fighting. It was given as a *bonne bouche* at a time when the Turks were obstinately refusing all the requests of the British Ambassador on more important matters. The monuments survived with only slight damage from the war, but this happy result was due more to bad shooting than to respect for the firman.

† See map on p. 284.

insisted on prevented a repetition of Peta. He extricated his little force to safety with the loss of a few Philhellenes and vowed he would never again fight in company with the irregulars. In October however, when Ghouras was killed by a stray bullet and it looked as if the Acropolis was about to surrender, Fabvier was prevailed upon to attempt another operation to cut off the Turkish supply route north of Athens, but again it proved impossible to co-ordinate the two types of forces. The irregulars, whose task was to hold the passes in Fabvier's rear, failed to appear at the proper time and again the regulars and Philhellenes had to retreat hastily to avoid being surrounded.

Fabvier had now taken the field with his regulars four times, first at Tripolitsa shortly after he assumed command in July 1825, then at Euboea in February 1826, and now twice in Attica in the autumn. At Euboea his lack of success was due to the inexperience of his men, but he felt that on the three other occasions he had been let down by the irregulars. Perhaps, he began to wonder to himself, he had been deliberately let down just as in 1821 and 1822 the captains had deliberately discredited and destroyed the Regiment. Fabvier was well aware that it was only his own experience and coolness in crisis that had prevented his little army from being totally destroyed. He had achieved nothing, received no thanks, but had seen some of his old revolutionary comrades uselessly killed.

As the autumn of 1826 gave way to winter, Fabvier shut himself off in the fortress at Methana, his disgust and suspicion of the Greeks growing steadily stronger. He seemed more than ever determined not to endanger his little army again by trusting to the captains. Then in the middle of December the Greek Government sent a special envoy to Methana to beg his help for a very difficult task. A party of Greek troops had succeeded in entering the Acropolis at Athens to reinforce the garrison but, as a result, the fortress was running short of ammunition. Would Fabvier be willing, the Government begged, to try to run ammunition into Athens? Fabvier was touched and relented from his previous resolutions. He agreed to make the attempt, stipulating only that he should not be required to stay in the Acropolis.

On 12 December 1826 when the moon was up he landed at Phaleron with 530 regulars and 40 selected Philhellenes in the lead. Each man carried a sack of gunpowder. The intention was to throw the sacks to the Greek outposts and then retreat, but at the crucial moment the alarm was given and Fabvier and his men were obliged to charge with the bayonet and seek the safety of the Acropolis. They were now caught in a besieged fortress with no prospect of escape unless relief came from outside. Fabvier felt that he had again been betrayed; that he had been deliberately enticed into the Acropolis to remove him from the scene and to strengthen the garrison; and that the garrison deliberately roused the Turkish sentries outside if he gave signs of preparing to leave. The siege of the Acropolis of Athens became, more than ever, the focus of attention. If it were to fall not only would the way be open to the isthmus but Greece would have lost her best trained regular troops.

At this depressing moment Fabvier was subjected to a new mortification. The story was gradually substantiated that the Greeks intended to appoint an Englishman* to the chief command over his head. The prospect of Lord Cochrane's arrival Fabvier could accept. Cochrane was a violent devil-may-care liberal of the type that Fabvier could almost admire despite his nationality, and in any case he was bound to confine himself to the sea on which the British were the acknowledged experts. But to appoint an Englishman to command the land forces was an insult which Fabvier would find it hard to forgive.

Sir Richard Church† had seen almost as much fighting as Fabvier.[3] As a young officer he had taken part in the invasion of Egypt in 1800, and from then until the peace of 1815 he was in numerous campaigns, often under fire and several times wounded. It was during this period that he first made the acquaintance of the Greeks. He took part in the capture of Zante, Ithaca, and Cephalonia in 1809 and was seriously wounded in leading the assault on Santa Maura in March 1810. While he was stationed in the Ionian Islands he raised a regiment of Greeks, the Duke of York's Light Infantry, and led them with outstanding success. When he left the Ionian Islands on leave in the summer of 1812 he was presented with several letters of gratitude by his men, praising him in terms usually reserved for the safety of obituary notices. He won the affection of men from all parts of Greece which neither he nor they could ever forget. In particular, the first of forty signatures in one of the letters of eulogy was that of Theodore Colocotrones who had experienced his first taste of Western ways in the Duke of York's Greek Light Infantry.

Church's success in the Ionian Islands was recognized in London and he returned with a mandate to raise a second Greek regiment and with plans to employ them on the Continent in the great allied offensive against Napoleon. In 1814, however, the Turks protested successfully to the British Government that it was a breach of their sovereignty to recruit troops in Greece and the regiments were disbanded.

Church was by now more Greek than the Greeks and looked forward to the day when the revolution against the Turks would come. He became spokesman for the Greek cause in London and was asked to brief the British delegation at the European Congress of 1814 on the situation in the Ionian Islands. His efforts no doubt played a part in the decision, when

* Actually he was an Irishman.
† His Hanoverian Knighthood was bestowed in 1823 for services with the allied armies in 1813.

peace finally came in 1815, to retain the islands under British protection.

In 1817, with the approval of the British military authorities, Church entered the service of the restored Bourbon King of the Two Sicilies in the rank of Major-General, and for the next three years he applied himself vigorously and successfully to the suppression of brigandage in Southern Italy. Endowed with power of summary execution which he did not hesitate to use, Church restored the authority of the government over the provinces of Apulia. 'A few months were sufficient', he himself reported, 'to totally destroy the assassins and brigands, and to break up the different revolutionary societies, to receive the submission of their chiefs and the surrender of their arms.'

After this success Church was appointed in 1820 to the command of the army in Sicily and he soon began to understand why that island has remained obstinately ungovernable since the fall of the Roman Empire. Before his programme of pacification had really started, however, the constitutionalist revolution broke out. Church attempted to maintain the royalist cause but he was attacked by a mob, arrested, and imprisoned. After six months his release was secured and he returned to England, but he was soon back in Naples after the rebellion had been put down.

When the news of the outbreak of the Greek Revolution arrived in 1821, Church 'sighed to be with them' and immediately chartered a small vessel and set off. He got as far as Leghorn before he was persuaded that it would be unwise to go without money or adequate preparation. He nevertheless felt guilty that the old commander of the Duke of York's Greek Light Infantry was not fighting in Greece. Because he had known something of the Greeks' plans for revolution before it started, Church never doubted that he should be their leader, and wrote:

One great and sublime idea occupies me and renders me insensible to everything else. . . . Conceive the great glory of my being instrumental toward the Emancipation of Greece. . . . The banner that I gave them floats in front of the Grecian armies, but the recreant general is absent, lost in the pleasures and extravagances of the Neapolitan capital.

The Greek deputies in London approached him several times with offers of command in Greece, but although his commitment to their cause was total, for years no agreement could be reached. In part this was probably due to worries about money. It is no light matter for a family man to give up regular pay and the prospect of a pension to fight in a cause officially disapproved of by his own government. The first negotiation seems to have fallen through because the deputies could not pay Church enough. On a later occasion, however, when money from the loan was plentiful, the deputies seem to have offered him too much. No doubt they had in mind their recent experience of the appetites of Napier and Cochrane, but Sir Richard Church was a different cast of Philhellene. The implication in their invitation that he would be principally interested in his salary, offended him deeply. He protested vehemently that he was eager to go, that he was ready 'to sacrifice everything to the cause', and that they had only to invite him and he would rush to their side.

Why then, the reader of his correspondence is often tempted to ask, if Church felt so passionately about going to Greece, did he not go instead of wasting time in fruitless recriminations. It is a poor lover who is prepared to spend five years in the preliminaries. The explanation lay in Church's attitude to the war. He felt that he had a very special place among the Greeks which they ought to recognize. He wanted desperately to go, but he would only go if he was asked properly, formally, by the Government of Greece and by the other leaders. Nothing less than an official invitation would do, but he was quite ready to spend time engineering one. At last early in 1827 he received a flattering letter of invitation from the Government in Nauplia dated 30 August 1826, which had been carefully contrived by the ever-resourceful Edward Blaquiere. Colocotrones added his own message in a letter in September:

My soul has never been absent from you—We your old comrades in arms. . . are fighting for our country—Greece so dear to you!—that we may obtain our rights as men and as a people and our liberty—How has your soul been able to remain from us? . . . Come! Come! and take up arms for Greece, or assist her with your talents, your virtues, and your abilities that you may claim her eternal gratitude!

Thus reassured that he would be welcomed and properly treated in Greece, Church decided to go, but even so proceeded slowly, choosing to appear in Greece in the capacity of a private traveller before committing himself further.

It is easy to see why the prospect of his arrival should have annoyed Fabvier. If anything is more exasperating than to be constantly reminded of a famous predecessor, it is to be constantly assured that he is coming back. And then Church was an Englishman most of whose life had been spent in fighting the great Napoleon, and who had personally taken part in the last harsh campaign in 1815 in the South of France when the few surviving pockets of Bonapartist resistance had been mercilessly crushed.

Most unattractive of all was Church's service to King Ferdinand of Naples, whose pay he drew right up until January 1827 when he set sail for Greece. How could a man who served one of the most hated and most despotic régimes of Europe claim to be a fighter for liberty? One man's terrorist is another man's freedom fighter, one man's brigand is another man's patriot, as his old friend Colocotrones might have explained to him. The Bourbon Government in Naples, like most dictatorships, found it expedient to pretend that its political opponents were criminals, to lump together carbonari and liberals with bandits and vendettists, and Church was quite content to carry out the Government's orders according to the simple notions of military justice, priding himself on never putting a man to death without a court martial. It never seems to have occurred to him that there might be a contradiction between suppressing liberty in the Two Sicilies and fighting for it in Greece. His commitment was entirely and exclusively to Greece and in this sense he can be regarded as one of the few true Philhellenes. He fought for Greeks as Greeks and Modern Greeks at that, not for liberty or for religion or for the sake of Homer, Plato, *et al*. But how could Fabvier and his little army of failed revolutionaries, French and Italian, regard such a man? His life had been devoted to destroying everything they held dear. Colonel Pisa, the leader of the Italian exiles and commander of the Company of Philhellenes, had personally fought against Church's forces in Sicily in 1820.

At the beginning of December a rumour suddenly swept Greece that new help was at hand: thirty thousand troops, it was said, were on their way from Bavaria. In fact there was a grain of truth in the story, but only a grain. The number of Bavarians who had come to join the fight for Greek independence was twelve.

Colonel Karl Heideck,[4] often called Heidegger, was a new type of Philhellene. He was an officer of the Bavarian army and the party of officers, sergeants, and military doctors whom he led were directly under his command. They wore Bavarian uniform and they had been officially and openly sent by King Ludwig, as a direct philhellenic gesture. It was a gesture which could be made by only a small power with few interests at risk in Turkey. The great powers, however much they interfered in one another's affairs, always carefully respected the proprieties. They took care never to support their Philhellenes to the extent of endangering their position in Turkey and their support was always, if necessary, disavowable. Ludwig's grand gesture was to produce a handsome dividend later when, in the absence of anyone more suitable, the powers chose Ludwig's son Otho to be the first King of Greece.

Heideck's description of his first encounter with the Greeks in December 1826 could, with a few changes, be an account of one of the early German Philhellenes. In four years the essentials had not changed. Heideck was shocked when on being introduced to the members of the Government he found them crouching on the floor in oriental style and he noticed with horror a huge louse on the Secretary of State for Foreign Affairs. Nevertheless he proceeded to present his letter of introduction and to outline his plans. He had come because of Bavaria's sympathy to the Greek cause; he had money and arms; he and his men would raise a force of Greeks and teach them tactics; he already had a system in mind and was eager to begin; he had no self-interest to promote and would happily serve under the Greek commanders; he would not even (a new point) write articles for newspapers.

To Heideck's surprise, the Government in a short speech of appreciation, seemed unenthusiastic and gave no word that they accepted his offer. He was affronted when Dr. Bailly, an agent of the French Philhellenes, tried to warn him against the Greeks and told him to take his time and look around. Such words from a Philhellene! Bailly, Heideck concluded, must have a personal grudge against Fabvier. Soon afterwards Heideck was taken aside and it was explained why the Greeks had turned down his offer. If he was allowed to raise a force of Greeks, he was told, many men would join, they would accept uniforms and arms but, as soon as they were ordered out to fight, they would desert and join the *palikars*. Heideck, the Greeks explained, would be angry, he would lose all his money and his equipment, he would have to report his disappointments and failures to the King of Bavaria, and the Greek cause would suffer as a result. Heideck, much perplexed, decided to accept the advice to wait and look around.

In December, too, the frigate *Hellas* eventually arrived from the United States bringing, among other things, the armament for the *Perseverance* which had arrived three months earlier. At last Greece had two powerful vessels which might be put to use immediately. Hastings was asked to remain in command of the *Perseverance*, which was known henceforth by her Greek name of *Karteria*. The *Hellas* was put under the control of a commission of Admirals from the islands.

The obvious strategy was to exploit the sea power which the two ships provided to make another attempt to relieve the siege of the Acropolis. Communication with Fabvier was maintained by carrier pigeon and it was learnt that water was short. The fortress could not hold out much longer. An elaborate plan was therefore drawn up to make use of all of Greece's forces in a desperate attempt to raise the siege. The *Hellas* was to blockade the north coast of Attica, the *Karteria* was to give artillery support off the Piraeus, and two bodies of troops were to land on the south of Athens and advance on the city.

The command of the operation was entrusted to Colonel Gordon who agreed to provide some of the money. Since his return to Greece in the spring, Gordon had insisted that he was not a Philhellene but a travelling gentleman who happened to be interested in Greek affairs. He cruised around in his yacht flying the British flag spending on any worthwhile cause he could find the remnants from the loan money with which he had been entrusted by the Greek deputies in London. He was thoroughly disgusted with the senseless quarrelling and armed clashes among the Greeks and vowed that he would not rejoin their service until Lord Cochrane arrived. In February 1827, however, when the various Greek leaders pressed him to take command of the operation to relieve the Acropolis, he could not refuse and agreed to provide money from his own fortune. Heideck consented to serve under his orders.

It was a bold scheme. One force was to land at Eleusis and attempt to do what Fabvier had failed to do in the autumn—advance on Athens over the rocky terrain to the north. At the same time another force under Gordon's direct command would secretly land at Phaleron, which is almost the nearest point on the coast to Athens, and surprise the besieging Turks.

The command of the Eleusis force which included a detachment of regulars was entrusted to a recently arrived French Colonel called Bourbaki. He came originally from Cephalonia, but had spent his life in the French army and was a convinced Bonapartist under suspicion by the secret police. To the amusement of more experienced Philhellenes, Bourbaki, who was now fat and unathletic, put on a splendid Albanian costume covered with gold braid, with pistols in his girdle and a jewelled sword.

At first the operation seemed to proceed according to plan. Bourbaki and his men landed at Eleusis and prepared to march towards Athens. Then at midnight two days later Gordon and his troops were put down by the *Karteria* at Phaleron only a mile or two from their objective. But this operation, like so many others, foundered on the deep-seated differences between the Europeans and the Greeks. Despite orders to preserve silence and secrecy, as soon as the *palikars* were safely ashore at Phaleron, they started to fire off their muskets out of high spirits to relieve their tension and to announce their arrival to their friends in the Acropolis. The Turks were of course immediately aroused and were able to attack Gordon's forces before they could move from their bridgehead. Disaster seemed certain and Gordon, rightly, wanted to re-embark since an advance on Athens was now out of the question. The Greeks in several days of severe fighting maintained the bridgehead and regarded the affair as a great victory although nothing of any strategic value had been achieved. The *Karteria* proved herself in bombarding the Turkish positions but her engines failed at a critical moment and only Hastings' skill and seamanship prevented her from being destroyed.

Meanwhile, Bourbaki and his force also repeated the same mistakes and misunderstandings which had occurred whenever Europeans and Greeks had fought together throughout the war. They were caught on the plain by the Turkish cavalry and the irregulars immediately fled. Bourbaki and his regulars were left exposed and were cut to pieces. Over 500 men were lost, one of the biggest disasters in battle (as distinct from massacre) of the war. Bourbaki himself was killed, his jewelled weapons and golden dress making him the favourite target. Two other Frenchmen and a German doctor[5] were captured alive but their heads were soon added to the general trophy.

At the end of February Gordon gave up his command in disgust at the continued insubordination of the Greeks. He did, however, recommend to the Greek Government that Heideck should be given a chance to attempt to cut off the Turkish supply line to the north by landing a force on the north coast of Attica and attacking the fort at Oropos. But Heideck had no more success than Fabvier or Gordon. A force of about 500 men was transported to Oropos mainly in the *Karteria* and the *Hellas,* but when they landed and attacked the fort it proved too strong for them and they had to retire with losses.

Meanwhile, Greece was slipping into anarchy. At Nauplia, the nominal capital, one captain was in possession of the fortress and another of the town. Sporadically their armed bands would clash and sometimes the guns of the fortress would be turned on the town. It was a shot from the fortress during one of these encounters that killed young Washington in July 1827. The Government had to move out, first to the fort in the bay and then to the islands, but as the area of Greece declined, the number of her Governments increased. Colocotrones established his own supporters at Castri and claimed that they formed the legitimate National Assembly. The islanders had also split up, one party led by the former president Conduriottis, was established at Hydra and was planning to attack by force his opponents who were established on the neighbouring island of Poros. Naval operations against the Turks had virtually ceased. Each of the leaders of the Greek Revolution struggled to ensure that, if by some good fortune Greece survived, he would be near the head of affairs.

On 23 February 1827 Colocotrones' assembly opened its sesssion at Castri. Shortly afterwards the followers of the old Government convened their rival assembly at Aegina. The two quarrelling island parties were physically restrained from fighting by the British naval squadron and gradually they attached themselves to one or other rival Governments. Meanwhile, the signs of famine became increasingly obvious.

The Greeks had never lacked for advice that they should settle their differences and pull together for the benefit of the nation as a whole. Edward Blaquiere, who had attempted the role in 1823 and again in 1824, now reappeared in Greece for the third time and thrust himself confidently into the political argument. Blaquiere's main task was to ensure that the way was well prepared for the imminent arrival of Lord Cochrane and of Sir Richard Church, but he had prudently ascertained the views of the British Government before he left England.

Blaquiere bustled ceaselessly between the rival Greek Governments trying to persuade them to sink their differences. He was unsuccessful but he did establish a fund of information about their views which was to be of value later. He also contacted the party in the Ionian Islands which, under the guise of being a charity, was working to have Capodistria invited to Greece. Blaquiere was able to establish that all the main parties and Governments would now be willing to accept Capodistria as leader of Greece in preference to any of themselves. He knew too that, contrary to earlier fears, this outcome would not be rejected by the British and French Governments since they had come to accept that Capodistria would not be simply a tool of the Russians. As far as the Greeks were concerned, Capodistria had certain huge advantages. Not only was he the only Greek political figure of any reputation or experience outside Greece, but he had never been in Greece. None of the Greek leaders knew him personally and he had no political debts. To the powers Capodistria seemed to be the only man with a civilized European background who had a chance of holding the country together.

On 17 March 1827, the long-awaited Lord Cochrane at last arrived in Greece with his pitiful little navy of the brig *Sauveur* and the two yachts. His reading of the fifty books on Greece during his enforced wait in France had taught him the appropriate sentiments for such occasions. After his first sight of the Acropolis he noted in his journal:

> The Acropolis was beautiful. Alas! What a change! What melancholy recollections crowd on the mind. There was the seat of science, of literature, and the arts. At this instant the barbarian Turk is actually demolishing by the shells that now are flying through the air, the scanty remains of the once magnificent temples of the Acropolis.

Cochrane presented himself to the Government at Poros where he was given a huge welcome. The next day Colocotrones invited him to go instead to his rival Government at Castri. Again Cochrane knew the proper philhellenic response: he quoted to Colocotrones the famous passage from the first Philippic in which Demosthenes exhorts the Athenians to lay aside their differences and unite against Philip of Macedon. Cochrane declared emphatically to both groups that he would do nothing unless they united.

A week before Cochrane's arrival, Sir Richard Church stepped ashore in Greece. He naturally made first for the Government of his old friend Colocotrones at Castri. 'Our father is at last come,' Colocotrones declared in presenting Church to his men. 'We have only to obey him and our liberty is secured.' Church however insisted that he was a travelling gentleman and would take no part in the war while the two Governments were at odds.

Since neither of the two saviours would act without the other and each Government had a saviour of its own, offers of mediation were soon made. After a good deal of patient diplomacy it was agreed that the two rival assemblies should meet on neutral ground and elect a new leader. Damala, the ancient Troezen, was chosen since it was almost physically half way between Aegina and Castri. In March and April a series of conferences were held in a lemon grove near the ancient ruins. After numerous setbacks, threats of resignation and attempts at treachery, agreement was at last reached on three important points. On 10 April Lord Cochrane came

18 The French entering the Ruins of Tripolitsa in 1828

19 The Monument to the Philhellenes in the Roman Catholic Church at Nauplia

ashore for the first time, took an oath of loyalty before the assembled Greek leaders, and gave his promise to fight until Greece was free. On 11 April the Greeks proclaimed Capodistria (*in absentia*) President of Greece for seven years. On 15 April Sir Richard Church accepted appointment as Commander of the land forces and a new Greek title corresponding roughly to 'Generalissimo' was invented for the occasion. Greece now had leaders, their main qualification for office being in each case their total lack of experience of Greek conditions.

A month had passed in these discussions and the Acropolis of Athens was still under siege. Cochrane and Church both tried to treat Fabvier with consideration, sending him encouraging letters and offering their co-operation, but Fabvier never responded to kindness. Despite his total dependence on the new arrivals for any hope of being relieved—and even of escaping alive—his characteristic reaction was sarcasm, implying that the Greeks were holding back out of cowardice although they outnumbered the enemy by about three to one. Fabvier also announced that the men in the Acropolis could not hold out for more than a few days longer and this was a deliberate exaggeration intended to mislead.

Cochrane decided that an immediate operation should be mounted to relieve him and various methods were considered. In the end the plan chosen was remarkably similar to the ones that Fabvier himself and then Gordon had attempted before his arrival, namely an advance simultaneously from the neighbourhood of Eleusis and from the bridgehead near Phaleron, with the *Hellas* and *Karteria* providing off-shore support.

It was to be on a larger scale and new bodies of troops were specially recruited in the islands. Everything seemed to be set for a great decisive battle and Greeks and Philhellenes arrived from all parts of Greece to play their part. At last all quarrels between the Greeks and the rivalries between the Europeans seemed to have been set aside. The Moreotes would fight alongside the hated Hydriotes, the regulars with the irregulars.

The Philhellenes were now united as never before. A commission had been set up to control the money arriving from Europe. It represented the philhellenic committees of Paris, Berlin, Dresden, Munich, Geneva, and the other Swiss Cantons. Heideck and his Bavarians co-operated unreservedly with Church. Gordon agreed to command the artillery.

New volunteers arriving from Europe usually preferred to join the land forces. Fabvier's force inside the Acropolis was almost entirely French and Italian, but the regulars outside, although still mainly French and Italian, now also contained Germans, Swedes, Swiss, and others.

The Greek Navy on the other hand now took on a distinctly Anglo-American appearance. Cochrane had brought with him a few dozen British and American naval officers and seamen, some of whom had been with him in South America. Other Americans came in the *Hellas*. Captain

St. George[6] had assumed his patriotic name to ensure that Lieutenant Hutchings could continue to draw his half-pay from the Royal Navy and would not be prosecuted under the Foreign Enlistment Act on his return. Mr. Thompson,[7] who died on the voyage out in the *Karteria*, was really a naval officer called Critchley. Lieutenant Kirkwood was a pseudonym for Downing.[8] These English were good sailors and fearless as everyone recognized, but they seem also to have been brutal and mercenary. Other Philhellenes were aghast at the ease with which they adopted the Greek practice of killing off prisoners, outdoing the Greeks in their atrocities.[9] They gained a reputation for violence and drunkenness.*

In announcing his intention to relieve the siege of the Acropolis, Lord Cochrane tried to put into effect the methods that he had used successfully in the past. Addressing the Greeks through an interpreter, he produced a huge blue and white flag with an owl in the middle which he had bought at Marseilles. A thousand dollars, he promised, would go to the man who raised the flag on the Acropolis, and ten thousand dollars would be divided among the men who would accompany him. Church, on the other hand, behaved as if he was at the head of a European regular army with headquarters and staff. He installed himself in one of the yachts offshore so as to be able to keep in touch with the different elements of his motley army and seemed determined to give most of the orders in writing. Soon the Greeks began to accuse him of being a yacht-General afraid to set his foot on the land.

Towards the end of April 1827 the preparations seemed to be complete and the forces began to land at the bridgeheads. On the 25th Cochrane himself went ashore and saw an engagement in which the Greeks overran some of the Turkish outposts near the coast and killed about sixty men. That day he wrote confidently to the Government, 'Henceforth commences a new era in the system of Modern Greek Warfare', but three days later he was disproved in one particular at least. About 200 Turks and Albanian Moslems had been surrounded and were induced to surrender on terms. As soon as they emerged, however, the Greeks attacked them and one hundred and twenty-nine men were massacred on the spot. Chaos ruled for hours until the leaders restored order by shooting down some of the Greeks, but an

---

* On one occasion at the beginning of 1828 one of the officers of the steamship *Epicheiresis*, Hesketh, was involved in a drunken brawl with a Frenchman on board Cochrane's yacht. He drew a knife and in the mêlée killed a Hydriote sailor by mistake. Lieutenant Kirkwood was promoted to the command but a few months later he too was involved in a disgraceful incident. The British and Americans at Poros were used to meeting three times a week for a heavy drinking session. Kirkwood, returning home very late one night, mistakenly rapped on the door of the house of one of his neighbours thinking he was at his own lodgings. When eventually the Greek answered, Kirkwood still did not realize what had happened, but thinking the man was his servant he began to abuse him for being so slow. A quarrel broke out and Kirkwood drew his sword and killed the man.[10]

advance on Athens was now impossible for the time being. To the more experienced Philhellenes such as Gordon, who watched the massacre through his telescope, the fault lay entirely with Church and Cochrane who refused to listen to any advice from men with experience of Greek conditions. Cochrane himself was deeply shocked and threatened to give up the attempt to relieve the Acropolis, but he was persuaded to give it one more try. Already in his few weeks in Greece he had become cynical and sarcastic, implying strongly in many of his pronouncements that, with a little pluck, the Greeks could have relieved the Acropolis long ago.

The 6 May was set for the next attempt and the operation was planned as almost a repeat performance of Gordon's disastrous expedition in February. The Greek forces, mainly irregulars but with a small contingent of regulars and Philhellenes to act as spearhead, were to land near Phaleron at night and advance directly on Athens from the south. The plan or variants of it had now failed on three occasions and it now failed again. The irregulars using their traditional methods built little redoubts to give themselves cover from which to fire and did not respond to an order from Church to go to the aid of the forward column. The Greek forces were scattered and when the Turkish cavalry appeared they were cut to pieces. 700 dead were left on the battlefield and 240 more were taken prisoner and put to death. Many more would have lost their lives if the Turks had not abandoned themselves to a riotous victory celebration and so allowed numerous survivors to be evacuated.

Cochrane reported tersely to the Government that 'the use of the bayonet would have saved most of those who fell on this occasion and would have rendered unnecessary those redoubts which delay the progress of your arms'. In other words, if the Greeks had not been Greeks but disciplined European troops, then the dispositions which Cochrane and Church made might have been successful. It was an apologia which might have been made by General Normann about the Battle of Peta.

The day after the disaster Cochrane sailed away to Poros. He sent a letter to the naval commanders of the powers to say that all hope of relieving the Acropolis was now lost, and urged them to try to prevent a massacre. This had its effect. On 5 June, after complex negotiations in which the commander of the French naval squadron took part, an agreement was reached whereby the Acropolis should be surrendered to the Turks. The Greeks and Philhellenes of the garrison were escorted to Phaleron and taken in French warships to the Greek camp. They were lucky to escape with their lives. Fabvier still haughtily refused to co-operate with Church and in July he retired again with his men to Methana nursing his resentment against Greeks and English alike.

The names are known of forty-two Philhellenes—nineteen Frenchmen, eight Germans, five Corsicans, three Hungarians, two Spaniards, two Italians, two Swiss, and one Belgian—who lost their lives in or around Athens during the few months leading to the surrender.[11] A few died of disease or were killed by sporadic shooting within the Acropolis and others were killed in the unsuccessful operations of Fabvier, Gordon, and Heideck. The majority were killed on 6 May, the day of the final disaster, when only four survived out of twenty-six Philhellenes who took the field.

Most of the casualties were men who had arrived in the great French philhellenic movement of 1825 and 1826, but there were still two survivors of the German Legion to be numbered among the dead, and one man who had been at Peta. Among the wounded was the brother of the Whitcombe who had taken part in the assassination attempt on Trelawny in the cave in Mount Parnassus in 1825. The British Ambassador in Constantinople later visited the Seraglio to inspect the exposed trophies and especially to identify a head with a fair beard thought to be that of an English Colonel. It had in fact belonged to Colonel Inglesi, an officer of Cephalonian origin.[12]

With the loss of the Acropolis it seemed only a matter of time before the last corner of Free Greece was overrun, although the Turks showed no hurry to mount an offensive. The main hope of the Greeks now lay in the powers although it was doubtful whether their attempts at 'mediation' could now save them. In July the Treaty of London was signed, which committed Britain, Russia, and France to intervene actively if their proposals were not accepted within a limited time, but the Turks were unlikely to yield now when complete success in Greece seemed within their grasp. The Greek leaders eagerly accepted the terms of the armistice proposed in the Treaty but it is impossible to observe an armistice unilaterally. Instead, they decided to try to restart the war in as many parts of Greece as possible. If the powers were successful and it was decided that Greece should become independent, then the question of boundaries would at once arise. Many captains were uncomfortably aware that they could hardly claim to be included in Free Greece if they were actively co-operating with the Turks. Plans were made to try to rekindle the war in Western and Central Greece and to renew the fighting with Ibrahim in the Morea.

Lord Cochrane meanwhile attempted to keep the war going at sea, but it was no easy task to take on two modern navies, one of which was under the direction of French naval officers. Cochrane realized that his only effective weapon was his reputation and he tried desperately to find some spectacular imaginative stroke that would transform the war such as he had accomplished in South America. In June he suddenly set off with the *Hellas* and the *Karteria* to the north-west corner of the Morea, an area of no apparent strategic importance at that moment in the war. Cochrane had heard that the Turkish Pasha was in the area in a small ship and he hoped by a lightning raid to capture him alive and negotiate the freedom of Greece in exchange for his release. The Pasha was not captured although it was a near-run thing. His harem was captured, but harems, although useful, are of little value for political bargaining.

Cochrane next made a sudden dash across the Mediterranean and on 16 June appeared off Alexandria itself, the great new naval port of Egypt in which Mehemet's fleet lay at anchor. 'One decisive blow', he announced, 'and Greece is free', and so with luck it might have been. But the fire ships which were sent into the harbour burned out before they reached their target, and the Greeks refused to obey Cochrane's order to attack. Instead of striking a decisive blow Cochrane was forced to retire, pursued by the Egyptian fleet. It was clear, however, from the way that Mehemet's sailors conducted the pursuit that they were prudently ensuring that they would not catch up or come within range. Again Cochrane's reputation was his defence. On their way back to Alexandria the Egyptian ships encountered the *Karteria* whose engines had, as usual, broken down but they gave her a wide berth. Again it was only reputation which prevented her from being sunk or captured. Cochrane, on his return to Greece, continued the psychological warfare by sending another rude letter to Mehemet Ali telling him that he would be back.

Then suddenly, in one day, Greece's survival was assured. On 20 October 1827 the combined squadrons of Britain, France and Russia carelessly destroyed the combined Turkish and Egyptian fleets in the bay of Navarino. For four hours until darkness fell the guns roared in the last great battle of the sailing ship era. When dawn broke next morning only twenty-nine out of the Turkish-Egyptian fleet of eighty-nine vessels were still afloat and they were badly damaged. About eight thousand men had been killed or drowned. On the allied side some ships had suffered damage but none was sunk. One hundred and seventy-six men had been lost.

The Battle of Navarino, despite all later attempts to glamorize and justify it, was the result of muddle. The allied powers who had signed the Treaty of London in July, which committed them if necessary to physical intervention, did not expect that force would be necessary and discussions were started with Mehemet Ali to try to persuade him to withdraw his forces from Greece. The naval commanders of the allies, however, were expected to enforce a policy on which they had only been given the most general instructions. They were to be neutral and yet to prevent the Greeks and their enemies from fighting—a virtually impossible mandate. Admiral Codrington, the British naval commander who acted as Commander-in-Chief of the allied squadrons, frankly favoured the Greeks and maintained a benevolent liaison with Cochrane, Hastings, and Church, which went far beyond the dictates of neutrality. He permitted and even encouraged them to continue and extend the war, although this was forbidden by the

Treaty. With Ibrahim, on the other hand, he was more strict and he instituted a blockade of the Turkish and Egyptian fleets in the bay of Navarino.

Crisis management was not then studied in the Royal Navy, and the word escalation was probably unknown to Admiral Codrington. Nelson's captains were not accustomed to defusing complex situations or to peace-keeping operations. Yet when all allowances are made, the affair was handled with astonishing lack of regard for the consequences.

On 20 October the allied fleets entered the bay, not with any direct hostile intent but to ensure that they could, if necessary, prevent the Turkish and Egyptian fleets from leaving. A rumour had been heard on the allied side that the Turks might sail to attack Hydra and, on the Turkish side, that their forces in the Northern Morea were being hard pressed by Cochrane and Church. It seemed certain that the Turkish fleet would try to leave Navarino and suspicion on both sides was intense. As the allied fleets entered the bay, a boat was sent to investigate the Turkish fire ships which were apparently being prepared for use. This boat was fired on with musket fire. Another larger boat was therefore sent to lend assistance but it too was fired upon. At this point two of the allied ships began to provide musket fire to cover the boats but this caused one of the Egyptian ships to fire its guns. Thereafter, as they say in the navy, the action became general. In other words every man in the five fleets struggled to kill or to avoid being killed without any further regard to the rights and wrongs of the situation.

The Philhellenes of Europe greeted the news of Navarino with rapture. At last the great powers of Europe had done what they had been urged to do since 1821, to join in the war for liberty, religion etc., and attack the enemies of Greece; but it is no light matter to destroy the fleet of a friendly power without any very clear reason. The Russians alone were delighted as the battle gave them an excuse long wanted to declare war on Turkey and prepare to invade the Balkans. The French were at first embarrassed before deciding to ride on the tide of congratulation and adopt an openly pro-Greek policy.* The British Government had the courage to admit embarrassment, but did so without grace. Admiral Codrington was relieved of his command but not avowedly for his action at Navarino, and in a speech from the throne the battle was officially mildly regretted as 'an untoward event'.

It took many years of patient diplomacy to rebuild the international order in the East. In Greece itself, however, the significance of the battle was

* The leader of the French naval mission to Mehemet Ali, Letellier, was present at the battle. The other officers were prudently taken off by the French Admiral when the crisis first developed so as to relieve them of the prospect of having to fire on French ships. Letellier also would have been taken off if there had been time.

recognized at once. It was now impossible for the Turks to win the war. Without a fleet to reinforce their troops and to attack the Greek island bases, Greece could not be reconquered. A corner of the mainland and a few of the islands were in the hands of a band of self-seeking quarrelling leaders but it was enough. Greece was free.

During the winter of 1826 a new danger had begun to threaten the fragile existence of Greece. For those that had eyes to see, Greece's worst enemy was not now the Turks or the Arabs but starvation. The country was in the grip of famine. Hundreds of people had already died and thousands more were quickly sinking into hopelessness.

For six years the country had been at war and in many areas cultivation had long since ceased. In Roumeli the inhabitants, back under Turkish government, returned to the land, but in Free Greece the situation was desperate. The Morea had been fought over by the rival chieftains in civil wars and a final devastation had been added by Ibrahim. Most of the towns were in ruins and their inhabitants had fled. In the islands, cultivation had continued without interruption but the islands were crammed with refugees. In Greece there lay scattered the broken human flotsam and jetsam of the ghastly tidal wave of the Revolution, refugees from Kydonies destroyed in 1821, from Chios destroyed in 1822, from Crete and Psara in 1824, from Ibrahim's devastations of the Morea in 1825 and 1826, from the destruction of Missolonghi in 1826, from Athens, Euboea, Thessaly, Salonika, Constantinople, Smyrna, Cyprus, Egypt, from every part of the Eastern Mediterranean area where Greeks and Turks had once lived together.

The fighting and devastation of 1826 exhausted Greece's last reserves of food and money. The Greeks were now wholly dependent on the charity of other nations to bridge the gap between starvation and survival. The crisis continued until the harvest of 1828.

In 1826 and 1827 the Swiss banker Eynard and the Paris Greek Committee between them sent seventeen shiploads of provisions to Greece, and Eynard employed an agent, Petrini, to arrange for the forwarding of the cargoes from Zante to Nauplia. The citizens of the Swiss cities and cantons had been the first to establish philhellenic societies in 1821 and they were still making their regular contributions at the end. Alone of all the Greek societies of Europe and America they continued in active existence throughout the war, seeing the leadership of the movement assumed first by the Germans, then by the British, and finally by the French, co-operating with them fully but continuing their own work even when the spurts of enthusiasm elsewhere had died away. The Swiss were the first to recognize that the most useful service that philhellenism could perform in 1826 was to send supplies to relieve suffering, and gradually an increasing proportion of their funds was devoted to this purpose. In later years Eynard also gave relief to distressed Philhellenes on their return to Europe, whether deserving or not. It was a remarkable achievement and contributed to the establishment of Switzerland's magnificent reputation of being the Good Samaritan of Europe.[1]

Eynard commuted ceaselessly between Geneva and Paris, keeping the ashes of philhellenic enthusiasm alight even after Navarino when most Europeans assumed that there was no need for further effort. In Greece the arrangements were made by a commission consisting of Doctor Gosse, a Swiss, Colonel Heideck, and a mysterious German calling himself Körring.[2] This man had astonishing organizing ability and obviously had occupied some position of great responsibility in his home country. It was never discovered who he was, but it was known that he had adopted a pseudonym because of some unknown incident at home.

According to Finlay,[3] whose exaggerations were always on target and delivered with the bitter relish of personal experience, the efforts of Eynard and his friends rendered more real service to the cause of Greece than the whole proceeds of the English loans. The supplies sent by Eynard were, however, almost entirely devoted to sustaining the Greek war effort. It was Greek soldiers who received the provisions not because their need was greatest but because their plight imposed itself on the attention. The starving and the destitute are too feeble to demonstrate and the worst misery was hidden from sight. In the caves in the mountains were thousands of homeless families, widows and orphans, huddling together for warmth and subsisting on tortoises, snails, herbs, grass, and anything green or living that they could grub up.

It was to bring relief to these people that the last great operations of philhellenism were mounted. That curious and marvellously deep-rooted complex of ideas about Modern Greece had generated many schemes since the first distorted news of the Revolution arrived in 1821, most of which had ended in disaster. The relief efforts of 1827 and 1828, however, make a fitting end to the tale. For the first and last time the vast reserves of enthusiasm, sacrifice, and good will which the name of Greece aroused throughout Western Christendom were mobilized in a manner which was wholly and intrinsically good, and the measures were carried through with intelligence and efficiency. At last the slogans of philhellenism were put into practice and it was found that the slogans were not needed. The credit for this result belongs exclusively to the people of the United States and in particular to three remarkable American Philhellenes. They each deserve a few words of introduction.

George Jarvis[4] was the son of the American consular agent in Hamburg, and was born and educated in Germany. Although he could speak English, German, and French with apparently equal facility, he was not the master of any of them. His education had been so mixed that he appeared to be only half educated, and it was perhaps because of a sense of being *dépaysé* that Jarvis, who never set foot in the United States, was so defiantly proud of being an American. Like so many Germans, Jarvis had set out from Hamburg in 1822 to make the long journey on foot to Marseilles. His father tried to dissuade him but consoled himself with the thought, which he reported to the Government in Washington, that his son would be well qualified to be the first United States official emissary in Greece. Heise, the friend in whose company Jarvis began his journey, was killed at Peta, but at Marseilles Jarvis met Frank Abney Hastings and they went together to Greece. Like Hastings, Jarvis volunteered to fight at sea and so he too escaped the brunt of the terrible disappointments which overcame most of the 1822 generation of volunteers. After a few months in Greece Jarvis virtually abandoned his European ideas. He learnt Greek, assumed Albanian dress, and taught himself to despise lice, filth, and discomfort, and became a rough, tough, minor Greek captain leading a band of a few dozen armed men. Probably less than ten Philhellenes* made a success of this role during the whole course of the war.

Jonathan Peckham Miller was said to have been an 'unruly dissipated youth'.[5] He was a non-commissioned officer in the United States army when he suddenly underwent a form of religious conversion. Immediately his whole way of life changed, he left the army, and he saved up to go to the University of Vermont. He was at Vermont in May 1824 studying the Greek classics when the college buildings caught fire and all his books and possessions were destroyed. It was just at this moment, as the news of Lord Byron's death came through, that philhellenic enthusiasm reached its peak in the United States. Miller presented himself as a volunteer to the Boston Greek Committee and in November 1824 arrived at Missolonghi with 300 dollars and a letter of introduction. Jarvis took an interest in him, welcoming him as the first Philhellene from the New World and Miller soon learnt the language under Jarvis's tutoring. He took part in the

* Notably the Marquis de la Villasse, a Frenchman, and the Poles Dombrovsky and Dzierzavsky, but they were exiles with no other home to go to.

fighting outside Nauplia when Ibrahim's army appeared there in June 1825, and he established a reputation as the 'Yankee Dare-devil'.

Samuel Gridley Howe[6] came from a proud and old-established Boston family. He studied medicine and surgery and graduated fully-qualified from Harvard in 1824. Like Miller, Howe found himself at a turning point in his life in 1824 at the precise moment when philhellenism was at its height in the United States and he determined to go to Greece as a volunteer. To his doubting father Howe explained patiently that the experience would assist him in his medical career, that he would learn French and Italian, and that he would have more varied opportunities of practising and improving his surgical skill in war-stricken Greece than in the genteel suburbs of Boston. But Howe's protestations that he was acting from rational motives or economic self-interest fail to convince. As his father no doubt knew, Howe was essentially romantic. The moment of his departure from university coincided with a personal crisis. At the time Howe was 'ardently attached to a lovely young woman who returned his affection, but from whom circumstances had permanently separated him'. But it was probably Lord Byron, the news of whose death had recently arrived, who led Howe to Greece. He was intoxicated by Byron's poetry, he admired and envied the freedom and spaciousness of his life and his active commitment to great and good political causes. If the harsh conventions of self-satisfied, small-minded Boston prevented him from making an unsuitable match, he would go to the lands of Lara and Conrad, Haidee and Zuleika, where such matters could be seen in their proper perspective.

Howe arrived in Greece early in 1825 and was given a commission as an army surgeon and for the next two years was sometimes soldier sometimes doctor, taking part in several battles. When Hastings arrived with the *Karteria* he joined the crew as ship's doctor. He became one of the most admired and best-liked Philhellenes in Greece.

The American Committees followed with close interest the adventures of the volunteers whom they had sent to Greece, and it seems to have been part of their conditions of service that they should supply regular reports on their activities. Apart from Miller and Howe, the men chosen by the Committees mostly fell into disrepute for one reason or another or rushed back as soon as they set foot in Greece, but a steady stream of informative and interesting letters from Jarvis, Miller, and Howe were widely published throughout the United States.

Towards the end of 1826 they began to report on the poverty of the country. At the same time letters arrived in America from some of the Greek leaders, including Colocotrones, asking for help. Miller himself decided to return to America for a while to give first-hand evidence of the state of the country. The three Philhellenes found themselves launching an appeal for American help.

Many Americans were ashamed at the scandal of the frigates. They felt that the Greeks had been cheated and that something should be done to restore the good name of the United States. Others recalled the situation of their own country at the desperate moments of the war against the British. On the whole, however, the great revival of philhellenic feeling which began at the end of 1826 was a spontaneous outburst of pity and generosity.[7] Edward Everett, who had led the initial movement in 1821, began work again in Boston. Matthew Carey, one of the instigators of the revival in 1823 and 1824, resumed in Philadelphia.

In January 1827 a huge meeting was held at the City Hall in New York and a new committee was elected. It immediately issued a fresh appeal which was to be taken up throughout the United States. This appeal struck a new note. Neither Epaminondas nor St. Paul were mentioned. There was no call to fight a new crusade or to send arms or volunteers. The appeal simply declared that the Greeks had been fighting a long and bitter war and were now reduced to beggary. Could their appeal to their 'Christian brethren of this republic' be refused by men who 'abound in all the necessaries and comforts of social existence'? The Committee declared that if anyone made a contribution of provisions, clothing, or money, they would 'pledge themselves to use their best exertions to appropriate it, without diminution or abatement, to the sole object of feeding and clothing the necessitous inhabitants of Greece'.

In 1824 and 1825, when contributions had been sent to the Greek deputies in London through Richard Rush, the United States Minister, the Committees had queried whether they should not instead send arms or men. The deputies had been obliged to write letters explaining that, in the view of the Greek Government, it was best simply to have the money as money, and the Americans had accepted this advice. By 1826 the Committees knew that their earlier contributions had been largely wasted. They had read the accounts in the newspapers and reviews of embezzlement and incompetence in London, and had noted the remarks in books by travellers from Greece which reported how the warlords had seized the loan money for their own purposes. Requests by the American Committees to the Greek deputies for accounts to be rendered were met with a bland statement that this was impossible—as indeed it was.[8]

These humiliations were accepted, but the Americans were not going to be fooled again. If they were to make further contributions to Greece they determined to supervise the whole operation, to send exclusively food and clothing, not money or anything which would be of any direct military value, and to keep hold of the stores until they could be given directly into the hands (and even mouths) of the people who most needed them. Not only would they send nothing military, they decided, but they would even forbid the stores to be used by Greek soldiers. Only non-combatants would be permitted to have a share. It was to be work of pure charity, non-political and neutral, performed entirely for humanitarian reasons.

The appeal of this new type of philhellenism had a success which over-whelmed everything that had gone before.[10] All over the United States new committees sprang up to arrange fund-raising activities,* or to collect food and clothing. A small community would contribute a few bags of flour, a village might buy a barrel of salted pork. Shopkeepers would give some of their merchandise, boxes of shoes, lengths of cloth. The ladies of Westerfield prepared 300 suits of clothes; those of Pearl Street, New York, made 733 pieces of women's clothing; those of Norwich, Connec-ticut, made 1,000 suits. At Baltimore 600 barrels of flour were donated. Charleston sent 350 barrels of meat, 9 barrels of wheat, some clothing, and a small sum in cash. Long lists of subscriptions were published of contributions by individuals, committees, and organizations all over the country. As a result the Committees of New York, Boston and Phila-delphia acting as the leaders, were able to send to Greece during 1827 and 1828 eight shiploads of relief supplies valued at nearly $140,000 and consist-ing entirely of food and clothing. Each of the ships had an agent to ensure that the stores were distributed properly to those for whom they were intended. Jarvis, Miller, and Howe resigned from military service to devote themselves exclusively to the work of charity.

The letter of instruction from the Committees of America to their agents included the following passage:

> As it is not the object of the Executive Committee to take any part in the con-troversy between the Greeks and the Turks, these provisions and clothing are not designed to supply the garrisons of the former but are intended for the relief of the women, children, and old men, non-combatants of Greece.

The Cause of Greece, the Cause of Liberty, Religion and Humanity, the recalled debt to Ancient Hellas, the new Crusade, the Sacred Struggle of the Christians against the Infidels—the Greek Revolution had now become, for its last and most generous friends abroad, simply 'the contro-versy between the Greeks and the Turks'.

To ensure that the supplies only went to those for whom they were intended was a difficult and even dangerous task in the anarchic conditions of Greece. Yet the Americans were remarkably successful largely owing to the efforts and experience of Jarvis, Miller and Howe.

The first relief ship, the *Tontine* arrived in May 1827. The agent, Joseph

* Attempts were made to persuade the Congress to vote public money for the relief operations, but the proposals were turned down to avoid the charge of a breach of neutrality. In fact the United States Government was still pursuing an ambiguous policy, apparently favouring the Greeks but trying to secure the commercial treaty with Turkey. After Navarino the Americans pressed the Turks to make a contract with them to rebuild the fleet and Americans took over the direction of the dockyard at Constantinople.[9]

Worrell, knowing no better, handed over the cargo to the Greek Government at Poros on receiving promises that they would distribute it according to the instructions of the Committee. The Government immediately sold it to raise money for their own puropses, and according to Howe accepted $2,500 for flour which had cost $12,000 in Philadelphia.

The second ship, the *Chancellor*, went not to Poros but to Nauplia where the two rival captains, one in possession of the castle, the other of the town were still conducting a sporadic war. This time Howe took personal charge of the distribution. A French relief vessel had recently put in to Nauplia, but all the provisions were seized by the soldiers and several people were killed in rioting during the distribution. Howe deliberately handed over a third of the cargo to the soldiers in the hope of saving the rest for the really poor and he had some success. If anyone unacquainted with Greece had attempted a distribution, he wrote 'he would probably have lost his own life, would have lost all the property and would have involved the town in a scene of blood and desolation'. Only a man such as Howe who had built up a reputation in advance could have dared to defy the captains and their armed bullies. When he began distributing the remainder of the cargo outside, he received an order from Colocotrones to stop. ' "By what authority." said I. "By the authority of Colocotrones." "I know nothing of Colocotrones, I shall obey none of his orders." '

As each ship arrived, the leaders of the various Greek factions tumbled over themselves in attempting to wrest the supplies from the inexperienced American agents with Jarvis, Howe, and Miller desperately trying to save as much as they could for the poor. The supplies were locked up under armed guard in the castle in Nauplia bay to prevent looting, but still they were not secure. On one occasion the keys were seized by force by one of the captains, until an American warship was summoned and they were restored. On another occasion a small vessel which was carrying a consignment of stores to the outlying areas was forced to seek shelter in Nauplia harbour in a storm and was ruthlessly plundered. When the *Jane* arrived from America in November, despite repeated warnings from Howe and Miller, the new agent 'was weak enough to allow himself to be flattered out of five hundred barrels of flour which the persons in authority promised to deliver to the poor'. Only eighty barrels were distributed, the remainder and seventeen boxes of clothes were sold to raise money.

The three Philhellenes and the new agents journeyed all over Greece seeking out human beings hiding in caves and holes in the ground, almost naked, diseased, and starving. In the towns they were mobbed by thousands of beggars and every distribution was a potential crisis. To try to maintain order and fairness, tickets were distributed, each one of which entitled the recipient to a portion of food and sometimes a piece of clothing. In some areas the priests were entrusted with the duty of distributing the tickets, but it was found that they were favouring their friends and Howe had to make new distributions of tickets.

They were besieged by letters from all over Greece begging for help or recommending needy cases to the Americans. The terms of the charity were strictly observed. Fabvier begged a few clothes to relieve the misery of some of the Philhellenes who had been made destitute by their time under siege in the Acropolis, but he was reminded of the rule that only non-combatants were eligible. Miller did, however, make an exception for one old Pole whom he had known since he arrived in 1824 and who was now in misery.

An extract from Howe's journal describes how the American agents spent a typical day:

Monday, July 30th, Lerna. Started at daylight on horseback and rode over the plain south four miles to Chevadi, a little ruined village with a mill, where we found thirty-seven families in great misery and gave them orders for flour. Then rode on to the west, finding here five, ten, and fifteen miserable families, refugees from their native villages, and living under the projections of rocks, or in caves or little huts made by sticking up poles, slanting, and thatching them with branches of trees. Most of these were not only hungry but half-naked, and I gave them large orders, even to an hundredweight, with the greatest delight. Hearing that up in the mountains were hidden many others, we began the ascent, and after a tedious climbing of two hours we came to a little plain where we found about six hundred persons, but not a single house, only the aforesaid huts, if they even merit that name. Here was a sight! Six hundred persons, mostly widows and orphans, driven from their homes, hunted into the mountains like wild beasts, and living upon the herbs, grass, and what they could pick up about the rocks. Many women came to me haggard and wan, their skin blistered by the sun, their feet torn by the rocks, and their limbs half exposed to view from the raggedness of their clothes, and they swore upon their faith that for many weeks they had not tasted bread. Here I gave them orders for about ten hundredweight of flour, and each one, seizing the billet, ran toward the road to the sea, blessing God that he had created men like the Americans to succour them in their distress. Repaid thus for my toil by the pleasure of relieving such wants, I jogged on to find more misery, and, after giving many orders upon the road, returned at night to the ship.

The Americans described the Modern Greeks as they found them, with sympathy but without sentimentality. Gone are the presuppositions of earlier philhellenic ventures. The captains in Nauplia, whom in earlier days Howe might have fashionably described as the 'true Greeks', are now 'two brigand chiefs (God's curse light on both of them)'. At last foreigners were looking at the Modern Greeks unhampered by the accumulated weight of centuries of misleading allusion.

Tens of thousands of Greeks owed their survival through the terrible year 1827 to a few pounds of flour donated by the citizens of some small far-off American town and brought to them by the three Americans who had fought in their war, learned their language, assumed their style of dress, and had now taken the side of the poor against the great men of Greece. The scenes of abject gratitude which they witnessed brought tears to their eyes. Years later, travellers in Greece would find old Greeks still speaking with wonder of the generosity of the Americans of 1827.

Some of the miseries of war cannot be cured by charity. Everywhere the Americans were confronted with examples of the studied cruelty and the arbitrary disregard of fellow humans which marked the East. Some of the beggars had lost their ears or their hands, and one man came to the distribution point on his knees, having had both feet cut off. At Poros, Miller met an eleven-year-old girl whose nose and lips had been cut off close to her face so that her gums and jaws were entirely exposed. The poor creature had lived in this state for over a year. In Laconia, Howe found a boy of about twelve leading his blind mother. She had been raped and then her eyes put out by her attackers. Her son was gathering herbs and grass and snails for her to eat.

When the empty relief ships sailed back to the United States, they usually carried a few orphan boys and girls to be adopted and given a chance of a new life. The Governor of Massachusetts set an example by accepting an orphan in his household. Both Howe and Miller adopted Greek boys into their own families. Miller described in matter-of-fact terms how he came to adopt his boy at Poros:

While walking the streets I observed a boy and girl hand in hand almost naked. The girl appeared about nine and the boy about seven years of age. On inquiry I found that they were orphans, and that their father had been driven from Haivale (a town in Asia Minor)* and had nobly fallen in battle. This boy I have taken as my own with the consent of the Government, and by the blessing of God who early taught me to feel the loss of a father, I am determined that in me he shall find a friend and protector. The little girl when she found her brother was preferred, wept most bitterly but what can I do?

Loukas Miltiades Miller was educated in the United States, entered the American Army and reached the rank of Colonel. He was eventually elected Congressman for the State of Wisconsin in 1853. The fate of his unfortunate sister is unknown.

By the end of 1827 Howe decided that the problem was of far greater dimensions than he had thought and that distributing relief supplies to indigent Greeks was not enough. He determined to attempt a more ambitious programme. In a letter to the Boston Greek Committee he reported that he had departed from the strict instructions of the Committee and had used part of the cargo of one of the relief ships to establish a free hospital at Poros. If the Committee knew the actual conditions of Greece's sufferings, he said, they would have done the same.

* Kydonies or Aivalik, a Greek town destroyed in 1821.

Many a poor object have we seen lying upon the bare ground by the roadside or under a tree, parched with fever, whom all the flour in America could neither solace nor save—many a poor soldier whose long undressed wound, full of little maggots, was hurrying him to an untimely grave from which a little care and cleanliness might have spared him.

With the aid of a few Philhellene doctors from Europe Howe established a hospital in a large building in Poros. There were fifty beds at first and the number was gradually increased to about two hundred. Aid was given free to anyone who needed it, whether combatant or civilian.

At the beginning of 1828 Howe decided to return to the United States for a few months to raise more funds and to canvas support for new ideas he was developing. To his horror he discovered that enthusiasm was flagging and he threw himself into the work of reviving it. The energy he displayed was amazing. He wrote dozens of letters to philhellenic organizations and prominent men all over the country urging them to help. These letters are full of vivid sketches drawn from his own experience, so different from the usual clichés of the pamphleteers. To the New York Committee he described how the wounded in Greece envied the dead:

Sometimes a number of them, saved from the field, are removed to some neighbouring village. In a few days there is an alarm of the enemy's approach; every soul flies. The wounded rush out, pale and emaciated, and attempt to fly with the crowd, but soon sink down from weakness, struggle on again as they see the enemy gaining on them, but are soon overtaken and their heads dangling at the cavalry's saddle-bows.

To the Philhellenes of Boston, Howe described the results of their earlier charity:

Greece expects it of you; she has tasted your bounty and expects a continuance of it, and I will venture to say that of those encamped on her sea shore, thousands of women and children are watching every sail that comes from the west, and flattering themselves with the hope that it may be an American ship with provisions for them.

Howe hastily composed a *Historical Sketch of the Greek Revolution* and it was rushed through the press to help his campaign. It was a more substantial work than its title suggests. He also set out on a long lecture tour to raise funds. From Albany in April 1828 he wrote to his father:

I wrote to you from West Point where I was most politely received by Colonel Thayer and all the officers; after delivering an address there, I went to Newburg, from N. to Poughkeepsie, from P. to Hudson, from H. to Kinderhook at all which places I had large and respectable audiences, and have reason to hope that my statements will be the means of rousing the feelings of the people, and getting extensive contributions for the suffering Greeks.

Y

Howe hated lecturing because it was fatiguing and embarrassing and also, in his own eyes, not an occupation for gentlemen. His father disapproved strongly but Howe persisted, considering it 'a sacred duty to go on'. He would prefer to serve Greece in any other way, he declared, but he honestly recognized that the encouragement of contributions for relief was the most effective service he could perform.

At the end of 1828 he returned to Greece on board one of the relief ships. The country had changed in the year that he had been away. Capodistria had arrived at the beginning of the year and gradually more orderly government was being established. The hospital at Poros which Howe had established had closed—it had been left in the charge of an American relief agent, Dr. Russ, who had left promptly on the day that his year's contract expired.* George Jarvis had died in August at Argos at the age of thirty-one, succumbing at last to the terrible diseases of Greece. Miller had returned to the United States at the beginning of 1828.

At first sight Howe thought that the crisis of the famine had passed but, as before, he found that the poor were merely concealed from sight. The work of distribution was accordingly continued. He decided, however, that the main effort should now be devoted to a new, more constuctive, form of relief, the provision of employment. The Greek Government was at this time established at Aegina and Capodistria had given work to hundreds of families by building an orphanage on the island. Although most of them had by now returned to their native villages to resume cultivation of the land, Aegina was still crowded with refugees from the areas which were still in Turkish hands, Athens, Roumeli, Crete, Chios, and elsewhere. Without charity, Howe saw, thousands would still die of starvation. Accordingly, he devised an ambitious scheme to provide employment for the refugees of Aegina. He described his idea in his journal:

After revolving in my mind various plans of relief to these suffering beings, I have resolved to commence a work upon which I can employ four or five hundred persons, give them their bread, and at the same time benefit the public; viz. the repairing of the port here which, from the destruction of the piers and the accumulation of mud and filth, is reduced to a state near resembling a marsh upon its border, preventing the boats from approaching near the shore and giving out an unpleasant and unwholesome odour. To remedy this and render the port at once commodious, salubrious, and beautiful, requires only that a solid wall should be built around the border of the port a little way within the water, and

* During his year in charge of the hospital at Poros, Russ attended nine hundred patients. He loyally fulfilled his undertaking, hating apparently every minute. Describing his impulsive offer to take over the hospital from Howe, he wrote:

Unacquainted with the Greek language, amidst a nation of robbers, and sharpers, and without a friend to aid or assist me, it was an act approaching madness. I not only perform all operations, prepare all medicines, and make all purchases—but the halls would not be cleaned, the beds shifted, or the comfort of the patients attended to unless I ordered it. The patients are mostly thieves. The women are the most immodest, and the men are the greatest poltroons that ever disgraced civilized society.

then filled up behind with stones and earth; after that is done the mud should be dredged from the port within the wall and the whole filling be covered with stones. In this way a fine wharf will be formed along the whole border of the port; boats can approach and unload at it; all the dirt will be removed, and the port rendered excellent.

It is impossible to think of a scheme which could have more precisely suited the needs of the situation. Howe's idea was bold, imaginative, and practical. The project would require large numbers of labourers. Men and women, boys and girls could all lend a hand, if only in carrying baskets of earth and stones. The most brilliant feature of the plan was that virtually no skilled labour was necessary at all. The skilled work of providing shaped stone blocks with which to build the walls had already been done two thousand years before.

Outside the town of Aegina on a promontory by the sea stands a solitary Doric column of an ancient temple, one of the most romantic spots in Greece and still an inspiration to poets. In 1828 the column was surrounded by the ruins of the temple. Howe determined to use the stones from the old temple to build the new mole in the harbour. For once the Ancient Greeks could be of direct help to the Modern Greeks, their putative posterity, over whose lives they exercised such a disturbing and persistent influence.

Work began on 19 December 1828. Howe engaged one hundred men and two hundred women to be paid three pounds of Indian meal per man per day, two and a half pounds for a woman. They were divided into companies of twenty and leaders appointed. Howe instructed them, before they began to make the sign of the cross and bow several times and declare aloud: 'Here's to a good beginning, and may the evening be happy; success to the Americans.' With this little ceremony the pickaxes were struck into the ruins to prise out the ancient blocks. Howe gave orders that the Doric column should not be touched, but modern archaeologists, an unromantic breed, still regret the ruination of the site.

The day after work began two hundred Greeks arrived at Aegina from Egypt, redeemed from slavery by the French Government. Howe looked on as the authorities attempted the heart-breaking task of compiling a list of the names and villages of the new arrivals. There were numerous children who had been torn from their parents or who had seen them die in Egypt. Some could faintly recall the name of a town where they thought they came from, and perhaps the first name of their father but nothing more. Others could no longer speak their native language. Some had their ankles sore from chains or were mutilated. Most were suffering from the terrible eye diseases of Egypt and some were permanently blind.

Every day Howe was surrounded by crowds of Greeks begging for work, and in many cases he could not refuse. Within a week of the start of the work, he was providing work for over six hundred persons and the number continually increased. Every detail of the work was personally supervised. He rose between three and four o'clock and spent the hours till daylight writing letters or examining the vouchers for the poor; at daybreak the workmen were mustered and Howe spent the rest of the day at the port; dinner was at six o'clock, and bed at ten. The work proceeded steadily, interrupted by storms and saints' days, and Howe's house was still surrounded by crowds encamped outside begging for work.

By March 1829 the work was nearing completion and he began to lay off his workers. They begged him to continue but he was firm. As the warm weather set in the need for his charity was less pressing. On 24 March he dismissed the majority of his labour force with a special payment and a donation of clothes. As he surveyed his work, Howe noted with satisfaction in his diary, 'I have enriched the island of Aegina by a beautiful, commodious, and permanent quay, and given support to seven hundred poor during nearly four months of the most rigorous weather of the year.' The American Mole can still be seen, one of the few surviving monuments to the philhellenism of the Greek War of Independence.

Howe was already thinking of new schemes and the inhabitants of Megara put another idea into his mind. Their corner of Greece had suffered terribly by the devastations of Turks and Greeks and they were so poor that they did not even have seed to sow. Howe intended to distribute flour but the Megarians represented that they would prefer to have seed. Howe sold some of his supplies to buy a small quantity, but he made it a condition of giving it that every recipient would sign an undertaking to contribute to the costs of a Lancastrian school in their village. The seed was distributed; the Megarians immediately sowed it, and in a few days it began to shoot. Howe calculated that, for the expenditure of less than $100 on bean seed, he had provided work for four hundred families, and produced $4,000 worth of beans, including $1,300 for the support of a school. Unfortunately, the experiment was only a limited success. The Greek soldiers of the Government helped themselves to the young shoots for salad and parties of marauding Turks came down from the north and carried off several families. Howe implored Capodistria to do something but he knew that the Government was powerless.

Howe now proposed to the Greek Government an experiment in establishing a refugee colony on some of the lands taken from the Turks, but Capodistria was suspicious and there were ugly rumours about Howe's motives in wishing to set himself up as a landlord. Howe had given up in despair and was about to go on a well-earned holiday when word arrived that approval had been given. He immediately cancelled his holiday and began work. He had selected a site on the isthmus at the village of Hexamilia and the Government agreed to lease 2,000 acres, tax-free for five years. In March 1829 twenty-six destitute families, refugees from Athens,

Chios, and Kydonies arrived to found the colony. Two hundred other people were employed as day labourers to help with the building of a new village. Soon the settlement was thriving. Howe obtained agricultural implements from the United States and succeeded in constructing himself a crude wheelbarrow, 'to the great amusement and astonishment of the people who had never seen such a complicated machine'. A Lancastrian school was established under the direction of one of the Greeks who had been sent to the school in London by Colonel Stanhope. Howe planned to rebuild the harbour and construct a new mole.

Near the new village could be seen traces of the work begun by the ancients to dig a canal across the Isthmus of Corinth, 'at the spot where they left off work as though but yesterday'. Howe seems to have considered the possibility of digging the canal himself, but he realized that, with his limited resources, he was unlikely to succeed where the ancients had failed. He did, however, have a vision that one day a great new commercial city would arise on the isthmus and that the settlement which he had founded would be the centre. With an eye on the Bostonians who were providing the funds, he decided to name his new town Washingtonia.

Howe's efforts at Hexamilia nearly cost him his life. No Philhellene could expect to live in Greece for more than three years without falling victim to the constant epidemics. He was taken ill with malaria and was to suffer from it intermittently for the rest of his life. Although his colony continued to thrive—it was an overwhelming success by philhellenic standards—Howe was disappointed, most of his friends had left Greece, and he seemed to be involved in growing friction with the Government. At the end of 1829 he left Greece to return to the United States, conscious that he had done more than any man to help Greece in her years of distress. He took with him one of the helmets which Lord Byron had taken to Missolonghi which had been put up for sale at Poros.

On his return to the United States at the age of thirty, Howe had already accomplished more than most men do in a lifetime. His connection with Lafayette in the July Revolution of 1830, his work for the Poles, his imprisonment in Berlin, his campaigns against slavery in the United States cannot be described here. For most of his life Howe devoted himself to the care of the blind and the deaf, and was the first to devise a means of education and communication for those who had previously been regarded as unapproachable lunatics. His achievement was described by Dickens in *American Notes*. During his long career as one of the greatest of American philanthropists Howe never lost his interest in Greece and he revisited his colony in 1834. In 1867 at the age of seventy, when Crete was again in desperate revolt against the Turks, Howe and his famous wife Julia Ward Howe, authoress of 'The Battle Hymn of the Republic', returned to Greece to extend again the charity of America to the suffering victims.

31. *Later*

Not until five years after the battle of Navarino was the independence of Greece formally recognized and the international situation regularized. The three allied powers, after failing to negotiate terms with the more suitable candidates such as Leopold of Saxe Coburg,* installed a son of King Ludwig of Bavaria, as Otho King of Greece. For the first years of its independence Greece was virtually a Bavarian colony.

In the years between Navarino and Otho's accession the centre of the action moved from Greece to London, Paris, St. Petersburg, and Constantinople, as the powers bargained with one another and coaxed the Turks towards a settlement.

For years the Ottoman Government would not recognize the inevitable, that Greece was free, and that nationalism had arrived among the peoples of the East. They stubbornly insisted on some settlement which would preserve the phantom of Ottoman sovereignty even when all power was lost. But without a fleet, active operations against the Greeks were impossible and, in any case, they were again involved in a desperate war with their old enemies the Russians. In 1828 the French Government persuaded the allies to permit a French expeditionary force to be sent to the Morea to arrange for the evacuation of the Turkish and Egyptian forces. The French, whose appetite for military glory had not been nauseated by Waterloo, were disappointed when in most places the Egyptians and Turks consented to depart without the need for compulsion.

At the insistence of the allies the French forces were not permitted to operate outside the Morea, since it was by no means certain that the final settlement would award any other part of the country to Greece. Meanwhile

* Leopold obtained the throne of Belgium, which was set up under the protection of the powers when it broke away from the Netherlands.

the two belligerents continued to fight. The Greeks were fighting not now to win the war but to ensure that the new country incorporated as much territory as possible. In 1828 two expeditions were mounted with the specific aim of ensuring that areas which had borne their share of the Revolution should benefit from its success. Church led an army into north-west Greece, a region that had been firmly under Turkish control since the Battle of Peta in 1822. Fabvier led an expedition to Chios in the hope that the dreadful sufferings of the 1822 massacre should not appear to have been totally in vain. Characteristically the British Philhellene and the French Philhellene chose their battle grounds as far away from each other as possible.

Fabvier's expedition was a failure for the usual causes and Chios remained a part of the Ottoman Empire for another eighty-four years. Church had some success in the north-west but his reputation as a general steadily diminished and he was fortunate to escape disaster. Lord Cochrane remained in Greek waters until the end of 1828, but the spectacular success for which he craved never came, and in the long success story of his life, Greece features as an embarrassing interlude. Only Hastings, patiently coaxing his defective steamship to work, achieved military success but he was killed in 1828.

After the arrival of the French expeditionary force in 1828 the excitement departed from the Greek war. Gradually the Philhellenes drifted off. Fabvier, still smarting from the humiliation of Church's appointment, quarrelled with Capodistria over the future of his regular corps, the need for which had greatly declined since the arrival of the French army. He returned to France in 1829 where, after considering whether to arrest him as a traitor, the French Government joined the public and hailed and fêted him as a national hero. He was reinstated in the French army, became a General, and was a prominent politician until his death in 1855.

The friends of the cause in Europe turned their attention to new topics. Edward Blaquiere was drowned in 1832 dashing off in a leaky ship on a characteristic mission to promote the liberal cause in Portugal. Jeremy Bentham took to sending long condescending letters of utilitarian advice to Mehemet Ali, an even less promising pupil than the Greeks. Colonel Sève, the much hated Frenchman responsible for training Mehemet's troops, rose to be Generalissimo of the Egyptian Army and, as Soleiman Pasha, was to sleep in Napoleon's bed at the Tuileries as a guest of King Louis Philippe and to be received by Prince Albert at Buckingham Palace.

A few Philhellenes remained in Greece after the war, as officers in the Greek army, lawyers or teachers, but their position was difficult. The Bavarians were disinclined to employ men who had taken part in the war unless they were exceptional in some way, and in the tempestuous politics of Greece purges were frequent. Hane, one of the volunteers of 1822, died in poverty and misery in 1844, having miraculously survived death by violence or disease during the war. Two other Germans of the 1822 vintage, von Rheineck and Dr. Treiber, eventually rose to high positions in the Greek Army.

Gordon continued his intense love-hate relationship with Greece. He had left in disgust for a second time in 1827, but returned and decided to settle in the country. He built himself a house at Argos and devoted himself to collecting material for his astonishingly accurate and comprehensive *History of the Greek Revolution*. During the 1830s he was Commander-in Chief of several expeditions aimed against the *klephtic* bands who had now reverted from patriots to their traditional role of bandits. He died on a visit to his native Scotland in 1841.

George Finlay, who had come first to Greece in 1823 to worship at the feet of Lord Byron, finally decided to make his home in the country. Throughout his long life an intense romantic philhellenism struggled in his breast with a bitter cynicism against the Modern Greeks. He fought back the romanticism, but he remained bewitched. He wrote a long history of Greece from its conquest by the Romans until his own day which has a touch of Gibbon about it.

Henry Lytton Bulwer (later Sir Henry), who had been sent on the abortive mision to Greece by the London Greek Committee in the autumn of 1824, became violently pro-Turkish in the Greek-Turkish questions later in the century. David Urquhart (later Sir David), who had fought in the later campaigns and whose brother was killed in Crete, also became a noted mishellene. Doctor Julius Millingen, Lord Byron's physician who changed sides in 1825, was a well-known figure in Constantinople for nearly fifty years and acted as personal physician to successive Sultans. His son, who called himself Osman Bey, was one of the pioneers of modern obscene antisemitic literature.

Greece continued to be racked by civil strife and much of the history of the early years of the Greek kingdom is concerned with the attempts of governments dominated by Europeanized Greeks to impose national unity on the captains. In 1831 the *Hellas* and the *Karteria* were destroyed as a deliberate act of spite in an outbreak of civil war. Capodistria was assassinated in Nauplia by a disgruntled Greek who saw himself as a latter-day Harmodius or Aristogeiton. Of the original complex of ideas which had contributed to the Revolution, the imported notion of regeneration made steady progress and eventually vanquished all others. Its only rival was the notion of re-establishing a Greek Empire in the Eastern Mediterranean, the 'Great Idea' which has regularly reappeared at times of international crisis.

During the nineteenth century the warlords and brigand chieftains were gradually brought to heel under the authority of the Government at Athens, and in time most Greeks came to believe that they were, in fact, the same as the Ancient Greeks. The seventeen hundred years or so between the Emperor Hadrian and the outbreak of the Revolution in 1821 came to be looked upon as a regrettable, even shameful interlude in the country's history. If in any respect Greece did not appear to be a fully mature Western European state with all the appurtenances of national culture and identity, the blame could always be put on the past and especially on the Turks.

In 1830 the German historian Fallmerayer published a theory that the Ancient Greek population had been ousted by Slavic immigrants in the in the early middle ages, and that the Modern Greeks were mainly of Slavic race.[1] Fallmerayer's ideas were looked upon as a deadly heresy, and the supposed identity of the Ancient and Modern Greeks became a question of intense political feeling.

Innumerable measures were introduced to emphasize the link with the remote past. Ancient names were resurrected or devised for the coinage, for offices of state, for ranks in the army and navy, for the law. The streets of Athens were named after the famous and obscure men of antiquity whose names have been handed down. It became customary to call Greek children after ancient heroes in preference to saints.

Few signs were allowed to remain in Greece to show that the country once contained a large Turkish minority. The minarets and mosques were destroyed. The Acropolis of Athens was stripped of everything but its ancient remains and rendered a lifeless desert. The marvellously impressive Frankish tower which had stood at the entrance to the Acropolis for hundreds of years was knocked down without regret. An interesting structure on the top of the pillars of the temple of Olympian Zeus, apparently the hermitage of some Byzantine stylite, was removed as being non-ancient and therefore not respectable. Only shortage of money prevented the Parthenon from being 'restored' and rebuilt as part of the campaign to emphasize the alleged continuity of the Hellenic race.

The Greek language is one of the undeniable links between Ancient and Modern Greece, representing a largely unbroken tradition. But that was not considered enough. The Modern Greeks must learn to speak the language of Pericles, or if that seemed too difficult, at least a language purged of foreign accretions, with the ancient words replacing the modern and a simplified ancient grammar. Generations of hapless school children were unsuccessfully inculcated with different versions of 'purified' Greek.*

Attempts to replace the unwieldy purified versions used in literature and for official purposes with the ordinary speech of the people, known as demotic, were regarded as blows directed against the feeble unity of the

---

* The vocabulary and grammar were changed, not the pronunciation. Present-day Greeks are inclined to insist that the modern pronunciation was used in ancient times even though this implies that the bleat of classical sheep (βῆ βῆ) sounded like 'vee vee'.

country and its life-giving national myth.[2] There were riots in Athens
following the publication in 1902 of a demotic version of the New Testament. Those who advocated the abandonment of the unequal struggle to
popularize the pure language have been accused at various times of being
traitors to the country and to the Church, freemasons, and tools of the
Panslavists. In modern times the charge has usually been of sympathy with
Communism, with strong anti-Slavonic overtones. In the twentieth century
the battle for a more general use of demotic seemed to have been almost
won when the Colonels, none of whom is personally at home with the pure
language, renewed the attempt to 'correct' the speech of the whole nation.
In innumerable ways the life, culture, and politics of Modern Greece are
still profoundly influenced by the men who inhabited the country in
ancient times.

It was the intention of the Greeks who assembled at Argos in July
1829 to confer the Order of the Saviour of Greece upon all the Philhellenes
who had taken part in the war. They also intended to record their names in
a book of remembrance and to erect a monument to the dead in a church
at Missolonghi. But even in providing memorials to express their eternal
gratitude—a theme which had featured in innumerable philhellenic poems
and addresses—the Greeks did not come up to expectations. The promised
lists were not drawn up and soon the names of many of the Philhellenes
were forgotten.

The casual visitor might remark upon the tomb of Müller at Nauplia[3]
or wonder about Marius Wohlgemuth who carved his name flanked with
torches of liberty so prominently on the wall of the Theseum in 1822,[4] or
about Ducrocq who whiled away the time during the siege of the Acropolis
in 1826–7 by carving his name on a column of the Parthenon,[5] but there
was no one to tell him who these men were, why they had come to Greece,
or what they had done.

In May 1841 a few former Philhellenes gathered in the Roman Catholic
Church at Nauplia for the dedication of a simple monument. It was built
by the French Philhellene Thouret and can still be seen. It consists of a
miniature triumphal arch of black wood across the doorway of the church.
The workmanship is crude, the lettering absurdly uneven, the spelling
poor, but the total effect is gloomily impressive. The inscription is in
French, '*To the Memory of the Philhellenes who died for Independence. Hellenes,
we were and are with you.*' On the columns are inscribed the names of two
hundred and seventy-eight Philhellenes who had been killed in the war
or had died in Greece, with the places where they died. Some of the names
are repeated more than once, many are hopelessly corrupted, or wrongly
transcribed. Gordon who died in Scotland has somehow crept in. First
names and titles are given but these are not always known or correctly
recorded. Against one name it is noted admiringly that he suffered thirty-

four wounds. Over fifty places in Greece are recorded as containing the bones of some Philhellene, soldier, student, runaway, disappointed lover, mercenary, adventurer, impostor, romantic, revolutionary, philanthropist, traitor to the Greeks, traitor to the Turks, duellist, suicide.

Plans were made at various times to erect a more permanent monument to the Philhellenes. Research into names was undertaken but the monument was never built. In 1861 the European colony at Athens was asked to name a few Philhellenes who deserved to be commemorated among the Greek heroes of the War of Independence.[6] They chose Byron (British), Fabvier (French), Meyer (German and Swiss), and Santa Rosa (Italian), and these names were officially received into the Greek Pantheon. The story of the Philhellenes had itself now passed into myth; reinforcing the myths about Modern Greece which the Philhellenes themselves had found so cruelly disappointing.

It is impossible to make confident statements about the Philhellenes in general without building up a picture of as many individuals as possible, and I have tried to ensure that there are no generalizations in the text about the characteristics of any particular group which are not solidly based on a study of the individuals who composed it. I had hoped to list in an appendix the names of all the Philhellenes whom I have been able to identify and to give a few words of biographical information and source references for each, but this plan had to be abandoned for reasons of space. However, it may be useful to provide a short analysis of the main features which emerge.

The materials for compiling a biographical index of Philhellenes are plentiful. The Monument at Nauplia contains a list of names of Philhellenes who had died before 1841 compiled by the French Philhellene, Hilarion Thouret. A fuller list which made use of Thouret's work was compiled by the Swiss Philhellene, Henri Fornezy. Schott's German edition of Pouqueville's *Histoire de la Régénération de la Grèce* listed the Philhellenes who sailed in the expeditions from Marseilles in 1822. The documents published by the Paris Greek Committee contain numerous names including lists of the Philhellenes besieged with Fabvier in the Acropolis. The series of paintings by Zographos of the Greek War commissioned by Makriyannes includes a list of Philhellenes. Other lists are included in the works of Raybaud, Phrantzes, and Byzantios (derived from Rheineck), and among the papers of Gordon, Eynard, Treiber, and others, and in the *Archives Nationales* of France. In addition there are innumerable scattered references in books and collections of documents of the time and later.

Collating the references presents great difficulties. Many of the names are rough transcriptions from one language to another; and misreadings, printers' errors, nicknames and pseudonyms abound. Without care it is possible to derive an entirely false picture of the number of volunteers at large in Greece during the war. It is relatively easy to establish that von Pieren, von Bieren, Byren, Biring, de Birn, and von Byern is one person (not Lord Byron), and that Le Croix, de Croze, de Crosse, Ducros, Dugros, Ducroz, Ducrocq, and Δουκρὸ are two. It is, however, not immediately obvious that Torti is the same as Forli, that von Astarelli is Tarella, or that Thunst is the same as Dunze. There are numerous Mayers,

Müllers, and Hahns to be sorted out. One imaginary Philhellene, Kirkman Finlay, has even won himself a sympathetic entry in the *Dictionary of National Biography*.
Byron, as usual, has a few apposite words:

> Then there were foreigners of much renown,
>   Of various nations, and all volunteers;
> Not fighting for their country or its crown,
>   But wishing to be one day brigadiers;
> Also to have the sacking of a town;
>   A pleasant thing to young men at their years.
> 'Mongst them were several Englishmen of pith,
> Sixteen called Thomson, and nineteen named Smith.
>
> *   *   *
>
> And therefore we must give the greater number
>   To the Gazette—which doubtless fairly dealt
> By the deceased, who lie in famous slumber
>   In ditches, fields, or whereso'er they felt
> Their clay for the last time their souls encumber;—
>   Thrice happy he whose name has been well spelt
> In the despatch: I knew a man whose loss
> Was printed Grove, although his name was Grose.
>
> (*Don Juan,* VII, xviii; VIII, xviii)

Then there is the problem of who should be counted as a Philhellene. The old lists tended to include friends of the Greeks who were not volunteers, for example members of the British and French armed forces in the area, members of the French expeditionary force of 1828, and prominent men who favoured the cause who never left Europe.

Despite these difficulties, it is possible, making a number of judgements, to identify with reasonable confidence some nine hundred and fifty individual volunteers who set out from Europe or America to lend their strength and skill for the cause of Greek independence. Biographical material about most of them is sparse but it is possible to give their country of origin and to divide them into one of three main periods of philhellenic activity, the first period from the outbreak in March 1821 until the sailing of the German Legion and the closing of the port of Marseilles at the end of 1822; the second period roughly corresponding to the Byronic interlude from early 1823 until mid 1825; and the third period, which began roughly with the arrival of refugees from Spain and the rebirth of philhellenic enthusiasm in France.

For the second and third periods the indications are that the figures are reasonably complete. For the first period the volunteers of 1822 are fairly well documented but there are large gaps for 1821. In particular, only a small fraction of the Italians who are known to have come in that year are individually recorded. I would estimate that during the war the number of volunteers who made their way to Greece was between 1,100 and 1,200.

The table shows a breakdown of the individual Philhellenes whom I have been able to identify by time and nationality. I have included only genuine volunteers who actually reached Greece with the intention of joining Greek service, omitting other friends of the cause, missionaries, relief agents, travellers, loan salesmen, and Knights of Malta.

I have noted, where known, the number of Philhellenes from each group and period who died in Greece before the final achievement of independence in 1833. As the table shows, the death-rate was high, usually about 30 per cent. When one considers how many Philhellenes stayed in Greece for only a few weeks or months it is obvious that the risks were extremely high. Apart from the great battles at Peta in 1822 and Athens in 1827, the majority of the fatalities were from disease.

ANALYSIS OF KNOWN PHILHELLENES
BY NATIONALITY AND TIME OF ARRIVAL IN GREECE

	Early Period 1821– end 1822	Middle Period 1823– mid 1825	Late Period Mid 1825 onwards	Time of arrival uncertain	Totals
Germans	265	10	50	17	342
Died	*116*	*9*	*13*	*4*	*142*
French	71	2	114	9	196
Died	*19*	—	*39*	*2*	*60*
Italians	62	12	48	15	137
Died	*19*	*4*	*13*	*6*	*42*
British	12	31	56	—	99
Died	*4*	*7*	*10*	—	*21*
Swiss	19	—	14	2	35
Died	*8*	—	*3*	—	*11*
Poles	24	—	3	3	30
Died	*10*	—	*1*	—	*11*
Dutch and Belgian	12	1	4	—	17
Died	*1*	*1*	*1*	—	*3*
Americans	1	5	10	—	16
Died	*1*	—	*2*	—	*3*
Hungarians	4	2	3	—	9
Died	*3*	—	*3*	—	*6*
Swedes	5	—	3	1	9
Died	*3*	—	—	*1*	*4*
Danes	7	1	—	—	8
Died	*3*	—	—	—	*3*
Spanish	3	—	5	1	9
Died	*1*	—	*3*	—	*4*
Others and unknown	4	—	8	21	33
Died	—	—	—	*3*	*3*
TOTALS	489	64	318	69	940
Died	*188*	*21*	*88*	*16*	*313*

The Principal Philhellenic Expeditions

Year	Ship	Port of embarkation	Sailing date	Estimated number of Phil-hellenes	Sponsors	Remarks
1821	*	Trieste	June	?	Demetrius Hypsilantes.	Baleste and his party.
	*	Marseilles	July	15	Greek ex-patriates.	Mavrocordato and his party.
	Amédée et Alexis	Marseilles	August	6	Colonel Gordon.	Gordon and his party.
	St Lucie	Marseilles	October	42	South German and Swiss Societies.	

The information for 1821 is very incomplete. There were numerous other expeditions, particularly from Italy, precise details of which are not known.

Year	Ship	Port of embarkation	Sailing date	Estimated number	Sponsors	Remarks
1822	*Pegasus*	Leghorn/ Marseilles	January	23		
	St. Marie	Marseilles	January	35		
	Madonna del Rosario	Marseilles	January	47		General Normann's Expedition.
	La Bonne Mère	Marseilles	March	24	South German and Swiss Societies.	
	Duchesse d'Angoulême	Marseilles	March	30		
	Félicité Renouvelée	Marseilles	June	17		
	St. Jean Battiste	Marseilles	August	17		
	Scipio	Marseilles	November	115		German Legion.

* Name unknown.

Year	Ship	Port of embarkation	Sailing date	Estimated number of Philhellenes	Sponsors	Remarks
1823	*Hercules*	Genoa/ Leghorn	July	13 (including 8 servants	Lord Byron.	Lord Byron's party.
	Ann	London	November	16	London Greek Committee.	Parry and the arsenal.
1824	*Florida*	London	March	?7	London Greek Committee and the Greek deputies in London.	These voyages were mainly to convey the proceeds of the loans to Greece but passage was given to a few volunteers.
	Little Sally	London	May			
	Florida	London	August			
	Little Sally	London	November			
1825	*Nimble*	London	January	—	Greek deputies in London.	Conveying the Loan.
	Lively	London	March	2		
	Little Sally	London	April	—		Italian exiles living in England.
	Elizabeth	London	July	36		
	? *Elizabeth*	London	September	18		
	*	Marseilles	September	20	Paris Greek Committee.	Raybaud and his party, including Arnaud and the arsenal.
1826	*La Nouvelle Adeline*	Marseilles	January	24	Paris Greek Committee.	Mainly Frenchmen.
	Heureux Retour	Marseilles	January	46		Mainly Frenchmen.
	Epaminondas (Greek ship)	Marseilles	February	12	Private.	
	Achilles (private yacht)	London	April	?5	Colonel Gordon.	Gordon and the remains of the loan money.
	La Spartiate (Greek ship)	Marseilles	May	27	Private.	Mainly Frenchmen.

* Name unknown.

Year	Ship	Port of embarkation	Sailing date	Estimated number of Philhellenes	Sponsors	Remarks
	*	Marseilles	May	16	Private.	Pisa and other Italian exiles.
	New Albion	London	July	1	Greek deputies.	Coal and cannon for the *Karteria*.
	Jeune Emilie	Marseilles	July	40	Paris Greek Committee.	Mainly Frenchmen.
	Harriet	London	September	—	Greek deputies.	Arms and stores.
	Pegasus	Ancona	December	12	King of Bavaria.	Heideck and his party.

* Name unknown.

Relief Ships

Year	Number of shiploads	Port of embarkation	Sponsors
1826	12	Ancona	} Eynard and Paris Greek Committee.
1827	5	Ancona	
	6	Philadelphia, New York, and Boston	} United States Greek Committees.
1828	2	New York	

z

NOTE ON THE SELECT BIBLIOGRAPHY

The primary sources for a study of philhellenism are numerous since it was an important political and literary topic in Western Europe and the United States for many years. The secondary material is also very great, but much of this is of little value. Many later writers have confined themselves to the Philhellenes of their own nationality, and some have picked up the habit from the accounts of the original Philhellenes of dismissing volunteers of other nationalities than their own as 'foreign adventurers'. Other books on the subject are mainly interesting as examples of present-day philhellenic writing and a few verge on the conventions of hagiography.

With notable exceptions therefore I have relied principally on primary sources or works containing a good deal of primary material, and in particular on the accounts of their experiences written by the Philhellenes themselves. These are much more numerous than is generally realized and I have attempted to compile a list, *Works by Philhellenes*, in as comprehensive a form as possible. Many of these books are of extreme rarity and there are a few of which I have not been able to trace copies.

The second list, *Other Useful Sources*, contains the names of contemporary works not by Philhellenes which contain evidence of their activities and of the chief secondary sources which I have found helpful.

It has not been my intention in this book to reconsider the general history of the Greek War of Independence, although I hope that I may have helped to illuminate some aspects of it. For the main facts of the war I have relied on the usual sources and I have not thought it necessary therefore to include a bibliography of the Greek War as such. As far as the Philhellenes are concerned, few of the Greek authors give them more than casual mention.

There seemed to be little point too in including a lengthy list of the pamphlets and books of verse about the war, important though these are for making judgements about the state of public opinion. Remarks on these books are included in appropriate places among the Notes. In the Notes to each chapter I have indicated the main sources relevant to the theme. Works referred to in the Select Bibliography are abbreviated to the name of the author in italics as, for example, *Kiesewetter*, or, in cases where he wrote more than one book, by the author's name and a short title, as *Finlay, Greek Revolution*. The titles of other works which are not in the bibliography are given in full.

In order not to slow too much the momentum of the narrative by overloading it with proper names, I have consigned the names of some of the characters who are seldom mentioned to the Notes. This is a compromise made inevitable by the decision not to include a nominal list of all known Philhellenes.

SELECT BIBLIOGRAPHY

1. *Works by Philhellenes*

MANUSCRIPT

Church Papers, British Museum.
Finlay and *Hastings Papers*, British School at Athens.
Gordon Papers, King's College, Aberdeen.
Stanhope Papers, National Archives, Athens
Washington, W. T., Copy of fragment of a diary, Gennadios Library, Athens.
Whitcombe, Thomas, Campaign of the Falieri and Piraeus in the year 1827, Gennadios
  Library, Athens.

PRINTED

'Albano', *Reise und Abentheuer*, Gotha, 1823.
Aschling, Nils Fr., *Försök till Grekiska Revolutionens Historia*, Stockholm, 1824.
Bellier de Launay, Wilhelm, *Einige Worte über Griechenland*, Berlin, 1823.
Blaquiere, Edward, *Report on the Present State of the Greek Confederation*, London,
  1823.
Blaquiere, Edward, *The Greek Revolution*, London, 1824.
Blaquiere, Edward, *Narrative of a Second Visit to Greece*, London, 1825.
Blaquiere, Edward, *Greece and her Claims*, London, 1826.
Blaquiere, Edward, *Letters from Greece*, London, 1828.
[Bojons, C. F.?] 'Auszug aus dem Schreiben eines teutschen Arztes, aus Athen
  vom 30. Sept. 1822', *Taschenbuch für Freunde der Geschichte des Griechischen Volkes*,
  Heidelberg, 1824.
Bollmann, L. de, *Remarques sur l'état moral, politique et militaire de la Grèce*, Mar-
  seilles, 1823.
[Brengeri], 'Adventures of a Foreigner in Greece', *London Magazine*, 1826 and
  1827.
Browne, James Hamilton, 'Voyage from Leghorn to Cephalonia' and 'Narrative
  of a Visit in 1823 to the Seat of War in Greece', *Blackwood's Edinburgh Magazine*,
  1834.
Bulwer, H. Lytton, *An Autumn in Greece*, London, 1826.
Byern, E. v., *Bilder aus Griechenland und der Levante*, Berlin, 1833.

Cochrane, George, *Wanderings in Greece*, London, 1837.

Collegno, *See Ottolenghi in list of 'Other Useful Sources'*, p. 366.

Dannenberg, Carl Wilhelm, *Harmlose Betrachtungen*, Hamburg, 1823.

Elster, Johann Daniel, *Das Bataillon der Philhellenen*, Baden, 1828.

[Elster, Johann Daniel], *Fahrten eines Musikanten*, Frankfurt, 1854.

Emerson, James; Pecchio, Count; and Humphreys, W. H., *A Picture of Greece in 1825*, London, 1826.

Emerson, James, *Letters from the Aegean*, London, 1829.

Féburier, Théophile, *La Corse, L'Ile d'Elbe, Les Grecs, et Sainte Hélène*, Paris, 1827. In verse.

Feldham (*sic* on title page, should be Feldhann), Gustav, *Kreuz- und Querzüge oder Abentheuer eines Freiwilligen*, Leipzig, 1822.

Finlay, George, *History of the Greek Revolution*, Edinburgh, 1861.

[Finlay, George], 'An Adventure during the Greek Revolution', *Blackwood's Edinburgh Magazine*, 1842. A letter from Finlay claims that this represents a true incident.

Friedel, Adam de, *The Greeks, Twenty four Portraits*, Paris and London, 1825–6.

Gamba, Count Peter, *A Narrative of Lord Byron's Last Journey to Greece*, London, 1825.

Garston, Edgar, *Greece Revisited*, London, 1840.

Gordon, Thomas, *History of the Greek Revolution*, Edinburgh and London, 1832.

Gosse, Louis-André, *Correspondance entre deux philhellènes*, Paris, 1919.

Gosse, Louis-André, *Lettres à sa mère pendant son séjour en Grèce*, Paris, 1920.

Grasset, Edouard, *Souvenirs de Grèce*, Nevers, 1838.

Hahn, A. E., *Brief des Philhellenen Em. Hahn aus Griechenland*, Berne, 1827.

Hahn, Amenäus Emanuel, 'Memoiren über seine Beteiligung am griechischen Freiheitskampf', *Berner Taschenbuch*, 1870.

Harring, Harro Paul, *Tragikomische Abenteuer eines Philhellenen*, Stuttgart, 1910. An extract from *Rhonghar Jahr* published in 1828.

Heideck, Karl Freiherr von, *Die Bayerische Philhellenenfahrt*, Munich, 1897.

Hodges, John Monins, *Diaries and Letters*, privately published, 1953.

Howe, Samuel G., *An Historical Sketch of the Greek Revolution*, New York, 1828.

Howe, Samuel G., *Letters and Journals*, Boston and London, 1906.

Humphreys, W. H., *First Journal of the Greek War of Independence*, ed. Sture Linnér, Stockholm, 1967.

[Humphreys, W. H.], 'Adventures of an English Officer in Greece', *New Monthly Magazine*, 1826.

Humphreys, W. H., *see also Emerson*.

Jarvis, George, *Journal and Related Documents*, Thessalonika, 1965.

Jourdain, *Mémoires historiques et militaires sur les événements de la Grèce*, Paris, 1828.

Kiefer, Heinrich Joseph, *Nachrichten über Griechenland*, Mainz, 1823.

Kiesewetter, Ferdinand von, *Reise eines teutschen Officiers nach Griechenland*, Parchim, 1823.

[Koesterus, M. C. I.], *Schicksale eines aus Griechenland zurückgekehrten deutschen Offiziers*, Darmstadt, 1822. I have not been able to trace a copy of this book. Some extracts are reproduced in *Deutsche Philhellenen in Griechenland 1821–1822*, ed. Karl Dieterich, Hamburg, 1929.

[Kotsch, Maximilian von], *Reise eines deutschen Artillerie-Offiziers nach Griechenland*, ed. F. W. Mauvillon, Essen, 1824.

Krazeisen, Charles, *Portraits des Grecs et des Philhellènes*, Munich, 1828 and 1829.

Krøyer, Henrik, *Erindringer af Henrik Krøyers Liv. 1821–1838*, Copenhagen, 1870.

[LeFebre, W. de], *Relation de divers faits de la guerre de Grèce*, Marseilles, 1822.

Lessen, Friedrich August, *Schilderung einer enthusiasmirten Reisen nach Griechenland*, Görlitz, 1823.

Lieber, Franz, *Tagebuch meines Aufenthaltes in Griechenland*, Leipzig, 1823.

Lübtow, Adolph von, *Der Hellenen Freiheitskampf i. J. 1822. Aus dem Tagebuche des Herrn A. v. L., bearbeitet von Ludwig von Bollmann*, Berne, 1823.

Marcet, Frank, 'Un Voyage en Grèce en 1826', *Revue Hebdomadaire*, 1915.

[Masson, Edward], Φιλελληνικὰ *or Poetic Translations . . . by a Scottish Philhellen*, 1852.

Miller, Jonathan P., *The Condition of Greece in 1827 and 1828*, New York, 1828.

Millingen, Julius, *Memoirs of the Affairs of Greece*, London, 1831.

Morandi, Antonio, *Il Mio Giornale dal 1848 al 1850*, Modena, 1867.

Müller, Albert, *Erinnerungen an Griechenland*, Aarau, 1872.

Müller, Dr. Christian, *Journey through Greece*, London 1822. Translation from the original German edition.

Müller, Friedrich, *Denkwürdigkeiten aus Griechenland*, Paris, 1833.

Müller, Gottfried, *Reise eines Philhellenen*, Bamberg, 1825.

Palma, Count Alerino, *Greece Vindicated*, London, 1826.

Parry, William, *The Last Days of Lord Byron*, London, 1825.

Pecchio, Count, *see Emerson.*

Persat, *Mémoires, 1806–1844*, Paris, 1910.

Pisa, Vicenzo, *Résumé des luttes de l'armée regulière*, Athens, 1841. I have not been able to trace a copy of this book.

Raffenel, C. D., *Histoire des Événements de la Grèce*, Paris, 1822 and 1824.

Raybaud, Maxime, *Mémoires sur la Grèce*, Paris, 1824 and 1825.

[Rosenstiel, Karl Emil] Nelisteros [anagram], *Tagebuch eines Griechenfreundes*, Liegnitz, 1824.

Schack, F.-R., *Campagne d'un Jeune Français en Grèce*, Paris, 1827.

Schrebian, C. M., *Aufenthalt in Morea, Attika und mehreren Inseln des Archipelagus*, Leipzig, 1825.

Sketches of Modern Greece . . . by a Young English Volunteer in the Greek Service, London, 1828. This book seems to contain some genuine material.

Stabell, Johann H., *Schicksale eines dänischen Philhellenen*, Leipzig, 1824. Translation from the original Danish edition.

[Staehelin, J. A. ?], 'The Siege of the Acropolis of Athens in the years 1821–22 By an Eye-Witness', *London Magazine*, 1826.

Stanhope, Hon. Colonel Leicester, *Greece in 1823 and 1824*, New edition, London, 1825.

Stauffer, Fridolin, *Die zwei Philhellenen*, Münster, 1823.

Striebeck, C. T., *Mitteilungen aus dem Tagebuch des Philhellenen C. T. Striebeck . . . Nach dem Manuskript von Fr. Lindes*, Hanover, 1828.

Tagebuch einer Reise nach Morea, Tübingen, 1824.

Tagebuch und Erläuterungen über den Kampf der Hellenen in Griechenland, Dinkelsbühl, 1823.

Treiber, Heinrich, Ἀναμνήσεις ἀπ' τὴν Ἐπανάστάση τοῦ *1821*, Athens, 1960. The German original of this diary has not been published.

Trelawny, E. J., *Recollections of the Last Days of Shelley and Byron*, London, 1858.
Trelawny, Edward John, *Records of Shelley, Byron, and the Author*, London, 1878.
Trelawny, Edward John, *Letters*, London, 1910.
Urquhart, D., *The Spirit of the East*, London, 1839.
Villeneuve, Eugène de, *Journal fait en Grèce*, Brussels, 1827.
Voutier, Olivier, *Mémoires sur la Guerre Actuelle des Grecs*, Paris, 1823.
Voutier, Olivier, *Lettres sur la Grèce*, Paris, 1826.

2. *Other Useful Sources*

MANUSCRIPT

Colonial Office Records, Ionian Islands, Public Record Office, London.
Fauvel Papers, Bibliothèque Nationale, Paris.
Hobhouse Papers, British Museum.

PRINTED

Anderson, Rufus, *Observations upon the Peloponnesus and Greek Islands*, Boston and New York, 1830.
Argenti, Philip, ed., *The Expedition of Colonel Fabvier to Chios*, London, 1933.
Arnold, Robert F., 'Der deutsche Philhellenismus', *Euphorion*, 1896.
Asse, Eugène, 'L'Indépendance de la Grèce et les Poètes de la Restauration' in *Les Petits Romantiques*, Paris, 1900.
Barth, Wilhelm, and Kehrig-Korn, Max, *Die Philhellenenzeit*, Munich, 1960.
Bartle, G. F., 'Bowring and the Greek Loans of 1824 and 1825', *Balkan Studies*, 1962.
Booras, Harris J., *Hellenic Independence and America's Contribution to the Cause*, Rutland, Va., 1934.
[Bowring, John], 'The Greek Committee', *Westminster Review*, 1826.
Brewer, Josiah, *A Residence at Constantinople*, New Haven, 1830.
Byzantios, Christos S., 'Ἱστορία τοῦ τακτικοῦ στρατοῦ', Athens, 1837.
Carne, John, *Letters from the East*, London, 1826.
Church, E. M., *Sir Richard Church*, Edinburgh and London, 1895.
Cline, Myrtle A., *American Attitude toward the Greek War of Independence*, Atlanta, Ga., 1930.
Crawley, C. W., *The Question of Greek Independence*, Cambridge, 1930.
Dakin, Douglas, *British and American Philhellenes*, Thessalonika, 1955.
Dakin, Douglas, ed., *British Intelligence of Events in Greece, 1824–1827*, Athens, 1959.
Dalleggio, Eugène, *Les Philhellènes et la Guerre de l'Indépendance*, Athens, 1949.
Davesiès de Pontes, Lucien, *Notes sur la Grèce*, Paris, 1864.
De Beer, E. S., and Seton, Walter, 'Byroniana', *Nineteenth Century*, 1926.
Débidour, A., *Le Général Fabvier*, Paris, 1904.
Dimakis, Jean, *La Guerre de l'Indépendance grecque vue par la Presse française*, Thessalonika, 1968.
Dimopoulos, Aristide G., *L'Opinion Publique française et la Révolution grecque*, Nancy, 1962.
Documents relatifs à l'état présent de la Grèce, publiés d'après les communications du Comité Philhellenique de Paris, Paris, 1826–9.

Dontas, Domna N., *The Last Phase of the War of Independence in Western Greece*, Thessalonika, 1966.

Driault, Edouard, and Lhéritier, Michel, *Histoire diplomatique de la Grèce*, Paris, 1925–6.

Earle, Edward Mead, 'American Interest in the Greek Cause, 1821–1827', *American Historical Review*, October 1927.

[Finlay, George], 'Biographical Sketch of Frank Abney Hastings', *Blackwood's Edinburgh Magazine*, October 1845.

Finnie, David H., *Pioneers East*, Harvard, 1967.

Frankland, Charles Colville, *Travels to and from Constantinople in 1827 and 1828*, London, 1829.

Green, Philip James, *Sketches of the War in Greece*, London, 1827.

Hartley, Rev. John, *Researches in Greece and the Levant*, London, 1831.

Irmscher, Johannes, *Der Philhellenismus in Preussen als Forschungsanliegen*, Berlin, 1966.

Isambert, Gaston, *L'Indépendance Grecque et L'Europe*, Paris, 1900.

Jurien de la Gravière, *La Station du Levant*, Paris, 1876.

Kennedy, James, *Conversations on Religion with Lord Byron*, London, 1830.

Lane-Poole, Stanley, 'Sir Richard Church', *English Historical Review*, 1890.

Larrabee, Stephen A., *Hellas Observed*, New York, 1957.

Lauvergne, H., *Souvenirs de la Grèce*, Paris, 1826.

Leake, William Martin, *An Historical Outline of the Greek Revolution*, London, 1825.

Lemaître, Alfred, *Notes sur la Guerre de l'Indépendance Grecque*, Paris, 1895

Levandis, John A., *The Greek Foreign Debt and the Great Powers*, New York, 1944.

MacFarlane, Charles, *Constantinople in 1828*, second edition, London, 1829.

Marchand, Leslie A., *Byron, a Biography*, 1957.

Mengous, Petros, *Narrative of a Greek Soldier*, New York, 1830.

Ottolenghi, Leone, *La Vita e i Tempi di Giacinto Provana di Collegno*, 1882. Includes Collegno's diary of the siege of Navarino.

Penn, Virginia, 'Philhellenism in England', and 'Philhellenism in Europe', *Slavonic Review*, 1935, 1936, and 1937.

Post, Henry A. V., *A Visit to Greece and Constantinople*, New York, 1830.

Roma, Dionysios, Ἱστορικὸν Ἀρχεῖον, Athens, 1901.

Rothpletz, Emil, *Der Genfer J. G. Eynard als Philhellene*, Zurich, 1900.

Rothpletz, Emil, *Bernische Hilfsvereine für die Griechen*, Basel, 1932.

Slade, Adolphus, *Records of Travels in Turkey, Greece, etc.*, London, 1832.

Spencer, Terence, *Fair Greece, Sad Relic*, London, 1954.

Swan, Rev. Charles, *Journal of a Voyage up the Mediterranean*, London, 1826.

Waddington, George, *A Visit to Greece in 1823 and 1824*, London, 1825.

Walsh, Rev. R., *A Residence at Constantinople*, London, 1836.

Wilson, Rev. S. S., *A Narrative of the Greek Mission*, London, 1839.

Woodruff, Samuel, *Journal of a Tour to Malta, Greece etc . . .* , Hartford, 1831.

1. *The Outbreak*

The facts of the initial massacres and counter-atrocities are mainly taken from *Gordon* and *Finlay* with a few details from other sources, e.g. *Walsh*. These authors are also useful for the causes of the Revolution, as is Douglas Dakin, 'The Origins of the Greek Revolution', *History*, 1952.

2. *The Return of the Ancient Hellenes*

For the effects of the classical tradition on eighteenth-century European civilization the best general guide is Gilbert Highet, *The Classical Tradition*, London and New York, 1949. For the development of literary conventions about the Ancient and Modern Greeks, see *Spencer*. The revival of Hellenism in Greece is illustrated in many of the old travel books (see Note 3 below) and in such histories of Modern Greek literature as C. Th. Dimaras, *Histoire de la Littérature Néo-hellénique*, Athens, 1965.

1. Quoted in full in slightly differing versions in, for example, *Green*, p. 272; *Gordon*, i, p. 183; and *Raybaud*, ii, p. 463.
2. It is comparatively easy to trace the extent to which famous politicians, writers, and artists were influenced by the classics, and to make some assessment of the view which they held about life in ancient times. To make a judgement about the generality of educated public opinion, it is probably preferable to consider the works of the forgotten authors, the bad poets, and the schoolmasters, and particularly the best-sellers.

The influence of Fénelon's *Adventures of Telemachus*, for example, must have been out of all proportion to its value or interest, great though that is. First published in French in 1699, it is said to have gone through twenty editions in that year alone. Thereafter it was reprinted year after year in every major town in France. It was used as a school book, to teach morals, to teach language and to teach history. It was abridged, selections were published separately, it was put into verse, all manner of illustrations were added. In France alone there were well over a hundred reprintings during the eighteenth century. Dozens of editions also appeared in English, German, French, Italian and other languages. Similarly, many thousands of European readers must have ploughed their way through Barthélémy's *Travels of the Young Anacharsis in Greece*. It first appeared in French in 1788 and was regularly reprinted in the main European languages. New French editions appeared almost every year, usually simultaneously in quarto, octavo, and duodecimo to cater for a wide range of pockets. Another work of the same type, Lantier's *Travels of Antenor* which was first published in 1796, was in its fifteenth edition by 1821. These were fictional works, in the style of novels but written not so much for the story as for the information and atmosphere about the ancient world which they contained.

3. The following table gives an indication of the opportunities available in Western Europe to learn of the conditions of Greece in the half-century before the Revolution. I have listed the separate editions which I have been able to identify. Only books which contain some description of the condition of Modern Greece are included. I have not listed works which are confined to descriptions of the antiquities, picture books, or travel books which ignore the Greeks or mention them only incidentally. I give the title in the language in which the book was first published. Those marked with † consciously identify the Modern with the Ancient Greeks. Those marked * discuss or advocate the possibility of a revolution.

	English	French	German
1770–9	*†Guys 1772 *†Guys 1773 †Chandler, Richard, *Travels in Greece*, 1775 †Chandler 1775 †Chandler 1776 †Chandler 1776	*†Guys, M. de, *Voyage Littéraire de la Grèce*, 1771 *†Guys, 1776	†Chandler, 1777
1780–9	*†Savary, 1788	*†Choiseul-Gouffier, Comte de, *Voyage Pittoresque de la Grèce*, 1782 *†Guys, 1783 *†Savary, M., *Lettres sur la Grèce*, 1788	
1790–9	*†Eton, W., *A Survey of the Turkish Empire*, 1798 *†Eton, 1798 *†Eton, 1799	*†Savary, 1798 *†Eton, 1799 *†Eton, 1799	

	English	French	German
1800–9	Olivier, 1801 *†Eton, 1801 *†Sonnini, 1801 Pouqueville, 1806 *†Eton, 1809	*†Stephanopoli, Dimo et Nicolo, *Voyage en Grèce,* 1800 *†Sonnini, C. S., *Voyage en Grèce,* 1801 Olivier, G. A., *Voyage dans l'Empire Othoman* 1801 Olivier, 1801 Scrofani, Xavier, *Voyage en Grèce,* 1801 Pouqueville, F. C. H. L., *Voyage en Morée,* 1805 †Chandler, 1806 †Chandler, 1806 *†Bartholdy, 1807 *†Castellan, A. L., *Lettres sur la Morée,* 1808	Olivier, 1802 *†Bartholdy, J. L S *Reise in Greichen- land,* 1805 *†Eton, 1805 Pouqueville, 1807 *†Castellan, 1809
1810–21	Clarke, Edward Daniel, *Travels in Various Countries,* 1810 Clarke, 1811 *†Chateaubriand, 1811 *†Chateaubriand, 1812 Pouqueville, 1813 †Galt, John, *Letters from the Levant,* 1813 *†Hobhouse, John Cam, *Journey through Albania,* 1813 *†Hobhouse, 1813 *†Douglas, Hon. F. S. N., *Ancient and Modern Greeks,* 1813 *†Douglas, 1813	*†Chateaubriand, F. A. de, *Itinéraire de Paris à Jerusalem,* 1811 *†Castellan, 1811 *†Chateaubriand, 1812 Clarke, 1812 *†Chateaubriand, 1813 Clarke, 1813 *†Tancoigne, J. M., *Voyage à Smyrne,* 1817 Pouqueville, F. C. H. L., *Voyage dans la Grèce,* 1820 *†Castellan, 1820 *†Hughes, 1821	*†Holland, 1816 Clarke, 1817 Dodwell, 1821 *†Hughes, 1821 *†Tancoigne, 1821 *†Castellan, 1821

English

1810–21	*†Holland, Henry, *Travels in the Ionian Islands*, 1815	Walpole, Rev. Robert, *Travels*, 1820

1810–21   *†Holland, Henry,
                 *Travels in the Ionian
                 Islands*, 1815
             Clarke, 1816
             †Chandler, 1817
             Walpole, Rev.
                 Robert, *Memoirs*,
                 1817
             Walpole, *Memoirs*,
                 1818
             Dodwell, Edward,
                 *Classical and Topo-
                 graphical Tour*, 1819
           *†Holland, 1819
             Pouqueville, 1820

Walpole, Rev.
    Robert, *Travels*,
    1820
*†Hughes, Thomas
    Smart, *Travels in
    Sicily, Greece, etc.*,
    1820
Turner, John,
    *Journal of a Tour in
    the Levant*, 1820
Williams, H. W.,
    *Travels in Italy,
    Greece, etc.*, 1820
Laurent, Peter
    Edmund, *Recollec-
    tions of a
    Classical Tour*, 1821

The only books of consequence which attacked the philhellenic conventions of the time were Cornelius de Pauw, *Recherches Philosophiques sur les Grecs*, Berlin and Paris, 1787; English translation 1793; and Thomas Thornton, *The Present State of Turkey*, two editions, 1807. De Pauw had never visited Greece.

3. The Regiment

The sources for the history of the Regiment are sparse compared with later periods. Some useful material can be found in *Byzantios, Raybaud, Persat*, and *Humphreys' First Journal*.

The anonymous author of an interesting series of articles in the *London Magazine* for 1826 and 1827, entitled, 'Adventures of a Foreigner in Greece', was also one of the earliest volunteers. I have attributed the authorship of this piece to the Italian *Brengeri* who is named by *Gordon*, i, p. 459, as one of the four Philhellenes who endured the first siege of Missolonghi. The siege is described from his own experience by the author of the articles. Also, it is known from other references in the Gordon Papers that Brengeri was a Roman and that he came to England, both points shared by the author of the articles.

1. Quoted in the *Examiner*, 1821, p. 232.
2. Ibid., p. 372.
3. Ibid., p. 689.
4. Ibid., p. 372.
5. Ibid., p. 456.
6. Ibid., p. 631.
7. Quoted ibid., p. 632.
8. *Raybaud*, i, p. 422.
9. *Humphreys, First Journal*, p. 29.

10. *Brengeri*, i, p. 462.

11. *Aschling*, p. 28.

12. *Raffenel*, i, p. 10.

13. For example *Brengeri*, i, p. 462. Hypsilantes himself encouraged this rumour. *Humphreys, First Journal*, p. 55.

14. *Examiner*, 1821, p. 242. This story is noticed in an enthusiastic philhellenic letter by Alexander Pushkin of March 1821. See *The Letters of Alexander Pushkin*, ed. J. Thomas Shaw, Bloomington and Philadelphia, 1963, i, pp. 80 ff. Pushkin joined a masonic lodge in order to help the Greek cause and his friend Karlovich Küchelbecker seriously considered volunteering, but by 1824 Pushkin was disillusioned.

15. See his *Mémoires*.

16. See his *First Journal*.

17. Emil von Z. See *Byern*, p. 108. This Philhellene cannot be definitely identi-fied with any of the Poles whose names are known.

18. Mierzewsky, killed at Peta. *Elster, Fahrten*, p. 319.

19. *Raybaud*, i, p. 269.

20. *Brengeri*, i, p. 466.

21. Ibid., pp. 462 ff.

22. *Humphreys, First Journal*, p. 40.

23. *Voutier, Mémoires*, p. 171.

24. *Christian Müller*, Preface. The two Englishmen are described as Mr. N. and Mr. S.

25. Not identified. *Raybaud*, i, p. 367.

26. Identified only as G. *Raybaud*, i, p. 368.

27. *Brengeri*, i, p. 467.

4. Two Kinds of War

Again, the main philhellenic sources are *Brengeri, Raybaud, Persat*, and *Humphreys, First Journal*.

1. See, for example, *Brengeri*, i, p. 469.

2. *Raybaud*, i, p. 290.

3. *Examiner*, 1821, p. 632.

4. Phrantzes, quoted by *Finlay, Greek Revolution*, i, p. 263.

5. *Humphreys, First Journal*, p. 28; *Raybaud*, i, p. 397.

6. *Brengeri*, i, p. 469.

7. *Gordon* who saw the aftermath dared not describe the horrors in his history (i, p. 245). He did, however, relate his experiences to Dr. Thomas whom he met at Zante soon afterwards and they were reported to London. Colonial Office Records 136/1085 reproduced as an Appendix to *Humphreys, First Journal*.

8. This surprising detail is asserted emphatically by *Brengeri*, ii, p. 41, and there is no reason to doubt it.

9. *Persat*, p. 100.

10. Wilhelm Boldemann from Grabow in Mecklenburg. *LeFebre*, p. 9, speci-fically says he committed suicide. Others say he was left to die of neglect.

11. *LeFebre*, p. 21.

5. The Cause of Greece, the Cause of Europe

The books by *Dimakis* and *Dimopoulos* discuss the reaction of the French press to the news from Greece during the Revolution. One of the main sources for the state of public opinion is the pamphlet literature, and I have tried in Note 7 to enumerate these works and draw a few general conclusions.

1. Many contemporary writers give examples of the transformation of the news, e.g. *Aschling, Raybaud*, and *Waddington*. Sir William Gell published his *Narrative of a Journey in the Morea* in 1823 specifically to combat the false newspaper stories.

2. *Examiner*, 2 July 1826, quoting Sismondi.

3. *Elster, Fahrten*, pp. 219 ff., recalling a quotation from Goethe's *Faust*.

4. See Note 8 to Chapter 26.

5. See *Irmscher, Arnold*, and Gaston Caminade, *Les Chants des Grecs et le Philhellénisme de Wilhelm Müller*, Paris, 1913.

6. Translated from *Constitutionnel*, 26 July 1821, quoted by *Dimopoulos*, p. 60.

7. Translated from de Pradt, *De la Grèce dans ses Rapports avec l'Europe*, Brussels, 1822.

The pamphlet literature published in Western Europe during the Greek War of Independence is huge. All but a tiny proportion of these works were intended to promote the Greek cause. A full bibliography would be of doubtful value since copies of most of the titles are not to be found outside a handful of libraries and, in any case, the sentiments of such works are predictably uniform. It might be useful, however, as an indication of public opinion, to have the following table of the numbers of pamphlets which are known to have been published in the three main European languages. I have included only political pamphlets and appeals published as separate works in their own right, excluding histories, memoirs, biographies, books of verse and articles in magazines and newspapers. When a pamphlet went into a second edition or was translated I have counted these as if they were new works. The great majority (except in England) had apparently one edition only, although one or two especially influential works went to as many as four editions. It is difficult to draw more than very general conclusions from the figures. The practice of conducting political argument by pamphlet was not equally developed in the countries concerned and they cannot be directly compared. In addition it is easier to be confident that the English and French figures are nearly complete, since many of these were printed for national distribution in London or Paris, than it is with respect to the German pamphlets, which were published independently for small circulation in several cities. Nevertheless, the figures do seem to illustrate a few points about the state of public opinion. They seem to confirm, for example, the success of the censor and the disillusionment with philhellenism in the German-speaking countries which occurred after the return of the early volunteers; and the astonishing revival of philhellenism which occurred in France alone in 1825 and 1826. They also seem to lend weight to the view that philhellenism was not as strong in England as in Continental Europe.

	French	German	English
1821	16	14	2
1822	15	23	10
1823	4	10	10
1824	10	4	6
1825	22	2	—
1826	31	3	3
1827	14	1	—
	112	57	31

8. J.-G. Schweighauser, *Discours sur les Services que les Grecs ont rendus à la Civilization*, Paris, 1821.

9. Giraud de la Clape, ex-étudiant en droit, *Appel aux Français en faveur des Grecs*, Paris, 1821.

10. For the early philhellenic movements in Britain see *Penn* and *Dakin*.

11. Rev. T. S. Hughes, *An Address to the People of England in the Cause of the Greeks*, London, 1822.

12. Thomas Lord Erskine, *A Letter to the Earl of Liverpool on the Subject of the Greeks*, London, 1822.

13. *Address in behalf of the Greeks*, Edinburgh, 1822.

14. Rev. T. S. Hughes, *Considerations upon the Greek Revolution*, London, 1823.

15. Charles Brinsley Sheridan, *Thoughts on the Greek Revolution*, London, 1824.

16. Quoted in *Booras*, p. 159, and elsewhere.

17. *Larrabee*, p. 55.

18. Ibid.

19. For the politics of philhellenism in Prussia and elsewhere in Germany, see *Irmscher*.

20. From the English translation, *The Cause of Greece, The Cause of Europe*, published anonymously in London in 1821.

21. Translated from Karl Iken, *Hellenion*, Leipzig, 1822.

22. Quoted by *Barth* and *Kehrig-Korn*, p. 95.

23. Translated from the second edition of Wilhelm Traugott Krug, *Griechenlands Wiedesgeburt*, Leipzig, 1821.

6. *The Road to Marseilles*

1. Some details of the eight expeditions are given in Appendix II. The members who have given accounts of their experiences are

Ship	Authors
St. Lucie:	Bellier de Launay, Koesterus, LeFebre.
Pegasus:	Kiesewetter, Treiber.
St. Marie:	Byern, Harring, Krøyer, Lieber, Lübtow, Rosenstiel, Stabell, Schrebian, Striebeck.
Madonna del Rosario:	Feldhann.
La Bonne Mère:	Albert Müller, Stauffer, Elster, Jourdain.

Duchesse d' Angoulême:	*Dannenberg, Lessen,*
	Author of *Tagebuch,* Tübingen 1824.
	Author of *Tagebuch,* Dinkelsbühl, 1823.
Félicité Renouvelée:	*Bollmann.*
St. Jean Battiste:	*Kotsch, Gottfried Müller.*

Most of these authors describe their journeys to Marseilles. There is also useful material in *Jarvis,* who set off in a Swedish merchant vessel.

2. *Elster Fahrten,* i, p. 219.

3. *Kiesewetter.*

4. *Schrebian.*

5. *Feldhann.* The book was published from letters. Feldhann himself was killed at Peta.

6. Author of *Tagebuch* of Dinkelsbühl.

7. *Dannenberg.*

8. *Harring.* Harring survived his experiences in Greece and on his return resumed his career as painter, poet, and dramatist in Italy, Switzerland, Germany and elsewhere. He served for a time as an officer in the Russian army but by the early 1830s he had become a professional revolutionary. Thereafter he moved restlessly from country to country through Europe, South America and the United States, constantly being driven out by the authorities. Half genius, half madman, he eventually committed suicide in London in 1870 by eating phosphorus matches.

9. Translated from *Krøyer,* p. 1.

10. *Harring,* p. 13.

11. *Penn,* quoting *Morning Chronicle,* 9 November 1821.

12. Ibid.

13. *Gottfried Müller,* p. 67.

14. Charles Tennant, *A Tour through Parts of the Netherlands, Holland, Germany etc.,* London, 1824, ii, p. 96.

15. *Krøyer,* p. 22.

16. Ibid., p. 27. Their names were Remi and Brugnatelli.

17. Rothermel.

18. Hochgesang.

19. Franz and Benjamin Beck who both died at Missolonghi in November 1822.

20. The twin brothers Fels from Leipzig. One, an apothecary, was killed at Peta; the other, a merchant's clerk, survived the battle but later returned to Greece and died at Missolonghi in September 1824. Deiss, a sixteen-year-old from Weimar, died of disease in 1822 at Anatoliko.

21. Josef Wolff, killed at Peta.

22. Benoit. According to *Bellier de Launay,* he later joined the Turks but he was one of the authors of a curious letter begging a passage home from the French Navy, quoted in *Le Maître* from the French naval archives, and we may doubt Bellier's story.

23. Wilhelm Heinrich Seeger, killed at Peta. His brother also died in Greece.

24. Johann Andreas Staehelin.

25. *Albert Müller.*

26. Johann Kohlermann.

27. Heinrich Stammler, committed suicide in Greece, July 1822.

28. Mignac, who killed Baron Hobe in the duel at Comboti (see p. 96) and was himself killed at Peta.

29. Friedrich Sander, killed at Peta.

30. Unidentified. Described by *Harring*, p. 17. Probably Krusemark, killed at Peta.

31. Said to be the wife of Onate who came in the *Madonna del Rosario*. *Elster* and *Albert Müller* also mention the wife of Toricella setting off dressed as a man; she was said to have died in Greece before Peta.

32. Descheffy, killed at Peta.

33. Eduard von Rheineck who confided this detail to *Collegno* during the siege of Navarino in 1825. Rheineck never returned to Germany but, unlike most of his contemporaries, lived out a long and successful career in Greece and now lies in a magnificent tomb in Athens cemetery.

34. von Katte was the name he used. His real identity is unknown.

35. Johann Jakob Meyer, one of the most famous of all Philhellenes. He set up a dispensary at Missolonghi, married a Greek girl, and adopted the Greek Orthodox religion. He became editor of the *Greek Chronicle* established by Stanhope and died in the fall of Missolonghi in April 1826. See pp. 187 and 242.

36. Frank Abney Hastings. See Chapter 29.

37. The fullest accounts of the Alepso incident are *Tagebuch* of Dinkelsbühl, *Lessen*, and *Tagebuch* of Tübingen.

38. *Elster, Fahrten*, i, p. 231 reports some of the details. The French naval officer was Jourdain who was later to be closely involved in the affair of the Knights of Malta. His own book contains little autobiographical information. The commander of the Greek Navy was Scholl.

39. This incident is described in numerous accounts, for example, *Elster*, *Harring, Stabell, Striebeck, Krøyer*.

40. *Krøyer*.

41. For Normann's earlier career see *Byern* and the short biography by Albert Schott in *Taschenbuch für Freunde der Geschichte des Griechischen Volkes*, Heidelberg, 1824.

42. *Feldhann*, killed at Peta.

43. *Examiner*, 1822, p. 72.

44. The four Frenchmen were Persat, Micolon, Delaurey, and Paulet. The incident is described from the French side by *Persat*. There are descriptions of the same incident from the German side by *Dannenberg*, by the author of the *Tagebuch* of Tübingen, and by *Lessen*.

45. *LeFebre*, p. 29.

46. *Bollmann*.

7. *Chios*

The main documents relating to the history of Chios have been published in a magnificent set of volumes by Philip Argenti. *The Massacres of Chios*, London, 1932, transcribes the chief contemporary accounts of the massacre in the diplomatic archives of several countries. Many of the details of events in Constantinople are supplied by *Walsh* and *Waddington*.

8. *The Battalion of Philhellenes*

The chief sources for this chapter are the authors listed in Note 1 to Chapter 6 together with *Brengeri*, *Raybaud*, and, where he can be trusted, *Voutier*.

1. This incident, which happened when the *St. Jean Battiste* arrived, is described by *Gottfried Müller* and *Kotsch*.
2. See, for example, *Byern*, p. 58.
3. *Lieber*'s narrative breaks into Latin at this point (p. 73) to spare the blushes of his female readers who were presumed not to have the education to understand it.
4. See, for example, *Stabell*, p. 21.
5. *Gottfried Müller*, p. 158.
6. Georg Grauer, a lieutenant from Württemberg, who came in the *St. Marie*.
7. Karl von Descheffy, killed at Peta.
8. An unidentified Alsatian.
9. Both Moring and Mulhens are recorded as duelling with d'André who claimed to be a marquis.
10. *Stabell*, pp. 40 ff.
11. *Striebeck*, p. 95.
12. *Stabell*, p. 50; *Striebeck*, p. 100.
13. Gustav Reichard from Vienna. Other accounts say from Frankfurt.
14. Hans von Jargo, a lieutenant from Berlin.
15. Anemat.
16. Hastings Diary, 6 July 1822. Hastings Papers.
17. The number is variously estimated. *Striebeck*, p. 154, gives two hundred and twenty. *Stauffer*, p. 53, gives as many as three hundred.
18. See especially *Byern*, p. 144. Friedel eventually established himself as an engraver in London and married the sister of Hodges, one of the artificers at Missolonghi with Lord Byron.
19. Waldemar von Qualen, killed in Thessaly in 1822.
20. See especially *Byern*, p. 135.
21. For the establishment of the Battalion see especially *Striebeck*, p. 208, *Kiesewetter*, p. 16, *Schrebian*, p. 112, *Byern*, p. 99, and *Raybaud*, ii, p. 238.
22. *Raybaud*, ii, 242.

9. *The Battle of Peta*

1. Rev. Robert Walsh, *Narrative of a Journey from Constantinople to England*, 1828, p. 63.
2. Vincenzo Gallina. See *Raybaud*, ii, p. 167.
3. These incidents are related by *Mengous*, pp. 185 ff., and *Elster, Fahrten*, i, pp. 328 ff.
4. *Brengeri*, iv, p. 340.
5. There are several accounts of the duel between Hobe and Mignac, the fullest in *Elster*.
6. Johann Bohn.
7. C. W. Van Dyck, a captain of cavalry. He returned safely to Holland.
8. Monaldi. See especially *Brengeri*, iv, p. 347.

9. Johannsen.

10. The wife of Toricella.

11. The best first-hand accounts of the battle are *Raybaud*, *Brengeri*, and *Kiesewetter*.

12. I include the following:

German	*Italian*	*French*	*Poles*	*Swiss*	*Dutch*	*Hungarian*	*Mameluke*

German
Bahrs
Beyermann
Dieterlein
Eben
Eisen
Fels
Feldhann
Heise
Kaisenberg
Krusemarck
Lasky
Lauricke
Lucä
Mandelslohe
Maneke
Nagel
Oberst
Oelmeier
Ohlmeier
Range
Rüst
Sander
Sandmann
Schmidt
Schneider
Schröder
Seeger

Seeger
Staël Holstein
Suri
Süssmilch
Teichmann
Wetzer
Wolff

Italian
Batilani
Briffari
Dania
Fozzio
Mamiot
Plenario
Rocini
Tarella
Tassi
Tirelli
Toricella
Viviani

French
Chauvassaigne
Frêlon
Guichard

Mignac
Seguin
Viel

Poles
Dieselsky
Dobronowski
Kosinsky
Koutselewsky
Miolowitch
Mierzewsky
Mlodowsky
Paulowsky
Tabernocky

Swiss
Chevalier
Koenig
Wrendli

Dutch
Huismans

Hungarian
Descheffy

Mameluke
Daboussi

13. Karl Weigand from Würtzburg, Friedrich Schweicart from Baden, and probably Deiss, a schoolboy from Weimar at this time.

14. The brothers Benjamin and Franz Beck.

15. J. Winterholler.

16. H. Pruppacher from Zurich.

17. Known only as Johann.

10. *The Triumph of the Captains*

This chapter is mainly taken from the usual sources for the general history of the war, especially *Gordon*, *Finlay*, and *Waddington*. The account of the fall of Nauplia by *Kotsch*, who was present, contradicts the usual version in some particulars. *Brengeri* gives an interesting account of the first siege of Missolonghi.

11. *The Return Home*

Almost all the surviving Philhellenes who left accounts of their experiences devoted a good deal of their book to their adventures on the way back from Greece: e.g. most of the authors referred to in Note 1 to Chapter 6, plus *Brengeri*; *Humphreys, First Journal*; *Persat*; *Aschling*.

1. *Elster, Fahrten*, ii, p. 35. The names of the two dead Philhellenes are given as Bollini and Daminski. Elster's account is, however, very fanciful at this point and is contradicted by more reliable sources.

2. *Stabell*, p. 89.

3. *Striebeck*, p. 234.

4. *Gottfried Müller*, p. 46.

5. *Elster*.

6. *Kotsch*, p. 60

7. *Lieber* mentions the Italian and two Frenchmen without identifying them. The doctor from Mecklenburg, Boldemann, has already been referred to (Note 10 to Chapter 4). The other German from Hamburg mentioned by *LeFebre* as committing suicide may be the same as the dancing master said by some to be from Rostock, Heinrich Stammler.

Dannenberg, p. 120, mentions the Württemberg officer who tried to kill himself. He gives his name as H——n, perhaps Hahn. C. M. Woodhouse, *The Philhellenes*, London, 1969, p. 121, suggests that the malaria which infects the area immediately north of the Gulf of Corinth produces acute depression in its victims, which often leads to suicide.

8. See, for example, *Lieber*, pp. 66, 113; *Schrebian*, p. 68.

9. *Finlay, Adventure*. This article is written in the first person and contains a number of points intended to make the reader think that the anonymous author is George Finlay himself, but he was not in Greece at the time. A letter from Finlay to the editor of *Blackwoods* of 21 September 1842 (National Library of Scotland MSS. 4061) claims that 'the facts happened as nearly as they are narrated and the persons whose names occur would almost feel inclined to vouch for the perfect accuracy of the tale'.

10. Monaldi. See p. 97.

11. *Brengeri*, iv, p. 351.

12. Unidentified. *Kotsch*, p. 27.

13. *Dannenberg*, p. 207.

14. For example Mari and St. André. See pp. 89 and 235.

15. August Christian von Schott, step-brother of Albert Schott, President of the Stuttgart Greek Society.

16. *Waddington*, p. 1.

17. *Aschling*, p. 88

18. *Examiner*, 1822, p. 551.

19. I include the following: *Aschling, Stabell, Christian Müller, Lieber, Schrebian, LeFebre, Bollmann, Dannenberg, Kiefer, Koesterus, Lessen, Kotsch, Rosenstiel, Stauffer, Kiesewetter*, Anonymous of Dinkelsbühl, Anonymous of Tübingen, translations of Christian Müller published in London and Paris, a translation of Lieber published in Amsterdam, and a translation of Stabell published in Leipzig. The work by *Gottfried Müller* published in Bamberg is of the same type but since it did not appear until 1824, I have omitted it. There were also numerous warnings in the newspapers, e.g. by Baron Wintzingerode at Munich.

12. *The German Legion*

The main source for the fortunes of the German Legion is the querulous account by *Kiefer* who was a member of the expedition. Other details are supplied by *Gordon, Millingen, Stanhope, Kotsch*, and N. Speliades 'Ἀπομνημονεύματα, Athens, 1851, i, pp. 344 ff.

1. *Lieber*, p. 157. In the United States he became a distinguished political philosopher and university teacher. He was founder of the *Encylopedia Americana*.
2. A copy of Kephalas' proclamation is reproduced in *Statuts della Societad d'ajüt per ils Grecs in Engadina*, 1822.
3. The anonymous author of the *Tagebuch* published at Dinkelsbühl in 1823.
4. Amand Gysin.
5. *Gottfried Müller*, the Philhellene who survived, related this incident. He mentions that his companion who died, Georg Dunze, had never left Hamburg, his native town, before he came to Greece.
6. *Millingen*, p. 28.

13. *Knights and Crusaders*

The attempts of speculators to persuade the Greeks to accept loans are described by *Dakin*, and there are numerous references in *Levandis, Dalleggio*, the Colonial Office records and elsewhere. The affair of the Knights is described in detail by *Jourdain*, who was personally deeply concerned.

1. British Museum Additional Manuscripts 30,130, f. 73.
2. References to the later activities of the Knights are in *Lauvergne, Hodges*, and *Blaquiere, Second Visit*. See also G.-J. Ouvrard, *Mémoires*, Paris, 1827, iii, pp. 353 ff.

14. *Secrets of State*

The British interception service at this period is described in Kenneth Ellis, *The Post Office in the Eighteenth Century*, London, 1958. The Ionian Island interceptions are among the Colonial Office Records. Some of the most important documents are in *Dakin*'s collection, *British Intelligence*. Quotations from the French secret police archives which show the concern with philhellenism are given in *Persat* and *Débidour*.

There are interesting references in M. Froment, *La Police Dévoilée depuis la Restauration*, Paris, 1829, and *Le Livre Noir de MM. Delavau et Franchet*, Paris, 1829.

15. *Enter the British*

For philhellenism in English literature *Spencer* is an excellent guide, and much of the story of the British Philhellenes is given by *Dakin*.

1. There is much about Gordon in *Dakin, British and American Philhellenes*. An article of mine based on Gordon's surviving papers is to be published as an Introduction to a reprint of the *History of the Greek Revolution*, due to be published in 1972.

2. Hastings' papers are in the Library of the British School at Athens. *Finlay*'s *Biographical Sketch* is the fullest account, see also Chapter 28.

3. *Jarvis*' papers are published. See also Chapter 30 for Jarvis' later activities in Greece.

4. *Humphreys, First Journal* and other works.

5. Haldenby does not appear in *Dakin*'s list. He is described by the author of the *Tagebuch* of Tübingen. It is also clearly Haldenby who is described by *Carne*, pp. 533 ff.

6. Hausmann from Colmar.

7. E. His full name is unknown, *Carne*, pp. 545 ff.

8. N. and S. *Christian Müller*, p. 6.

9. Hoistin mentioned by *Elster, Fahrten*, ii, p. 32. I doubt whether he existed.

10. *Finlay, Adventure*. See Note 9 to Chapter 11.

11. C. Brinsley Sheridan, *Thoughts on the Greek Revolution*. Pamphleteer XLVIII, 1824, p. 424 ff.

12. *Palma*, p. 7.

13. Quoted by *Gordon*, ii, p. 85.

14. Printed prospectus among Gordon papers.

15. Charles Brinsley Sheridan, *The Songs of Greece*, London, 1825, p. 98.

16. Henry Renton to Gordon, 22 February 1825, Gordon Papers.

17. Thomas Moore, *Memoirs, Journal, and Correspondence*, London, 1853, p. 88.

18. Bowring to Hobhouse 24 December 1823. British Museum Additional Manuscripts 36,460 f. 178.

19. Examples from which the quotations are taken are in *The Works of Jeremy Bentham*, edited by John Bowring, Edinburgh, 1843, and *Dalleggio*.

16. *Lord Byron joins the Cause*

For the details of Byron's life there is no substitute for *Marchand* who has made best use of the original documents.

1. Blaquiere to Reeves to be passed to Lord Liverpool, 28 October, 1823. British Museum Additional Manuscripts 38,297 f. 166.

2. Blaquiere to Byron 28 April 1823. Copy sent to Gordon by Bowring with the news that Byron had told the Committee that he would proceed instantly to Greece if the accounts contained in Captain Blaquiere's letter were confirmed in his next communication. Gordon Papers.

3. This incident is described in *Gamba* and in letters by Byron. The two men cannot be identified for sure, although one was perhaps *Adolph von Lübtow* who was later killed at Missolonghi.

4. *Trelawny* and *Hamilton Browne*.

17. *'To bring Freedom and Knowledge to Greece'*

The official papers of the London Greek Committee are in the National Archives at Athens. They were used by *Penn* and a short account of some of the more interesting documents is given by E. S. De Beer and Walter Seton in *The Nineteenth*

Century, September 1926. There are many relevant documents among the Gordon papers including copies of some of the Committee's papers.

See also *Gamba, Parry, Millingen, Bowring, Stanhope*, and, among later writers, *Dakin* and *Marchand*. These works also provide the main sources for the following three chapters.

1. Blaquiere to Hobhouse from Marseilles, 27 March 1823. British Museum Additional Manuscripts 36,460 f. 24.
2. Byron to Bowring 12 May 1823. Quoted in Thomas Moore: *Letters and Journals of Lord Byron*, London, 1830, ii, pp. 655 ff.
3. See Note 1 to Chapter 15.
4. *Parry* is one of the best of the contemporary accounts. He was assisted in writing his book by Thomas Hodgskin. See my note, 'Postscript to *The Last Days of Lord Byron*', *Keats-Shelley Journal*, 1970.
5. William Gill, E. Fowke, James Grubb, W. Watson, J. M. Hodges, Robert Lacock, James Hampton, and Richard Brownbill.
6. Hon. Leicester Stanhope, *Press in India*, London, 1823, p. 193.

18. *Arrivals at Missolonghi*

1. This conclusion is explicitly confirmed by *Trelawny, Recollections*, p. 201.
2. *The War in Greece*, 1821; *Greece in 1824*, 1824.
3. Quoted in *Marchand*, iii, p. 1136.

19. *The Byron Brigade*

1. *Gamba*, p. 157.
2. Ibid., p. 201.
3. There were at least two Philhellenes called Sass. According to the ships' lists Adolph Sass came in the *Félicité Renouvelée* and Karl Sass came in the *Duchesse d'Angoulême*. For Adolph see *Barth and Kehrig-Korn*, p. 214, and *Parry*, p. 57. There is a tombstone at Missolonghi said to be of Gustav Adolph Sass who died in 1826, and there is some evidence that a Swede called Sass was drowned there in 1826.

Borje Knöss, 'Officiers Suédois dans la Guerre d'Indépendance de la Grèce' in *l'Hellénisme Contemporain* 2me série, 3me année, Fasc. No. 4, pp. 319 ff., quotes letters of 1824 and 1825 from contemporary Swedish newspapers allegedly by Adolphe de Sass who is said to have died in 1829.
4. *Dakin, British and American Philhellenes*, sets out most of the information that can be gleaned about this group.
5. *Larrabee*, pp. 145 f.
6. Maitland to Colonial Secretary, Colonial Office Records, C.O. 136/1086 f. 379.
7. *Barth and Kehrig-Korn*, p. 118.
8. Ibid., p. 175 from *Treiber*.
9. Ibid., p. 177.

10. *Millingen*, p. 183; *Walsh*, i, 172; *Wilson*, p. 485; *The Literary Life and Correspondence of the Countess of Blessington*, ed. R. R. Madden, London, 1855, ii, p. 127; several letters are quoted in *Blaquiere, Second Visit*. See also the remarks of Charles Armitage Brown quoted in *The Keats Circle*, ed. Hyder Edward Rollins, Harvard, 1948, i, pp. lvii f.

11. *Palma*, p. 2.

12. *Krøyer*, p. 84.

13. *Treiber*, p. 130.

14. *Bulwer*, p. 123.

15. *Emerson, Letters*, i, pp. 39 ff. Compare *Howe, Letters* and *Journals*, pp. 98f. and p. 112. Wright's travelling companion, Railton, was at work on *The Antiquities of Athens* begun by James Stuart and Nicholas Revett.

16. *Wilson*, p. 495. Incidentally Wilson's chronology goes wrong at this point in his book. He could not have seen the body of Lord Byron at Zante at the end of his Greek tour of 1824 as he says.

17. See Doris Langley Moore, *The Late Lord Byron*, London, 1961.

18. *The Life, Writings, Opinions and Times of the Right Hon. George Gordon Noel Byron . . . by an English Gentleman in the Greek Military Service, and Comrade of His Lordship*, London, 1825.

20. *Essays in Regeneration*

The principal source for Stanhope's activities is his own book and the quotations are from *Stanhope*, except where otherwise noted. The *Stanhope Papers* show that he drastically edited the material for his book.

1. See, for example, *Gordon*, ii, p. 180.

2. Sir William Gell, *Narrative of a Journey in the Morea*, London, 1823, p. 303.

3. *Gordon*, ii, p. 121.

21. *The New Apostles*

The main sources are *Anderson, Brewer, Hartley*, and especially *Wilson*. The curious work by *Kennedy* throws light on the point of view of the missionaries, and also incidentally reveals something of the charm of Lord Byron. There is much of interest in *Larrabee*. Quotations are from *Wilson* except where otherwise noted.

1. *Stanhope*, p. 105.

2. Rev. William Jowett, *Christian Researches in the Mediterranean*, London. 1824, p. 255.

3. *Wilson*, p. 203.

4. Ibid., p. 338.

5. *Hartley*, p. 4.

6. Ibid., p. 5.

7. *Anderson*, p. 31.

8. *Hartley*, p. 79.

9. *Wilson*, p. 400.

10. Ibid., p. 207.

11. Parry to the London Greek Committee, 24 February 1824. Gordon Papers.

12. Thomas Moore, *Letters and Journals of Lord Byron*, London, 1830, ii, p. 721.

13. *Swan*, i, pp. 189 f; ii, p. 34.

14. Ibid., i, 103.

15. *Swan*, i, p. 141.

16. *Slade*, ii, p. 459.

17. *Hartley*, p. 35.

18. *Fifteenth Report of the British and Foreign Bible Society*, p. 212, quoted in *Swan*, i, p. 190.

19. *Slade*, ii, pp. 462 f.

22. *The English Gold*

For the loans, see especially *Dakin, Levandis,* and *Bartle*; for the economic background, Leland Hamilton Jenks, *The Migration of British Capital to 1875*, New York and London, 1927.

1. Jenks, op. cit., p. 49.

2. Figures from the *Journal of the Royal Statistical Society*, June 1878, pp. 313 ff.

3. Bowring to Hobhouse, 24 December 1823. British Museum Additional Manuscripts 36,460 f. 178.

4. *Blaquiere, Greek Confederation*, p. 28.

5. *Blaquiere, Greek Revolution*, p. 302.

6. Ibid., p. 302.

7. Ibid., p. 302.

8. Ibid., p. 301.

9. Ibid., p. 305.

10. Ibid., p. 303.

11. Ibid., p. 303.

12. *Blaquiere, Second Visit*, p. xiv.

13. Quoted by *Levandis*, p. 15.

14. *Examiner*, 18 December 1824.

15. Ibid., 22 February 1824.

16. Bowring to Gordon, 21 June 1824. Gordon Papers.

17. Bowring to Hobhouse, 18 July 1824. British Museum Additional Manuscripts 36,460 f. 242.

18. Humphreys to Gordon, 17 August 1824. Gordon Papers.

19. *New Monthly Magazine*, xii, 1824, p. 515.

20. *Bulwer*.

21. *Examiner*, 5 March 1826.

22. *Waddington*, p. 1.

23. *Blaquiere, Greece and Her Claims*.

24. Quoted by *Bartle*, p. 70, from a MS. in the John Rylands Library.

25. *Bartle*, p. 71.

26. Quoted in *Quarterly Review*, January 1827.

23. *The Coming of the Arabs*

1. *Wilson*, p. 273.

2. *Gordon*, ii, p. 182.

3. See, for example, *Stanhope*, p. 376; *Bulwer*, p. 116.

4. *Palma*, p. 10.

5. *Wilson*, p. 274.

6. *Finlay, Greek Revolution*, ii, p. 39.

7. There is a full biography of Sève by Marie E. Aimé Vingtrinnier, *Soliman Pacha*, Paris, 1886. Several contemporary writers give further details, notably *Lauvergne* and *Swan*.

8. For Doctor St. André see J. S. Mangeart, *Souvenirs de la Morée*, Paris, 1836, p. 29.

9. Collegno's diary of the siege of Navarino, *Ottolenghi*, pp. 242 ff.

10. *Swan*, ii, p. 240.

11. There are several biographies of Trelawny but none since the important article by Lady Anne Hill, 'Trelawny's Family Background and Naval Career' in the *Keats-Shelley Journal*, 1956. Trelawny's own books and letters have to be treated with scepticism. The most prominent other romantic Byronists of this period are George Finlay in his early phase and William Humphreys—see especially the lush descriptions in the latter's *Adventures of an English Officer*. There are some revealing passages in that strange compilation, *Sketches of Modern Greece by a Young English Volunteer*.

12. There are numerous accounts of the affair in the cave. Documents in *Jarvis* leave no doubt about the plot. *Humphreys, Adventures of an English Officer*, confirms the outline of Trelawny's own account.

13. Quoted by William Mure, *Journal of a Tour in Greece*, Edinburgh and London, 1842, i, p. 167.

14. *MacFarlane*, ii, p. 53.

15. *Emerson, Picture of Greece*, i, p. 282.

16. Alphonse Nuzzo Mauro, *La Ruine de Missolonghi*, Paris, 1836, p. 16.

17. Quoted by W. Alison Phillips, *The War of Greek Independence*, London, 1897, p. 203.

24. *The Shade of Napoleon*

For the life of Fabvier see especially *Débidour* who had access to much primary material. Other details are in *Davesiès de Pontes* and *Grasset*. A pamphlet published in Paris in 1828, *De l'Empire Grec et du Jeune Napoléon*, throws an interesting light on the aspirations of the Bonapartists in Greece. The author argues that an independent Christian empire should be established in the Near East as a bulwark against the Russians. To survive, such an empire would need a stiffening of European immigrants and these could be provided by the warlike Bonapartists and failed revolutionaries of Europe. The son of Napoleon could be appointed emperor, so ensuring that the new state did not fall too far under the influence of any of the great European powers.

1. Humphreys to Gordon, 21 December 1823, Gordon Papers.

2. *Stanhope*, p. 27.

3. *Villeneuve*, p. 9.

4. *Le Livre Noir de MM. Delavau et Franchet*, Paris, 1829, iii, pp. 347 ff. Gibassier was put to death by the Turks after being captured near Athens in 1827.

5. Ibid., Froment, *La Police Dévoilée depuis la Restauration*, Paris, 1829, i, p. 168. Bourbaki was killed near Athens in 1827.

6. Berton was met by Humphreys. See *Humphreys, Adventures of an English Officer*.

7. Howe (*Letters and Journals*, p. 250) was present at Bonaparte's death on board the *Hellas*.

25. 'No Freedom to Fight for at Home'

The title of this chapter is taken from a poem which Lord Byron sent to Tom Moore about his own activities in support of the Italian liberals in 1820:

> When a man hath no freedom to fight for at home,
> Let him combat for that of his neighbours;
> Let him think of the glories of Greece and of Rome,
> And get knock'd on the head for his labours.
>
> To do good to mankind is the chivalrous plan,
> And is always as hotly requited;
> Then battle for freedom wherever you can,
> And, if not shot or hang'd, you'll get knighted.

First-hand accounts by Italian Philhellenes are surprisingly sparse. I have used those of *Brengeri, Pecchio*, and *Palma. Gamba*'s book is concerned solely with his first visit to Greece. Collegno's diary of the siege of Navarino is in *Ottolenghi*. There are also passages of especial interest in *Morandi*.

1. *Brengeri*, vi, p. 84. The name is supplied from *Persat*, who was involved in the project on his return from Greece.

2. *Memoirs of General Pepe*, London, 1846, iii, p. 251.

3. *Brengeri*, i, p. 466.

4. Ibid., vi, p. 91.

5. Letter of Rossaroll, 10 December 1824, C.O. 136/33 f. 28.

6. *Palma*, p. v.

7. *Pecchio, Picture of Greece*, ii, p. 10.

8. *Millingen*, p. 241.

9. *Dalleggio*, p. 121.

10. Froment, op. cit., i, p. 278.

11. For example, the author of *Sketches of Modern Greece*, i, p. 216.

12. Quoted in *Œuvres de M. Victor Cousin*, Paris, 1849, iii, p. 414.

13. *Palma*, p. vii.

14. *Pecchio, Picture of Greece*, ii, pp. 190 ff.

15. Ibid., ii, p. 7.

16. *Morandi*, pp. 75 ff.

17. *Dalleggio*, p. 124.

18. Collegno, Rossaroll, Santa Rosa, Palma, Romei, Barberis, Barandier, Aimino, Morandi, Ritatori, Isaia, Gambini, and Ferero are all said to have received a death sentence. Pisa, Porro, Pecorara, Pecchio, Andrietti, and Giacomuzzi may also have been condemned.

19. *Hahn*, quoted in *Barth and Kehrig-Korn*, p. 199.

20. Georges Douin, *Une Mission Militaire auprès de Mohamed Aly*, Cairo, 1923, p. 4.

21. Most of the details about Romei and Scarpa are extracted from correspondence among the Colonial Office records, the more important of which are reprinted in *Dakin, British Intelligence*. Scarpa was met in Crete before the invasion by R. R. Madden (*Travels in Turkey*, London, 1829, i, p. 172), and his name appears among the defenders of the Acropolis in 1827.

22. *Dakin, British Intelligence*, pp. 50 ff.

23. *Gordon*, ii, p. 199.

24. Ibid.

25. Collegno's diary in *Ottolenghi*, pp. 242 ff. Collegno gives the Pole's nama as Schutz. The same incident seems to be referred to by the author of *Sketches of Modern Greece*, ii, pp. 39 ff., who says the Pole—a former Philhellene with a long white beard, whom he calls Statoski—told Collegno 'For forty years I have bared my arm for liberty and never gained a para.'

26. *Villeneuve*, pp. 120 f.

27. *Pecchio, Picture of Greece*, ii, p. 274.

28. *Gordon*, ii, p. 257.

29. Calosso appears in the Thouret-Fornezy list of Philhellenes as having taken part in the Battle of Chaidari in 1826. For his later career see *MacFarlane*, ii, pp. 175 ff. and *Slade*, i, pp. 132 ff. The destruction of the Janissaries is described by *Walsh*.

26. *French Idealism and French Cynicism*

The development of French policy towards Greece is discussed in *Dakin, British and American Philhellenes* and *Dakin, British Intelligence*. The general context is described in Harold Temperley, *The Foreign Policy of Canning*, London, 1925. On aspects of French philhellenism see *Isambert, Asse, Dimopoulos*, and the *Documents* of the Paris Greek Committee.

1. *Dakin, British Intelligence*, pp. 104 ff.

2. Ibid., p. 29.

3. For this society see Jean Dimakis, 'La Société de la Morale Chrétienne de Paris et son action en faveur des Grecs', *Balkan Studies*, volume 7, 1966.

4. Quoted, ibid.

5. The growth in the activities of the Paris Greek Committee can be easily followed in their bulletin, *Documents relatifs à l'état present de la Grèce*.

6. See *Asse* and Edmond Estève, *Byron et le Romantisme Français*, Paris, 1907.

7. Quoted, ibid., p. 120.

8. The books of verse which were published in France during the Greek War of Independence on philhellenic themes provide an interesting indication of the state of public opinion. Most of the titles were collected by *Asse*, but others are known from other references. The following table gives an indication of the numbers. Only books published separately in their own right are included—innumerable other philhellenic poems were, of course, published as part of larger collections and in reviews and newspapers. The numbers by themselves give a guide to the ups and downs of public interest which rose to a peak in 1826. The fascination with Lord Byron and with Missolonghi can also be seen from the frequency with which they are mentioned in the titles.

Year	Number of books	Number which mention Byron in the title	Number which mention Missolonghi in the title
1821 (after the outbreak of the Revolution)	10	—	—
1822	18	1	—
1823	5	—	—
1824	30	14	—
1825	20	3	1
1826	40	2	13
1827 (until Navarino)	16	1	3
TOTAL	139	21	17

9. Translated from J. J. Hosemann, *Les Etrangers en Grèce*, Paris, 1826.

10. *Féburier*.

11. By Beauchène, quoted by *Asse*, p. 99.

12. *Note sur la Grèce*, Paris, 1825.

13. The best source is the *Documents* from which many later accounts are derived.

14. *Stanhope*, p. 483.

15. For the history of the French Military Mission in Egypt, taken mainly from the French archives, see Georges Douin, *Une Mission Militaire auprès de Mohamed Aly*, Cairo, 1923.

16. Ibid., p. 137.

17. Again the main official papers about the provision of the warships have been published by Georges Douin, *Les Premières Frégates de Mohamed Aly*, Cairo, 1926.

27. *Regulars Again*

The main sources are *Débidour*; *Documents*; and *Dakin, British Intelligence*.

1. *Larrabee* gives most of the story of Washington from original sources such as *Howe, Journal*, and *Swan*. A copy of a fragment of Washington's own diary is in the Gennadios Library, Athens, the original MS. being now in private hands.

2. Translated from version in *Swan*, ii, p. 156.

3. *Dakin, British Intelligence*, p. 77.

4. Letter from Arnaud, 19 October 1825, Colonial Office Records, C.O. 136/33, volume 2, f. 544.

5. *Davesiès*, pp. 23 ff.

6. Marcet and Romilly. See *Marcet*.

7. *Gordon*, ii, p. 299. Characteristically, Gordon does not mention himself by name.

8. Letter from Arnaud, 19 October 1825, Colonial Office Records C.O. 136/33, volume 2, f. 544.

9. Correspondence among the Gordon Papers relates to Gordon's successful attempt to have Justin's narrative suppressed. It is likely that Gordon himself

made use of it for his history. See *Gordon*, i, p. 504, where he refers to the 'Ms memoirs of a Philhellene then serving in Crete'.

10. *Schack*, p. 9.

11. *Harring*, quoted in *Barth and Kehrig-Korn*, p. 88. Byern describes his second visit in his own book.

12. *Jourdain*, ii, p. 212; *Villeneuve*, pp. 115 ff.

13. Young Garel was said (*Millingen*, p. 291) to have distinguished himself as flag-bearer at Navarino in 1825. His father was killed at Athens in 1827.

14. *Voutier, Mémoires*.

15. *Raybaud*, ii, p. 275 and elsewhere. *Persat* also remarked on Voutier's romancing but his book was not published until much later.

16. *Millingen*, p. 63.

17. Gordon to Robertson, 18 December 1826. Gordon Papers.

18. Chardon de la Barre.

19. General Dubourg. *Schack*, p. 79.

20. *Documents*, June 1826, p. 61.

21. *Heideck*, p. 35.

22. Legracieux, who had worked on the *Courrier Français*. Killed near Athens 1827.

23. *Schack*.

24. *C. D. Raffenel*, killed Athens 1827. Some accounts give the Philhellene different Christian names but the identity seems to be established.

25. Perhaps Rigal. *Byern*, pp. 236 ff. Etienne was killed near Athens in 1827.

26. *Palma*, p. 291. According to *Millingen*, p. 54, British seamen deserted in 1823 and 1824 to join Lord Byron's brigade.

27. Lassberg known as Wolf and Schaffer known as Reinhold, both killed at Athens 1827. *Barth and Kehrig-Korn*, pp. 216 ff.

28. von Vangerow. See *Gosse, Lettres*, p. 25.

29. *Barth and Kehrig-Korn*, pp. 233 ff.

30. Wohlgemuth. See *Byern*, p. 250. Another Wohlgemuth came in 1822.

31. Letter of Fabvier, 10 May 1826. *Roma*, ii, pp. 189 ff.

32. *Pecchio, Picture of Greece*, ii, p. 76.

33. *Slade*, i, p. 135; *MacFarlane*, i, p. 517.

34. September 1826 in Aegina. Howe performed the autopsy.

35. *Morandi*, pp, 74, 77.

36. *Miller*, p. 143.

37. Names unknown. *Hahn*, quoted in *Barth and Kehrig-Korn*, p. 24.

38. *Roma*, ii, pp. 189 ff.

28. *A New Fleet*

The fullest account of the events surrounding the ordering of the steamships and the frigates and of their performance is *Dakin, British and American Philhellenes*.

1. A sketch of Hastings' life was published by *Finlay* in *Blackwood's Edinburgh Magazine*, 1845. Hastings' papers came into Finlay's possession after his death and are now in the library of the British School at Athens.

2. Reproduced as an appendix to *Finlay, Greek Revolution*.

3. The development of philhellenism in the United States is described in *Booras, Cline, Earle*, and *Larrabee* from whom most of the following section is drawn.

4. Howe's estimate. *Historical Sketch*, p. 446.

5. For American dealings with the Turks and the career of George English, see *Finnie*.

6. The affair of the frigates is described by *Dakin, Earle*, and *Levandis*. Many of the details are derived from the controversial pamphlets of the time, William Bayard, *An Exposition of the Conduct of the Two Houses . . .*, N.Y., 1826; Alexander Contostavlos, *A Narrative of the Material Facts . . .*, N.Y., 1826; John Duer and Robert Sedgewick, *An Examination . . .*, N.Y., 1826; *A Vindication of the Conduct and Character of Henry D. Sedgewick*, N.Y., 1826; H. D. Sedgewick, *Refutation of the Reasons assigned by the Arbitrators*, N.Y., 1826; and especially *Report of the Evidence and Reasons of the Award between Johannis Orlandos and Andreas Luriottis, Greek Deputies, of the one part, and Le Roy, Bayard and Co. and G.G. and S. Howland, of the other part*. By the arbitrators, N.Y., 1826.

7. For the life of Lord Cochrane see his own, *The Autobiography of a Seaman*, London, 1860; E. G. Twitchett, *Life of a Seaman*, London, 1931; Christopher Lloyd, *Lord Cochrane*, London, 1947; and Warren Tute, *Cochrane*, London, 1965. For Lord Cochrane's activities in Greece see especially the work by his nephew, George Cochrane, *Wanderings in Greece*.

8. *Slade*, i, p. 182.

9. *MacFarlane*, i, p. 197.

10. *Dakin, British Intelligence*, p. 45.

29. *Athens and Navarino*

For the diplomatic developments which led to the Battle of Navarino see *Crawley*, and Harold Temperley, *The Foreign Policy of Canning*, London, 1925. For the operations near Athens see *Dakin, British and American Philhellenes*, and *Débidour*, as well as the general histories. Some new details are in the recently discovered journal of Thomas Whitcombe.

1. Quoted Temperley, op. cit., p. 346.

2. Quoted *Crawley*, p. 55.

3. For the career of Sir Richard Church see *Dakin, British and American Philhellenes, Lane-Poole*, and the curious work by E. M. Church. Church's papers are in the British Museum.

4. For Heideck's expedition see *Heideck*. For the false rumours see the letter from Heideck to Eynard, 4 November 1826, Colonial Office Records, C.O. 136/42, f. 16.

5. Gibassier, Gasque, and Bohn. The French naval commander in the area made a plea for them to be spared.

6. Described in *Dakin, British and American Philhellenes*.

7. Letter of Hastings, 11 September 1826, Hastings Papers. 'Mr Thompson alias Critchley died of bilious fever 8 September.'

8. Described in *Dakin, British and American Philhellenes*.

9. *Howe, Letters and Journals*, p. 235.

10. For these incidents see *Miller*, p. 163; *Woodruff*, p. 87; *Post*, p. 195. Hesketh had visited Greece in 1823 and 1824 and worked with Byron. See also *Finlay, Hastings*, p. 508.

11. I include the following:

French		*Hungarian*
Berlin	Vitsche	Georg
Bourbaki	Woirion	Marc
Clement		Lasso
Darmagnac	*German*	
Dujurdhui	Becker	*Spanish*
Florence	Bohn	Lanzana
Garel	Bruckbacher	Riviero
Gasque	Lassberg	
Gibassier	Schaffer	*Italian*
Inglesi	Schweicard	Pecorara
Ledoux	Seiffart	Ritatori
Lefaivre	Zimmermann	
Legracieux		*Swiss*
Parat	*Corsican*	Doudier
Raffenel	Balzanni	Rival
Rigal	Galdo	
Robert	Gambini	*Belgian*
	Marseilleisi	Oscar
	Passano	

12. *Frankland*, i, p. 312.

30. *America to the Rescue*

1. Much information about the Swiss relief activities is in the *Documents* of the Paris Greek Committee. See also *Rothpletz*, *Eynard*, and *Penn, Philhellenism in Europe*.

2. *Finlay, Greek Revolution*, ii, p. 128. Körring was said to be 6 feet 7 inches tall. He took part in the campaign in Western Greece in 1828 but his *palikars* mutinied against his attempts to impose discipline and shut him in an oven. He died of disease at Patras in 1829.

3. *Finlay, Greek Revolution*, ii, p. 158.

4. See *Jarvis*; *Dakin, British and American Philhellenes*; and *Larrabee*.

5. *Dakin, British and American Philhellenes*; *Larrabee*.

6. *Howe, Letters and Journals*; *Dakin, British and American Philhellenes*; *Larrabee*.

7. See *Earle*, *Booras*, and *Cline*.

8. *Dalleggio*, p. 221.

9. For American policy towards Turkey after Navarino see *Finnie*.

10. The descriptions and quotations about the American relief work in Greece are taken from *Woodruff*, *Post*, *Miller*, and especially *Howe, Letters and Journals*. *Larrabee* is a useful secondary source.

31. *Later*

1. J. Phil. Fallmerayer, *Geschichte der Halbinsel Morea*, Stuttgart and Tübingen, 1830.

2. For the development of the Modern Greek language and the politics surrounding it, see Robert Browning, *Medieval and Modern Greek*, London, 1969.

3. Rev. Richard Burgess, *Greece and the Levant*, i, p. 257.

4. This can still be seen.

5. See Ernest Breton, *Athènes*, Paris, 1862, p. 139. The name of Ducrocq can still be made out but not the rest of the inscription quoted by Breton. Ducrocq was killed in a naval action in December 1827. On the same column of the Parthenon it is also still possible to read the carved name of the French Philhellene Daubigny who was also in the Acropolis during the siege.

6. Letter of Church to Finlay, 20 November 1861, Finlay Papers.

INDEX

Bonapartists, 29, 32, 76, 133, 234, 245, 247, 248, 257, 268, 279, 289, 321

Bonn, 69, 153

Borel: alias of Colonel Fabvier, q.v.

Boston, Massachusetts, 60, 177; Boston Poor House, 32

Botsaris, Marco, Albanian Suliote leader, 24, 36, 108, 179; 'the modern Leonidas', 269

Bouboulina, a woman of Hydra, dubbed 'the Modern Artemisia or the Greek Joan of Arc', 24

Bourbaki, Colonel, French Philhellene, former officer in Imperial army, 247; killed in unsuccessful advance on Athens, 324

Bourbons, 57, 133, 245, 265, 279, 289, 320

Bowring (Sir) John, Secretary of London Greek Committee, 141–3, 146, 147 and fn., 148, 153, 169, 186, 206, 210, 211, 254, 255, 299, 308; his personal speculations in Greek loan bonds, 211–20 *passim*; promotion of his own interests, 212; his anonymous article in the *Westminster Review* a piece of 'unscrupulous politics', 220; appointed secretary of investigating committee, 220; employed by British Government for commercial investigations, 222. 'The Greek Committee' (*Westminster Review*), 365, 381. Pl. 9

Boyer, General, member of French Government mission to Mehemet Ali, 274, 276

Brazil, 217, 305

Brengeri, Italian Philhellene, 251–2, 371

British Government, 30; receives first-hand reports from Near East, 29; attitude to Greek revolution, 58–9, 263–72; intelligence service, 132–3, 264, 279; rejects Greek offer to put their country under, 237, 279 (*see* Act of Submission); anxious to maintain neutrality, 308; Cochrane (q.v.) eludes prosecution under Foreign Enlistment Act, 308–9

British Philhellenes, 66, 138–49; equipment of expedition to Greece, 156–8

British and Foreign Bible Society, Fifteenth Report of the, 383

Broglie, Duc de, member of the Paris Greek Committee, 270

Brown, Charles Armitage, 382

Brownbill, 'a hypocritical canting methodist' (Parry, q.v.), 198

Browne, James Hamilton, 175, 178, 215–16; 'Voyage from Leghorn to Cephalonia' and 'Narrative of a Visit in 1823 to the Seat of War in Greece' (in *Blackwood's Magazine*), 362, 380

Bulgarians, 7, 92

Bulwer, Henry Lytton (later Sir Henry), 215–16, 350; *An Autumn in Greece*, 362, 382, 383

Bunyan, John: *The Pilgrim's Progress*, 202

Burdett, Sir Francis, M.P., member of the London Greek Committee, 146. Pl. 9

Burma River War, 307

Burton, London broker: identity revealed by *The Times*, after Louriottis' masking him as 'a friend of Greece', 220–1

Buskins, archaic footwear adopted by professors and students of the Hellenic University, Corfu, 21

Byern, Eugen von, Prussian Philhellene, ex-cavalry officer, 287–8; *Bilder aus Griechenland und der Levante*, 354, 362, 371, 375, 376, 388

Byron, George Gordon Noel, Lord, 32, 136, 145, 157, 209, 210, 214–15, 385; first visit to Greece, 17; publishes cantos I–II of *Childe Harold's Pilgrimage* and becomes a European celebrity, 17–19; *Don Juan*, 18, 139, 151; translation of the war-song of Rhigas, 20–1; wide influence of his philhellenic poems, 53; Blaquiere (q.v.) calls on him in Genoa, 150; his literary philhellenism, 151; decides to go to Greece, 152–4; takes flamboyant wardrobe and black American groom, 154; his illusions discarded, 167; decoyed by London Greek Committee, 167; receives requests from Mavrocordato and Colocotrones, 168; presses on Bowring need to raise loan for Greek Government, 168; lingers in Cephalonia as guest of Napier, British Resident, 168–9; reaches Missolonghi and receives regal welcome, 169; his quarrels with Stanhope, 170; the Byron Brigade, 173–84; his military plan, 174; death of, 180; becomes posthumously a cult figure of romantic revolutionaries, 183; failure